To the God of the Mountain,
Who bore us up on eagle's wings
and carried us to Himself~

The One, True, Living God,

Who was,

and is,

and is to come . . . .

Two years ago, the word "adventure" began to surface with increasing intensity in my life. Little did I know that I was about to embark on an adventure so wild, and so holy that the first fifty years of my life would pale in comparison. Penny and Jim Caldwell have lived an extraordinary adventure for far longer than I. They have seen and done things that nobody on earth has experienced. Penny's new book, *The God of the Mountain*, gives the reader a rare glimpse into the lives of two people who have been led on a very special mission by God. To be sure, it isn't easy to follow the call to such an adventure. In fact it can be frightening, dangerous, physically and emotionally draining, and very confusing. But, they have persevered, prayed, and have listened carefully to God. In return for their obedience, they have been rewarded on a supernatural scale. They have walked in the ancient footsteps of God's chosen people and have been asked to bring this knowledge back to them—in Israel. Penny and Jim have been entrusted with much, and they were uniquely chosen for just such a time as this. You MUST read this book. It may change your life.

— **Pete Windahl**, Co-Producer *The Exodus Conspiracy*

If you combine Indiana Jones with the Swiss Family Robinson, and then turn those fictional Hollywood epics into fact, you will just begin to appreciate the husband and wife adventurers, Jim and Penny Caldwell, as they searched the ancient land of Midian for the true Mount Sinai. Faced with the constant threat of arrest, torture, and possible execution for their bravery, Jim, Penny, and their two children answered the call of the Lord and followed the ancient writings of Moses on the most amazing adventure of modern times— equal in every aspect to the search for Noah's Ark and the Ark of the Covenant. What Jim and Penny found is of supreme importance for both Christians and Jews. It is the very mountain where Moses received the Ten Commandments, where Aaron fashioned the golden calf, where Moses built the Exodus 24:4 altar and twelve pillars, and where God stood in the pillar of fire when Moses struck the rock that would supply the Hebrew slaves with life-giving water. Penny's moment-by-moment account of their adventure is a must read.

Congratulations, Penny, on a spectacular book!

— **Roger L. Johnson**, Commander, US Navy

There are books and there are *different* books. This is a different one. Penny Caldwell writes about her travels in Saudi Arabia, together with her husband and their children. Travels that few have experienced: strange events, remarkable discoveries, dangerous situations in the Land of Midian, in the territory of Moses. This is a personal travel log; it tells of travels that were personal to Moses and his people, and in the same way they are personal for Penny and her family. I know what she writes about because I have also been there—with Penny and her husband in the middle of nowhere—in the Land of Midian.

Penny describes her travels as "a journey of revelation and destiny." And I can tell you, this is not the end of a story—it is a beginning of the future.

— **Dr. Lennart Möller,** author of *The Exodus Case*

In my twenty years of life in Saudi Arabia, sixteen of which was spent as the private physician rendered to the former governor of Mecca, I traveled to the northern part of Saudi twelve times over a period of seven years. This is not a place for a Christian to share his or her faith. It is a country where one can get executed for believing in God. Ironically, this is where the Holy Mountain is located, protected with swords, guns, and modern weapons. From the world of religious repression inside Saudi Arabia, God chose two families, one from the East and one from the West to do His work. This book is the incredible story of the Caldwell family, and how they came to the Mountain. This is how it began in January of 1987 and 1988 when our two families moved there, and today it is God's grace that we returned to Korea and America safely.

That mountain called on us all the time. We both traveled there many times. We connected with Jim and Penny deep in our soul when we met. It was our experiences that brought us together and binds us to a common identity. Together we pray that all the nations in the world will come to know the hidden mountain, and the God of the mountain.

— **Dr. Sung Hak Kim,** South Korea

The God of the MOUNTAIN

THE TRUE STORY BEHIND
THE DISCOVERIES AT THE REAL MOUNT SINAI

PENNY COX CALDWELL

Bridge-Logos
Alachua, Florida 32615

Bridge-Logos
Alachua, FL 32615 USA

The God of the Mountain
by Penny Cox Caldwell

Copyright ©2008 by Penny Cox Caldwell

Edited by Ann Blanton

Printed in the Canada.

Library of Congress Catalog Card Number: 2008933165
International Standard Book Number 978-0-88270-605-4

Scripture quotations in this book are from the *King James Version* of the Bible.

All photos copyright © 1992-2008 Jim & Penny Caldwell. All rights reserved.

Ark of the Covenant photo used by permission
Copyright © Tim Mahoney, Mahoney Media Productions

The names of certain individuals mentioned in this book have been purposefully changed at the author's discretion.

BP 07-29-13

THIS BOOK IS DEDICATED TO THE MEMORY OF MY DADDY

Who taught me the meaning of wonder
and how to dream among the stars.

CLAYTON CARLYSLE COX

For Lucas & Chelsea

You are the very breaths that I breathe and the greatest joys of my life! What you have braved being the children of your father and me is beyond anything normal kids usually have to tolerate! For your intrepid spirits and for strapping on heavy back packs and trudging up mountains with us over and over again while all your friends played baseball and soccer, I stand amazed and exceedingly proud! This story is your heritage, and that of your children to come.

For Jim

You are the living beat of my heart and my one true soulmate forever, as well as the most fearless adventurer I have ever known! You have taken me into the most remote regions of the planet and through some of the most harrowing experiences any human could endure, and even yet I would follow you again with but a glance. You alone know what our eyes have seen together on the high places of the earth, and to you alone will I always belong.

Special Thanks

Joyce Bordlee, my dear friend! You have been a constant encouragement to me since I made you aware I was writing this book a number of years ago. For your valuable help in editing and wonderful support in every area of this project, I thank you so very much!

And to Ann Blanton, my editor and teacher, you cannot begin to imagine how your calm and steady hand working with me on this book has settled my spirit and given me peace! For your endless hours of work, patience in hearing out my concerns and covering this whole thing in prayer, I am eternally grateful!

Contents

Foreword

What would you do if you realized that the foreign land you were living in possibly held the ancient location where Moses and the Israelites received the Ten Commandments?

Would you investigate? What if you found artifacts that perfectly matched the biblical story, but are now hidden, locked and guarded behind barbed-wire fences, not to be seen by outsiders. What if you could see evidence of one of the biggest stories of the Bible lying in front of you and no one in the world knew it existed. What would you do? Would you photograph these locations? Would you tell others?

This was the dilemma that faced Jim and Penny Caldwell. In January 1988, they left Louisiana with their two children Lucas and Chelsea. Jim had taken a job as a digital technician in the oil fields of Saudi Arabia. It was during an Egyptian vacation to the traditional Mount Sinai in the Sinai Peninsula that a series of unusual events transpired, events that would change the Caldwells' lives forever. Events that led them right to the base of what many believe is the real Mount Sinai, known today in Arabic as Jebel al Lawz.

Over the next eight years Jim and Penny made fourteen trips to the Jebel Lawz area. They documented, photographed and video-taped the entire area, with their work demonstrating a pattern of evidence that matched the exodus events. The Caldwell family was arrested and harassed numerous times, even though they had official permission to be in the area. They soon learned that the Saudis did not want anyone to see these "potential" biblical evidences. As Penny would say, each time they encountered trouble, it made them more determined to continue their mission as field reporters—a mission to document evidence revealing ancient truths of the God of the exodus and the story of Israel that was lost for thousands of years in the ancient land of Midian.

This is a story of a family traveling deep into the wilderness of northwest Arabia. They risked arrest, climbed mountains, survived the scorching sun and the 120 degree heat of the desert, went without water, and dealt with an abundance of scorpions, snakes and secret police. What would drive anyone to take these monumental risks in Saudi Arabia?

In the following pages you will read about the unforeseen and the supernatural events that led this couple with their two small children into one of the most closed and sensitive countries in the world. You will follow them on each journey as they go camping in this volatile location in Arabia. You will experience each step of their incredible expeditions as they hold a Bible in one hand and a walking stick in the other, discovering location after location, each matching the story of the exodus. Like the Caldwells, you will gain new insight into the biblical scriptures and a new understanding of the Bible's relevance.

You may question their sanity but will certainly praise their courage. You will anguish as they did when security forces pointed guns at their children, Lucas and Chelsea. You will experience the joy and wonder of a family truly on an adventure—an adventure that their children to this day cherish beyond any remembrance. They long to return.

There is probably no one in the world, outside of the Bedouins in northwest Saudi Arabia, who have spent as much time exploring this ancient Land of Midian as the Caldwells. You may have heard of adventurers who have traveled into Saudi Arabia looking for the real Mount Sinai, only to be caught. Those escapades lasted a few days and none produced much, if any photography or video.

This is how I came to know the Caldwells and to learn that the vast majority of the photography attributed to this area was taken by them, even though others claimed credit. The Caldwells could not be linked to this remarkable collection of photography for their own safety while they were still in Arabia. For several years I knew that photographs which matched the biblical account of the exodus were leaking out of

Saudi Arabia, but the identity of the photographers was a big secret. I then received a call from a rabbi in Jerusalem who knew about my film, called *The Exodus Conspiracy*. This is a scientific and forensic investigation into the story of the exodus, with Dr. Lennart Moller, a DNA research scientist who had conducted extensive investigations concerning this topic.

We talked by phone and then arranged a meeting. Wow! The investigative materials started to come together and the Caldwells' fieldwork was indispensable in the making of *The Exodus Conspiracy*. Over the years, more people confirmed the work that the Caldwells had started. A pattern of evidence was beginning to unfold. In May of 2003, the Caldwells returned to the ancient land of Midian accompanied by myself and Dr. Moller, Dr. Glen Fritz, and a few others. Although we had been granted permission to enjoy the Arabian landscape and to camp in these areas, we were soon asked to leave by armed and determined security forces. However, during this trip, it was possible to confirm the fieldwork recorded by the Caldwells. With our own eyes, we attested to the validity of these locations and artifacts.

Since returning, I have continued to work on the film, spending hundreds of hours reviewing the video footage of the Caldwells' now fifteen journeys into the Jebel Lawz region. Along with several scholars, I truly believe that Moses and the Israelites received the Ten Commandments in this location. I have enormous respect for the willingness and faithfulness of the Caldwells to find and report the potential evidence of these events.

Finally, as you continue to read this amazing story you will learn what the Caldwells, myself, and others have learned: that this key event at Mount Sinai testifies that God made a covenant with the people of Israel and that this covenant was everlasting. I believe that the events that are occurring today in the Middle East are directly related to the event at Mount Sinai.

I believe that the Caldwells' effort to document the pattern of evidence surrounding this area now known as Jebel Lawz, is quite possibly the result of God's direct revelation, thus helping a very secular world to remember the exodus and not to forget the covenant that God made with the Jewish people.

Today most of the world hates Israel. Moses and the prophets warned the people of Israel many times not to forget what God did by bringing them out of Egypt and into the land he promised their forefathers. Today, most have forgotten. The book you are about to read records the journey of a family of four who were catapulted on an adventure to help the world *remember!*

Tim Mahoney
Director
The Exodus Conspiracy

Preface

Originally I began writing of my family's wild adventures simply to create a history for my future grandchildren. However, matters too great and weighty to be easily confined within a family, matters of import and significance, demanded a permanent record to testify to their reality. Therefore, I was persuaded to detail the story in book form so that it would be available to others. And so this project was born.

This is the record of what happened to the Jim Caldwell family between December 1, 1991, and April 3, 1992. Within those four months, we experienced and filmed happenings that defy any material or scientific explanation to this day. We cannot fathom the whole scope of what they signify. As fantastic as it may seem, what you will read is based upon an accurate log of the events as they happened, taken directly from the journals penned by my own hand as each occurrence unfolded.

Yes, this story is true from beginning to end! It is difficult to recount events of such consequence by way of pen and paper, or keyboard and computer screen. The journeys we made throughout the Middle East which are told in this book have given our eyes and our spirits a horizon point that is just not easily shared, particularly if others have not witnessed the vast distances these desert and mountain regions encompass, nor been moved by the recorded histories of them. These lands are as wild and untamed as they have been for thousands of years and have remained equally enigmatic and alluring through time. And history isn't over.

Penny Caldwell
April, 2008

JIM'S THOUGHTS ON *The God of the Mountain*

The words contained in this book are as dear to me as my life itself. It is right that the love of my life, my wife Penny, be at my side and be the one to have witnessed these things first hand and then be able to chronicle all that was seen, said, and done, into this work. It was also her passion and love for the Word of God which led her to instruct and to share, always recognizing the importance of recording the miracles of life as they happen. Then she also wanted to build altars of remembrance simply to have a legacy for us, our children, and grandchildren-to-come, to learn and hold to what God has done for us and can do in people's lives.

This book is a record of the remarkable events that happened to us in Arabia from late 1991 to 1992, specifically the first three trips to the Jebel Lawz mountains and surrounding areas. It is as accurate as a soul could possibly make it, written from Penny's own diary as the events unfolded around us. I can testify that there has been no embellishment in this writing, for it would pollute the power of the truth. And be prepared, because what this reveals is only the beginning.

Jim Caldwell
April, 2008

I WILL GO BEFORE THEE,

AND MAKE THE CROOKED PLACES STRAIGHT:

I WILL BREAK IN PIECES THE GATES OF BRASS,

AND CUT IN SUNDER THE BARS OF IRON:

AND I WILL GIVE THEE THE TREASURES OF DARKNESS,

AND HIDDEN RICHES OF SECRET PLACES,

THAT THOU MAYEST KNOW THAT I,

THE LORD, WHICH CALL THEE BY THY NAME,

AM THE GOD OF ISRAEL.

ISAIAH 45:2-3, KJV

The *God* of the MOUNTAIN

THE TREE ABOVE THE CAVE AT JEBEL LAWZ

CHAPTER ONE

The Tree

LATE FEBRUARY 1992 – NORTHWEST SAUDI ARABIA

The tree. There it was, sandwiched between two gigantic slabs of granite at the peak of the mountain directly in front of Jim Caldwell. It was most certainly this same tree that had buried its way deep into his psyche only two weeks before when he had laid eyes on it the very first time. And now, peering into the brilliant blue sky against which it seemed to stand as a timeless memorial, he felt it difficult to concentrate on the near impossible task that lay before him.

As he gazed upward he was amazed at how conspicuous it was. He knew instinctively it must have meaning linked to the ground upon which he stood; the very ground where, in all likelihood, Moses and the children of Israel once peered upward in wonder and trembling at the glory of the Living God, resplendent and terrifying alike. *Holy ground that it had been prophesied he himself would walk on.*

It was notably more obvious to him this time how very much the two enormous blocks of rock on either side of the tree were reminiscent of the stone tablets of the Ten Commandments. What a fitting marker for this location, he thought to himself. Was this the clue he had been looking for? He felt his pulse racing as the possibilities in his mind led him right back to the real reason he was standing here at all. Much warfare and prayer alike had carried him and his family to this place at this time, and there was no denying what Jim was really seeking. Clearly visible below and to the right of the two stones and the tree was a large cave. And everything within him was screaming out that the Ark of the Covenant could be hidden inside!

* * *

To the left rose the rounded mountain we'd nicknamed "Belly" Mountain on that first trip. It billowed out and was smooth as glass in places—so smooth, in fact, it seemed to have been designed that way. Scanning from its middle downward, Jim became quite aware of the focus of his purpose again. In a direct line running toward him like a sneering watchdog, stretched the fence; and it continued without breach in its enclosure of the area he wanted to explore. Not a single unexposed point for our entry, he noted with disgust. He raised his camera in a defiant motion and began snapping away while the tracks were clear.

The day had begun on a more promising note. Jim and I, and our children Lucas and Chelsea, had risen early and gathered our whittled-down supplies for backpacking into the mountains, which lay on the far northwestern frontier of Saudi Arabia. It would be the first time we'd carried our gear on our backs, and we had all looked forward to it for more reasons than one. It had been a quick series of flights the day before from the east side of the country where we'd been living for four years, to the Al Adel Hotel of Tabuk, following the rental of a four-wheel drive vehicle. Refreshed and expectantly watching, we dreamed of adventure, each of us in our own way, and we intended to find it.

It was still dark as we began our trip. Lucas and Chelsea were balled up under fluffy jackets, snoozing on-and-off, while Jim and I balanced the time between rambling, hushed whispers of our mission and staring into the blackness that lay before us. This was the road out of Tabuk to Duba, where we would intersect a desert track at Bajda leading off to the north. We had followed this route only once before and remembered a gas station just beyond the turnoff as the only landmark that could keep us from driving past and missing the track all together. This morning had been clicking as smooth as clockwork though, and neither of us had any fears that we'd miss it.

The Toyota Land Cruiser we'd rented was a black and gray two-door model, with a four-cylinder engine and a wonderfully short wheelbase. This pert little truck was in Jim's opinion a fun toy he could play around with, not having the usual concerns one must have for the well-being of his transportation. Some things were not certain, however, such as the all-important range of the vehicle with regard to fuel consumption. Jim knew his own truck, a Nissan Patrol, like the face he saw in the mirror every morning and knew exactly how far he could push fate, so to speak—which he had a knack of doing on a regular basis. This trip had to be planned down to the liter, and even Jim had curbed his appetite for "riding the edge," which raised him a few notches of respect in my eyes.

After a few minutes of driving, the sky behind us had begun losing its rights to the dawn; pale blue replaced the deep ebony of the desert night. Ahead of us the jebels, the Arabic word for mountains, appeared as random lumps and shadows amid the waves of sand, like so many islands scattered across a sea of tan. It was the landscape we had come to cherish in the years of living in Arabia; the desert had been virtually unknown to us before, having been born and raised in the deep South, in Louisiana. We were accustomed to great stretches of greenery and the endless winding bayous that had formed so much of our childhood memories. The land here first seemed harsh, barren, and devoid of life, but as we ventured out on our camping expeditions, little by little we came to know just how full of activity it really was. The freedom of the frontier had birthed in us a desire to roam it whenever possible, and the prospect of finding traces of the past enveloped in the shifting sands had grown irresistible. It was just such a desire that drove us this morning, as the first rays of sunlight slipped over the horizon and landed squarely onto the Bajda sign we sought. We looked at each other in triumph—with a knowing glance that we gave each other when we knew events were falling into place in a master plan that was beyond us both.

Off-road travel was not by any stretch of the imagination a smooth ordeal. With a bounce, a dip, and a jolt, the little jeep adjusted itself to the desert floor, which in this area lay strewn with sharp-edged rock. This track was obviously well used by the local Bedouins, and as is common with frequented trails, had several sister tracks on either side of it which had been born out of attempts to avoid some rather serious wash-boarding on the main drag. Following it would be easy enough, but the choice between being jostled to pieces, or risking getting stuck on a sandier path, was a difficult one. After all our teeth began complaining loudly from the severe chattering and jarring of the stones, Jim made the decision to switch off to the track on the left side of the main one, and almost as quickly we found ourselves quite immobile and stuck. A quick shiver of fear ran through Jim and me alike, though neither of us allowed the other to see it. In our own truck, this was rather routine, and a simple whipping out of the shovel and sand boards could take care of the matter in seconds. But this was not our truck; there was no shovel, and sand boards were nowhere in sight. We looked at each other with a grin, however, and as was our custom, bounced out of the truck with a positive hope that the importance of the journey would somehow overcome any obstacles that had been sent forth to detain our progress. Five minutes later, with two large hands and four small ones pushing against the back of the jeep, Jim was back on the main track, waiting for his family, to catch up and join him again.

The day was shaping up nicely around us. When we traveled this track before, a howling wind had whipped up the sand and cast a dull haze over the entire area, making it difficult for any of us to see much at all on the horizon. We'd stopped numerous times that trip, taking compass readings and straining to see the mountain peaks in the far distance to get a bearing on the direction we needed to follow, but the quantity of dust in the air had slowed us up considerably, and distinguishing anything at all ahead of us was nearly impossible. Remembering the hassle, Jim found himself sending up a quick prayer of thanks for our good fortune this morning. Blue skies became brighter as the sun rose, and the outlines of the various rock formations on either side of the jeep were as crisp as the air around us. We knew if the calm prevailed, before long the distant range would be apparent, though still several hours drive off. And true to the spirit of the day, they suddenly popped out ahead, sentinels of time and space, majestically towering toward the sky.

On and on we traveled cross-country, switching back and forth between the sister tracks at random, following the ones that seemed less rocky. We watched the sandstone formations with their "melted" look change into harder rock outcroppings that resembled volcano cones and rifts. These actually were small mountains, rising here and there across the plain, and would eventually grow into the monstrous giants further on, where our little family was headed. As the landforms were changing, so was the variety and texture of the sand. In places it was as nondescript as beach sand, but in others it was a beautiful reddish-purple color, and in other places a pebbly consistency and bright orange. I recalled the mental landmarks I'd placed in my mind on the previous jaunt and knew, as did Jim, that we were right on target.

Kilometers silently clicked themselves off as excitement and tension mingled and tugged at our imaginations. Off to the right, the three circular tower-like pillars stood where they'd been painstakingly carved over the years by the elements—another signal of our proper whereabouts. By 10:00 A.M. the object of our adventure loomed huge in front of us: the highest peak in the region, named Jebel Lawz centuries before by the peoples of what was then the land of Midian. Standing there in the clear air as it had for all of time, the mountain was as shrouded in mystery now as it had been when Jethro, the Priest of Midian, regarded it as the Holy Mountain of Yahweh. As for us, there had come to be only one explanation for this piece of breathtaking scenery—it was, indeed, the very site of the true Mount Sinai, where as the biblical narrative confirms, Moses received the Law of Almighty God.

There was still a good deal of country to cover, even with Jebel Lawz in view. As Jim and I had evidenced before, not taking just the right track could put you in a dead end wadi, which is what the Arabs call a dry river bed, where the path would vanish into either a sheer wall rising or a straight wall down. Backtracking cost valuable time, but unfortunately it was to be the case this morning. We had strayed a bit too far north and missed the wadi track that sloped gently into the valley we needed to traverse in order to reach the bottom of Jebel Lawz. When we attempted to find a way down, the track had disappeared into a field of boulders, and there was nothing to do but turn back toward the south and search for the main way in. It was not all in vain, however, as our wrong turn took us past some sights we had not encountered on our first visit to the range. We came upon some outcroppings of pure white quartz, embedded in the hillside here and there. It rang a note in Jim's memory of the circular pieces he'd seen at the base of Jebel Lawz, which had been cut out of a white stone. A bit further on still, Lucas, who'd spotted more arrowheads in the desert than any nine-year-old boy should have been allowed to find in a lifetime, called our attention to a long row of rock formations sticking up at right angles from another hillside. Carved into the tops of many of the pieces were petroglyphs, or ancient rock carvings, of the same variety we'd seen the time before, yet in an entirely different area, and much closer to Jebel Lawz. We made time to stop and photograph some of these, and Jim shot a bit of video for good measure. Jim hated to miss any little bit of information that might be valuable, especially if it could shed further light on the proof we were gathering on Jebel Lawz. Beside that fact, he always felt more comfortable with a video camera in his hands.

A little further on we came upon a graveyard—a unique sight to see in any part of Arabia. The graves appeared to be both old and recent, with worn down stone piles and freshly dug mounds of dirt. Each hillside gravesite was marked with well-placed stones in half-moon configurations; we thought after examining them further that they must all be pointed toward Mecca, as would be the Islamic way. More camera shots, more video.

Jim found himself suddenly distracted by a sound he'd hoped he wouldn't be hearing this morning: a clear and distinct noise he knew so well—the whine of a small truck engine. He looked at me with a face that knew it was only a matter of time before we'd all be intercepted by a Bedouin who'd spotted us on his territory. And there, over the ridge, the little white truck appeared.

Happily, we did not know the man—the Bedouin we had met before who held the keys to the fence was not a man Jim wanted to see again. Now, faced with an encounter before he even reached the area, Jim was not so positive the day would turn out as well as he'd hoped.

Anxiety has a funny way of speeding up your thinking, as though some rapid-fire brain circuit gets attacked and pushes reason and ability right out of the way, allowing for the incredible and bizarre to take over. The difficulty already produced by the language barrier was enough to cause misunderstanding, but Jim knew that if he could push back his fear and just stern up his face enough to act as if he had a perfect right to be there, this desert Arab would sense that mindset and let us go by. It had been an established plan of Jim's to slip into the area undetected from the south, thereby gaining the photo opportunity he wanted.

The man in the white truck seemed cordial enough. With his best "*Sa-laam allay-kums*" and "*kaif-ha'aliks*"—the usual and most friendly way to greet an Arab you've never seen and try to establish trust—Jim began the ping-ponging of English to Arabic, Arabic to English, that usually accompanies these sort of meetings. Normally, when the first few words of understandable Arabic had played out, he'd offer the Bedouin cigarettes, or charcoal briquettes, water or fruit; and both parties would be satisfied that neither one was interested in way-laying anyone, nor in carting off either one's wife and children. This was similar, but quickly turned in the very direction Jim had prayed it wouldn't.

This guy began making references to a black sierra, the Arabic version of *truck*, and Jim realized that the story of our former trip through the region must have spread like wildfire among the nomadic community. It was only the travel letters he had obtained somewhat miraculously the week before from his company, Aramco, that floated our family out over the edge of the mistrust this Bedouin was sitting on. For there, in blatant written Arabic, stamped and sealed on February 17, 1992, stood the words: "Permission to travel to Jebel Lawz."

With a wave of his hand, and an expression that really didn't spell out much trust, the Bedouin wandered back to his truck and drove off, albeit as slowly as gears would allow. Jim tucked his letters back into his Iqama, the national passport of sorts that identified a man and his family as legal residents of Arabia. His thinking had halted during the episode with the survival of the mission being at stake, but seeing the dust behind the Bedouin's truck seemed to jolt him back into awareness. To the right of our jeep, he noticed two shallow rises, the one on the left bearing the remnants of a rather squarish ancient dwelling, and the one on the right having evidence of three neatly rounded bases of the same type. I had, during the conversation, noticed them, too, and recognized them as the markers of the course we'd chosen the last time. That route had eventually parked us at the foot of Jebel Lawz. Jim bounded back into the jeep and whirled it around toward the landmark.

The moment of worry was instantly replaced by the logical, procedural Jim's return. I knew the sound of his voice told the state of his being—fourteen years had etched his patterns inside my head like a stonemason's chisel carves out reliefs in granite. I marveled at the change I'd witnessed in him over the last month . The Gulf War the year before had done some serious damage to our normalcy, what with the children and I being exiled to the States for almost an entire year, and Jim stuck in Arabia alone. It was the first time we'd ever been separated, and the months had been agonizingly slow. Even after I had returned to Saudi Arabia with Lucas and Chelsea in July, the after-effects of being apart so long had a grip on us that just wouldn't let up. Financially, we were a disaster because of being a family living in two different locations of the world. It was this very fact that had necessitated our going to Egypt instead of to the States for our month's vacation and had led us into the wild series of events that had us hot on the trail to Jebel Lawz this very morning.

Egypt had been neutral ground for us to settle back into our old familiar lives once again. Ras Tanura, where we lived on the company compound belonging to Aramco, had almost no traces of home for me and was a reminder that Jim was accustomed to living alone. And he felt awkward about having us there again with him, a feeling which he had not been able to either shake or deny. But neither of us had ever set foot on Egyptian soil before, and we'd decided if anything would knit our little clan back together again, it would be living in our truck for thirty-five days, with no choice but to do everything together. And the days had done just that—ticking away their magic reconstructive powers, weaving the threads in and out of the four of us in memories of temples and tombs, pyramids and sphinxes, obelisks, and hieroglyphs.

Now, as I retraced these things in my head, I found it difficult to imagine that a war had ever taken place. The kids sat laughing in the back of the jeep, the sky above me was a crystalline blue, and the ruggedly handsome face of my husband was within the reach of my hands. A sigh of relief and thanks to God for the miraculous healing of my marriage had caught me up in a daydream, when Jim's insistent voice snapped me back to attention.

No one had ever accused Jim Caldwell of not being an able-bodied slave driver. It wasn't that he meant to act bossy; it's just that in his own mind, he had all the steps worked out for any particular job he was attempting to accomplish, and every bit of the gumption required to tell anybody around exactly how to do what he wanted done. He had this knack of talking people into helping him without their realizing quite what was happening until long after the job was finished. Then and only then, would he allow others the luxury of relaxing in thought, in which state he distastefully found me in at that moment. When he dared glance somewhere other than the rough track under our vehicle, he knew beyond a shadow of a doubt that I had gone off in that poetic mental venue I like to enjoy so often. He had allowed me the longest space of time he could stand, partly because he knew how much I loved to daydream, and partly because he enjoyed watching the expressions change on my freckled face. But the moment had stretched to the point that he feared himself getting caught up in it, and he no longer could hold back his supervisory personality. After all, time was of the essence and this was no ordinary joy ride through the desert. There was work to be done, and he was bound and determined to undermine these hostile descendants of the Midianites by carting off the proof—in video and print—that Mount Sinai was smack in the middle of Saudi Arabia.

I was instinctively at his beck and call in such circumstances. We'd proven over and over again what an effective team we really were, and it would be absolutely necessary to complete this job. Jim ran down the list of what he wanted done: as soon as we had the mountain in sight, I was to begin snapping pictures from inside the jeep as rapidly as the camera would allow. Jim would be attempting to video from his side wherever possible, just in case we were caught before nightfall by the gatekeeper Bedouin, who we both knew would remember us well. Jim surmised he could hide the jeep over a small hill which stood in front of the mountain, and from that vantage point, be free to photograph at will. Then, with the film and tapes removed and hidden from sight, we would be able to enjoy the area and explore, having rid ourselves of the task we'd set out to undertake. It was a good plan, and had concealment been our friend, would have worked with amazing accuracy. But another scenario was fated that day, and the shock of what happened next came close to scrapping our objective permanently.

As planned, with camera in hand, I scanned the horizon behind us the whole time as we crept closer and closer to Jebel Lawz. Lucas and Chelsea were in charge of side-to-side clearance, and Jim kept tabs on the front. When the rotund bulge of Belly Mountain appeared and the sharper peaks of Jebel Lawz could be seen rising imposingly in the background, I leaned out of the window and focused squarely on the tree between the two huge stones that seemed to scream out to the entire valley, "Look up here!"

And look at it we all did. The two giant slabs of granite so high above us with the tree standing in between seemed for the world to be a symbol of the event that had shaken the earth: the delivery in flames of fire of the Law of the Almighty—the Law, written by His very own hand! Could that tree be a witness? Could those two huge stones actually represent the two tablets of stone Moses came down from the mountain with? The very tablets upon whose surface were written the laws that still frame the governing councils of all civilized societies today?

We were transfixed for a time remembering all that took place there so long ago. In the sight of such holy ground, in the presence of such awesome power, the feeling we'd had on that spot the trip before had flowed upon us again, and I even saw Jim let down his guard for a moment to bask in the spirit of the place.

A moment was all it took for the gatekeeper's truck suddenly to screech to a halt alongside us. The gatekeeper! We froze for what seemed an eternity before our senses returned. Reading the expression on the old Bedouin's face told us two things immediately: he had remembered exactly who we were, and he wanted us off that mountain!

I tried my best to remain calm and let the normal course of conversation take place. The usual greetings rapidly gave way to a barrage of guttural Arabic, along with sweeping gesticulations and gleaming anger in the eyes of the gatekeeper. His countenance today was not the same as "the friendly old man" who on our first trip had offered us lodging for the night—in the very cinder block style building inside the fence which barred any visitor to Jebel Lawz. This man before us appeared to have changed from the trusting Bedouin that had allowed his young son to open up the gate and show us, step by step, the ancient altar site Moses himself had stood upon; the circular white pillar remains that had been erected by Moses on a holy site; the double-walled stone corral that had led the innocent animals up to the fire as sacrificial beasts required to hold back the wrath of Almighty God against the hideous sins of the people.

What had caused the change in his attitude? Had threats been made against this nomad and his family such that he feared our very presence? Had we fomented such a stirring in the community after that first trip that all the Bedouins had banded together and determined that under no circumstance should these white faces be allowed upon the mountain again?

So many questions raced through our minds that it was impossible to light on one and wait long enough to reach an answer. Whatever the event, we were caught red-handed the moment we reached the mountain. A wave of fear, and the horror of failure in our assignment, loomed heavily over our heads. Searching what to do first seemed to muddle Jim's thinking. (Should he argue? Should he remain silent?) The volley in his head was threatening to dissolve his nerve when he remembered his travel letters giving him permission to travel to Jebel Lawz, and also to another site called Madain Saleh, where carvings of tombs in sandstone had been shaped by the Nabateans centuries before. Out of his pocket Jim came with the folded papers and into the outstretched hand of the gatekeeper they went. The flash of hope that burned momentarily in Jim's heart was swiftly doused as the old man's brows knit together in a frown, and he shouted out loudly, "Mafie Jebel Lawz!"

The words we were hearing seemed incredulous to Jim's ears! What did he mean, "No Jebel Lawz?" Only the week before Jim had his Arabian fellow workers back home in Ras Tanura translate the letter into English for him. Had they not assured him that Jebel Lawz was clearly and neatly written in classical Arabic across the face of the letter? Jim tried to assert calmly that the letter should be re-read and that it surely did mention Jebel Lawz—which was quickly received by the Bedouin as hostility. Around and around, the Arabic chased the English, neither man willing to budge, and neither growing any more peaceful. By this time I myself felt the rising heat of anger building to an explosion inside me and found that holding my peace any longer was quite out of the question.

In the midst of the world of man, I burst out of the jeep in a flare-up of emotion that carried a surprising wallop. A product of Louisiana's Cajun South, my indignation had climbed dangerously to all time level. I had watched the bantering getting nowhere fast, seen the inflexibility of the tight-lipped Bedouin, and I was sure of the appearance of "Jebel Lawz" on that travel letter. Knowing good and well that the miraculous series of events that had brought us here to this place were not of our own doing, but from a Heavenly power, a righteous indignation had taken hold of my logic, and I began shouting right back into the old man's face with every threat I could fathom—from his being in serious trouble, to my hauling him up before the King of Saudi Arabia. I found myself grabbing our Saudia Airline tickets, and in a move that still boggles my mind to this day, saw my own hand reach up with those tickets and shake them violently only inches from his face, screaming out all the while in every tongue imaginable that we had a perfect right to be there! The shock of my daring to yell at him was more than he could take. He began to rapidly back away from me, mouth hanging wide open in shock. Then he began to yell at Jim all the louder. One word was all we could make out, and it shook us hard: "POLICE!"

Our previous incident with the Frontier Forces police had not left us with a warm glowing feeling toward them: on that first trip in, a truckload of police had pulled up and harassed the Bedouin and his son severely for even allowing us to enter the gate, much less carrying binoculars inside the perimeter. The police leader—a swarthy, leather-faced man with a huge ammunition belt and pistol strapped across his chest—had forced us at the point of an AK-47 machine gun to leave the site at dusk, in weather so cold that snow flurries were in the air! Then we had to find our way out of the unfamiliar desert landscape with no road visible and get as far away as Tabuk to spend the night. It was a most unusual demand, as Bedouin ethics will normally at least permit a desert traveler to camp for the night and depart at the first light of dawn.

Whatever they had enclosed inside that fence, they wanted no human alive to see; that was for certain.

And now, from behind us came the sound of another small truck. A younger man stepped out after parking behind us, and from the best we could tell, asked the gatekeeper what the problem was. Again the Arabic flew in circles around our heads, and Jim and I looked at the sons of the desert, awaiting a chance to speak. For the second time in twenty minutes of mumble and shouting, a recognizable word wafted up off the tongue of the younger man—he actually read the name "Jebel Lawz." Hope surfaced, paddled around for a moment, then received a torpedo blow to the starboard side and sank. "Wrong date," came the reply from the other man.

"What!" Jim's face reflected his disbelief that any of this was happening. Now what did they want? Would he and I simply be knit-picked to pieces about this travel letter and how it was written? Would the next complaint be the color of the ink on the paper? Bewilderment was written all over him, and Jim threw up his hands and came over to where I sat scowling. I had begun my own series of threats and abuses again inside the jeep and heard my own voice growing louder and louder as the stand-off continued. "Just take us to the police then," I said before I thought. "Now!" Jim agreed in a second and braced himself for the response. The garbled language rose steadily, in a crescendo ending in a finger pointed at Jim alone, and "Mafie madam" repeatedly spoken in rapid-fire succession. What they wanted was to escort Jim alone to some Frontier Forces outpost in the region, and leave me, whom they had dubbed a wild woman, and my children, sitting like ducks on a lake where the reeds were full of hunters. It was the last straw for Jim. With eyes blazing with renewed zeal, and a sudden burst of adrenalin, he waved off the two men and leaped up into the jeep with us, and shouted back to them, "Police!"

As if commanded by a much Higher Authority, the two Bedouins silently retraced the steps to their individual trucks, clambered inside, and proceeded to sandwich our jeep between them for the cross-country trek to the outpost. The momentary success and exhilaration of victory caused a smugness to invade our jeep. Basking in it without saying a word, we set off in the custody of the Bedouins, wondering what in the world would happen to us next, and enjoying our crazy, adventurous life.

It was then, and only then, that I realized what I'd seen on the front seat of the old man's truck—the long, worn stock of a well-used shotgun.

Moments have a way of lasting eternities when fear creeps up and knocks at your door. It was no surprise to either of us that we'd been apprehended—neither was the old Bedouin's response one that had caught us off guard. It was, indeed, quite an expected thing—just not so soon as it had appeared. And there in the heat of the exchange of stubborn wills, it had even struck a pleasingly resonant tone inside us both, to stand on terra firma right up there against all odds, like some great pre-climax to an Indiana Jones flick. But this image of the gun represented a new twist; and it was as though an electric shock had been applied to my brain just for that instant when I spied the stock. I thought to myself, "Children! Watch out! I've got children in this jeep!" The thought circled the airport of my head once, then came in for an emergency landing—what would I be able to do to protect the kids?

Little did I dream that it was probably their very presence with Jim and me that day that kept us secure in the very safety I so sought at that moment. As we raced off bumping and bouncing down the rough desert track, following the Bedouin and his gun in the lead, I felt anger and resentment building up inside me once again. Just who were these descendants of the Midianites to cordon off the property of the Almighty? Who were they to block His purpose from coming to pass? Even worse still, who were they to threaten my kids!

It was simply impossible to hold all my feelings inside, and I found myself spitting out my various complaints right and left, much to the satisfaction of Jim, who, in listening, smugly chalked up another mark on the windshield of the truck testifying to how well he knew me. Knowing his expectation of my verbiage, I expounded all the more, letting the indignation flow against these "uncircumcised Philistines," a term I held against these native land inhabitants with a real vendetta. My curses for their defeat rang out across the desert as we went along, now into uncharted territory toward the Frontier Forces outpost. By the time we saw the rambling, makeshift shelters of cinder block and tin which housed the desert police force, fear itself was afraid to come near to us! It had been choked out completely by verbal insults, replaced with the fervor of a righteous infuriation.

Within a minute or so more, the first Bedouin came to a halt in front of the quasi-command center, which was one of the last shanties on the right. We had passed a few Saudis walking in and amongst the collection of lean-tos and were stared at in the usual manner we'd grown to expect. Here, surrounded by hostilities, was not the place for a woman to expand her innermost feelings verbally, and I was well aware that to accomplish anything further, I would have to button up and suck it in. With the three vehicles stopped now, a small crowd was beginning to form around the two Bedouins and Jim, who'd already gotten out and begun walking toward the door. I watched Lucas plop down out of the jeep and thought to apprehend him quickly, until I saw Jim motioning for him to come on inside with him. I thought to myself that Jim had been hit with a sure stroke of genius to bring Lucas inside. Children tend to calm the intense suspicions of these locals somewhat, and we needed all that kind of nerve relaxant possible here. It was nearing twelve noon, and I knew that Friday Muslim prayer services were due to blast forth from the minaret of the mosque at the front end of this village of cops at any moment. I wondered what they would do if they knew how serious my own prayers had suddenly become and how fast and furiously they were rising from my lips.

Chelsea and I sat in the jeep for a good while before we realized how hot it was getting. Thermal underwear, jeans, t-shirts, and flannel shirts with sweatshirts over them had been the order of the day, and it was all starting to make itself well known. I pouted with disgust in the unwelcome warmth, realizing that there was absolutely nowhere to go to shed some of these clothes, and even if I had found someplace, local custom would have kept me roasting. Chelsea could disrobe to the level of t-shirt and jeans, which alleviated her complaining and whining, at least, but the best I could do was a half-hearted attempt at rolling up my flannel sleeves. I reached to roll the windows down in an effort to get some cross ventilation going on our behalf, just in time to catch two Saudis hanging out the door that Jim and Lucas had disappeared into moments before, staring and giggling in hushed tones under their breaths. I knew it was at the sight of a female face in public, and I really had to fight to control my desire to jump out of the jeep and give them cardiac arrest right then and there. "The purpose, Penny, the purpose," my reasoning told me in an almost audible voice. Playing the part of the rebellious woman would not be to our advantage at this point. By the time the third series of onlookers had appeared in the doorway, however, it was becoming more and more difficult to hold myself back. Thankfully, and right on time, "*Allah-wahkbar*" began it's off-key resonance in the air around us, and the thoughts of impropriety drizzled into the dust below the truck. It would be a long afternoon, I thought to myself.

The sky above my head remained cloudless and a deep azure; the dust blew around the tires of the jeep in whistling little eddies every so often, and time seemed to stand very, very still. With so many possibilities, I could not allow myself to think at all. The burden of what could happen threatened to unwire my peace at any moment, yet a strange knowing of assured safety never really left my insides.

It was in a period of blank daydreaming that my eyes fed me the sight of Jim and Lucas walking toward me and Chelsea, and it took an active effort to bring myself back to reality long enough to realize that they were actually coming out of the command post. I sat straight up in the seat and sought the face of Jim for the verdict, but I could not catch his eyes long enough to ascertain what he was thinking. All I knew is that he was not in shackles, nor being walked at gunpoint, both of which had been distinctly probable. I did, however, think I had seen a few new patches of white gleaming in the brilliance of the sun as it shone on Jim's temples. I was beginning to understand that encounters of the God-kind had a way of causing hoary hairs to appear before they were due.

There were very few words exchanged as Jim and Lucas stepped up into the jeep. Nods and smiles were all I had for a clue for the first few minutes. Nods and smiles to the Saudis on the outside, that is, for Jim still persisted in his silence toward Chelsea and me. When the crowd of men who'd been inside with them began making their way toward the mosque at the entrance, then and only then did Jim speak, and even at that point, through a false smile and gritted teeth.

He filled me in on the view: a darkened room, with men all around in a circle and a fire right in the center of the floor. Amongst the coals sat a pot of tea and various cups filled with what resembled the notorious stump water that Jim had remembered avoiding as a young boy in a rather dirty little watercourse named Hurricane Creek near his childhood home. He recounted to me how he and Lucas's worst fear was that they would be offered tea and have to drink out of one of those cups! A fate far worse than being arrested and thrown in jail!

He told me that they had been motioned to sit, and did so; and with hearty smiles and pleasing tones of greeting, they'd tried to appear as innocent and unobtrusive as possible. Some of the men were stone-faced and suspicious anyway; others appeared to be amused and fascinated that white faces had ventured alone this far out into the wilderness. He'd already handed over the infamous travel letter and his Iqama, and could do nothing but sit back and await the response from this archaic counsel. Of all the daydreams Jim had been cultivating before the onset of this trip, none had even vaguely resembled this one. *Nightmare* came to mind, as he grinned and nodded to each one there, hoping to find favor and praying like crazy that God would be merciful and show him the way out.

The minutes went by like hours, and each tick of the second hand on his watch seemed to bring about a rising crescendo of the voices of the men interrogating them. The papers Jim had with him had been sent back and forth time and time again to each set of hands inside that building. With each pass, the arguments got more out of control. He was just about to give up when his captors beat him to the punch. With papers in hand, one of the men motioned for Jim and Lucas to move toward a partially open doorway further inside the shanty. Inside this room was a large desk with a man who must have been the Chief of Police sitting behind it. The man was looking downward at some other paperwork on his desk, and didn't immediately look up to see who'd come into his office. It was one of those moments you never forget in a lifetime when he finally did. As if in slow motion, his eyes gazed upward and met Jim's, and suddenly glory filled the vacant space in Jim's head that was awaiting the answer to all his prayers! Like the first rays of sunlight pierce the blackness of a long cold night, the realization of who the man was shone brightly in Jim's mind, and hope rose to the surface once again.

On our first pass through this territory in January at the end of our trip to Egypt, we'd been searching for Jebel Lawz and had been forced to camp without any success that night. Finding a mountain as big as this one would be a cinch, Jim had figured, but after an entire day of traversing every crack and crevice of the range, no such mountain could we find. Jim had gone to bed that night restless, disturbed that we only had one day left to locate this place, and then we'd have to begin the long trek back across the entire country to our home in Ras Tanura. If our luck continued on this level we'd miss it all together!

We'd gotten up the next morning somewhat refreshed, but under the intensifying pressure that sought to sow fear of failure into the fibers of our conscious minds. After breaking camp and setting out, several hours went by and we were no closer to a clue of the mountain's whereabouts than we'd been the day before. As a matter of fact, we were rather hemmed in by a wadi that led to the edge of the mountain range directly in front of us and were blocked by the rock formations from crossing it to reach the higher peaks that showed up from behind. As we stopped that morning to assess where we were, we saw an army-green pickup slowly moving down the track that crossed ours. It went on by, and we thought it would keep on going when it suddenly just stopped, a little beyond where our tracks crossed.

Jim decided to get out of the truck and walk over to the guy, and as soon as he did, noticed the same idea had occurred to him. Jim started to chat with him in his best broken Arabic and communicated that we were looking for Jebel Lawz, and with a shrug and a wave of the hands, the man pointed in the proper direction and showed him exactly how to get there! He even bent down and drew the exact pathway in the sand at Jim's feet, as if to be sure he understood what he'd just seen waved in the air! Shocked and excited by the wonderful response, Jim said his thanks and goodbyes, and was headed back to us in the jeep with a huge, broad grin on his face. Just as he reached the truck, he looked down through the open window and spied his prized can of honey roasted cashew nuts. Within a moment Jim decided that this gracious man's willingness to give us directions must be rewarded with proof of our thankfulness, and he grabbed up the can and headed back in the direction of the green truck. At first the guy didn't want to take them, but with Jim's insistence, he humbly accepted, and away the two trucks went in opposite directions.

There, standing in the midst of judgment at the desk of the Chief of Police, it dawned on Jim that the face he saw before him now who held the power to apprehend him, or set him free, was the same face that had been so pleased to receive the can of cashews! Yes, there was no doubt that the hand of God was orchestrating every little detail. Jim knew as he stood there that this man must surely have recognized him. Not only was he a foreigner, but a very conspicuous one, what with his 6'3" frame, his blonde hair hanging down to his shoulders in the back of his head, and his bright blue lapis lazuli scarab beetle earring stuck in his left ear. Not a common sight in the desert to be sure, much less in this world of men.

The chief looked over at Jim, and a broad smile spread across his face. He recognized Jim, all right! It wasn't another three minutes and Jim and Lucas had the freedom they'd been praying for all of the early afternoon! With a few crisp orders shouted out in Arabic, the chief had effectively silenced the whole lot of others that had kept them incarcerated until now and set them free!

Speaking in broken English to Jim and Lucas, he informed them that they would be permitted to camp around the area of Jebel Lawz, but they must not take any pictures whatsoever. Jim paused to think of the wonder of this incident, knowing now for certain that this angel of a man had been placed there on our first trip into the area just to save our skins on this one! And after taking a written copy of the letter for the file at this outpost, the Chief had set Jim and Lucas free!

Now that he and Lucas were safely back in the jeep, a scheme had begun to form in the overactive mind belonging to Jim Caldwell. I knew it when I saw the expressions beginning to change on his face, and I braced myself for the next wave of adrenalin which was surely on it's way to crashing into the shore of my conscious mind. Had I heard him right? In his excited repetition of the impulse, I was afraid I had.

Jim relayed to me the plan: we would drive slowly and nonchalantly out of the outpost region until the track took its swing out of sight to the right, then I was to prepare myself and the kids for *light speed* through the wilderness. I felt joy attempting to mingle with my apprehension, but it was having a hard time to say the least. A window had been opened before us, and albeit a short one, we were bound and determined after what had just happened to us to blaze through it with all the gusto we could muster. Our fortune had held, even in what seemed like sure doom, for the armed escorts that had brought us there to the Frontier Forces outpost would be at the mosque for at least the next thirty minutes! This fact, coupled with the blessing of a familiar leader who had just set him free, had renewed the fervor inside Jim. I found myself as intent as he was to get back to that mountain and grab every photographic opportunity we could before these Bedouins got finished with their prayers. It was the perfect chance. It was the only chance!

Just as he'd planned, Jim smiled and waved to the remaining Saudis filing toward the mosque as innocently as he could act, seeing as how just the opposite of innocence had the veins in his neck twitching.

Exuberance and thankfulness filled exactly half of his being, while the other half seethed with concentrated indignation at the chaotic morning we'd had to endure. He was absolutely determined now not to be undermined by these modern day Midianites.

We set off slow and sure, as though we were enjoying a meandering drive through the countryside, slowing to look at shrubs and trees or anything else we could think of to prove ourselves simply a family of campers in the desert. The right turn in the track we expected was beginning to appear on the horizon in front of us now, and I, filled with the knowledge that what Jim said he'd do, *he'd do*, began strapping down the backpacks, coats, cameras, and kids for the warp drive that was about to begin. With everything prepared, Jim shot me a glance and swung into the turn without a change of pace until we were good and out of sight. A bell was clanging somewhere in the deep recesses of my mind at the face Jim had just given me, and I winced at the vivid recall it flashed before my eyes. There was no time for fear to even enter in when I realized when I'd seen that face of his like that the last time. It was July, 1978. New Orleans, Louisiana. At the top of the first and highest incline of that ancient but terrifying old roller coaster, the Zephyr!

A smile was all I could get by with before the G-force smashed me back against the front seat of the little Toyota jeep. Lucas and Chelsea in almost perfect unison, screamed "Yeeee-hah!" as we began to accelerate at a ridiculous rate down the rocky track back toward Jebel Lawz. It was a struggle to hold myself down to the seat as we bounced along, and soon we all had the giggles at banging our heads against the roof of the vehicle. The kids were having a ball toying with the conclusive evidence that their father had finally cracked and lost control. He had lost something, because the normal "Boy Scout Safety Leader," who was constantly preaching caution to them in the desert, had suddenly become an Indy 500 race car driver! Who cared anyway what had happened, as long as this joyride continued? I was cracking up right along with them, as it was not possible to be serious with all that had happened anyway.

But I caught the steely determination that danced on the fringes of Jim's laughter. I knew beyond a shadow of a doubt right then and there that the pictures of the tree were as good as developed.

Chapter Two

The Vision

I t was not the thrill of the chase that had drug us back to the mountain for the second trip. Nor was it the little victories that we won along the way that prompted our future trips. It was indeed the historic ground itself that called out to both our subconscious and surface thoughts.

The series of events we had lived through had all been so crazy, so miraculous, so ridiculously impossible, they could not have been planned so perfectly by humans—they were obviously orchestrated from a vantage point somewhere in the heavens!

Looking all the way back to December of 1991, before we knew of Jebel Lawz, the events that were glaringly obvious to us now were then just items of somewhat noteworthy importance.

Beginning with Jim's rededication to God and turning his back on the sins of his past, he had as of early December, begun a new and fresh relationship with me, his children, and his Heavenly Father. I had lost my own integrity in much the same manner and had also sought repentance. I was determined to start the upcoming year with my heart set like flint not to fall prey to the temptations of my past. Both of us had been through an onslaught of the worst darkness that a couple could ever suffer, and it had reached such a point that the searing white light of the Sword of God was the only hope our life together had. Yet, true to His Word, there was the Spirit of Grace, ready to save to the utmost.

Living in Ras Tanura had always held its unspoken benefits. Jim and I were seashore fanatics, and our house was positioned so that a view of the Persian Gulf in all its turquoise glory was available outside our front windows. After our vows of the fifth were made to God, we had begun a week's fast, both for direction and thanksgiving. Each morning before dawn we would go for a jog down the beach path, and then return to the house to pick up a thermos of coffee and head back to the beach where a park bench conveniently had been positioned. It was on such a morning as this that the sky captured our rapt attention.

Saudi Arabia is not normally a wet country by any stretch of the imagination, yet this winter had been unusually rainy and damp. On this particular morning, clouds filled the pre-dawn sky, and the light of the flares from the oil refinery south of our compound cast a pinkish-orange glow against the southern horizon. Jim was convinced that in turning his life around and seeking God's will for it, we were in store for something big, something far-reaching. He felt that God had big plans up ahead for us, as yet unknown, and all of hell was stirred up against us to try to stop them from ever coming to pass. That was quite frankly the reason we had been through such an intense battle. Now, as we made our way along, we looked up almost simultaneously and noticed that right there above our heads, a huge round hole had appeared in the clouds, leaving room for an entire constellation of stars. An impressive, significant constellation to be exact. There, with its stars glistening in the crispy morning air like perfectly positioned diamonds, was the Big Dipper—upside down—as if by calculated gesture pouring out goodness from His throne above on top of our heads. Jim felt the goose bumps rise on his flesh, and out of his mouth came the Scripture: "I will open the windows of heaven, and pour you out a blessing you cannot contain ..." (Malachi 3:10). These words were to become a predominant focus in our lives over the next several months, for indeed a window had opened, and the supernatural had begun to flow.

The very next morning, following our routine Jim and I were at it again, bounding down the beach path in the bare light before the sun began to rise. Facing toward the south, we were headed for the end of the row of beach houses where we'd turn around and walk back to our awaiting coffee. Remnants of clouds were wisping by here and there, and a stiff breeze chilled us even in the heat of the jog. As we neared the turn, again the sky captivated our attention, and we froze in our tracks—we stood witness to what was surely another sign in the heavens. Out over the pounding surf was the perfectly formed finger of a man's hand in the clouds, pointing out in front of us with exacting precision. We stared at each other in disbelief. What was this? What did it mean? Did it mean anything at all? Were we just looking so hard for signs that everything appeared to be one? We had too many questions with no certainty to back the answers up. Yet neither of us, skeptical though we were, would turn loose of the possibility that the Creator of Heaven and Earth was trying to get our attention. Jim again felt the goose bumps rise on his arms and was impressed with but one word—"*Go!*"

In the midst of such rapid-fire spiritual directions, normal life was still going on. But it was Christmas time in Ras Tanura and with that came a confusion of different rules and regulations because of Islamic practices. Aramco was responsible for the behavior of its employees during this season, as the locals could be horribly offended if blatant celebrations of the birth of Jesus Christ were offered for public view. Two years previously Jim had hung a modest string of Christmas lights around our door and front windows and been forced via threat of losing his job to take them down. It left a bad taste in his mouth that he was quite able to recall and stew upon right now. With this in mind, he'd been one step ahead of the game and phoned the personnel section of Aramco before hanging any lights this year and was informed that this year it was acceptable, just so long as no religious symbols were depicted by design and moderation was observed. With this kind of approval, Jim, being true to his own nature, had gone absolutely berserk and was determined to out-do the entire camp by way of twinkling lights. Over the course of a few days we outlined every window, every door, every corner, and every line of our home. The tree in the front yard certainly did not escape a covering, and we even added a secondary Christmas tree in Lucas's upstairs window. It was in admiration of the job well done that the outrageous idea popped into Jim's head, and he hesitated for mere seconds before he decided it was a must.

Now Jim was already known all around the neighborhood for having the highest and most ridiculous antenna conglomerate this side of the camp, and the true probability was that all our neighbors were in secret fear that he might just use that advantage to celebrate the way he felt about Christmas. It was already a foregone conclusion by the next morning as the shopkeeper in the adjoining Saudi town of Rahima sold out of his remaining stock of Christmas lights. Jim's determination in everything he did was beginning to shine again. Out went the phone calls inviting friends over—most notably, the stronger and more agile ones. Over came the unsuspecting suckers, ready for the promised cup of cappuccino on the chilly Friday afternoon. Out rolled the bribery from Jim's mouth, smooth as glass. Up went four duly bribed friends along with Jim and myself to the second story roof of our home. Round and round went the twinkle lights, covering the six guide wires holding the antenna down. Round and round went the regular lights, covering every inch of the center pole the antenna sat on. After two and a half hours the connections were all made, and the final plug went into the wall. What we'd done did not immediately appear—not until after dark. When we saw it, the implication was obvious. The coerced crew had unknowingly formed the shape of a perfect pyramid on the roof of our house! Pyramids spelled Egypt!

The days of December were beginning to click by rapidly now, and a very important decision we had to make before December 31 was also hanging in the balance for us. Certain expatriate employees in Saudi Arabia were required to take a leave outside the confines of the Kingdom each year, and Jim fell into this category. Normally this would be a simple thing: we'd buy four plane tickets back to the USA and spend a month or so with family and friends. This year, we already knew that would be impossible. We simply did not have the money to fly all the way back home. We had been agonizing back and forth for the past couple of weeks, studying the only viable choices we felt we had. Those options narrowed down to driving our truck to the island country of Bahrain and sitting there for a month, or driving all the way to Egypt and spending our required leave there! And based not only upon what had been happening to us in the last few days, but the soon upcoming series of supernatural events, Egypt would win this decision hands down!

From what we'd experienced so far, we knew our trip to Egypt was not simply being forced because of financial reasons—we were beginning to think the financial situation had appeared only to cause the trip. After all, here was the hole in the clouds dumping blessing out, the finger in the clouds saying "GO," and unbeknownst to the hands stringing the lights, a pyramid now sat blazing forth in grandeur atop our house! The possibility of all this being coincidence was fading fast, yet we could not grasp just what it all meant. We simply knew that the days were passing quickly, and we were soon to be on our way.

All throughout the evenings and nights during this time, Jim twitched with a secret dream he had only vaguely shared with me. It was so out of reach, so utterly fantastic, and yet so absolutely a part of him that he couldn't shake it; and soon matters got to the point that he wasn't even trying to. He'd been overwhelmed with the notion of climbing all over Mount Sinai in the Sinai Peninsula of Egypt on our vacation trip. He was filled with the zeal for finding a heretofore unknown cave system there, and discovering abundant and lost treasures that explorers have been looking to find for centuries. Yes, he'd even entertained the unbelievable notion that he and Lucas would squeeze their way into a tunnel inside a cave, and burst into a room that would reveal the lost Ark of the Covenant!

The genesis of this astonishing vision that was now driving him had all started one evening when he went in to work. It was early December. He had been placed on an evening shift at the refinery and wouldn't get off until around eleven o'clock. This one particular evening he had gone in to work, and after making his usual rounds, came to his office and sat down at his desk as he always did. The office was illuminated only by the soft glow of LED lights attached to various pieces of equipment. As he sat there in the semi-dark, something completely out of the ordinary disturbed his usual preparations for the night's work. He looked up at the white board that hung there in front of him—and was mesmerized as he watched. It was as though a movie screen had suddenly appeared on that white board, and he found himself gazing transfixed at a small procession of robed men slowly moving across the desert. They were carrying a large object that was completely covered so that he couldn't see it plainly. Yet strangely enough, in that very instant it seemed to be conveyed to him in his innermost being that this was the Ark of the Covenant of Israel, and it was being carried back to where it had been made!

He came in after work that evening as white as a ghost. I didn't know what could have been wrong. I was about to panic when he assured me that it was *awe* that rendered him speechless. And hearing all that had happened to him only hours before, I understood fully that something far greater than our own ability to plan a simple trip to Egypt was indeed in full swing over our lives.

Jim was fueled at every turn to hold tightly to this vision that was driving him; he began to read the book of Exodus with a fervent ardor to see if his expectations could be even close to reality. He and I studied the whole book of Exodus from beginning to end in great detail. He

Jim's original vision of the Ark of the Covenant

pulled down the video tape we had of *The Ten Commandments* and made us all watch intently the plight and rescue of the Israelites by God's mighty hand. Although the Hollywood version of the movie was not completely accurate, it did cover most of the major highlights of the story very well. The Hebrews had come to Egypt during a time of severe famine from the land of Canaan. They prospered there, and their numbers increased substantially. The Pharaoh of Egypt then forced them into slavery, fearing an uprising among them would threaten his rule. He put them under severe burdens, so much so that they began to cry out to the God of their fathers for a deliverer. And God chose Moses as that man. Although this was a familiar story to Jim, for some strange reason, as he watched, it took on a whole new life, almost as though he had some part in it! He did not realize it at the time, but he was being filled with information that he would desperately need for what lay ahead of us.

The season did have its requirements though, even with all the wild and crazy adventures on the horizon. Buying the children's gifts was fairly simple. But Jim and I were especially intent about shopping for each other; we had determined independently to have this Christmas make up for the last one we had spent apart. As Christmas Eve came around, when he and I began our usual exchange of a few presents, a strange and wonderful trend began to be seen.

Christmas morning continued the surprise—and the astounding evidence of a Higher Hand at work was getting rather commonplace! Jim had purchased for me a pair of gold pyramid earrings—and what he thought would be the ultimate amazement, a rosewood trunk delicately inlaid with brass designs. He just knew it would blow my mind when I laid my eyes on it. And boy, did it blow my mind! Little did he know that I had bought a few surprises on my own for him: the very same gold pyramid as on the earrings he'd given me, except on a chain, and a wooden chest from Bahrain, decorated with inlaid brass! By the time all the wrappings lay around Jim and me in heaps on the floor, the true wonder of just what was going on had us speechless. We had been moved, unknowingly, to give each other the same gifts!

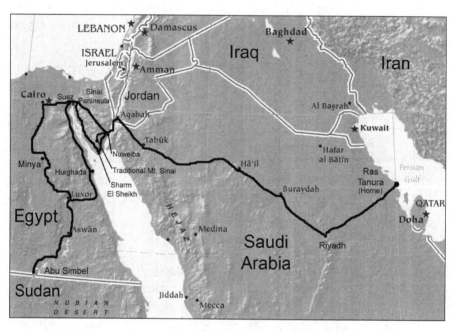

THE CALDWELL'S ORIGINAL ROUTE
FROM RAS TANURA, SAUDI ARABIA, TO ABU SIMBEL, EGYPT

CHAPTER THREE

The Beginning of Signs and Wonders

December 31 rolled in right on schedule, and with our truck packed beyond visual belief, we backed out the driveway and away from the corner of Surfboard and Seashore Drive. Fear, excitement, and the lust for adventure pricked at us from every angle. Knowing God was up to something in our lives spurred us on, yet it was hard not to look back as we watched our home grow smaller behind us. Jim had to work the day we were to leave, and as a result we would have to drive as far as the capital Riyadh and spend the night there. It was only four or so hours away, and the beautiful Intercontinental Hotel was awaiting us. What a way to spend the last hours of a year! Our wedding anniversary was the next day, January 1, and year fourteen looked a whole lot more appealing than the previous number, thirteen, which had been marked by so much tribulation. With minds as loaded as our vehicle, we watched the sun set toward the west and gave ourselves whole-heartedly to whatever lay before us.

Before even an hour had passed, the stomach of Chelsea in its usual insatiable way, forced us to begin looking for a place to eat supper. The capacity that this seven-year-old girl had for food was beyond any of our combined abilities to understand, and its making itself known right now was not the thing Jim had wanted to have happen. It wasn't that he minded stopping; it was finding somewhere that was not associated with the backside of a gas station that concerned him. With the closest McDonald's restaurant being at this time in London, and Riyadh being three and one-half hours away, this put her father in a serious bind. But hope gleamed on the horizon when we found a restaurant sign that was at least spelled correctly in English, which was something of a miracle. We pulled up just at nightfall and walked in, happy to see that the place was clean and the odors permeating it were great. Around the corner and into the family section we went, because in Saudi Arabia, all women must be separated with their husbands in privacy to be able to lift their veils to eat. It was a requirement even for Western families. As soon as we entered the cubicle, my eyes met Jim's with a look that was becoming all too familiar. There, across the table from us, formed by using pretty white tile, was a scene depicting ancient Egypt, complete with pyramids and the Nile River! If we had ever questioned ourselves before as to whether we'd made the right decision to go on this trip to Egypt, this little hole-in-the-wall rest stop meal had sealed it for us! It was time to look forward and only forward. Later, full and ready to move on, we scrambled back into our waiting Nissan Patrol and took off.

We arrived in Riyadh around ten-thirty and checked into the Intercontinental Hotel. After a most refreshing night, Jim awoke early and shook me awake, shoving me into the shower first. Not too nice a thing to do on our anniversary, I thought, until I emerged a few minutes later from the bath to a lavish breakfast and a fresh rose, and presents and cards given as though to a queen! Jim had not forgotten the traditional anniversary gift of golden bangles and had wrapped me up two real beauties! Along with the exchange of words, thought about and written carefully, the glow that had never left us in all our years of marriage burned brightly that early morning. It would be a long day of traveling, but its beginning would make the weariness light.

We watched the countryside change and alter its scenery throughout the day, and soon reached the point where dusk was approaching, Somewhere—still far to the southeast of Tabuk, and just past the city of Hail—we pulled off road and into the desert. The sand was an orange hue and broken up here and there with twenty-to-fifty-foot high sandstone globules, which appeared to have been scooped out at random with a giant ice cream spoon. A pretty stiff wind was rising, and it was tricky finding a spot that offered any reasonable wind block to keep the tent from flapping all night long. We finally chose a rocky ledge up next to one of the sandstone formations and proceeded to set up camp. The weather was turning quite cold with this intensifying wind, and the fire we'd started was whipping orange flames first to the right and then left. I wondered just how cold it really was, as I struggled to prepare our supper of black-eyed peas and cabbage. Yes, even in the most remote desert possible, the southern U.S. tradition of having black-eyed peas and cabbage on New Year's Day was a must! My hands were freezing, it seemed, and that was a very unusual sensation to have here in the desert. Jim wondered himself when his breath began to form clouds in the air before him. But we dismissed it as our tiredness and climbed into our tent before it was late. I fell asleep immediately but awoke to find myself shivering hard in just a few hours. We had all left our sweat suits on to sleep in, with t-shirts and socks underneath and had huddled into the goose down sleeping bags that were supposedly rated to a minus 20 degree temperature. On top of that we had laid out our *bisht*—the long wool robe-like coats lined with sheepskin that the Saudis wear in the winter. I had not expected to feel even a draft, much less to suddenly be frozen! It plagued me the rest of the night, and I was quite happy to see dawn that morning. Jim and I both got out of the tent to make the fire, and the all-important coffee began to brew noisily there on the stove.

The serious cold was all we could talk about, and neither of us could remember ever feeling it this bad. As the light chased the darkness from the sky, we began seeing gray puffy clouds marching out of the southwest rapidly, and we figured we had better get the kids up and moving just in case we had to break camp rapidly. It was a very wise decision.

The rain began before we got everything put away and into its proper place in the truck. Most of our gear was taken care of, but some had to be smashed at the last minute into any crook or crevice into which it would fit in the back of the truck. It was a chaotic scene as we scrambled up into the truck, half frozen! The kids were chattering loudly in complaint, making incredibly funny faces at us and at each other, so I went right along with them, not realizing that Jim in his usual manner had already gotten the video camera up and running and was taking some perfectly awful close-up shots of not only the kids, but my own face which was not only iced over, but scrubbed clean of makeup. Film I just knew I would regret seeing later!

We managed to get only a slight bit wet ourselves though, which kept us from becoming really cold. Caps, gloves, overcoats, and even bisht were all being used this morning; Jim remarked that the cold seemed to be getting even worse. He was correct. As we made our way through the desert and toward the highway, praying the sand would let us pass unhindered, the full horizon was visible; we could see bands of cloud and breaks where the rays of the sun could peek through.

Here and there appeared both partial and full rainbows, which we took to be the first signs and wonders of the day. Like little half moons wherever a shaft of light broke through the clouds, the various rainbows were a phenomenon we'd never seen the likes of before.

But it was the next sign that we would never have expected in a million years: it would follow us throughout this trip like a guard round about us. It would again make its appearance late in the holiday to remind us of the great miracle it represented at the beginning of our trip.

It was the second day of January, 1992, and the laws of nature were about to be changed by an unseen Hand in the Heavens. Jim had looked forward and away, toward the southwest, and seen in the distance a very low, ominous cloud rolling toward us at a rapid clip. It disturbed him in that it seemed so full of wind; he really wondered if it could be tornadic in nature. We expected a tremendous gale, and probably a goodly portion of lightning and thunder. The boiling black roll cloud caught up with us, and it was as though we'd run into a solid brick wall at 60 miles an hour! It hit us full force, blasting the windshield of the truck with such force that it actually left tiny pock-marks all over the glass! Great globs of dirt and sand were within the cloud, and they began to hit the truck along with huge drops of rain. As the windshield wipers struggled against the torrent, it became nearly impossible to see out through the muddy, smeared mess that now covered the front glass!

What was strange is that this rolling cloud, even in all its fury, did not last very long at all. Behind the initial blast, it appeared to be only strong gusts with no following thunderstorm. It was not long before Chelsea and Lucas pointed out a whitish spray on the road, and as all kids would assume, they called it *snow*. With much assurance that it simply could not be, and massive explanations to disprove their theory, Jim and I told them it just wasn't possible in Saudi Arabia. Ten more kilometers down the highway and the impossible took up our challenge and was turning the sands of this ancient desert white! When we realized that the kids had perceived the truth, and that snow was indeed falling in Saudi Arabia, we as a family went quite literally out of our minds! This time I was the one that grabbed the ever ready video camera, and what it recorded is probably the most incredible video footage of our lives! We truly went nuts for the space of about fifteen minutes as we traveled in the winter wonderland.

Lucas and Chelsea had just completely gone crazy. They were yelling and clapping and crying all at the same time! Jim was wildly exclaiming that the ground was frozen as he noticed large ice patches on the highway that were at least half an inch thick! I just kept uttering strange sounds, except for the occasional outburst that this was "snow-hail," which just goes to show how ridiculous the scenario really was. Snow-hail?

The laughter, the jumping up and down inside the vehicle, and the demands that he immediately stop, forced Jim off the main road as soon as a rest area came into view. We leapt out, completely transfixed, while the miracle flakes whooshed by us in a furious tempest!

It was a ludicrous scene, but one right out of my own fondest dreams. Snow was the most special thing in the world to me and always had been. As a child growing up in Louisiana, I'd seen it so seldom, and at that time felt that it must fall upon the earth only at very special times, for very special reasons. The few instances I'd experienced it back home in my youth I recalled with vivid detail, and I just knew that God was speaking to me through those pure, perfectly formed white crystals. I had in all my teen-age and adult life carried forward the love of winter, and each and every year I tormented all who knew me well with my constant jabbering and pleading for snowfall. Jim, knowing this from the very beginning, had surprised me and whisked his bride away to a private condominium in Steamboat Springs, Colorado, for two full weeks for our honeymoon! He also gave me the same surprise for our ten-year wedding anniversary—a second honeymoon in the deep, mountain snow. No better gift could I have ever been given as one who loves the snow like I love the snow!

LUCAS AND CHELSEA IN THE SNOW

The first year we'd been in Arabia, just one month after we left the States, a heavy snow had blanketed the deep South. All my family and friends had called long distance to inform me about it. The news nearly broke my heart, for I had been looking for that snow for fifteen years; and the very month I left, it came. Now, standing ankle deep in what was an even more phenomenal display, I tucked away moment after moment inside the video of my mind and didn't have to make myself strive to remember this scene. I knew because of providence, I never would forget it.

We had already donned the full winter gear we had with us by the time the truck rolled to a stop at the rest area. This particular one was simply a blacktop addition to the highway that allowed one to pull over and stop without being in danger of the vehicles on the main highway crashing into you. Right next to the blacktop was a rock formation, like those we'd camped near the night before, so Jim pulled up against it to use it as a partial shelter from the howling wind, which had now turned completely around and was roaring in from the north.

As always, Jim had the video camera in hand and was almost immediately pulverized in his vulnerable condition by Lucas, Chelsea, and I with as many snowballs as could be quickly rolled together! "Stop pelting your Dad with snowballs," was all he could manage to get out through his chattering teeth! I gave him a break for a moment, even if the kids didn't, and just stared in total childlike wonder at the spectacle that was taking place all around me. I looked down at my arms, which were being kept warm by the dark brown bisht I was wearing, and began to notice that the icy white stuff falling in abundance from the sky was actually snowflakes! Tiny little perfectly formed beautiful snowflakes!

I quickly yelled for the kids and Jim to come see, and especially wanted Jim to get the proof on video that what I was seeing now was not plain ice, sleet, or some tiny form of hail! This was *snow*, and the snowflakes on film would be the *proof* we needed to show to all those back in our town of Ras Tanura, those that I knew would be doubtful of our story in a huge way! As the perfect little flakes kept landing on our arms, Jim zoomed in and recorded their reality as they came tumbling down from someplace high above the earth. We would not notice at that moment in time, in our joyous revelry, that something of exceeding importance was taking place before our very eyes. A happening so absolutely stupendous, so utterly fantastic, that not a single one of us could believe what our very own eyes were seeing.

But it was proven later: There on the video tape, recorded in full view for all of mankind to witness, it could be seen that the snowflakes were all identical to each other, as though a cookie cutter had stamped them all out from a perfect, cosmic mold in the sky! But even more incredible, not only were they all identical, they were all tiny six- pointed *Jewish stars of David*!

Unfortunately, we soon had to call quits to the revelry, not only because it was intensely cold, but also because we had an awful long drive ahead of us to get to Aqaba, Jordan before the end of that day. We drove along in astonishment at the view though, and kept stopping from time to time to shoot video or still camera shots of the gorgeous white desert. We were careful to even include some road signs, as proof to the whole of humanity that we were there at the right place and the right time, for the once-in-seventy-to-one-hundred-year snow event that takes place inside Saudi Arabia.

After about an hour on the road, the skies began to clear somewhat, and we noticed that the desert was but slightly dusted here and there with snow. We had passed through and were on the outskirts of the city of Tabuk, and Jim was in desperate need of some coffee. So I reached for the little plastic container, which I called the coffee pot, that I had bought for this trip. I could fill it with water and plug it into the cigarette lighter of the truck. When the coil inside would heat up, the water would actually become hot enough to boil, sufficing nicely for Jim on this incredibly long drive. I had placed a baby food jar full of instant coffee, and another one full of powdered creamer, in the glove box, along with a small container of sweetener and two mugs just for this purpose. And so far, it was working like a charm. Until this time, that is.

I got everything ready and plugged in the coffee pot; then I noticed that the little light that showed it was working did not come on. I tilted the thing to the right and left, and twisted the wires back and forth to see if maybe it was just a bad connection, but to no avail. After about twenty minutes, it was certain that we had a problem. And the larger one was that Jim had no coffee.

When he found a place he could pull off the highway, Jim went to digging into the truck's panel and found that a 10 amp fuse had been blown by the coffee pot. By this time we were flat in the middle of nowhere, with no possibility of finding a fuse. His brows knit together and a deep frown spread over his tired face. "Great!" he thought to himself. "Now I've got to rig something up."

So he got out of the truck and began hunting for what he could use to make a fuse with his trusty MacGyver knife, and found a few wires on the ground he thought he'd try. He carefully fashioned a homemade fuse to bridge the 10 amp circuit and plugged it into the fuse panel, with a rising confidence that already had him congratulating himself. About a half an hour later, we were sailing down the highway again and my little coffee pot's light was doing just fine. But just about the time the water was getting good and warm, a smell like something was burning began to infiltrate the truck, and sure enough, the little light blinked out just as it had before.

Just about that moment Jim caught a whiff of electrical wires smoldering and in a panic, swerved the truck off the road and onto the shoulder, where we went sliding and throwing a cloud of dust and rocks up into the air. The truck had barely come to a complete stop before he threw open his door, raced around the front of the truck to my side and ripped open my door, all but tearing it right off the hinges! Before I could even get out of the way, he leaned over and grabbed open the fuse panel door by my left knee, smashing me flat against the back of my seat. In another lightning fast move, his fingers found the wires he'd created a fuse from and tore them from the panel in a desperate attempt to stop the complete melting down of the truck's dash, which was already in progress.

"What a stupid idea!" he grumbled under his breath. "I need a real fuse." His voice was getting louder. "Maybe if I up the amperage to a larger size...." Now he was talking to himself and figuring out loud. He threw his head backward and looked straight up into the sky, heaving a huge cry of desperation. *"I need a twenty amp fuse!"* I was sure all of northwest Saudi Arabia heard him this time.

This was rapidly becoming a desperate situation. Jim's eyes were beginning to close on him as he drove, and as we were still in Saudi Arabia, it was not possible for me to drive and give him a break to rest.

It was obvious to Jim that his make-shift fuse had failed, and there was nothing for him to do except pray for the impossible: a 20 amp fuse to remedy the problem!

On down the highway we went, and as every kilometer went by with no gas station where Jim might be able to find a fuse, Jim became more discouraged. He really could not stop to take a rest because of the tight schedule we had to keep to get to the hotels we'd reserved in Jordan and Egypt on the correct nights. But he knew before long it would become dangerous for him to be behind the wheel if he didn't get some coffee to perk him up. We passed a little blue sign on the side of the road that said "Rest Area," and Jim decided maybe stretching his legs would help. The exit came up, and he took it.

What the Saudi's considered a rest area looked nothing like any rest area I'd ever seen. We were in the middle of a barren wasteland, with lumps of sandstone and rocks sticking up out of the desert floor here and there. This so called rest area consisted only of a blacktop exit that went off to the right, paralleling the highway for about 100 yards, and then led right back onto the highway. There was not a single building in sight, which answered my question about bathroom facilities immediately. In fact, the only thing at this rest area besides the exit road itself was a rusty oil drum that was being used as a garbage can, and that was of course overflowing with uncollected refuse. But it was at least a pull-over to do that stretching Jim needed, so pull over we did.

Lucas and Chelsea took off in opposite directions to look and see what the desert here had to offer. They had been well trained by us in all the camping we'd done in the Eastern Province to search the sands for relics of the past. We had found a number of arrowheads, pottery, and beads in the desert back there, and it was always a fun family adventure to see who could come up with the best find.

It would not be very long before Lucas would shock us all with the find of the century!

Jim was about ready to get on the road again. The skies above us were getting cloudy, and the wind had turned sharply cold all of a sudden. He yelled out to the kids for them to come on back to the truck and get in.

Lucas was reluctant to leave, as he always was, and walked as slowly as he could back toward the paved area, all the while searching the ground for that last, great find he was dreaming of. As he neared the truck, he stopped short, and wheeled around and bent over.

"Dad! *Dad*!" He yelled out over the sound of the now howling wind. *"Dad!"*

"Lucas, we have to go!" came Jim's reply. He too was having difficulty with the wind.

Lucas started running back toward the truck and came up behind me as I stood with my door open, preparing to get back inside. He reached his hand across me and over to Jim, and I noticed he was holding something between his thumb and his forefinger.

"Dad! I found a 20 amp fuse!"

The words hit Jim full in the face, as he whirled around in his seat to stare openly at his son. The first thought that hit him was that this was impossible considering where we were. His brain continued in its logical way to taunt him by thinking next that even if the boy had found a fuse, surely it would have to be a blown one! As he reached out to take in his hand what Lucas now handed him, he shook his head in disbelief as he verified the finding of a 20 amp fuse—a 20 amp fuse that had not been blown, but was in perfect working order!

Lucas scampered back to his own door and climbed into the Patrol, smug and satisfied that he knew what he'd found all along! Jim and I sat dumbfounded and silent in the front seat, totally blown away by the absolute miracle that had just transpired before our very eyes. It was a while before Jim could compose himself enough to pull off the cover of the fuse panel and plug the thing in. Moments later, the little coffee pot was bubbling forth in great working order, and no burning smell was emanating from the panel. The chances of this being just a coincidence were far, far more astronomical than to just believe that an Unseen Hand had reached down into the empty desert sands and filtered out of their contents a necessary bit of plastic and metal we needed to continue on.

As we traveled, the terrain was becoming more and more diverse. Now, on either side of the road, the sands had taken on a mauve color, and the sandstone formations were higher and higher. A few more kilometers down the highway and the desert was once again becoming white with a fresh snow that was now beginning to fall.

If I had been told that I would have been snowed on twice in Saudi Arabia in the same day, I would have been sure a lunatic was speaking! And yet, here I was, an eyewitness to just such an event, with actual miracles happening right before my eyes. What in the world was going on? All I could do was shake my head in awe.

Because it had started snowing again, Lucas and Chelsea were begging for another stop to play in it as before. One area in particular we thought was worthy of pictures involved some rather high peaks that had been thoroughly dusted with the white powder. We were in the mountains northwest of Tabuk now, and the road signs read Al Zetah, and Al-Khan. We figured this would be as good a place for the kids to romp as any. This very location was to become extraordinarily instrumental in our future, but for now it only meant recording the gorgeous, white scenery.

Onward we went from there down to Haql, the last Saudi town before we would cross the Saudi border into the tip of Jordan. The mountains of the Egyptian Sinai peninsula were clearly visible across the incredibly beautiful blue-green waters of the Gulf of Aqaba, and the sun was displaying its radiant brilliance in a setting that brought tears to our eyes.

It was a befitting way to end a day of such marked and obvious signs from Heaven.

CHAPTER FOUR

Border Crossings

Presently the Saudi guards came into our view, and we pulled up to the exit gates at the border; Jim gathered all the appropriate paperwork necessary to release us legally from Arabia. Usually this was just an experience in patience and the rubber stamping of documents, but today Jim saw a hint of delay, which puzzled him and brought worry. The guys inside were arguing in their usual manner amongst themselves, and all Jim could make out was the word, "tryp-tyche." The word rang a bell, and he remembered it was one of those pieces of paper that no one understood how to obtain inside Saudi Arabia, and no one knew what it was, either. He'd been told that Egypt required it if you were to drive your own personal vehicle in-and-out-again, but he'd also been assured he could obtain one inside the borders. Now that the guards were motioning for him to come over, Jim was informed of exactly what he did not want to hear. Egypt would not allow us entry in our own vehicle unless we held in our hands this elusive tryp-tyche document. Jim thought this was an interesting twist, but he proceeded to talk these Arabians into letting him through anyway. The Jordanian border was within eyesight and as tired as he was, along with the rest of us, this was no time to argue over what he could finagle tomorrow. Without too much hassle they let us pass unhindered, out of Saudi Arabia.

It was nearing 9:30 P.M. by the time we entered the gates where the customs offices of Jordan began. The friendliness toward Americans we had experienced the first time we'd been there in 1989 had been replaced by a guarded wariness on the part of the Jordanians. Knowing the vacillation Jordan went through between supporting the Allies of the Gulf War and supporting Iraq, it did not give us the easiest feeling to re-enter the country that was seventy percent Palestinian and loyal to Saddam Hussein. However, the supernatural signs of the day had been so absolutely burned into our minds, we figured if God wanted us to get through for a reason of His own, He was big enough to protect us through the short stay we would have in Jordan.

The paperwork at this border crossing was almost complete when a controversy ensued about whether or not we were going straight into Egypt or spending the night in Jordan. By this time we were so sleepy and travel weary there was no question but that we would try to spend the night in Aqaba and head for Egypt afresh in the morning. The border police decided that the cameras, tape player, and music keyboard we were carrying were items that were hot for sale on the black market, and would not allow us to leave before recording the serial numbers of each one into our passports, which we would have to produce upon our return to and departure from Jordan thirty-odd days hence. This was their way of making sure that we were not bringing these items in for sale to the locals for profit without paying customs duties. Understandable, but hardly the harassment Jim wanted to wait for at this hour. Eleven o'clock in the evening, and our Patrol finally pulled out of the gates of no-man's-land and into the country of Jordan.

Funny how familiar, even at this late hour, this coast road was to us. Neither of us had figured on ever passing this way again, yet here we were almost three years later on the very same highway. The streets were quiet, and the palms strained against the stiff wind that had been blowing on us all day. Our little family pulled up into the same hotel that we'd stayed at before, a former Holiday Inn that was now called "The Philadelphia," and we bounded into the soft, clean beds without much talk at all. The intensity of the day had overcome us, and sleep came in a moment. We were at rest at last!

The next morning we scrambled down to the restaurant we all remembered. It held an extensive selection buffet, and after surviving for the past few days on pop tarts and Vienna sausages, we dug in heartily to the hot meal. The day had dawned rather cloudy, windy, and cold and the anticipation of a rough ferry ride across the Gulf of Aqaba to

Nuweiba, Egypt, did not impress me the least little bit. We'd found out through the customs agents that we could not drive from Jordan into Israel, and then onward into Egypt, so our only choice was to take the ferry that was called "The Arab Bridge." Only weeks before, over four hundred people had lost their lives in a ferry disaster in the Red Sea, and the headlines were flashing in my head like neon nightmares! Aha! The resistance begins! We didn't know it at the time, but it was things like this that were sent to keep us from this trip at all costs, and the fear encroaching upon me was beginning to choke me off from all rational thinking.

Downtown Aqaba found us purchasing the tickets for ourselves and our vehicle, and suddenly we were in a panic to get through immigration services at the docks and onto the ferry before it set sail. The "Jimy" was its name, and it was rather huge by any standard ferry size to us. We waited on the upper deck for several hours, all the while watching streams of humanity shuffle down the lengthy ramp that led to the loading dock, then onto the decks below us. Semi-trailers, cars, and cart after cart of luggage of one kind or another piled on. With the weight of every item and vehicle I saw being placed on this ship, I was beginning to be assured that sinking under this great load was a real possibility. Almost three hours after we boarded, the Jimy finally trumpeted its departure, and we shoved off.

The ride was smoother than I expected, but extremely windy on the upper class deck, which was the only place I decided I could be truly safe. Inside, a swarm of people formed a moving sea that undulated in unison with the wave action of the ferry. Outside on this deck were a few Egyptians with me—one which I discovered was smiling at me just a bit too much. Before long, just as I knew he would, he came over and tried to bridge the language barrier between us and struck up a conversation.

The most I could make out of what he said was "Cairo," which was where he was from, and the fact that he was sure that I was Jewish! It was all I could do to keep from cracking up, what with the complexities that would entail if I had still been in Arabia. Imagine! Me, being Jewish and living in Arabia! I wondered why in the world an Egyptian man would think that. The attempt at conversation lasted for the better part of the three-hour journey, and before I knew it, the ferry was sounding

PENNY AND THE JIMYZ FERRY IN AQABA, JORDAN

off its giant air horns again, signaling its turn into the small bay at Nuweiba. I noticed then that the only beach of sand I'd seen the whole way down the Gulf was there in front of my eyes, while all the rest of the Egyptian side had been straight, jagged mountains, extending right down into the water. An odd thing, I thought.

Now the real trial was to begin, and little did we imagine what lay ahead of us. Coming in to port, customs was no big ordeal; we were specialists at Arab borders by this stage of the game. These crossings usually allowed us a great opportunity to roll our eyes at each other and do a little of what Jim referred to as "drizzling." It was his term for being overwhelmed with disgust or impatience, or having to put up with anything he did not want to do, especially when prompted by the stupidity of others. A few more hours beyond where we were at that moment and Jim was about to enter the rainstorm of his life.

The run-down, ramshackle buildings that comprised the immediate view of our entry into Egypt were overflowing with the humanity that had washed off of the Jimy and into the canal of concrete that led to immigration. It was like a scene from some movie I had seen years before; some nameless B-flick that played again in my head while my eyes focused on the sight. It crossed my mind how very little my world was before our move overseas—how little I had known about the plight of the peoples of other nations. The palette before me now held every color and tribe and tongue, a tapestry painted in living flesh as far as my eyes could see, and changing as the people moved closer to customs, like threads fading one into the next.

After driving off the ferry and up to the first gates, and finishing the initial proceedings of car searches and the multiple rubber stamps on our papers mania, we pulled over to the side of the cement area where we were gone over with a fine-toothed comb. Jim left with a handful of paperwork, thinking that within a matter of a few short minutes we'd be off to the hotel and a welcome rest after the never-ending ferry ordeal. He disappeared around the corner of the buildings to the left which were behind the truck, and I began to straighten out the truck to prepare for our trip to the El Sayadin Village, which would be our lodging for the next several days. I didn't notice at first how long he'd been gone, as my business was occupying much of my thought. When I did finally look down at the clock on the dashboard I almost panicked! Jim had been gone almost two hours, and I saw no sign of him anywhere. In a flash I remembered the Saudi border guards and their warnings about the tryp-tyche paperwork that Egypt supposedly required for the truck. "Oh, Lord," I said out loud, "please help us!"

The face of Jim Caldwell was as easy for me to read as the very large print on the top line of an eye-chart and as reliable in its forecasts as an aneroid barometer. By it, I had been able over the years, to predict vast periods of clear blue skies, or the inevitable days of severe cumulonimbus thunderstorms, coming in bands of tempest and whirlwind, seeking whom they could devour. It was one of the lowest atmospheric pressure readings I had ever witnessed when his eyes locked onto mine, as he rounded the corner heading back toward the Patrol.

His jaw muscles were clinched tightly, and his lip twitched to the side as it only did when he was doing his best to control his temper. I heard but one phrase escape his gritted teeth: "Tryp-tyyyche!"

Another movie instantaneously flashed across the ready cinema in my mind, as I plugged in to Captain James T. Kirk's response to being left on a lifeless planet with no hope of rescue: "Khaaaaaaaaaan!" he had screamed on the movie. It earmarked the event with multiple scenarios, none of which my overactive imagination and overtired body had trouble blowing up into scenes in a new movie it had just created, *Nightmare in Egypt*. Not so inviting was the prospect of spending the night in our truck with the Egyptian customs officials, since the truck was in the process of being impounded by customs at this point in time. Lucas and Chelsea were beyond tired after sitting inside the truck for so long with nothing to do, and Jim and I were just plain roasted. "Now what?" we both asked disgustingly and in unison.

Jim stood there for a moment, and then rounded the lot of us up, and one by one we filed across the blacktop and into the nearest immigration agent's room, which had little to offer in the line of comfort. Four uniformed Egyptian border guards sat sprawled in the vinyl chairs there in the office, and three of them got up and stood around so that each of us could sit down. I immediately began a display of excruciating tiredness, as sometimes in Arabia one could move upon the hearts of officials to get things sped up via having women and children in distress. I soon made a note inside my head that Egypt was not Arabia, and this game was going completely unnoticed. Well, maybe not completely, as I caught some sympathy out of the corner of the eyes of the youngest of the men, but it was certainly unfruitful. I couldn't even quite determine whether or not it was compassion I read in his face, or passive flirting. Disgust was creeping in quickly. The youth picked up my change of attitude and looked the other way.

One of the Egyptians had been walking back and forth from this office to another building, obviously speaking to some head officer, in a half-hearted attempt to help us. Two or three times he had been back to them with no apparent luck, and by this time Jim had endured enough. He made a deal with them that finally flew with the head honcho, allowing us to take a taxi from just outside immigration to the El Sayadin Village Resort, which was only about a thousand yards from these archaic proceedings, to spend the night. This was conditional upon our Patrol maintaining its impounded status and remaining inside customs until we could come back and continue the argument in the morning. It was a chance we would have to take.

We gathered what we would need for one night and filed like a battle-fatigued caravan of weary pilgrims toward the concrete wall that led to the iron gate of freedom. Jim wondered why it seemed that all hell had suddenly opened its doors and dispatched hoards of demons to keep us from getting into Egypt. Or so it seemed as we piled into the taxi's back seat, covered in rugs and sheepskins and reeking of Eastern incense, our minds clouded and unsure of our destiny. The horizon wasn't even visible at this juncture, and sleep would have to be intravenously given to be enjoyed at all. I was not so tired, however, to miss the fact that the rugs on the floor of this little taxi were there to keep items from falling through the giant rusted out holes that allowed me to see the ground passing by beneath us.

Only five minutes away, lights gleamed from the little resort village where hopefully, we had reservations awaiting our arrival. The outside had been decorated with a conglomeration of Christmas lights, but in the shape of a large fish, which didn't seem too bad a sign as we drove up the circle and to the front office. Jim mustered up his wits, totally scrambled from the evening's events, reaching deep inside him to that reservoir of supernatural strength he'd known personally for so many years, and even managed a smile as he greeted the guys behind the counter at the reception desk. A kindly looking man with jet black hair and gold rimmed glasses looked over the travel voucher Jim had handed to him, and began the registration paperwork immediately. Jim had been almost afraid to show the voucher, as it was a day behind the date of arrival we'd originally given, but this man had waived it off as though it meant nothing. Already Jim liked him and introduced himself and the rest of our crew. His name was Ziyad Taleeb, and he held the position of manager at this resort. "A good man to know well," thought Jim, as the wheels began turning in his mind as to how in the world he could coerce Taleeb into helping him get our truck out of hock. But one look from me and the children's combined whines told him he could think tomorrow. Tonight it was past time to put his family to bed.

JIM IN FRONT OF THE TRADITIONAL MOUNT SINAI
IN THE SINAI PENINSULA OF EGYPT

CHAPTER FIVE

To St. Katherine's Monastery

The morning dawned cold and mostly cloudy. From our hotel room, my little family made its way down the sidewalk that eventually joined itself to the main building, then on to the restaurant. We had seen only a few people late the night before and ascertained that very few guests must have actually been here at this time. The eatery itself was spacious, with glass all the way around the eastern and southern sides, which faced the Gulf of Aqaba and the bay, respectively. Furnishings were simple but it was neat and clean, and the smell of fresh coffee was a beckoning familiarity we all needed desperately. The food was already partially served, as is European style; an array of cheese, jellies, and breads, accompanied after seating with a hard-boiled egg. There on the edge of the Sinai Peninsula in Egypt, a new Caldwell breakfast tradition was birthed that we wound up observing with regularity for the entire rest of our trip. It consisted of combining strawberry jam with cream cheese, then spreading it over fresh Arab bread like a slab of butter. This was a truly unique new taste to us as hearty Westerners, eager to try anything at least once.

As we relished and savored the flavor of our newly found treat, I caught a strange looking protrusion gathering momentum at the base of the clouds that were streaming quickly to the south, right down the center Gulf. From our vantage point, the mountains of Arabia were clearly visible to the east, and we'd been watching the rays of the sun occasionally stream through the random breaks that dotted the cloud cover. But now, the openings had become fewer and fewer, and the dark rain clouds had the appearance of being stirred with some giant, celestial spoon into a boiling mass of turbulence. Just as I was about to give my usual report of the weather status, a perfectly formed funnel dipped quickly down, and hovered approximately one third of the way to the water! Jim and I saw it simultaneously, and our mouths fell open wide in utter amazement. It was not often that either of us found ourselves speechless, but neither one of us could at that moment, utter a sound.

I felt the hair beginning to stand up on my arms as the first waves of goose-bumps flushed across my skin. Funny, I thought, because this sensation usually only occurred to me during times of close proximity to the Spirit of God in His divine operations among the brethren. I knew good and well what I was seeing because of my years of interest and study in the field of meteorology, yet something here was not quite fitting to scientific explanation. For one thing, the clouds were moving at a visibly rapid clip to the south, while this funnel didn't move at all. It just hung there as if in suspended animation. Secondly, I knew that spouts of this kind have been known to stall before reaching the ground, but it was highly uncommon for one to extend to a certain point and just stop completely, as this one was doing. I was transfixed in awe and amazement, and my mental conflict rose to a fevered pitch—was this a normal funnel cloud or not? But if it wasn't, then what in the world was it? Something was sparking a memory in my head, but I couldn't quite put it into focus. While I tried to remember what it reminded me of, the funnel slowly uncoiled itself right back up into the sky and was gone. My whole family sat there motionless for a moment, then shook it off as a wild and crazy event, one of those "one in a million" of nature, and proceeded to finish our breakfast.

There are certain times in the course of revelations to mankind that the supernatural breaks forth upon the scene both unexpectedly and profoundly, leaving no room for explanations of logic or reason. Such was about to enter inexplicably into our morning just as blatantly as before, carrying along with it the implication that what was meant to be understood in the first attempt was missed altogether. Jim had just finished spreading the jam and cream cheese onto another piece of bread and was about to put it in his mouth, when his eyes grew wide with wonder and disbelief at the sight he was witnessing again. He made no sound, but motioned for me to look up and over toward the mountains on the Saudi shoreline. As my eyes rose to the sky, I felt the electricity dancing all over my body in wave after wave of chills. There again was a perfect funnel cloud, hovering in exactly the same position that the previous one was, exactly the same distance from the water. And exactly like the one before, it too suddenly uncoiled itself, and sucked right back up into the clouds!

Within the space of three or four more minutes, in the very same place, the funnel made its third dip down from the clouds and hovered the very same distance from the water again. *Three times* it came down in precisely the same manner, in exactly the same fashion, at exactly *the same place.*

Dumbfounded would have been a good word to describe us. There we sat, mouths gaping open, in dead silence and with frozen limbs. How in the world could this be? And much more, what in the world did it mean? It would be another three and a half weeks before I remembered when I saw the first funnel dance down out of the dark layer of clouds, like a giant finger pointing to the mountains below it—the same sort of finger we'd seen over the Persian Gulf in the early morning hours at the beginning of December, saying to us, *"Go!"*

But initially, nothing clicked except that we should retain this vividly in our minds, for it surely must mean something. While pondering the implications, Ziyad Taleeb breezed into the restaurant and came directly over to us and pulled up a chair. He was quite inquisitive about our comfort and our meal and sought to serve us in any way possible. Jim and he would attempt to go to customs this morning, and with Ziyad there to translate, he was certain he could get some sort of arrangements worked out to free the truck from its incarceration. Attitudes refreshed and positive thoughts abounding, we pushed away from the table and hopped into the cab Taleeb had waiting to take us off to the border. A thousand footsteps between buildings, thirty-eight stamps upon as many pages—and a whole lot of arguments later—the two men stepped up into the Patrol, started her up, and triumphantly drove out of bondage and into the world of freedom. It had taken them almost four hours to do it, and wear and tear on several mighty angels, but the officials had been moved to release it and nothing apparent now stood in our way. It was time to turn our thinking toward Jebel Musa, the traditional Mount Sinai, and nearby St. Katherine's Monastery, in the south of the peninsula, and to test the mounting number of signs that seemed to point to us finding something there. The vision he'd had of the Ark of the Covenant blazed brightly in Jim Caldwell's mind. He spent that night in dreams of adventure.

* * *

Another dawn was beginning to break casually over the western mountain range of Saudi Arabia. Jim had been up and outside already in the pre-dawn darkness. In a habitual response, he had awakened me and both of us had slipped out quietly to the truck; we grabbed the kitchen box and the Coleman stove out of the back. Having to wait until seven for a first cup of coffee was totally unacceptable to us both, but even if it hadn't been, this was our way of introducing normality into what was fast becoming a completely unconventional vacation. Still in relative darkness, Jim had fired up the stove behind the little wall that separated each bungalow, for the wind was howling out of the northeast. I prepared the coffeepot and put the water on to boil, and we sat there, snuggled up tight against each other, waiting for the sun to pop out above the mountains that the funnel cloud had pointed to the day before.

This day was starting out very chilly, and we wondered how much colder it would be at 8000 feet when we got to the peak of the traditional Mount Sinai, Jebel Musa. This was the special place we were headed for, where Jim expected to find a cave holding the Ark of the Covenant.

Fueled with our morning liquid and warmed by communion with our Creator as the glorious rays of light streamed across the Gulf of Aqaba and onto our faces, we stood and went to wake the kids and get ready for breakfast. Ziyad Taleeb was our guest again, and he had American omelets prepared for us and also the national food of Egypt, which was called "fool." This bean dish was much like pinto beans in olive oil. He explained to us that if this mixture was mashed, it was called tahini, which we politely pretended to understand. It did have a unique and delightful flavor, and we left the restaurant quite a bit fuller than the day before. Taleeb bid us farewell as we set out for St.

Katherine's Monastery, and off we went. It looked like the beginning of a wonderful day. One full of hope for us.

There were no clouds in sight. The mountains before us to the west seemed to have no entry, and as we followed the road up higher and closer to them, we wondered where in the world we could get through. Just as it appeared we would crash into the mountainside, a narrow valley opened up before us and the two-lane highway meandered off to the right, following the natural wadi, called Wadi Watir. It was here and only here that there seemed to be any break in the mountains whatsoever. Just as before, around another corner and it seemed the same blockage would be repeated; but once again a pathway opened up, to the left this time, and we were able to travel on. The climb was steady, winding through this natural pass, but it finally opened up into a wide plain, with peaks surrounding it in the distance. It was rather strange to see a desert inside the mountains, at a higher elevation than one would have expected.

About an hour later we saw some rather high sandstone formations off in the distance, swathed in many hues from earth tones to brilliant mauve. Following a huge bend to the left, we looked across the flat sandy floor of this basin and saw what appeared to be a cave way up high in one of them. Jim would have jumped off road immediately to investigate it but for the fear of missing visiting hours at St. Katherine's. This is exactly the sort of thing he'd been searching for; maybe this cave held the mystery he knew he'd been sent to locate. In the event he didn't find what he wanted at Jebel Musa, the traditional Mount Sinai, this site could hold a victory. He made a note of precisely where the site was located, and determined to get back there by afternoon for an exploratory mission. Three *Hear, Hear's* from the rest of us and it was set.

Presently the turnoff appeared, and it was not long before the highest mountains we had yet seen came into view off to the left in front of us. Judging the distance on the road signs to St. Katherine's, we knew these monstrous peaks had to contain Jebel Musa. Thrilling was not the word for it. This was the event, so we thought, that had brought us to Egypt. This visit to such a holy and crucial place in the history of our God had us silent in reverence before we ever got there, and the prospect of Jim's finding what he had seen over and over again in his mind, hidden away in the mount, was threatening to thump his heart right out of his chest. The Ark of the Covenant was fashioned at Mount Sinai, his inner voice kept repeating over and over. For no apparent reason, and for every ludicrous one, the Holy Spirit kept connecting the two in his head. This struggle to fit the two together had plagued him in a constant battle since early December. What in the world was going on, he wondered.

The summit of the highest mountain there was covered with snow, and the nearer we got, the more snow we saw, filling every ridge and valley along the highway. Yes, snow again. Was I dreaming? I was certain that this was the most sign-filled few months I had ever experienced in my life. Right now it was the mountain that had me spellbound, but later I would recall the snow, and just what a special messenger it really had been!

The road dwindled down to the base of the brown granite pinnacle that was the traditional Mount Sinai, and seemed to end in a circle. In reality, it continued onward into the little village behind Jebel Musa, but our direction was to the left, down the dirt trail that led to St. Katherine's Monastery. A thought was already forming inside my head about this valley in front of this mountain, because it seemed way too small to have ever had a huge Israeli encampment below it so many years ago, in antiquity. Right behind that one, another thought sailed down into my psyche: this mountain seemed too, well, too short! I remembered in the text of Exodus that we had so carefully studied that the Israelites argued among themselves, asking each other what had become of Moses. Standing there at the base of this mountain, I thought of how easily they could have looked right up at the top and seen him standing there! But these thoughts were not the ones I wanted to be having. This place was to be the whole focus of our Egypt trip in the first place! What was I doing doubting it so immediately? I looked over at Jim, who was filled with hope and anticipation and searching for the fulfillment of his vision, and kept my mouth shut.

The storm that had come through here several days previous must have been a big one, for even now the snow was clinging on tenaciously in drifts of up to three feet! We pulled up near one of the drifts and parked the truck, intending to go into what looked like a bookstore or information shop of sorts. Once inside, I was overcome with a sensation of darkness I could not at all understand. The Egyptians behind the counter were not unfriendly, but when a tall, thin monk walked in, I knew where the source of my feeling had originated. He had a scraggly beard, and glaring eyes that never left us for a moment. Not exactly what we took to be a welcome. We purchased a book about the monastery and left rather quickly. I was glad we were moving onward, but knowing how much this sight had been built up in Jim's mind, I dared not tell him how strange I was beginning to feel there.

We proceeded back to the truck and deposited the book, then picked up the cameras for the hike behind the bookstore and on up toward the actual monastery. A dirt road led the way, and before long we were greeted by an Egyptian dressed as a Bedouin, walking a camel toward us. He immediately began his sales pitch, trying to get the kids up for a camel ride. Now Lucas and Chelsea had lived among camels for over three years now, and it was no big thrill to them to see one up close. But this guy kept on, and finally Lucas decided to sit on it for a picture. It was then that we experienced our first "Baksheesh" harassment. "Baksheesh"—the Egyptian way of demanding money for anything and everything. Jim became hardened to it long before, but this time we were suckered. It was inevitable, we figured, but it didn't have to happen again. We walked on, wiser and less a few Egyptian pounds.

In meeting several people passing down from the vicinity of the monastery, we were informed that the snow on the pathway to the top of the mountain had caused it to be closed. Great, Jim thought. It looked like this trip was a total failure. Nothing was going to be found here, and it was blowing his mind. Surely he couldn't have missed all those signs! He just couldn't have made all this up! We half-heartedly walked up maybe one hundred feet, and I gathered a few rocks, but the enthusiasm had been lost, never to be recovered in this site. Jim signaled it was time to get out of there and tried to hide his disappointment by focusing on the cave we had spied earlier on the highway. His head was hung low—he had needed to find something. He had needed it desperately.

I didn't know how to react. I was upset myself, but I was really worried about Jim. What a letdown he must be feeling! I searched for words to comfort him, and when we got back to the road, finally found them. In my best fake optimism, I said "Jimmy, what you're looking for isn't here!" As soon as the words left my mouth, I looked down to the road at my feet, and saw something golden in color gleaming in the dirt. Now I had this radar about me that could find a coin in a sand dune if I really put my mind to it. I'd found two very old Arabic coins in Arabia right under the noses of my colleagues, and disgusted everyone early in our desert adventures. But even I was not prepared for what I saw when I picked this one up and held it in my hands! The writing was absolutely Hebrew, and the English on the other side proved it out: an Israeli coin, right there in the middle of Egypt, at the base of Jebel Musa! I couldn't believe my eyes, though, when upon the back I also saw pictured the seven-tiered candlestick, or menorah, that was to stand near the Holy of Holies in the temple of God. It was such an obvious answer neither of us knew what to say, except that this surely didn't seem to be holy ground. In fact, by now we were totally convinced this could NOT be the real Mount Sinai! But if it wasn't here, where was it? Too much wondering was going on, with no way to get any answers. So we got in the Patrol, drove back out to the entrance, and right up into the restaurant to eat. Food to our family had a way of answering everything.

After lunch, we headed toward a series of little shops, poked around a bit, and listened to some locals talking back and forth about various things. In one, a merchant had some beautifully colored rocks and quartz, with turquoise here and there interspersed. Jim asked the guy where they came from and was told that a mountain somewhere in the vicinity, named appropriately Color Mountain, produced them all. So after receiving some cryptic directions from the shopkeeper, we decided to take off and search for it, and wound up on a trail behind Jebel Musa. All that panned out was a pack of Bedouin dogs and a group of children that ran out into the track, chasing our vehicle. On Jim's time clock it was time to move out of there and off we went, back down the highway and onto the main road again. In about forty-five minutes we came upon the spot with the cave that we'd seen earlier. Now Jim was extremely glad he'd marked it coming in. There sure wasn't anything to be found at the traditional Mount Sinai!

Before long, the sign we were searching for appeared to us again, and afar off we could see the cave, high up in the side of the range. There was an extended area of sandy plain that we'd have to cross before reaching it, but that was par for the course in Arabia. It took us about fifteen minutes or so to get over to the edge of the escarpment and we followed a natural cut in the rocks as far back as the truck would go. Much to our surprise, the cliffs narrowed to the point where the vehicle wouldn't fit, and continued to do so until only a person could pass through. We got out of the truck and readied ourselves for the hike.

The cliffs rose up maybe twenty feet, and turned right, then left, then right again every one hundred feet or so. I thought if I could see this from the air, it would look like a giant, continuous zigzag. For the better part of the afternoon, we wound our way and climbed through what we named the "Siq," after the one so similar to this in Petra, Jordan. All along the way we found fossil after fossil of seashells and marine life imbedded in the soft sandstone. The colors were beautiful, and also reminded us of the similar strata in Petra. But time was beginning to be a problem for us, as the sun was sinking lower and lower and losing itself behind the range that intersected our "Siq" from behind. Already we'd been in it for almost an hour, and the walk out would take at least that. What we didn't want was to be in the dark out in the desert in unfamiliar territory. So at the last, Jim himself climbed up a cliff on the left, straining to see if he could reach the cave which, much to his disappointment, turned out to be not a cave at all, but simply a shadowy depression in the rocks. He decided then to turn around, filing away the fact that the Egyptian Sinai peninsula was dead ground when it came to the things of God. They just weren't there. He did feel better though, than on Jebel Musa; at least here we had a family adventure to write home about.

We had hardly been on the road for half an hour when the stars began making their appearance in the sky. The scenery was breathtaking there in the mountains as light gave way to deeper and deeper blue, all the while changing form and breaking out in distant suns like twinkling diamonds here and there at random. It always amazed me to see the sky at night. For years and years, my own daddy had taken me ritually to the roof of our garage when meteor showers were predicted or comets forecast to shine in the heavens. Watching there, the heavens were so quiet and so distant and so big. And so directionally positioned toward the throne of the living God. "He calleth the stars by name...." I pondered the Scripture over and over in the back of my mind.

Jim, as if entranced by the same celestial glory, found a track off the road to the right, and drove down it so that we as a family could get out and just look up for a while. There we were, awash with wonder: four children in a desperately beautiful wilderness, alone and looking up to our God! But the tired little faces of Lucas and Chelsea soon noted that they needed sleep. We got back inside the truck and moved onward, until the final turn between mountains gave us sight of the glimmering lights of Nuweiba and the sea. Once inside our bungalow, sleep came quickly, and took us all away.

CHAPTER SIX

The Road to Cairo

N ow the next morning was the sixth of January and deemed the day to drive to Cairo. In all actuality it had not been our decision, nor was it in the original plan. Not only that, it had quite rearranged our entire vacation schedule because we would now have to exit the country via the same port we had entered. This ditched our visit to Alexandria altogether, and also our tentative arrangements to see Cyprus at the end of the trip. It also totally hacked me off because I would have gone via Alaska to avoid riding that ferry again. The intricacies of the tryptyche deal made by Ziyad Taleeb and the Egyptian customs officials dictated that we now had to take along with us a representative of Cairo Automobile Association, who was in possession of my passport as part of the surety that we would not sell the truck and run off without paying duty on it. Not our idea of a joyride, but probably not his either. Cairo was six hours across the peninsula, and as loaded as the Patrol was, we were squashed inside like sardines.

The day was long and arduous and passed slower than our driving stretches usually did because having a stranger in the truck limited our conversation considerably. Besides having an unexpected passenger, it didn't help matters that we realized all too late that this was one of the Egyptians that had not taken a bath for a number of days. The smell arising from his body was atrocious. To make matters worse, he must have attempted to overcome his body odor by showering himself with cheap cologne, and the combination of the two was producing a thick stench that was curling our noses. The scenery was nice though and

THE SPRAWLING CITY OF CAIRO, EGYPT

changed from mountains to desert to mountains again. Nearing Cairo, the flatness became hugely monotonous, and everyone was beginning to feel the edge of irritability coming on. The lack of fuel stations was putting a silent horror in the back of Jim's mind too, and though he

hadn't said anything yet, he himself knew he'd been gliding on fumes for well over an hour. At the moment he couldn't think of a worse thing that could happen to us, but it was beginning to look inevitable. Every kilometer that went by, a gas station was nowhere in sight. In his desperation he prayed silently, hoping his faith would bring a swift result. Before fifteen minutes had passed, the answer showed itself on the right side of the highway, and we all heaved a gargantuan sigh of relief!

Later, Cairo at first glance was the most outrageous commotion we had ever seen. It seemed to reach out and envelope us before we knew it and began to digest our vehicle into its bloodstream of traffic, as if billions of red and white cells were pulsing at slow, then rapid, then slow speeds to some unseen, humongous nerve center. In the few short days since we'd left Ras Tanura, enough awe had boggled us to last a lifetime already, but Cairo was doing its best to scramble our thoughts for good. This was awe all right, but awe in the negative—a fearful nightmare of moving machines and nameless faces, all having places to go, yet going nowhere at all. The honking and beeping was never-ending noise pollution, and the halting speed with which this bumper-to-bumper traffic traveled was maddening. Even Jim, who surely must have the blood of Mario Andretti flowing somewhere in his veins, was paling at this onslaught of chrome and steel. I detected his wavering and felt myself slipping down a spiral staircase of uneasiness. Never had either of us felt so out of place, or so all alone.

The worst problem was one undeniable fact: we had to reach the auto association before three-thirty, and it was now already two-thirty. In a city of eighteen million strong, three hours to drive across this town was not uncommon, and whether we'd make it in this traffic or not preyed upon us. Fear was banging down our doors now, and the gloomy tone of our psyches could have been cut with a knife inside the truck. Our fragrant passenger finally got us within sight of the building we needed at 2:45. "Ah," I thought. "We've made it!" But it was not yet to be.

For the next hour, we marked in inches the forward motion of the Patrol. With the business in sight, we still could not move in the worse traffic-jam-to -beat-all-traffic-jams we'd ever witnessed. We were on a one-way street, and there were three lanes, with parking on either side. The grisly part was that the cars were smashed five deep, and as a result, no one was pointing in exactly the right direction! When the traffic cop would blow the whistle for us to move, no one could budge because we were all in one way or another blocking our own forward motion. Jim was reeling, both in frustration at not making our deadline, and in pure disgust that a city could be this out of control, when the most unbelievable happening of all took place before his very eyes. The small car in front of us was slinking slowly forward, when its back bumper caught the front bumper of a van on the side of it. Instead of stopping and freeing himself, the man continued to move forward, slowly but surely ripping the van's bumper cleanly and completely off! Jim and I gave each other the open-mouthed, gaping-eye look, and spoke not a word between us, stuck that way for at least two minutes. Where in God's world had we been sent? Warm feelings and pleasant salutations were not on the agenda today.

The next hour was to stand out as the most intense in our recorded journey. We finally got past the traffic jam and were able to make a mad dash for an illegal parking place, got a policeman to accept a verbal bribe not to haul our vehicle away, and raced upstairs to an office that surely could have made motion picture history. Four desks were crammed side by side in far too small an office to handle them. Sitting behind each, in the now familiar act of trying to appear to know what they were doing, were four Egyptian "businessmen," much concerned with their smoking and tea drinking, and phone conversations with what were obviously personal calls. Jim and I sat down dazed, but hopeful that our unwanted passenger of this drive up from Nuweiba would be able to do and say what was necessary to get us on our way. Very quickly we found out that this was simply not the way of Egypt. Another major blow to the old tryp-tyche was about to explode.

The arguments that began to break out soon drew the attention of a higher superior, who had been barking out orders from a hallway that ran perpendicular to the front four desks. As he emerged and came forward to get involved, we knew all was definitely not going as it should have been by now. It seemed that the presentation of the tryp-tyche was as guaranteed as a six-legged pig showing up. With all the promises that had been spoken in Nuweiba, with all the grueling hours spent just moments ago in Cairo traffic, with all the aching backsides from the day-long drive across the Sinai Peninsula, a numbing of understanding was taking place here that would have ended in violence if Providence had not been present once again.

We had been promised the documentation and denied it all in the same day. This Cairo Auto Association would not budge from their insistence that the U.S. Embassy guarantee our vehicle, that is guarantee that we would not sell it while in Egypt. The government offices also would not issue the tryp-tyche unless the Cairo Auto Association received such confirmation. I absolutely lost it and hit the roof, shouting at them as loud as I could about the mistreatment of Americans in Egypt. I threatened to withdraw myself and my family back across the Sinai that very day, and spend our entire month in Jordan. I reminded them of the loss of revenue to Egypt this would entail. I promised to advise all the peoples of the earth that Egypt was not the place to ever take a vacation because of how horrid the Egyptians treated their guests, as we were finding out! But the worst of all insults was when I called them liars, loudly, right to their faces.

"Your people promised us in Nuweiba that if we brought this man here to you and paid 600 pounds we would be given the tryp-tyche in Cairo! Now that we've come all this way as strangers and guests in your country, this is how you greet us and welcome us to Egypt? You tell us lies!"

As a matter of fact, I did everything but curse their mother's graves. Which, of course, was next on the agenda of my tongue, had not Jim grabbed me and shut me down.

Jim knew he had to do something, but had no idea what to do, when what we then didn't realize was an angel stepped forward to speak. Samir was his name, and he was an attorney for the company, and the mediator we so needed to take up our cause. Jim had watched Samir's face cringe while I was railing out my accusations of injustice, and seen him get up with a horrified look on his face when he heard the threats of taking a month's worth of hotel expenses out of Egypt and into Jordan. Unbeknownst to us before now, there seemed to be a standing feud between the two countries about such things as tourism. Finally, this was the advantage Jim was looking for!

After much haggling and terse conversation, it was decided that we'd be allowed to travel to the Cairo Nile Hilton for the night—and that without surrendering my passport, which was their previous requirement. From there, in the morning, Samir would take us to the U.S. Embassy, where we would seek a guarantee of personal property. Neither one of us expected such a thing would be possible, but with what we'd so far been through, a bed for the night was welcome. We left the place completely frazzled. I made up my mind then that I absolutely despised Egypt, and I hated Cairo worse than all of Egypt. I continued to rant and rave, albeit a bit more quietly, as we made our way back to the truck. It was a hatred that was subject to change.

Jim had been calculating his position in his mind during the whole ordeal, and as we wound our way down the dusty staircase to the outside it snapped back into his mind that the policeman he'd bribed to watch the truck in a no-parking zone just might have made off with the pounds and left it unprotected. Messing around with a man's vehicle is kind of like hassling his wife; both can get you into a heap of trouble. Fortunately, when the Patrol came into view, nothing appeared to be disturbed. Jim shot a glance of thanks upward, and turned his attention to the task at hand—finding the Nile Hilton in this undulating sea of automotive congestion. We headed in the general direction of the river and tried to follow the quasi-directional map a bystander had traced for us in mid-air. One thing we quickly realized: this moving organism of steel and tires allowed no room for error. There was no pulling over if you missed your turn. You were simply swallowed alive and went tumbling slowly in whatever direction the majority of the traffic was going.

In just such a move, Jim spied the Nile Hilton off to the right, and grimaced at his luck as he found himself in the left-hand lane of a major artery that was headed for a bridge over the Nile River. True to the enormity of Cairo traffic's healthy appetite, our truck was quickly and efficiently sucked up and over the bridge as Jim called out to the children, "Kids! Nile Hilton!" The next few minutes were spent trying to explain to the rest of us just why we found ourselves across the river from our hotel. Jim had no means to describe it, only that he meant to do it that way so we could see more of the area. A right turn found us paralleling the water, and soon enough another bridge back across the Nile appeared. Ah! One more right turn, and Jim figured we'd be over the river and able to jump right back to the right and straight up to the hotel. Wrong! Indeed, the bridge was navigated, but the road to the right that would have brought us straight in front of the hotel turned out to be a one way street, and naturally it was going the wrong way!

So, we followed the car swarm behind the hotel, and attempted to traverse the square that sat directly in back of the Nile Hilton. Lo and behold, it just so happened that there, behind the hotel, was the loading zone for the busses that were so smashed full of humanity. Driving in front of this zone was treacherous at best, if not impossible altogether. It took us another twenty minutes to go less than a block, which was all we lacked to reach the first highway we had seen the Hilton from.

"Patience, Jim, patience!" were the words echoing inside his head. Jim was not well known for his abundance of this trait, yet he'd had to restrain himself so long with the events of the day that he knew if he didn't get a break in the traffic here soon, he'd stand the chance of going completely berserk and using the Patrol like a battering ram against the obstacles impeding his forward progress. In a fortunate stroke of Sovereignty, when the traffic picked up again, Jim spied just the right exit; and in a move best described as a careening side-swipe, bulldozed his way over to it. Within two minutes, we were under the huge concrete canopy of the Nile Hilton Hotel. As usual, we sat for a moment of silence, aghast at the entire scenario, until the yelling and honking and beeping wafted back into our now deafened ears. This time we were responsible for the traffic jam, and the line of people behind us was growing by the second. Out we went, one by one, after very skeptically having to turn the keys over to the parking attendant.

Inside, the plush luxury of the cram-packed hotel was quite a contrast to the circus that we were beginning to believe was the normal state of things in Cairo. The high ceilings and chandeliers could be classed as normal for a five-star hotel. But the huge chunks of Egyptian antiquities that appeared to have been ripped in whole walls from tombs and temples, and now covered vast portions of the lobby, made us aware that we were quite a long way from home. It took a while, but reservations were finally confirmed, and our dusty, worn out crew headed up to the Executive Floor to find quite a nice room awaiting us. With what we had been through today, it was like finding an elusive oasis in a howling desert wasteland. Bed came early, and except for the noise of the never-ending car horns eleven stories down on the streets below, the night passed with much needed sleep.

January 7 started out with Jim and me sneaking to the floor above us for a cup of coffee on the balcony overlooking the Nile. The noise was deafening there, too, but we were almost getting used to it. A frightening thought, we mused! The Executive restaurant was set up with rolls and cereals, and sausages, or what was called such. Toast and jellies, Arab flatbread and honey, cream cheese, olives and fresh cucumbers were all a part of the usual morning meal. We found it was not much different than Saudi Arabia, although the bottles of scotch and gin against the wall at the bar were certainly indicative of where we were not. It felt sort of posh and surreal to us, that there we sat—the bayou Cajuns from Louisiana, high above Cairo, Egypt, eating breakfast! In reality, Jim and I had gotten only coffee at first, then twenty minutes or so later, crashed into our own hotel room, wrangled Chelsea and Lucas awake, and chased them up the stairs to the same table where our coffee awaited us. It was a pattern we would be repeating for the next four days.

After the tooth-brushing and hair-combing that was always a necessity after breakfast, we made our way down to the lobby and found ourselves to be about a half-hour early. No problem, Jim thought to himself. It would give us time to take in the large square of shops that lodged themselves here in the Hilton. At first glance, and surely confirmed by closer inspection, these were no trinket markets. I got the impression Paris had come to Egypt! Everything from exchange banks to fur coats could be found within a few walking steps. Most of them were not yet open, and that was all the better Jim discovered quickly, when he saw that for the price of one small pyramid-shaped clock, he could buy a new truck! As we made our way around a corner, we noticed an elderly gentleman in a three-piece suit walking toward us. He was an eccentric looking fellow, with his cane and Muslim prayer cap firmly in place, yet there was a wonderfully pleasing glow about him that drew us closer. His wide smile and radiance came along with his outstretched hand, as he introduced himself as Mr. Mansur el Sharif, private tour guide of Egypt. The depth of his voice was a real surprise, and we immediately took a liking to him. In the space of five minutes, Jim had arranged for Mr. Mansur to be our private guide to all the sights of Cairo for the next several days. That of course, was predicated upon our obtaining the personal guarantee from the Embassy, which none of us could calculate the odds of at this point.

Before much longer, Samir appeared in the doorway, and we were off to the U.S. Embassy, which was another mind-boggling drive that should have taken ten minutes and wound up taking forty-five. It was becoming clear to Jim that the city of Cairo had not had a functioning traffic light at any intersection since about 1954, which was also the approximate date it seemed, when these ancient traffic police had been stationed at their posts. The voluminous lines of automobiles, however, were not the current agenda on Jim's brain. His vehicular positioning and the rest of our vacation which at present hung in the balance was.

The building was massive and windowless, as was the current status of most Middle Eastern American Embassies, we assumed. Samir appeared to have been there before and led the way around the entire building, just to be turned back again to the very first set of entrance doors we'd encountered. Once in the interior lobby, we adult Caldwells breathed a sigh of relief, as the familiar things stood out like elephants at the proverbial party of mice would. There was the President of the United States, George Bush, grinning down on us from his position upon the wall. There was Old Glory, ever-so-still, yet proudly at attention in the heart of Egypt. It felt suddenly as if all would be worked out somehow, although the thought nagged Jim that we were now grasping for signs to bid us to go on in every nook and cranny. I, on the other hand, was taken by the amount of local Egyptians trying to get visas to enter the U.S. It was amazing how much of a wait and paperwork nightmare it was to the average man here even to visit my country, and here I stood—passport in hand—able to exit and re-enter at will. A good glimpse of my blessings, and our tryp-tyche troubles seemed to lessen even further.

After much explanation and much waiting, the Embassy staff called forward Jim Caldwell to the line of hopefuls awaiting word on their various requests. From where Samir and I sat playing cards with Lucas and Chelsea, the volume of chatter did not seem to be favorable for our cause. After a moment, Jim walked over to us and announced the plan to Samir, who, of course, had been sent to represent the Cairo Automobile Association. Since the Embassy did not know us from any other stranger, they could not give any personal guarantees of any kind to us. What they had agreed to do was to notarize a personal statement as a witness to the fact that Jim Caldwell would state and subsequently sign a document promising not to sell his vehicle inside Egypt. It was the best the agency could offer. It was the only chance this vacation had of continuing a moment further.

The next hour was possibly the longest thus far in the quest for the infamous tryp-tyche. Samir, having not the highest authority in the company he represented, could not agree or disagree with this plan. We would have to take the notarized document back to the office and try to get it approved. If we did receive approval, it would mean car tags would be issued to us for use in Egypt on the vehicle, which should stop us from getting pulled over and checked for the travel ticket booklet. Then we would not necessarily need to hold the tryp-tyche itself. If we were turned down, Egypt was finished. Unfortunately, this entailed another classic drive through the streets of doom, with tension so high both inside and outside the truck, that we feared spontaneous Caldwell combustion, as no one could forecast what would happen if implosion and explosion both occurred at the same time. Jim was already beyond any stress point he'd ever been to before. How little he realized then that it was a minor place to be, compared to what lay ahead!

Samir directed us to a parking tower near his office, and up the rickety ramp we went, with the overloaded Patrol and its roof rack barely skimming the ceilings. I had to completely close my mind down not to think of what the building standards must be like here. The cinder block construction seemed able to sway even in the slight breeze that circled it from the west, and I dared not calculate the weight of the crammed levels of cars and trucks that were jammed into every available inch. One good earth tremor, I thought, would level Cairo. We walked quickly to get out from under it just in case.

Within a few blocks, we were back to the same dusty, winding staircase that had led us up to the hassles of the day before. The office looked as though no one had moved since yesterday. Did they ever really do anything at all, Jim wondered in bewildered silence? We sat down to our own inner prayers and waited. It was all that was left to do. Arguing at this point was beyond use. After only a couple of demitasse-sized cups of very strong, very sweet tea, Samir emerged from down the dirty hall with a grin that looked as glorious to us as the sunrise. He himself did not see how, nor had he held out much hope, but beyond all odds, he held in his hands the permission to travel onward through the country of the Nile! It was almost ridiculous, the gushing relief that washed over us all. Even Chelsea and Lucas, who'd seemed to only care about the current moment's boredom, were overcome with it. The wave continued throughout the entire office of workers, and though all present knew none of our faces would ever see each other's again, we had been privy to share a moment where something extraordinary had taken place: something that set in motion the turning back of the pages of time itself.

We scrambled for the words to thank the Lord, and Samir, and were, even for Southerners, beyond speech. Jim was back to his joviality and traditional family harassments as we bounced down the stairs and around the block to the parking tower where the faithful Patrol sat shivering on her wheels, awaiting her removal from the creaking concrete dungeon. We didn't even notice the honking and beeping of the streets this time, and it completely slipped our minds that in our rejoicing, Jim Caldwell drove us straight up to the Nile Hilton Hotel. Later at lunch, when I realized it, I froze for a moment of reflection: had we been here so long already that Jim had learned Cairo? It was a frightening thought.

SHOPPING IN CAIRO, EGYPT

CHAPTER SEVEN

Merchants and Madness

M r. Mansur el Sharif turned up in the lobby as we had arranged, right on schedule, right after lunch. His character was already leaking out in major floods upon us all, and his power with the locals was obvious even before we got out of the hotel. It was as if all the employees of the Nile Hilton knew him well and respected him greatly. Jim had been taken by how quickly and accurately Mr. Mansur had answered the original questions he'd fired toward him, and how deep this older man's knowledge really went. With a Masters in Archeology, and a B.A. in English, and the communication gift he exuded with people, we knew right away that somewhere over the hotel hovered an immense angel, pulling strings above our heads. Thank you, Father!

The afternoon had been all laid out by Mr. Mansur. He was to ride with us in our truck and would be taking us to three classically Egyptian trading dominions: the jeweler for the khartoosh; the perfume-oil mixer; and the papyrus painter. A definite pattern formed upon our entrance to the second establishment, which would always remain a symbol of Egypt for us. But for now, we were the green, wide-eyed American tourists, goggling at every new event with wonder and amazement.

The first business was reachable only after the most intense and lengthy excursion into the bowels of Cairo's traffic that we had sustained since our date of arrival in the city of the eternal combustion engine. From the Nile Hilton Hotel it was westward, up and over the Nile, and down what must have been a major throughway straight into the middle of the most congested areas we'd yet seen. It was like traversing through a long canyon, except the walls were made of cement block apartment houses of varying heights instead of rock. The usual ten-car-width was in full swing, all pointing in different directions, all drivers waving and gyrating and shouting as per the norm. Here in this district, however, a new clatter arose to join its staff of harmonic notes with the melody already in progress. As we looked up in disbelief at how these barely mortared, rebar-exposed, leaning towers of humanity were even standing, it was a new sight and sound altogether to witness the inhabitants of these places screaming above the noise of the traffic below them to one another, two to twelve stories off the ground! What a way to visit, I thought, as I additionally thanked God to myself that I was not one of the occupants.

It seemed like we went on and on and on, never getting anywhere again. Just when exasperation was beginning to set in, Mr. Mansur called our attention to the horizon, or what you could find of it between the apartment buildings. Now the sun had been slipping slowly toward the west all this time, and though not nearing its setting yet, was already becoming enshrouded in the ever-present dust and sand haze that characterizes Middle Eastern skies. When the traffic again came to a grinding halt, we got our first glimpse of what made Cairo stand apart from all the other cities of the world: there, silhouetted against the sinking sun, between the plastered buildings of the modern, stood the monolithic enormity of the Great Pyramid. Even at the distance we still were from it, and even only being able to see the very tip of its massive height, the effect was breathtaking. The noise of the streets was even subdued to a minor undertone as we gazed upon what the ancients had erected upon the sands of the great desert floor. Much to my amazement, I noticed no change of expression upon the face of Mr. Mansur, except that of an ever-widening grin. He knew the exact moment people needed to be impressed and had become an expert in doing just that.

In the matter of a few short moments, the deep voice of our guide was motioning for us to make a left turn off the thoroughfare and onto the tiniest of side streets which was now set before us. A few shops from the corner stood an establishment called "The Rosetta Bazaar." It was our first destination. Immediately upon our entry, several of the employees, and what we would learn was the actual proprietor, were at our service as though they were personal servants we'd known for years. It was puzzling to us until we realized that the special treatment was a direct result of the presence of Mr. Mansur (Jim was becoming more and more impressed with him by the minute). He led us through the store after introducing us to all, hammering his cane against the floor until the children were given soft drinks and Jim and I were served Turkish coffee. Another note Jim filed away in his brain: when Mr. Mansur whipped out the cane, people snapped to attention!

And that cane would become a focal point for the next three days. Mr. Mansur was a very well-educated, intelligent man. He was proud of his country and of his heritage and had every right to be. His accomplishments were profound, to say the least. But Mr. Mansur literally despised the direction he felt a majority of his fellow Egyptians were taking. In one incident, right in front of us, he actually struck a number of beggars with his cane that were up under an overpass by the droves. While it shocked us at first and seemed cruel, he explained to us that these people had chosen to beg rather than to work, and he felt it was ruining the proud lineage of his country. He taught Jim to say in the Egyptian Arabic dialect, "*Al Ashan, eh?*" which meant, "What the hell for?" A retort for beggars who began to ask for *baksheesh*. We had no idea at the time just how often we would have to use that phrase during our Egyptian adventure!

Here in the Rosetta Bazaar we got our first lessons in metal working and jewelry-making. Some of the traditions of the ancient Egyptians were still being utilized currently. The creation of the *khartooshes*, for example, we learned about in great detail, and were even ushered behind doors to the actual fabrication shop to observe the process. The *kartoosh* was comprised of the name and qualities of a person written in hieroglyphs on stone or jewelry, and both Lucas and Chelsea had their own made in silver. Instead of a kartoosh, I went for the tiniest little golden scarab beetle ring I could find, in memory of my own mother's fine green scarab ring that had been given her years before and was now in a jewelry box in south Mississippi. Thinking about it sent my mind spinning; here I was actually standing in Egypt proper, buying my own scarab ring!

After thoroughly investigating everything from real ivory pieces fashioned into anything possible, to precious stones of great quality, we decided it was time to move on—but not before I marked it in my mind that lapis lazuli, a blue stone swirled with gold, was pricking my spirit for some unknown reason. I filed it away under "pending" in my brain-file, and followed the rest of my family out the door. I would not understand this connectedness to lapis lazuli for several years to come.

Away into the sea of cars we sailed again, only this time the ride was not one of any great distance. The shopping areas were generally within the same vicinity, and before long the arm of Mr. Mansur was again motioning to turn the Patrol off the main street to park. Upon stepping down from our vehicle, an extreme blending of strong aromas filled the air, and much to my delight, we found ourselves entering the Al Amirah Palace of Perfumes. I had always wanted to go into one of these places, but in all our wanderings around the Arabian Peninsula, we'd never quite made it in. Probably by the design of Jim, I thought, as I shot a "ha-ha-ha" smile at him and pranced my way through the door.

Inside the smell was almost too strong to withstand, but the kids had taken instantly to the multi-colored blown glass bottles that lined the shelves like Christmas ornaments, and they were at the back end of the place before Jim could protest. The shop was set up almost like a shoe store would be: rows of chairs side by side, and a center aisle of them back to back for sitting facing both ways. The colors therein were the only competition rivaling the smells for audacity, with their deep reds and violets, blues and greens. Quite as if on cue, the owner and his staff surrounded us and Mr. Mansur, and a servant from the back somewhere was already present serving Turkish coffee and soft drinks. Lucas and Chelsea were on cloud nine from the previous Coca-cola at the Rosetta Bazaar, and now being offered another was beyond their wildest dreams come true! I did not allow them to indulge in cola drinks very often, and this spot to them represented the mother-lode. Jim and I took our second cup of the thick, almost chewy traditional drink, and sat down to begin the sniffing of samples and the instructional advice that accompanied each. Again we noted the response of the people to Mr. Mansur and to us because he was with us. It was truly remarkable. We spent an hour there and did not escape without purchasing six small vials of the viscous oils. The second blast of extremely strong coffee was peaking in our systems about then, too, and Jim fired up the truck like a wild man, ready to storm the next bazaar.

Again, the distance between the Al Amirah Palace of Perfumes and our final destination for the day was not far. A few blocks down the street and Mr. Mansur had us pulling off the highway and parking on sort of a downward ramp that was situated between buildings. The exterior of this place looked a bit more elegant than the previous two shops, and the large lettering above the door told us what we were getting into next. "Ani Papyrus" was the name, and through the windows we could see the wall-to-wall hangings of prints and calligraphic Islamic artwork, all done on the papyrus plant's unique medium. Jim's eyes grew wide and excitement filled his face. It had been almost more than he could stand, having to endure the perfume-shop ordeal, and he'd been afraid of what this last stop could be—but this was his reward for having only made a few smirks and no disgusting comments at the Al Amirah. Before he even got out of the Patrol, he turned around and set his gaze into the packed-to-the-gills nightmare in the back end of the truck and started sifting through it bit by bit until he located the book he'd hauled all the way from home for this very reason. *The Mystery of the Pyramids*, by Humphrey Evans, surfaced through the cluster, and Jim bounded out a very expectant man.

Though he and I had owned this book for over ten years, we'd never even looked at it in detail until the trip to Egypt was being planned in December of 1991. In the first few pages of the book, a picture appeared that we'd both gone crazy over entitled "Israel in Egypt," painted by Sir Edward Poynter in 1867. An extremely meticulous and accurate work, it detailed ancient Egypt in all her magnificence and grandeur, while showing the horrid plight of the Hebrew slaves who, at that time, had yet to be freed by Moses via the great exodus from captivity. When Jim had first laid eyes on it he'd been determined to have the thing painted on papyrus, no matter what the cost. "It must be done in Egypt, as a memorial to our trip," he had demanded to me. I knew when he got that glazed look in his eyes that he just had to have it. There was no changing his mind. I prepared myself for the inevitable cost that was sure to use up all our vacation money. Better that, I thought, than it being an impossible thing for him to obtain. If it couldn't be done, I'd have to spend the next twenty-five days in the confines of our truck with a jilted Jim. That scenario was too dreadful to even think of.

Once inside, the now familiar scene of the former two shops was repeated in expanded detail. This place was truly of a finer quality than the previous, and when the ladies that worked up front saw Mr. Mansur, their complete attention was focused upon us at once. One who appeared to be in charge clapped her hands, and a servant boy came forth with Coke and Turkish coffee one more time. "Be nice," I whispered under my breath to Jim. We were literally swimming in the stuff already, but rejected courtesies were not looked favorably upon among the Egyptians. And here in this place, Jim would be requesting what we considered the impossible.

Presently, a plump young man with a very agreeable face came racing over with his arms outstretched to Mr. Mansur. Par for the course, we figured. Here was another of our ever-famous guide's hatchlings. This was the head of Ani Papyrus. This was the boss, the main man, the grand pooh-bah, the big hamour, as they would say in Saudi Arabia for "the big fish." If anyone could get this painting done for us, it would be him. After many salutations and hand shakings, Jim explained what he wanted, and the owner then took away the book and the instructions. It didn't look really hopeful, as the painting was so very detailed it would take a fine artist and a load of time to get it done. But the trying was there, so Jim went on to tour the gallery and learn a bit about this ancient custom. We were shown the actual papyrus plant, and the step-by-step procedure of how the stalk was stripped, cut, and flattened, then finally pressed together for a soaking and drying process that would eventually yield a thin sheet of useable paper. Jim carefully videotaped the whole thing, confident that both his Mom and my parents would be quite interested in seeing this. He was thinking as I was, and would do so many times during the course of our trip, how very much our folks would thrill to see what our eyes were seeing. We went from our instructional lesson through the finished work gallery, where we selected several pieces to purchase and one to have personalized with our own khartooshes. When we were finished, the owner again came out to us to say goodbye and promised to return Jim's book on the night before we had to leave Cairo, hopefully with an artist ready to paint. We crossed our fingers and walked outside to greet the dusk. Night was rapidly falling on the busy city, and fatigue was overcoming us, the caffeinated Caldwell's. The Nile Hilton glowed as an oasis in our minds as we journeyed back toward it and the Executive Floor luxury that awaited us somewhere on the eastern horizon.

THE CALDWELLS AT THE PYRAMIDS, GIZA, EGYPT

CHAPTER EIGHT

Pyramids, Temples and Tombs

J anuary 8 dawned with a foggy haze that hung out over the Nile like a hand-woven carpet. Up on the twelfth floor balcony we sat: the ever-amazed Caldwell adults, sipping our morning ritual liquid and trying to wake up. The day before us would be crammed to the maximum: a veritable sight-seeing extravaganza, sure to impress and fatigue at the same time. On schedule today were the Pyramids, Memphis, Sakkara, The Village, and the "Life." None of it made any sense to us then, but before the evening was over we assumed we'd be quite Egyptianized.

After the formalities associated with breakfast, Jim led us back down to the lobby of the Nile Hilton and wandered to and fro, searching out Mr. Mansur. His faithful form appeared right on schedule, with many salutations and blessings sprouting from his mouth as he went along greeting the people who all knew him so well. He proceeded to take the lead up from Jim as if on cue, and our expedition into the bowels of pharonic Egypt began.

As we left the lobby and exited to the right toward the car park, the cane of Mr. Mansur reached for the sky and his deep voice bellowed out some commands in Arabic to the attendants. Much to our surprise and within a mere few seconds, valets were scurrying and the familiar thrum of the Nissan Patrol came whistling into our ears. Jim and I locked glances, beginning to feel excessively smug in our choice of guides. We watched him struggle up into the truck and marveled at just how well we were really being taken care of. We also wondered why.

Memphis was the first stop on our agenda this day. The ancient capital of Egypt, called the "city of the living," was little more now than a few alabaster and granite relics in the midst of the black farmland of modern life. From the moment we'd left the noisy congestion of Cairo traffic to follow the road down the Nile it had been quite apparent that the bulk of the people worked as peasant farmers to this day, and that they all lived within 1 square kilometer of the great river that offered them life. It was also abundantly clear that poverty had an iron-clad grip on the country with very little else to offer. Even this great ancient city whose streets once held the imprint of the feet of pharaohs was incapable of stopping the ever-increasing population's advance. It was ironic to us both that the majesty and glory of such works lay falling to ruins among cane fields and donkey carts. "Judgment of God," I mused. It is irreversible but by His fingertips.

We toured each of the monuments at Memphis and were particularly taken with the huge granite form of Rameses lying prostrate on the ground there, the only fairly enclosed piece and the most impressive. The attention to detail these stone masons had was outrageous. The smoothness and curve of the statue almost gave it a life-like sensuality and had a way of drawing you to itself and into its past. Its very presence represented such a different Egypt than that of what we were seeing now. I thought more than once that the ancients would be turning in their tombs if they could see for themselves what had become of what they thought was the greatest nation on the face of the earth.

Just outside the gates of Memphis, the dirt groundcover gave way to a sloping vale of sorts, and away to the left, behind a cyclone fence that had been twisted out of shape, the sparse grasses gave way to marsh reeds. We could tell water from the Nile must somehow come into the area, but the actual river was not within our eyesight. As we were heading back to the truck, Mr. Mansur called our attention to the spot, and explained how the Nile used to flow in that very area naturally. This was the place, according to legend, where the baby Moses had been plucked from the water by the daughter of the pharaoh. It left more of an impression on us than had the ancient city itself. Lingering was not an option today, however. The agenda was too tight, and Mr. Mansur was ready to go.

Sakkara was up next. Just as Memphis was called the city of the living, Sakkara was its counterpart, being called the "city of the dead." It was the burial site for the people of Memphis and was situated up on a ridge farther west. When we reached the top of the escarpment, the landform lost the rich green of the Nile valley and was the sharply howling desert wasteland that forbids travelers even to this day. Here upon the ceaseless plane of pale tan sand and rock stood the massive form of the Step Pyramid, and farther off in the distance, several other much smaller ones. A huge, multi-colored tent was semi-permanently set up here for the tourists, and a restaurant of sorts was within its shade. Mr. Mansur led our way to the ticket booth, and as would be the course for each sight we visited, demanded the best for his friends and got it. This morning we were earlier than the tour buses that swarmed the area and would catch a glimpse of our first hieroglyphs within the walls of the tombs of several priests and nobles.

The pathway led down toward the level of what once were the streets of Sakkara. A turn to the right and a few more steps down took us up to what appeared to be a small pyramid that was in a sad state of disintegration. The casing stones were all gone, and the actual building blocks of the structure were deteriorating badly. Teti's pyramid, it was called, and it was of great interest because of the stars etched in the ceiling of the burial chamber. This was not common for pyramids in general.

We stood at the entranceway which consisted of an opening of about four feet by four feet—barely enough room to crunch down and crawl through. Wooden railings and makeshift steps had been installed to facilitate the tourists' descent down into the structure, and every so often a single light bulb hanging precariously by an unraveling wire glimmered dimly. But the corridor's first light bulb was burned out, and as a result, only the first ten feet or so down was illuminated by the outdoor light. Jim and Chelsea eagerly tromped right on down after the Bedouin guide who had come on the scene as we'd neared the sight, but Lucas and I lingered at the entrance, fighting the claustrophobic tentacles that were rapidly closing in around us. It had gripped me so suddenly: the dank, dusty smell of the ancient gravesite; the scenarios of horror if Sakkara was hit by earth tremors at this very moment; the dense darkness that lay before us. I felt as though I was almost being commanded by hell's demons not to enter that tomb. I had enough sense to know that if I couldn't make myself go into this little pyramid, I'd never have the strength to get to the heart of Cheops, the Great Pyramid.

"What an idiot," I said to myself. "I've come all the way to Egypt and fear is locking me out of this experience!" But it wasn't only feeling stupid that gave me the gumption I needed to take that first step downward. Somewhere, deep inside my spirit, a still small voice told me, "Be brave! Be strong! Much courage you will need in the days to come. This is only a beginning." In a moment's time my feet were moving, and Lucas was right behind me.

Just beyond that availability of surface light, the guide stopped and our little group came to a complete halt in the most dense, clammy darkness we'd yet seen. Obviously we were in a section where that infamous bulb had burned; too far down to turn back, and in too much blackness to go forward safely. "Great!" I sighed. "Just when I thought I'd made it over the fear." The feeling of being stuck was overwhelming. The tiny shaft we were in left not even enough room to turn around. Once we started going down inside, we would have had to go all the way in order to enter a chamber large enough to turn ourselves around and go back. There the Bedouin decided to stop and try to fix the bulb. After ten minutes of unfruitful effort with a new bulb and a dying Bic lighter, he finally gave up and motioned for us to follow on by feeling our way to the next light. Now touching cold, ancient stone was just the thing I wanted to do, especially after having struggled so hard to even set foot into this pyramid, but I found it was quite necessary. Within about five feet, a stone on the left wall was jutting out into the passageway, and had I not been groping forward, it could have knocked one of us out cold! In moving as much as I could to the right, which wasn't any farther than a few inches at best, I plodded onward away from the hazard just to find a larger, unseen stone barring straight movement on that side! I stopped for a moment to think on the situation and to try to regain my nerve. This was beginning to have all the hallmarks of a faith test from God. And I knew perfectly well that if my faith was being tried, there would surely be a purpose to fulfill in the near future. But here, inside the dank pyramid of Teti, I had not a clue of what was to come before the end of this trip.

Thankfully, a few more steps led us to the dull luminescence of one of the few poor bulbs that still had enough juice getting through to it to work. It shone down into a straight pathway, which was a great improvement over the slanted angle of the one we'd just had to follow. This was short-lived, however, and another downward shaft appeared before us which led directly to the burial chamber at the base of the pyramid. We could see from this point the very well lit opening, and upon entering ,were all too glad to be out of the tunnels that had led us to this point.

Standing up straight was all Jim could think of at first. His 6' 3" frame had been literally crawling along to get there and the cramps in his legs and back were getting unbearable. What a relief it was for us all to stretch! And what a worthwhile torture the getting there had been! The chamber was a large room with a cathedral ceiling, and stars had been etched deeply into the whole of it. It was completely amazing to us that such enormous effort and energy had been spent on the afterlife, when none of it was to have been of any avail. Here was the proof of a civilization that had erected such huge monuments on such a grandiose scale to the life beyond the grave, never having found the key to eternal life at all. With all the current day hysteria over the mystical powers of pyramids, there truly remained nothing behind in this tomb but cold stone and musty, dank air. The hype of New Age culture, where these things are concerned, was absolute hogwash. This place was totally spiritually dead.

None the less, it was indeed an awesome sight to behold. We spent only a few moments pondering, and turned to make our ascent back above ground. From there Mr. Mansur led us down to the tombs of the nobles and priests, which were cut out of the local stone, and not in the classic pyramid shape. Inside were the still colorful and skillfully carved hieroglyphic writings and reliefs that had been chipped into the rock three thousand years before. The attention given to every little detail was superb, even in viewing the remains in this day and time.

After our tour, we got back into the truck and pulled over to the tent we'd first seen upon our entrance to Sakkara. Once inside, we got refreshments and relaxed for a time just to chat with our faithful guide.

It had already been wonderful having him and his extensive knowledge of Egypt at our disposal. His rapport with Lucas and Chelsea made things even more special. We would be reminded of just how great he was to them in the coming days throughout the land.

From the tent, we set out in the Patrol again but not very far. Mr. Mansur motioned for Jim to stop in what seemed like a rather remote area, until he explained that he wanted to get the Step Pyramid in the background and take a family photograph for us. Of course, as the ever-photographable Caldwells, we were always ready for a picture, and out we bounced with much hair fluffing and scarf adjusting. The wind was blowing fairly strongly, and the weather was still quite nippy because of it. Mr. Mansur situated us just the way he wanted, snapped the photo, and told us a little about Djoser's Pyramid. Then, to remain on our schedule, we had to move on. This was as close as we would be going to the site itself.

Once back out on the Nile road, we stopped briefly at a carpet weaving factory where children were employed to work. As par for the course, the owner knew Mr. Mansur well, and treated us with the usual Turkish coffee, tea, and soft drinks. One more purchase, and we were off to a restaurant called "The Village." Nestled in the fertile valley of the river, it sat among the farmer's crops as an open air bistro of sorts. The well known Mr. Mansur retired to a chair and we wandered around the curious place where life was bustling so cheerily. Near the entrance began the animal life: rabbits in cages, geese and ducks wandering freely about, a scattering of dogs and cats, birds and goats, and even a Shetland pony on a leash. The kids were beside themselves to run free safely for a while, and the vivid green grass was a very welcome relief to the harsh glare of the endless desert we'd just come from. Arabic bread was being baked right there in an open oven outside, and its unbelievably fantastic fragrance filled the air.

Just outside the gates of the establishment, life went on unawares; ladies walking with baskets of greens and huge cabbages turned upside down and balanced on their heads, men and boys riding on donkey carts filled to overflowing with sugar cane or palm boughs, and children running in every direction. The traffic on the highway was constantly blowing horns at the "life," as Mr. Mansur called the farmers and their families. To me, it was the most glorious conglomeration of sights and sounds, hustle and bustle, and just plain life I'd seen so far. Anything but the dull nothingness inside those tombs. "How could people think any psychic power was available there?" I said to myself, as we sat down to enjoy the premises.

Our meal came out in several stages, each being freshly prepared by hand. Every sample of Egyptian food possible kept heading our way from the kitchen via Mr. Mansur's demand that his newly found "family" must be filled to overflowing properly. Most of the samples we found to be quite delicious, and the bread we'd seen being baked in cute little rounds was most enjoyable. Lucas left the table to go over to the woman at the oven for a fresh piece, and returned with a huge disc of it, hot and breathing. We all got a laugh out of watching it rise and fall, until Lucas couldn't stand it anymore and stabbed out its life with the tines of a fork.

By this time Jim and I were stuffed and had laid back in the sunshine to let our meal digest, so the children ran off to bribe the cook for carrots to feed the pony. It had been tied up not far from us during our whole meal, and now and again would lift its head and make the funniest whinny we'd ever heard! Its eyes would appear to bulge out, and it would roll them back while its lips would quiver and this hilarious sound would come out of its throat. The kids were in heaven. It was such a relaxing stop for us all, but with a schedule to keep it could not last indefinitely. After a restroom clean up and sporting renewed vigor, away we all went again. This time, the major pyramids were our quest. As we boarded the truck, I thought back to the cramped and dark little tunnel I'd had to endure earlier that morning. I was glad it was a while yet before we'd reach our destination.

Back down the road whence we'd come, Jim savored the fresh air and the crisp, clear day. Thinking of how evil the darkness of the former year had been, he felt every bit renewed and squeakily clean on this wild and invigorating adventure—just what his family had needed to fuse itself back together again. He mused adoringly upon the power of his God to change things just in time, and with such superb detail to the inclusion of the desires of his own heart. Here, out on the Nile road with the massive silhouettes looming before him, yesterday was just that—yesterday. Gone. Dead and buried, never to rise again. And today, he would enter the world his father had spent a lifetime longing for, because he was now on his way to actually go inside the cavernous depths of the Great Pyramid at Giza!

He shook his head with a smile, and turned his gaze left toward the ageless sentinels rising so far off, right out of the barren desert. Huge seemed inadequate to describe them from this distance, for they were obviously monstrous and dwarfed the rest of what Jim could now see. In the foreground still were the green palms, and above them the three peaks pricked his memory, jogging loose stories of the ancient people and their obsession with the afterlife. He wondered if this great monument would be any different from the other one he'd seen earlier in the day. There was, before his combing of Teti's pyramid, a curiosity of sorts that had him wondering about all these rumored pyramid powers. With the impression of the little one he'd already encountered today, his hopes of them being true had dimmed. Still, this gargantuan tomb that lay before him had his radar up. If there was anything there, he was determined to find it.

The congested structures of Cairo were beginning to become more visible as we reached the outskirts of the mega metropolis. It was hard to imagine, but even the pyramids had been swallowed up from view by the endless high-rise apartment complexes and dilapidated old buildings of this busy city. As we wound our way through the traffic again, for the umpteenth time, Jim lost all thoughts of the mysterious past civilization and wondered how the ancients could have had their act together enough to produce what they did. We talked about it for a while, until Jim's comment ended the conversation.

"Their descendents surely knew nothing of what their forefathers must have, or they'd never have given birth to this nightmare they call Cairo," he muttered as the cars came to a thoroughly grinding halt. Once again, it took an hour to go the short distance necessary to enter the drive that led up to the Giza Plateau where the pyramids stood. This time though, the sheer size of these great works overwhelmed us so immediately that the traffic of Cairo lost out in a moment's notice its bid to ruin the day.

Before going to the ticket booth, the ever-ready Mr. Mansur shone again, thinking for us as we gawked with no perception at the massive stones. He led Jim up a side road that curved away from Chephren and Mycerinus to the right, the two lesser pyramids, and up onto a knoll overlooking the whole area. As if awaiting our arrival, two Bedouin youths approached us on camelback, signaling Jim that rides were available for the right amount of Egyptian pounds. One camel could carry Jim and Lucas together, and one could carry Chelsea and I together. "Why not?" shrugged Jim with a devilish grin, knowing Mr. Mansur had probably prearranged the whole thing. We moved over to the animals, which were presently being forced to kneel down so that they could be mounted. Jim and Lucas swung their legs over the huge beast's back. When the owner made the camel stand, he growled and grumbled so violently that Jim was convinced he'd soon be sailing airborne in the direction of the Great Pyramid, Cheops! Before I could protest and stop our own ride, Chelsea and I were scooped up and found ourselves atop the other camel, but fortunately without all the bellowing that accompanied the former. And within just a few moments, each of us found the rhythm of the "ships of the desert," as camels are often called, and were enjoying for ourselves quite a good viewpoint from so high off the ground.

Smiles gave way to serious stares before long, though. Two thoughts prevailed, and filtered back and forth from one to the other in my head. The magnificence of these great monuments was truly beyond words, and their very survival in such harsh conditions as the Sahara can provoke was hard to fathom, as was the ever-present wonder of how on earth were they erected in the first place. My imagination was building the scenario of how they must have looked in their day of completion, when suddenly I felt overwhelmed by the horrid state of ill repair the poor things were in today, and the atmosphere of degradation that surrounded them now. Way below the rise on which they now sat, at the base of one of the great wonders of the world, thousands of humans were scurrying about as though nothing of any significance was there. The traders were behind every stone trying to sell useless items of junk for the most part, and the beggars for baksheesh were hidden at strategic points all along the tourist route up to Cheops. The clamor could be heard from as far away as we were, up on the plateau. Beside the sellers who carried their wares on their person, sleazy looking tents and booths were seen lining the avenues by which the same tourists had to pass, each filled to overflowing with souvenir items of no worth. In addition to all the yelling and swearing, the noise of traffic jams there on the premises filled the air with the usual sounds and smells of Cairo: honking and beeping and the fumes of the internal combustion engine. What a contrast to how elegant and royal this place must have once been! And how different this once great nation of pharaohs and princes is today, I remember thinking. As Mr. Mansur noted, it had truly become a nation of beggars. They seemed to have little interest in the antiquities for their historical importance at all, but only for what they attracted to Egypt. The sadness wound up outweighing the majesty.

We rode on camelback around the hill for another ten minutes or so, then dismounted and drove on down into the chaotic mess we'd seen from up above. It was time for the ultimate test of nerves: the descent/ascent into the Great Pyramid of Cheops. Mr. Mansur would not be making this journey, which told us already that it was a long way down another cramped corridor and a long climb back up to the burial chamber. I braced myself and fell in line with the other hundreds that were crowding their way toward the tiny opening. It gave me the impression of a herd of cattle being forced into single file before being corralled and sent into slaughter pens. Not a good way to think before entering a tomb. It became quickly obvious that there was no turning back from this one either. With so many people in so tiny a crawl space, I could not turn around and go back once I got inside. Another great thought. But a wave of intestinal fortitude crashed over me anyway, and blaze forward at Jim's heels I did. I wasn't about to let him experience something that I didn't! It was the usual thing—Jim charging forth with me in his jet-wash! But that very reckless audacity and unconstrained boldness to charge ahead into the unknown is what made us an unstoppable team. It would be what kept us in the events that lay ahead.

There was not much difference in this huge pyramid and the small one we'd gone inside earlier in the day except for the immensity of its size. True, the burial chamber was impressive, and the feeling one got once inside was that of overwhelming awe at the building of this super-structure of antiquity, but the mystical properties associated with it were absolutely swallowed up forever. Dust was thick, the air was stagnant, and the stone was anything but alive. There were no spirits, no time warps; no psychic noise whatsoever. It was just a great big pile of enormous hewn stones. We gazed and pondered for a few moments, and turned back toward the exit chamber. Our adventure into this wonder of the world was complete.

Back out and into the waning sun, we found Mr. Mansur amongst the throngs, and loitered for a little while taking pictures in front of Cheops. Then back into the truck, we went over and around to the right for photographs of the Sphinx. We did not actually walk up to it, but opted for the balcony of the tourist restaurant to take its shots with the pyramids in the background. It, too, was in serious shape, seeming to crumble right before our eyes. Another deep sadness blew in on the breeze, as we realized we were witnessing the slow death of the most amazing antiquity of four thousand years. At this, we told the Giza Plateau goodbye.

It was not all without fun, however. True to her nature, Chelsea was hungry and had been pestering me to take her into the restaurant for food since the moment we'd begun the Sphinx photography. It wasn't sinking into her at all that the place was closed, and food was a total impossibility at that point in time. Now Chelsea had a stubborn streak about her—a trait that neither of us would claim, but sometimes exhibited. Her mood rapidly deteriorated, and the demands for groceries were growing embarrassing in the crowds. I had finally had enough, and drug her over to the owner who explained to Chelsea himself that they were not serving yet for the evening meal. Well, the brow of Chelsea became flint, and everything from that point forward was not right with her. The frown was imbedded, and she saw fit to enjoy nothing of the scenery, nor the fact that she was standing where so few children get to stand, seeing what so few children get to see. In her disgruntled mode, she clammed up tight, which was a grateful relief to the passers-by who'd been listening. Good things not being known to last forever, though, her next series of comments would follow her beyond the rest of our vacation, all the way back to Arabia.

She'd been listening to us talking of the Great Sphinx, and puzzling in her little mind as to how that could be its real name at all. She finally had heard enough, and blurted out in a very loud and disgusted voice, "That's not a Finx, it's a FINK! There's only one! You got to have two to be Finx!

I felt my jaw dropping open. Lucas curled up his lip and snarled, and looked at her with all the affection a nine-year-old boy usually has for his little sister. Jim's eyes goggled. Mr. Mansur closed his eyes and nodded a knowing nod. For once, we were all speechless. There was no more need for words, as we turned and walked back down the stairs and over to the waiting Patrol.

Darkness was approaching as we entered the arteries of the lifeblood of Cairo again. Jim was so thankful he didn't have to remember how to get us back to Ani Papyrus and then on to the Nile Hilton for the night. Mr. Mansur was doing all our thinking for us. The day had been so crammed with sight and sound, Jim had felt an information overload and was waiting for his brain to process the data. All the while though, in the back of his mind, the hope of getting his painting done at the art shop had floated in and out of his conscious thinking processes. Would we find an artist? Would he take on this huge project if we did? Would he be good enough to satisfy Jim's finicky taste? Only the getting there would tell.

As we neared the shop and parked, Jim could only keep his fingers crossed. Mr. Mansur had made it clear to the owner, whom he knew as well as a son, that Jim's book had better be there when we arrived from the pyramids. As we got out of the truck, Mr. Mansur started toward the door and out coming to meet him was this very man, shaking his head and babbling profusely in Arabic. Jim and I watched in utter astonishment and hilarity as the expression on Mr. Mansur's face went to disbelief, and his cane flew out, flailing wildly toward this poor merchant as he spat out curses upon his brother, his mother, his sister, and the rest of all he held near and dear! It was so shocking and funny to witness the passionate side of Egyptian personality that we didn't even mind much when we realized it would be another day's wait to get our answer on the painting. We were once again, being taken great care of.

CHAPTER NINE

The Papyrus

January 9 was being birthed with the dawn outside the eleventh floor balcony of the Cairo Nile Hilton Hotel. Jim's eyes opened warily, and he wondered where he was for a split second until his eyes adjusted to the darkness and he saw his children balled up across the room still sleeping, and me rustling beside him. The smile crept across his face as he leaned over and whispered those ever so magical, ever so traditional words into my ears ... "It's spoffee time!" The word "spoffees" had been our variation on "coffee" for years and had become the only proper way to greet the morning. Of course, this wasn't the common routine, but we had already attached a habitual pattern to this hotel's twelfth floor Executive Restaurant in that we had snuck out for the previous two mornings to drink the black gold alone, just as we were preparing to do this morning. We dressed without saying a word, knowing what we were each thinking, and off to the next floor we went. Today would be our last full day in Cairo, with the Islamic sights and the Cairo Museum on the agenda. The last order would be to Ani Papyrus to collect our book and, hopefully, word of an available artist to begin our painting.

The sky was overcast with medium to high clouds, and it was quite humid; but it was not as chilly as it had been the day before. After coffee Jim and I, as on the days before, went back to our room and awakened and tormented Lucas and Chelsea sufficiently, then fed them breakfast from our twelfth story bistro. Now all of us were ready to see Mr. Mansur, though a bit wistful and slightly concerned about having to leave him behind on the morrow. He'd become such a friend and caretaker to us, and he himself had grown quite fond of us. The children especially captured him. He was constantly reminded by our two of his own children in their young days and had taken to giving advice just as a grandfather would have done. This morning was no exception to our ever-growing fondness of the older gentleman. He was awaiting our arrival as usual in the lobby of the hotel, but he had a book under his arm and motioned the children over to him right away. Jim and I almost dropped our teeth when we saw the title, which read *Little Stories About God.* It was a beautiful book written expressly for children, and we could tell by the pictures inside it was old. As it turns out, Mr. Mansur's children were given this book oh so long ago, and he now was presenting it to Lucas and Chelsea to keep. What a touching moment it was! Mr. Mansur was now permanently secure deep within all our hearts.

Islamic Cairo was huge and overpowering. Right through the center of one of the poorest sections of Egypt we had yet to see, there stood before us the towering minarets and immense fortifications of The Citadel. It was situated way up on a bluff overlooking the vastness of the city, and from inside its gates we could see just how far Cairo really spread herself out. It was certainly clear why Cairo had been labeled "The City of a Thousand Minarets." Mr. Mansur showed us around, explaining all the history behind the place, and finally steered us over to the huge mosque that stood in the far corner of the complex. It was made almost entirely out of alabaster and had the capacity for being one of the most beautiful structures we'd ever seen, except for the two-inch layer of dust that covered the pretty bone-colored stone. Still, even dirty, it was an impressive sight to behold. We were allowed to go inside and strangely enough it was the first mosque any of us had ever been in. Of course, as is demanded, we removed our shoes in the outer courtyard before nearing the entrance to the main inner area.

The inside was one enormous room, with lights hanging on long chains from the ceiling which rose what seemed like one hundred feet up in the air. Brilliant colors of glass were placed inside great cupolas, and the light filtered through them lazily, casting a pale hint of each hue over the different areas of the room affected. Bright green was predominantly used, and that being our favorite color, it struck a fancy to us both. We stayed long enough to hear the call to prayer sounding out, and then left for the long drive back to the Nile Hilton. It was almost noon before we got there, and Mr. Mansur retired to parts unknown for all of us to rest and to have lunch.

Along about two o'clock, we took our previously purchased museum tickets and walked the block behind the hotel and over to the Cairo Museum. Inside, the treasured relics of the world lay in state, silently gazing up into the rafters of the old building. The singular beams of light that cut through the high windows, typical to the architecture of the era, cast eerie shadows and light effects across the granite and alabaster faces of the Pharaohs and their Queens. Here the ancients had truly achieved the immortality they so desperately sought. Statue after statue, glass case after glass case, pharonic boat after pharonic boat, and chariot after chariot came into view as we slowly strode across the room. With more than one floor, and an immensely large display area, we had to plan our progress quickly, for the halls would close in one and a half hours, and it would be impossible to see it all.

The treasures of the boy king, Tutankhamen, were all separated to one entire wing of the museum, and it was the one thing we all really wanted to see. The viewing room was packed with people, but when it came time for us to enter in, the entire trip to Egypt had been worth it. The abundance of gold was enough to spark off ancient treasure hunt stories in one's mind, but the exquisite workmanship of Tutankhamen's personal sarcophagus and burial mask were outstanding. The intricacies of the design, and the perfect cut of hundreds of precious stones, were so stunning—and the mirror-like shine on the smooth gold of his face was so life-like that it was enough to bring tears to the eye. We almost expected the headpiece to begin speaking at any moment. The wealth was astonishing. Once again, the thought permeated my thinking: how could a nation that had been first in architecture, first in literature, first in medicine, first in wealth and splendor, lie in the state that Cairo's inner city did today? It was beginning to plague me with relentless agony.

The rest of our time was spent pouring over the glass cases filled with every imaginable artifact, from ancient flint arrowheads and spear points to Roman and Greek coins. The wealth therein must be enormous, we figured. The afternoon shadows were growing long when we finally left the building and headed back over to the Hilton. Cairo was rapidly drawing to a close around us.

Around four o'clock, Mr. Mansur greeted us back in the lobby of the hotel for our final ride together through the tangled web of Cairo's streets. The feelings igniting inside my head were those of growing dread for the next morning when we would have to leave Mr. Mansur behind and journey onward alone. Jim had already mapped out our itinerary with him and extracted names and places that Mr. Mansur knew of personally and recommended, but it would not be the same without him. He was such a security; like an old teddy bear filled with memories and psychological comfort. Besides that, he would just plain be missed. We'd come to so depend on his taking care of everything for us, from the baksheesh hounds to the steely traffic cops who tried to harass us. When Mr. Mansur spoke, all of Cairo it seemed stood still.

We were now getting underway to approach Ani Papyrus for the collection of Jim's book, and news of the hoped for painting.

When we drove up to the building, no owner ran out to greet us this time. Instead we were ushered in and given refreshments, just as we were the first time we graced the premises. At first Jim thought that this was not a good sign. What if they'd lost the book? Then he would have no painting and not even a copy in a book to retain. Presently, however, the owner appeared, all smiles, and said the book was coming along with something for us to look over. It was in the nick of time, as the cane waver extraordinaire was poised to strike the owner once again. So our company sat down in the parlor of the gallery to sip our cokes, while we watched a busload of German tourists come in through the front door. We watched while the hostess went through the same papyrus explanation we had received only a few days before; we had just begun to reminisce when a courier came bursting through the front door with a huge cardboard scroll covering and Jim's book under his arm. He spoke in rapid fire Arabic, and the owner's face just about exploded into a wide, toothy grin. He told us nothing, but handed the book over to Jim and asked us all to step out of the limelight and into his private office.

Now his office had all the marks of being the big boss' office. The desk in the center of the room was tremendous, but what we saw being rolled out on the surface there was beyond the size of the desk's top.

THE CALDWELL'S ORIGINAL PAPYRUS FROM CAIRO, EGYPT

Our mouths were gaping as we watched the largest papyrus we'd ever seen completely enveloping the top of this desk. And from the moment the colors of what was painted there began to unfold, Jim knew the Divine had intervened on behalf of his request. There, across this desk and hanging over the edges was Jim's dream painting, finished to perfection and ready for purchase!

He was dumbfounded. He could only stand there staring. There were no words coming out of his mouth; only an astonished gasp could escape. I was awestruck. The several workers who'd come in to look were shocked and whispering their own comments on the incredible work. Mr. Mansur even raised a burly eyebrow and leaned closer to examine the magnificent copy of the old painting. Every tiny detail had been worked in. The attention given to keeping the integrity of the scene was phenomenal. Not one flaw could we find. Of course there was no questioning to see if we would indeed purchase the thing. It was sold from the moment it unfurled.

Jim couldn't stand it and had the workers take it and lay it out on the floor in the main lobby so that he could stand back and view it from a distance. The moment they laid it out on the floor, the entire German tourist group of forty or so people came running over and crowded around us all, gawking and squawking away in German. Jim beamed with pride as he knew that this masterpiece would be gone in a moment if he did not want it. But there was no doubting that. *This baby was given to him as a sign from above that he had business with the Egyptian/Israelite connection of old.* What it was, he knew not. He only knew that here, as darkness enveloped the city of Cairo, he had received his answer to move on. As he rolled it back up and handed it back over to the Ani Papyrus staff for packaging, he looked at me with blazing eyes, and it hit me right in the heart. I knew this was a sign of what was lying ahead, and the feeling flushed over me in waves of chills and goose-bumps. What a way to close our last night in Cairo!

Later on, driving down the freeway of congestion, we dropped off Mr. Mansur at his home and ventured the rest of the way to the hotel on our own. Jim needed only to be in any city for a few hours before he knew his way around, and even Cairo had become no exception to the rule. It took a bit more than a few hours, but he knew it now, and his confidence was bursting at the seams. Tomorrow would open a new window and a new road before us, but for tonight, Jim felt that all was not only well with the world, it was supremely well! He swung the Patrol up and into the parking lot attendants' hands and huddled us together with our new treasure inside the Hilton. Later that evening when he crawled into bed and wrapped me up in a tight embrace, we felt the Presence of our God blanketing us in love. Sleep was very, very sweet.

PENNY IN FRONT OF THE AKHENATON HOTEL, MINYA, EGYPT

CHAPTER TEN

The Akhenaton Hotel

I t was now Friday, January 10, and our stay in Cairo was over. The
traditional breakfast on the Executive Floor of the Nile Hilton had
been said good-bye to, the porters were on their way for the luggage,
and there sat Jim and I on the foot of the bed wondering what the
coming days would hold for us. We both felt a hesitation for a moment.
Leaving the now comfortable security of our guide for parts and people
unknown was not altogether settling. Beside that, the old gentleman
had wormed his way so deep within our hearts, saying good-bye to him
would not be easy. Time was of great essence, however, and that had
a way of causing a man to go when his heart says stay. It was to be so
this morning. We made our way to the elevators and soon wound up
standing in the huge lobby of the now very familiar Nile Hilton.

Jim was at the counter having the bill totaled when Mr. Mansur
walked up behind us, ready to bid us farewell. Just as we were about
to say the dreaded words, the desk clerk motioned Jim over, and much
to our amazement, declined our credit card! This card had almost no
balance on it, and it was obviously a major mistake that it had come
back declined. But this put us in a unique situation indeed! We didn't
have the cash to pay such a large sum, nor could we imagine any bank
cashing a personal check from the United States in any reasonable
length of time. It would have been a nightmarish dilemma had not the
ever present cane of Mr. Mansur figured into the scenario. After talking
rapid-fire Egyptian dialect Arabic to the clerk, Jim noticed the serene
face of Mr. Mansur turn to him, while the cashier began processing our

credit card at once. He had saved us, even in our moment of departure! "What a blessing to have found you! Thank you for all your help," I told him as he reached to hug me good-bye. The tears could not be stopped. With no further time spent, we were up and away and absorbed by the traffic of our wondrous Cairo.

The road to Minya was the same road we'd been on when we went to the Village Restaurant a few days earlier. For mile after mile, the scenery didn't alter its continuous showing of the "life," as our dear Mr. Mansur had taught us. Farm after farm—cabbage patches, and huge sugar cane fields that seemed to stretch on forever—were always before and behind us. Every now and again we'd reach a small town or village just large enough to have a few buildings and a guard shack of sorts where traffic slowed to be checked, causing a crowd of locals to gather and watch the vehicles go by. As traffic on the narrow, shoulderless highway would come grinding to a standstill at the checkpoint, Jim found himself stuck in a most harrowing spot. Not knowing the disposition of the residents of any of these small communities was no comfort, as our white faces and shiny black four-wheel drive truck stood out all too conspicuously! It was not uncommon for us to be swarmed by children, all pawing at the vehicle and smiling their often toothless smiles right into our windows! Here again, many of the men would simply hop up onto the running boards of the Patrol and hitch a ride to the next traffic light, then hop off again without ever even looking inside! Jim and I exchanged more glances in that first day on the Nile Road than we had in all the time we'd so far been in Egypt.

What topped our surprises, though, were the late 1800's horse-drawn carriages we were beginning to see making their way along the streets. It was beyond comprehension that these could be as old as they appeared to be, yet upon close inspection, it was every bit believable. The giveaway was the small lamp on the side of each one—ready to be fitted with a candle for night driving! It was no wonder Jim kept his thoughts to himself—and if I had known what fears were lying wait in his heart pertaining to his decision to go on this trip, I would have freaked! As it turned out, that emotion would be reserved for the days to come. Right now, the major concern was making our way through the little clusters of folks dotted here and there along the Nile, and finding the city of Minya.

It was nearing three o'clock in the afternoon when the somewhat larger and more civilized town of Minya came into view. After hours and hours of driving the dilapidated, narrow road we'd been on, Jim was frazzled and ready to have a good meal and a soft bed. Dodging traffic on this highway was a unique experience, to say the least. Jim had become quite well adjusted to the wild and wooly antics some of the drivers in Arabia tended to practice at regular intervals, but he was also quite used to the beautiful super highway systems and the ever available shoulder where one could get out of the way of these sorts of activities. Here, faced with a steep embankment on either side of him and berserk drivers coming in from every angle, he had to concentrate so hard he had developed a serious migraine. Whizzing at speeds no one would believe, 1955 Plymouth station wagons and 1958 Chevy's would fly around us. These old things had been converted into taxis and were crammed to the gills with Egyptians and other third world nationalities, all racing off into the distance going who-knew-where! Beside the small vehicular traffic, huge busses of varying ages would suddenly appear in Jim's rear view mirror and race around us, barely avoiding running off the embankment to the left as they swerved by. It got to the point where we'd watch for these guys coming up behind us to compare the nerve of one to another, as they'd challenge the huge benzene lorries, or gasoline tanker trucks, as they passed and sped away into the distance. Amazement was common this day.

Jim reached into his wallet for the few hotel listings Mr. Mansur had given him. One, The Lotus, was operated by a friend of his, although we'd been warned it was no Nile Hilton. The problem was finding the place. Minya was a network of extremely narrow streets, with everything from parked cars to mules and carriages serving as mini-blockades. We found ourselves circling around several times and always seemed to end up back near the taxi sheds behind the railway station; the process took more patience than Jim had at the moment. His mood had been deteriorating with the increase of his headache's pounding, as well as the grumbling from the rest of the occupants in the Patrol. It was all beginning to have the appeal of long fingernails scraping down the length of a chalkboard. In desperation he finally motioned a local over and tried his best to ask the guy where the Lotus Hotel was. Surprisingly enough, the man was able to point and give us a clue, and within a few minutes, we sat in front of a seven-story building that had every bit of the warmth and charm of a snake farm. The construction was typical of the apartment buildings in Cairo, and the nightmare of being in one in either a fire or an earthquake rushed over me like a tidal wave. Jim would have stayed in a tent by now and observing the horror on my face, he was not happy. After some very long, glaring looks from me, he finally resigned himself to driving on. It was no use to argue on this one.

There was another hotel listed in the Fodor's guide we'd been reading throughout our trip. Called the Nefertari Hotel, it was on the Nile's edge and relatively new, with good ratings. If we could find that one, maybe we had a chance of turning the mood of the day back to favorable. Down the tiny streets we went again, weaving in and out of the obstacles as before. We soon came to a lush garden on a corner. There, under the greenery and set back a way from the river, was the Nefertari Hotel, a beautiful white building. It was pristine after what I'd just seen, and surely the inn for the night! An armed guard paraded at the gate in front of the place, and our whole clan popped out of the truck and strolled into the courtyard just beyond him. Relief washed over me just as the fear had done earlier. I was already picturing the room in my mind and how good it would be to rest in such a nice place. It was lovely—while it lasted.

Up to the counter we went, to the well-dressed clerks and bell boys behind it. What was waiting behind their painted-on smiles was not at all the news we expected, nor dared to believe. There was not a single room of any type available for us to stay in, and my brilliant beam of sunshine was rapidly displaced by lowering black clouds and a tempest's fury! As it turned out, the counter was filled with diplomatic passports that the employees were trying to register, and the hotel was overbooked and brimming with people already. The Lotus came back into my mind's eye, and I could have sworn I saw a face on the front of the building, with the lobby elevators I had seen through the open front doors appearing as its huge mouth, grimacing in a grisly fashion, ready to eat us alive. It was a nightmare, I thought to myself. It had to be a nightmare. I lost track of time as the vision of doom swallowed me up inside itself.

Jim, in the meantime, had problems of his own. With no place to stay, and a wife determined not to set foot inside the deathtrap I suspected the Lotus Hotel to be, he wondered what his options were now. The desk clerk came to the rescue, and wrote down directions for him to another hotel called the Akhenaton. "My last chance," he murmured. "Let's get out of here and check out the next one." We were all hoping beyond hope, and tired beyond tired. This Akhenaton was the last chance. As if coerced by unseen forces of far greater strength than our present ability could overcome, we boarded our truck looking like walking zombies, afraid to see what lay before us.

Back down the Nile we went, slowly at first, searching for the hotel that had been promised. I was beside myself internally, and the pop valves were beginning to go off here and there in the form of snaps at my family's comments and sneers that shone with disgust.

"These buildings couldn't possibly withstand the slightest breeze," I spat out at Jim. "I've never in my life seen such as this! Jim, if you think I'm staying in any of these stupid shanties you're crazy. You hear me? Crazy. You'd better get ready to drive, cause drive you will if this Akhenaton isn't every bit as good as the Nefertari was!"

As we meandered down the corniche, the winding street next to the river, one of the shoddy, six-story cinder block constructions appeared in our view to the right, and next to it, what seemed like an old villa of sorts, having been built of stones unlike the current choices, and encompassed with verandas and wide, plantation style steps and columns. It looked ridiculously out of place in the center of all the tackiness of the current architecture, and we thought it a terrible shame to find what could be such a showplace falling down around itself in the sad state of what surely was once upon a time great splendor. We passed it on by, realizing after a moment that we'd probably gone too far, and knew the pricking of concern that then hit us: the Akhenaton must have been one of those horrid buildings before the old palace. I turned to Jim with but one statement: "No."

"Penny, shut up," Jim yelled right back at me. "I'll end up killing us all if I have to keep driving on that Nile road at night, and I will not endanger you and the kids that way. You have no choice, my dear. We're staying here for the night and that's final."

Jim's words were not negotiable. That tone of voice left no room for any further comments from me and I knew it. I knew it, as we made a u-turn and passed back in front of the old estate. I knew it as we discovered, half hanging down with some letters missing, the sign reading "Akhenaton Hotel" on the leaning building just to the right of it. I knew it as we pulled down the side street full of broken down, wrecked, and junked vehicles between the plantation and the Akhenaton. I knew it as we got out, dodging the cats amongst the old garbage, and entered the pseudo-lobby of the deathtrap. I knew, in my tired and miserable head, I would have to go through with it. The very best I could do and get away with it, was to use the weapon of my facial expressions. Heaving sighs, and contorting my face to the most grotesque contusions of eyes and mouth, I sought to convey my reactions as vividly as possible to this beast of a man who thought so little of me as to make me stay in this ramshackle, rundown atrocity of a hotel.

The smell of the place was musty and stale, and the ceiling was far lower than it looked like it ought to be. I stood there motionless, except for my occasional smirks, while Jim checked us into what would be our abode for the evening. As he finished up, the clerk behind the counter sent us toward the elevator to a room on the third floor. Ever the hopeful one, Jim tried to make the best of things, even against my stone-chiseled face. He tried valiantly to devise plans of spades games and family fun for the evening. He even tried dazzling me with his dimples, usually irresistible in my eyes and always producing a smile. It might have even worked this time had not the iron grating in front of the elevator opened just at that moment, and a very short fellow in the bellhop's outfit stepped aside to allow us in. I slowly raised my head and left my now pasty face expressionless; and I stared that "See-what-I-told-you" stare into Jim's face with my piercing eyes. Jim knew it was going to be a long, long night.

"What an appropriate end to my life," I thought as we searched for the door to shut the elevator, realizing all too late that there was no door to the elevator itself! I shut my eyes and tried to brace myself for what surely must lay ahead of me. It was with great effort that I blocked my thoughts, knowing all too well what they were capable of conjuring up. The trouble here was that most of what I could conjure up was less nightmarish than what I was actually seeing! I shuddered and waited, opening my eyes again. It was then that the soft spot in my heart turned and tugged at me, as I looked intently into the pleasant face of the little man standing before me. He was truly short, not even as tall as Lucas; and his whole life of torment flashed before me in a moment. Yet, here he stood, just as proud as he could be for his job as the elevator attendant. He looked back at me and smiled a huge smile, and slightly bowed.

"Object lesson well taken, Lord," I thought to myself. This little man had probably been born right there in Minya, and he'd probably die right there in Minya, never having seen any other parts of the world. The compassion I felt flooding my spirit for him was easing the sight of the cinder blocks lacking mortar that we saw through the open elevator as we ascended.

Finally we reached our floor, and the little guy smiled brightly again and gestured for us to step out and into the hallway. To the left, workers were doing something frightful looking with the wiring for some lights, with nothing but a dimly burning single bulb swinging back and forth suspended from a frayed electrical cord. But for that one light, none burned to the left. To the right, a hallway proceeded down and around a corner to the right again. I suspected our torment awaited us there, and within a moment I knew I was correct.

Jim went first up to the door, a wooden one with a little window at the top, very much akin to the ones I remembered from twenty-five years previous in my ancient, first grade classroom. "How ultra modern," came my sarcasm, sailed in Jim's direction.

"Well, now, let's just wait and see what's inside—it can't be that bad," was Jim's reply. He was still hopeful, though hope's glimmer was swinging ferociously just like that light bulb he'd seen a moment ago in the hall. He turned the key in the lock only to find, as he swung the door open, three more doors awaiting him inside!

"Whoa! See, babe, look at this!" he said in highest hopes. "This ain't no ordinary room—it's a suite!" He'd decided that was pretty fancy and expected at least a raised eyebrow look from me. One backward glance at my steely-eyed frown told him I was in no mood to provide the fuel for his expectations today.

He continued on, opening the door directly in front of him first, to find two single beds neatly made on the right and a set of French doors that led onto a balcony beyond them. A chiffarobe stood to the left, and a picture hung between the two beds at an angle out from the wall. It really wasn't too bad, considering what it had looked like from the outside.

Next Jim opened the door to the left, and found much the same room setup, with the exception that this one's balcony faced the Nile, and what must have been one of the first portable color television sets ever made sat atop a desk of sorts opposite that.

"Ooooooh! I wonder if the aluminum foil on these antennas will cost us extra," I again spat out caustically. I hadn't even tried to resist the statement. I'd been pushed beyond that usual filtering device, called my conscience, too much earlier in the day.

No comment came back my way from Jim this time. We turned to each other and took a deep breath before facing what surely must be beyond door number three—the bathroom! It was a scary enough thought considering what we'd seen already, but there was no getting around it now. We were stuck here for the night, no matter what it entailed.

Jim gingerly stuck the key in and turned the lock, and he cracked the door open as slowly as he could to minimize the shock. To the immediate right, a fairly recent looking pedestal sink stood, with a white porcelain shelf above it and a mirror above that. If he'd stopped there, it may have been all right—it could have been, indeed, if I hadn't poked my head in behind him just then and gotten the whole view at once before he could brace me for it.

"Oh, no way!" I just plain shouted out loud. There before me was the sink to the right, just like Jim had seen and thought wasn't the worst he'd looked at. But to the left rose the shower: its floor looked like a hundred rusty nails had recently been left to soak along its entire length. A moldy shower curtain had been half-heartedly placed along an aluminum rod that hung out of the broken tile on the wall as though it could collapse at any moment, and the faucets were partially ripped out of the wall and dripping quite regularly. From this awesome vantage point, one had only to glance further to see the real object of horror: the toilet! Rust was the key element involved, until closer inspection revealed that there, inside the bowl itself, was suspended a copper tube that had been curved upward by force to aim directly at the user. Where it was attached to the wall behind the commode, a faucet had been rigged in, again by breaking the tiles, and it too, dripped incessantly. This, in combination with the shower faucets, had left quite a pool of water in the area of the toilet, because that end of the room sort of slanted downward visibly. I collected my outrage as best as I could, and quietly composed myself as I silently smiled a tremendously false smile and backed myself out of the room. In my very politest and most strategic voice, I raised my head to look at Jim's face, which was now growing ashen, and said, "Camera, please." What followed would become the most famous scene recorded on video from our entire Egyptian adventure.

I guess I have to admit that I have an acting flair that can surface at quite unexpected moments, but catching the glint in my eye and the glaze on my face that usually signified another personality was about to come forth, Jim had a sneaking and correct suspicion that there was not really any acting going on this time. The twitch of tempest fury that played around on the edge of my lips served notice to Jim that he'd better do as I said and give me a full spotlight with regard to the camera's attention. I led him around the place with as disgusting a narrative as I could sarcastically spit out through clinched teeth, finally winding up on the balcony facing the Nile, and singing new lyrics to a familiar tune, begging him to take me back home to Arabia. Big time drama!

Jim, boggled and confounded, yet overcome with the hilarity of the state of our condition, gathered up his wits and clicked off the camera, and announced the times of disgust and frustration were over.

"Hey, kids. Get your coats on and let's head out across the street to that park over there. I think I see some swings."

I turned on a dime and glared at him, as though hired assassins were posted behind every bush in that park. "Surely you can't be serious?" I exclaimed.

"You bet I am, my dear," he shot right back at me. "I'm not going to sit here moping the rest of the afternoon. We can't go to supper yet, so we're going out to do what's available. If you'd rather sulk, stay here."

I followed all right, but at twenty paces just to make sure he knew how I felt. The walk was brisk, and the swings were rusty. The park was not exactly what you'd choose to bring your kids to, but it sufficed to keep them occupied until the sun went down and we could go to the restaurant that lurked atop the leaning building. I had dreaded it all evening, being up there at the top of this God-forsaken structure, especially with the wind howling the way it was. But hunger was beginning to take over the fear, and we cleaned up and went out to face the elevator bellhop and the scary elevator.

Right on time the iron grate slid open, and his cheery little features looked up at me, warming the dread inside. It wasn't but a moment before the smells of the kitchen wafted into the elevator shaft, and I had to admit it smelled mighty good. As we reached the top and made our way into the maze of tables and chairs that signified the dining hall, it was apparent that the supper would be buffet style, and our now familiar soup broth was on the menu.

"Well, that's a good sign," I remarked. "I was afraid to even imagine what sort of food would be served here, but it smells wonderful."

"Yep, it sure does," Jim smirked back at me. "I told you it wasn't so bad. It sure beats the Nile road, which is where we'd be right now if you'd had your way."

"Listen, I know it would have been a long road and I know how tired you were, but you have to admit this is no Nile Hilton," I said in an even tone.

"Okay, it's no Hilton. Now, can we end the hotel wars and get on with it?" It was his only response to my offered truce.

Jim was really not so serious as he made out to be. He had his own reservations about this place, but he dared not voice them until we were safely away the next morning. It was best just to enjoy this meal tonight and leave early the next day. And enjoy our meal we did! Steak and spaghetti were among the items on the menu; the food was truly delicious. As a matter of fact, I didn't even think I'd mind coming up the next morning for breakfast. Now that was a real breakthrough!

After supper we made our way back down to the room and played a few hands of spades with Lucas and Chelsea. Eyes were growing heavy with the weight of all the food we'd just consumed, so it wasn't long before we all had to turn in for sleep. Most of the night passed uninterrupted.

It was still dark when Jim woke up, puzzled at the feeling that was gnawing at his mind. He hadn't heard a noise, nor had he seen anything, but something was bothering him enough to disturb his usually sound sleep. He looked around. I was sleeping, and through the two doors, he could just see the kids enough to tell that they too were zonked. So what was it? That same discomfort he'd noticed during the afternoon was crawling all over him now, but he couldn't get a bead on it for the longest time. But then, like a sinister fog rolling through the rooms, he realized it was not a tangible thing he sensed, but an odor that was causing his spirit to recoil—a vile smell, not like that of garbage or something rotten; it was the stench of death!

It was a most thankful thing to him that his watch reported almost five o'clock and we'd all be rising soon anyway and could exit this shrouded place quickly. He didn't immediately tell me of the odor, knowing how I'd felt about the hotel to begin with. In the very first place, his pride wouldn't let him admit readily that it was possible all my ranting and raving of the day before had some solid foundation, unlike the Akhenaton. But he really didn't want to add to my concerns. I picked up on spiritual darkness ninety- nine percent of the time, while he did most of the time, and he knew I would flip right out of my skull knowing some evil was so strong that he'd go so far as to make a comment on it. No, it was best to keep this quiet until we were far beyond the grips of this time warp.

When everyone was shuttled awake and dressed, it was back to the elevator and to the little man who was so faithfully operating it. I felt ashamed—now that I was leaving safely and hadn't been killed—that I had mistrusted the little fellow in the first place. I filed his face away in my memory, so that I would not ever forget it.

The iron grate slid open and we stepped out onto the top floor restaurant.

We were set for a familiar Egyptian breakfast of Arabic bread, cream cheese with strawberry preserves, fool, and omelets. Across the table and through the large windows, we could see the sun rising above the Nile: a huge, deep orange fireball, sending streaks of radiance in laser-straight lines, slicing open rifts in the ancient riverbed. Beyond the locality of Minya lay a high bridge over the water, and it was that one I assumed we would cross on our way to the first stop of the day, Beni Hassan.

Our Fodor's guide had descriptions of some spectacular tombs there, and as it was on the way, we didn't want to miss it.

Because this time our eating held the promise of escape from the dreaded death tower, I—the ever-eager-to-depart Mrs. Caldwell—hurried the kids to stuff their first meal of the day down, and all but choked my entire family trying to save our lives. It was my twisted logic that sometimes forced an even bigger potential danger upon us to rescue us from the depth of my ominous fears. It was something only I understood.

It took me all of two minutes and twenty-three seconds to brush my teeth, pack my bags, and salute at full attention toward Jim-the-drill-sergeant-Caldwell at the door. Lucas and Chelsea, having been forced to submit to my desire to leave the Akhenaton, rushed along as well and stood beside me, and the troops got their morning pep talk from their dad. With all the gusto he usually had in the morning at his disposal, Jim Caldwell rang out his events-of-the-day calendar, ready to see his family jumping up and down and in awe at the potential scenery to be devoured. What he got was our looks of disbelief at where we had been forced to sleep, and worse yet, where he would take us next, seeing as how the star ratings of the hotels he'd chosen were dropping like shot skeet. He guessed he'd wait a while on the revelation of the death stench the night before. And with a wave of his hand, we bid the Akhenaton Hotel *adieu*.

CHAPTER ELEVEN

Beni Hassan and the Nile Ferry

With everything packed again into its rightful place inside the truck, Jim turned the faithful black Patrol around and headed south along the Nile, looking for the bridge's entrance. Once over, we recognized that on both sides of the river, the road was atrocious. Now on the eastern bank, we were to travel for about an hour to the tombs etched into the limestone at Beni Hassan. These tombs held particular interest to Jim, for they had been recorded as having some of the only hieroglyphic references to the Habiru, or the Hebrew slave faction that he was so interested in. And, of course, as in most cases, when finding what direction Providence bids you go, the perpetual enemy makes it as difficult as possible.

I picked up the *Fodor's Guide to Egypt* and began reading about the tombs we were headed for. "Hey, listen to this," I announced to the captive audience. "It says here that we should pass a bunch of what are called beehives. They are both Christian and Muslim graves, and they're supposedly everywhere along the way to Beni Hassan. "

"Yeah, I've read about 'em," Jim answered. "Really funny looking from what I understand, and unique to the region. We'll have to watch for them, okay kids?" Jim, ever trying to torment both Lucas and Chelsea, was doing his best to get them interested in the day at hand.

I think he wanted to make certain that sleeping in the death trap last night hadn't warped their personalities.

We went on for a few kilometers, following the Nile along at a fair distance to our right. Sure enough, before long a strange sight appeared in the distance that nearly boggled our minds. Like a network of elongated honeycombs, the cemetery of beehives was suddenly upon us. To call these structures unusual was a real stretching of the word. We'd never seen anything like this before. As far as the eye could see on both sides of the road, the domes stood, one almost upon another, some with crosses perched atop. Each one touched the one next to it without much space in between at the ground level at all. On the average, eight to twelve of these big domes would be joined together at the bases by walls of brick or mud. The hillsides were so crammed with these domes that it reminded us of sand on a beach that had been packed into a plastic cup and turned over, one right after another. We looked on in amazement.

Jim felt his skin begin to crawl, thinking of all those souls that had been laid to rest there. It was by far the largest gathering of grave sites he'd ever seen, and what with the aroma of death he'd smelled the previous night not but about twenty kilometers north of here, he was beginning to formulate a theory in his mind he really didn't like all that well. Thousands upon thousands of graves took up all the available landscape between the escarpment range off in the distance to the left, and the Nile River to the right. Haunting possibilities began tickling his psyche in a macabre lineup of nightmarish scenarios. He was startled to find he was getting cold and clammy, and at the same time he was breaking out into a fresh sweat. This was one creepy area, and anxiety was starting to take its toll. He told no one of his uneasiness, however; he knew if he wanted to keep on heading toward Beni Hassan I would never allow it knowing he had the willies as bad as he did. So onward he forced himself to drive, hoping soon we'd break out of these mists of spiritual darkness and into the brilliance of the January sun beyond. In the first few minutes of the trip, all had gone perfectly well, but now time and kilometers were passing without a sign of Beni Hassan. Jim thought by now he'd be getting close to some sort of apparent change in the escarpment ahead that would foretell the tombs' vicinity. What he did see that he wished he hadn't was the narrowing of the already tiny highway, and the pavement's giving way to more and more sand. When it had all but disappeared, and the road had become a typical desert track and even tire marks had vanished in front of our truck, Jim knew he was in trouble. The only sign of anyone civilized was the Filipino driving the bulldozer ahead of us. Two Egyptians were hanging onto the back of the big piece of machinery as it moved slowly down the pathway, and their gazes had become rather fixed on the perplexed looking strangers in the black truck behind them. Presently one of them jumped down and started moving toward us. Jim braced himself.

"We've got a visitor ..." he said in a small, wavy voice.

I just looked at him with a faked smile. "I see that, Jim."

"Well, maybe he can help us find Beni Hassan," came forth the even wavier reply.

"Yes. And maybe he can slit our throats and steal our truck," I responded with a sickly sweet, toothy grin.

The blank stare came back at me from him this time. He cleared his throat and recovered his normal voice, and said, "Just try to be nice, Penny, okay?"

"I don't think so, Jim," I purred smoothly, continuing to smile sweetly and retain as much sarcasm in my voice and demeanor as possible. It was all the dialog we had time for, before our next encounter with another angel began.

"Hallo, hallo," came the salutations from the stranger, who now had just about his entire head stuck inside our truck. "What you are looking for?"

The Arabic speaking people of the entire Middle East in general have a habit of putting words in the wrong places according to English grammar. I am certain the way they say things is absolutely correct in Arabia, but not to our Western minds. For these past few years, I had been listening to it with a rather comical interest, and I'd almost learned what to expect to hear before they spoke. I'd even found myself phrasing my own words in the same manner they did when trying to use the English language to expatriates such as myself and Jim. It also cracked me up that they pronounced all of our "p" letter sounds with a "b" sound, as there is no corresponding alpha character in Arabic for a "p." I turned to hear the dialogue that was beginning between my husband and this Egyptian.

"Hi!" Jim said full of hopeful enthusiasm. "I'm looking for Beni Hassan." Jim was short and to the point. It was the safest way to approach the subject, not knowing at all whether or not this man would help us or pull a firearm out of his pocket and kill us all.

"Bani Ha'sn?" the man asked again. "Bleese. I will go you there." Before Jim had even deciphered what he meant by that latest twist of the English language, the Egyptian was opening up my door and I found myself scrambling into the back seat with Lucas and Chelsea. It was now obvious what he meant. He was going with us, and as far as he was concerned the discussion was over.

I glared into the rear view mirror at Jim's eyes, which once again were widened by the passionate Egyptian way of doing things. He raised his eyebrows at me as if to say "What'd I do?" while I mentally made out my last will and testament. Yet, even so, I did not have a feeling of doom; after all, it was only someone trying to help. That's what I kept telling myself as we turned, bumping and bouncing back down the way we'd come in.

The man introduced himself as none other than Mohammed, which is the most common name for a male in the Middle East, and got it across to us in surprisingly decent wording that he was an English teacher. Jim and I shot each other another incredulous look in the mirror at the atrocious contradiction in terms. We hadn't gone very far when he asked to be let out, but not until he'd shown us a turnoff we'd missed, which was just the one we'd needed to take. Retrospect hit us both as we watched the broad smile of Mohammed waving goodbye, walking down the road. Now I felt bad for not trusting him in the first place. He didn't even ask for baksheesh, which was unheard of and completely impossible. He had appeared right where we needed him, spent only a few minutes with us, and then disappeared again down the road. Very strange, but very good for us! Now that the Patrol was pointed in the right direction, we were off again.

Around a long, wide curve in the track we came upon what looked like a village of sorts, albeit a tiny one, at the very edge of the last remaining beehive graves. Several mud brick and straw huts lay in a semi-circle arrangement, and an abundance of "the life" was beginning to become visible as we drew near. Jim, willing to face anything but a continuance of the horror he'd been feeling for the past several minutes,

LUCAS, JIM, AND CHELSEA AT BENI HASSAN, SOUTH OF MINYA, EGYPT

blazed on forward to greet the now apparent throngs of women and children in the vicinity of the dwellings.

"Aaawwwwwwwhhhh, woooooof!" came the disgusted scream from the back seat. True to her nickname, "The Nose" Chelsea had been the first to detect the stink in the surrounding air. Only mere wisps of it had entered through the vehicle originally, but now our whole family had quickly progressed from the frowning, crinkly-nosed "I wonder what that is" stage to a full fledged, vomituous gag!

"Phew!" Jim muttered. "Where in the world is such a thick stench coming from?"

It wasn't long before we knew. Now following the track ever so slowly in the very midst of a populated area, we saw the source of the fumes. As we drew closer, the tan color of the track had been getting progressively darker and turned finally into a deep, dark brown. On the edges of each of the huts, mounds of this dark dirt were scattered here and there, some up to six or seven feet high. Children played in and amongst them like sand piles. Cows and donkeys milled about freely, just as the children did. That's when we realized what the piles were made of.

"Penny," Jim said in a very pleasant tone of voice. "Do you see what I see? Am I seeing right, or am I crazy? Are those kids over there playing in a humongous pile of—well, poop?" He was inquiring of me as politely as he could, while motioning to the filthy, barefooted, rag-mop children who'd presently taken notice of the black jeep traipsing through their home territory. A new sort of horror had replaced his feelings at the gravesites. "How can those kids be playing in all that crap? Gross!"

"Jim, Jim!" I yelled. "Jim! They're coming over here! Oh, man, they're running now! Jimmy, they're gonna jump on the truck! "A crowd of green-teethed, terribly dirty children ranging in age from what looked like two to sixteen had dropped their games in the manure and were making tracks as fast as they could for our truck! Having fresh memories of Cairo traffic still in our minds, we knew it would only be a moment before all these offspring would be positioning themselves to catch a free ride on our vehicle wherever they could hang on.

Jim did the only thing he could, and that was to hit the accelerator and fly out of there before they could reach the truck. The wheels spun for a moment in the crumbling manure, but then caught a grip and moved us out! Fortunately, it was just in time, and we escaped with the only casualties being a few well-thrown poop balls hitting the back end of the truck. It took a few moments of silence for us to recover our wits, but we were not so stupefied as to forget to hold our noses. Nothing could have forced us not to do that!

Just beyond this menagerie of odor and life, the track entered a broad plain, where the escarpment to the left became quite clearly visible. It was at this point we noticed the limestone facades of tombs that were cut into the edge of it, even from as far away as we were. The carving had been done high upon the rock, and the notable rise in ground level between us and the tombs had become plain. From this vantage point, it was obvious why the tombs had been placed so high. The Nile, god and goddess alike to the pharonic age, lay spread out far below us, fertile and green as a living eternity. All the facades of the tombs faced it, as though peering in a timeless stare toward what they'd believed their salvation to be, yet ever stark and dead, being so far separated from the life-sustaining waters. The division between the living and the dead had never seemed more apparent.

We looked at each other in great relief as we made good our escape, and quickly decided that it could well have been worth all the efforts of the morning to get us to this locale. Beni Hassan was spoken of in Fodor's as having carved figures in various games of sport, even fighting resembling judo or karate. These tombs were positioned on the east bank of the Nile, which set them apart as the only such ones to be found from the Middle Kingdom of Egyptian rule.

"You think we can make it up there?" came my usual line of questioning to my "of-course-I-can-make-it-anywhere" husband. The track before us was veering to the left and upwards toward the tombs at an incredibly steep angle. Judging from how heavily the truck was loaded down, it was a question worthwhile.

"Well, we can certainly give it a shot, now can't we?" Jim slyly smiled back at me, knowing things like this little drive up a sharp hill scared me. My imagination could conjure disaster quicker than his, and that was really saying something!

He shifted down and gathered the speed he'd need to go for it, and we were on our way. Rocks and sand gave way beneath us as the powerful wheels were set in climbing motion. The truck frame squeaked and groaned under the pressure and the strain of the upward motion, but kept moving steadily forward. It only took a few feet, though, to eat up the momentum Jim had started with. Balancing such a load and put to such a test, the Nissan soon came to a halt, and it wasn't at the top. It really wasn't as bad as I had imagined, but the length of the drive and the angle did ultimately prevent us from going all the way. It would only be a short walk to the tombs from where we'd stopped, so Jim's momentary disappointment melted away as the dust cleared.

"Now, did I kill us all?" Jim said as he grinned and shot a quick glance and a gloating smirk at me.

"No, but you probably knocked off a few guardian angels," I replied smugly. But by now, the relief had a smile growing on my face, and I opened up my door to the chilly morning breeze that was blowing along the length of the River of Egypt. The sky was crystal blue, and the air up high upon the bluff was squeaky clean and fresh, unlike the stench of the valley we'd just escaped. Forward we climbed until we reached the level ground in front of the tombs. As we drew near, the now expected "guides of Egypt" descended upon us with gusto.

"Halooo, halooo," came the familiar ring of the very friendly but very greedy baksheesh hounds. At every site of possible tourist interest, the locals hung about like blood-thirsty buzzards; the crags and crannies of the cliffs were their perches, offering them the advance knowledge of unsuspecting prey. Today we were the first to arrive.

From this height far above the Nile, we could see clearly how the desert began where the fertile flood plain of the river ended. It was like a line drawn in the topsoil of earth: on one side, lush and life giving; on the other, harsh, rocky, and life-threatening. Vivid green versus stark tan: there was no in-between.

The tombs themselves had been carved out of the stone facing the Nile. These were the burials of nobles and governmental figures for the most part, and had been sealed with great metal doors and huge padlocks in recent times to keep robbers out. They extended as far as could be seen to the south within the hillside, and appeared to continue on around the corner as the formation of rock curved to the east.

Jim chose the first guide that got to us, and the others disappeared seemingly into nowhere. It was amazing how quickly they could vaporize when the opportunity to take you for all the Egyptian pounds you had closed. This man had a kindly, older face, but his expertise with the English language was quite questionable. And his name was, of course, Mohammed. He steadily led us through the several tombs that were open though, and seemed to have a fairly substantial knowledge of what he was showing us. Inside, the reliefs were in pretty good shape, and did, as our Fodor's guide read, include sports games and martial arts. These were in contrast to the tombs at Saqqara, which seemed to incorporate the more spiritual side of life and death. The stories here were ancient scenes of every day life. They had a quite personable effect on us. One group of carvings held particular interest and dealt with a people that had been artistically drawn differently from the Egyptians. They were of angular faces and pointed beards and basically described as Asians. They were probably slaves to the nobles of the day.

The tours didn't take much more than an hour, and we then were ready to embark on our continuing journey toward Luxor. At the beginning of our Beni Hassan experience, Jim had been thinking of how disgusting it was going to be to have to drive back through all the poop-piles and dirt roads we'd been picking our way through all morning. He'd decided if at all possible, he'd seek information from Mohammed about any roads further to the south that would lead to a bridge over the Nile so as not to have to venture back through that nightmare again. It was with great disappointment that Jim learned that the only option by road to cross the Nile was to return by the way we'd come in. However, Mohammed did come up with another solution: apparently he knew someone who ran a ferryboat! He told Jim if he'd just fork over a wad of cash up front, his companion would take his own boat across and fetch the captain of such a service, and have him come over to pick us up! Absolutely unwilling to re-experience our morning drive, Jim reluctantly agreed and gave in.

Now that we were finished with the tombs, Jim had turned his thoughts to wondering what we were in for. There was a chance the guide was shooting straight with him, and a ferry would come. There was the far greater chance that they'd ripped him off, and hell would freeze over before a ferry would appear on the east bank of the Nile. In any case, we had to get down there to the river to find out. So with a wave and a smile, we returned to our faithful truck and began the arduous descent to the makeshift road, which led to the banks of the river and the Nile cruiser docking station.

We wound our way down the road and found what appeared to be the only straight blacktop heading for the water. That's when we spied—not a ferry, but a cruise boat—one huge and fancy cruise boat filled with tourists riding in the lap of luxury. I gazed at it with a mixture of emotions, seeing how clean and coiffed these people looked, and envisioning in my mind's eye just how sparkling clean their bathrooms must be. With Minya fresh on my mind, this was not the kind of thinking that produced a great and abiding love lump in my throat for my husband who'd just forced me and my children to sleep in a death trap and await an uncertain ferry of unknown origins.

I forced the techniques of torture and revenge out of my psyche, however, and tried to concentrate on the gorgeous weather outside and the sparkling green water of the Nile before me. This too had its problems, as I felt myself drifting into the wonder of whether we'd be sitting here until mold began to grow on my body, or if we'd just all die of starvation before these ferry drivers showed up. One thought rapidly digressed into another, and before long, I had us all skeletons in the bottom of the water never to be found again, as the conjured ferry in my head overturned and drowned us all! A clattering noise shook me back out of my daytime nightmare, and I came to realize a boy of about eleven or so was rapping away at the window, holding up the dented remainder of a teapot, and evidently offering us some of the brew that was venting steam inside it. I turned from my side of the truck and slowly raised my expression of horror to Jim, who, by this time, was stir crazy and fit to be tied that he'd been waiting almost two hours for what would probably turn out to be a phantom ferry!

"Don't even say a word!" he spat through gritted teeth. He motioned in no uncertain terms that we were definitely not interested in his tea, and then gazed in abject disbelief as the boy began making motions back to him that undoubtedly were asking if we wanted a car wash! Jim swallowed hard to keep from exploding and turned back to me, hoping the boy would get the hint and leave. Fortunately he did, but not before giving us a look that said exactly what he thought of tourists that wouldn't give money to his cause.

"I'll give them until noon, and if they're not here by then, we leave," Jim remarked, becoming resigned to what he believed his fate would be. It was the final straw of patience that had begun to bend inside his head, and the audacity of a Egyptian lying to him about a ferry, taking his money and absconding with it, was about to snap that same straw right in two. He could just picture the Egyptian laughing as he smoked a hubbly-bubbly pipe with a group of his friends of the same caliber, and bragging about how he'd taken advantage so easily of the gullible American! It was true that Jim always tried to believe the best about folk, but being in Egypt these past nine days had already stretched that good-natured part of him completely out of shape. It was also painfully prickling, as he sat before the sleek new cruise boat named the "Nile Princess," to recall that some of our friends had luxuriously wined and dined through the ancient countryside in pure comfort on just such a cruise boat the month before, while we'd just spent the night smelling death at the Akhenaton Hotel! And to top it off, here he sat, awaiting God knows what to appear before him upon the river. He wondered, but not aloud, what he was doing here at all.

Before Jim finished the thought, he caught my face change expressions out of his peripheral vision. We were extremely good at noticing and reading each other's faces, and today was no exception. A whole new train of thought broke in with force onto the thoughts he was previously thinking when he saw the look of sheer disbelief and shock that laced itself in wide swaths across my countenance.

"Oh, please not!" The words came out of my mouth quiet and serene, like the last words of a death row prisoner, ready to face his own imminent demise. I smiled sweetly and batted my eyelashes at my husband, and ever so softly began to speak again. "Jim, darling? Jim, why is there a tin shanty with a tin roof moving among the Nile reeds?"

Jim recoiled instantly and frowned hard, gazing intently in the direction of the river. Here where we sat, the Nile had carved an island of sorts in its midst, and it was impossible to see the opposite bank because of it. All we could really see was the top of the masts of the feluccas, the small sailboats, as they sailed past. When he scanned to the right and found nothing, he turned his eyes left and had to rub them twice before he could gain focus on what he was seeing. It was not possible that the loosely joined frame of two-by-fours that was visible just above the reeds was our ferry—or was it? In a flash of Jim's thoughts, the lesser of two evils almost weighed out to be the Egyptians laughing at him for falling prey to their lies and stealing his money! Was it conceivable that their telling him the truth could be worse? He swallowed as best as he could and waited for the moving network of wood and tin to become fully visible.

When it kept coming nearer, but then went on past, Jim breathed a well thought-out breath of relief. He kept it in the corner of his sight, and wondered what in the world it was for a while, then froze ashen gray when it slowed its movement away from us. To our mutual horror, it appeared to reverse itself and its direction, and be once again headed for us! "This is not happening," he muttered to himself, all the while turning and grinning sheepishly at me. He'd hoped beyond hope that I had not seen it reverse back toward us.

But sure enough, it had. By this time, after Minya, nothing surprised me. "Great! Ha, ha, ha, ha, ha!" I began laughing hysterically at the contraption that was coming into full view in front of us. I just couldn't help myself. It was all too insane! A barge-like square platform, dented and ancient, was now moving directly at our truck. Attached to the

THE NILE FERRY

greasy steel foundation on the left side and the right were the two-by-four structures we had partially seen earlier, but now were revealed to be in two distinct segments divided by a space with room enough for maybe two or three vehicles. What looked like oil drums underneath the thing seemed to be the only items keeping this junk-pile afloat. Within the studwork on the left, a captain's stall had been sectioned out, and a great ship's wheel was barely visible. It was our ferry!

Jim and I just about lost all of our senses right then and there. This was too funny to be real. And we both knew by this time, it could only happen to us. But that was part of what made the two of us click so well. In all the worst of times we had the ability to laugh, though sometimes out of hysteria, and carry on in an innocent way that always knit us closer and kept us going. It would be a trait we would surely need in the days ahead of us, for our very survival. But for now, all I could get out as I gasped for air between guffaws was, "Our friends got the Nile Princess, we get the Nile garbage barge."

Jim cracked up incessantly, until he realized the true nature of the situation he was in. This makeshift ferry was about to be the only thing between his truck with its precious cargo and the Nile River, the fear of which was only exceeded by the six or seven toothless, grinning Egyptians that stood hungrily on the scrap heap before him. He watched anxiously as they docked the thing and knew he had no choice but to ride it across and take his chances. He had it in his mind to reach Luxor by nightfall, and that was six hours away on the opposite side of the river on the horrid Nile road. It was indeed, his only choice.

The smiley deckhands went into work mode as soon as the hydro-jalopy touched the bank of the river. With a loud, clattering clang, the ramp crashed down upon the shore, and six pairs of hands began waving us wildly aboard. Jim took a look at the flimsy metal ramp, and the very questionable deck of the contraption before him, and with one mighty burst of gusto, yelled "Away we go!" He gunned the Patrol forward and we were suddenly feeling wave action. The launch had been successful, and we were on. Amazingly enough we did not sink, and the ferry actually began moving toward the opposite bank of the Nile within seconds of the raising of the ramp.

"It's a miracle," I replied in an exhausted sigh of relief. "Are we going to get out, or should I just hide my face in a book and lock all the doors?" My reference was, of course, to the deck hands, now about six feet away from us, and glaring into the vehicle with obvious intent.

"You can get on out," Jim said. "I think they're harmless." He was now doing just fine, now that the whole junk-pile hadn't sunk immediately into the murky depths of the Nile. We opened the doors and got out and were quickly descended upon by the throng of curiosity seekers. In an instant the communication trials began, what with their no English and Jim's approximate twenty words of Arabic to aid us. Two of them came over to me and motioned at my notebook, then made like they were writing in the air. It was not anything new to us for the locals of any of these countries to ask for items of need. This time, we were prepared with cigarettes, water, and charcoal, all of which we'd found ourselves being asked for before. But it was indeed a new item, one of great personal importance to me, that they were in want of today. I couldn't believe my eyes, but it was true—what they were asking for.

I turned and looked over the hood of the truck, where Jim stood hand signaling to some of the others, and said, "Jim. It's the pens! These guys want my ink pens!" It was truly the worst thing to beg of a writer. My indignant mood vanished when Jim, through gritted teeth, said, "Penny, just give them the pens. Can't you see we are rather stuck here with these guys right now? Not a good idea to make them mad, wouldn't you agree?"

I knew he was right, and quickly began scrounging all the hotel pens I'd been collecting so far on this trip. "Good thing I kept all these," I walked off muttering toward the captain in the pilot house, with Lucas and Chelsea close behind me.

The pilot house itself was a makeshift box sitting above the rest of the framework of the barge, yet still within the roof's edge. The captain was a man of about ten teeth: a wiry, wizened-looking man whose face bore far too many wrinkles to be the fortyish years he must have been. The flock of helpers he had on board, the ones who'd just depleted the inventory of my ink pens, had my family surrounded and before him now. He surveyed us between glances at the water, and before the third look, the smile was playing at the edges of his mouth until it broke toward us in a face-crunching grin. He looked like he'd been out in the sun most of his life, as dark and leathery as his skin was, and gave convincing evidence that he was enjoying this excursion with these white-faced tourists immensely. Once again Jim did his best to communicate, but motions would win out over words this time. The only real breakthrough came when he motioned to the children and pointed to the captain, asking how many he was blessed enough to have. When the captain held up two fingers and pointed to me, then six fingers and seven fingers and pointed to the kids, Jim understood him to be the proud owner of two wives and thirteen children! Jim looked at me, then back to the captain and said, "Two wives? Mafie-muck!" In other words, YOU MUST BE CRAZY! Jim had no idea how funny the whole crew thought his reply was, until they were doubled over in laughter and started slapping him on the back in recognition. It broke the remaining bits of tension between us all, and I could finally let go and relax. After all, it really was funny!

At a position approximately halfway across the Nile, and nearing the small island that had previously blocked our view of the ferry, the captain motioned for Lucas to come closer and up into the seat with him. Lucas, being extremely reluctant to go, gave me a look of "What now?" and frowned with disdain when I took both hands and shoved him forward. Jim and I knew what was coming and knew that Lucas would never regret it once he made that first move—for the captain with the two wives and the thirteen children was about to turn the wheel of the Nile ferry over to my firstborn son! In realization of his destiny, a broad grin flushed over Lucas's face, and he moved right on in to assume the position just as calmly as though he was at the helm of his grandfather's boat named Snoopy in Three Oaks Bayou back home. Jim and I looked at each other and the silent thought occurred to us at the same moment: these were the sort of things that just didn't happen on the luxurious Nile Princess cruise boats we'd passed at their elegant dockings just a few minutes ago. Memories such as these came once in a lifetime, and we were quite proud suddenly of our son: Lucas Caldwell, Nile River Ferry Captain!

All strange things must come to an end, however, and after snapping out of our daydreams, we realized that the opposite shore was rapidly approaching us. Lucas, now beaming with pride in getting to do something his sister didn't get to do, strode down from his perch and sauntered across the barge and back into our truck. It was time we all did, the crew motioned. Reality being back in full swing now, the next feat of acrobatics would be getting the gate lined up with the rather steep ramp on the bank we were nearing. Already a small crowd was beginning to form on either side of the ramp, mostly children with a few passerby adults lingering to witness the attempt. They formed two lines like the guests at a wedding waiting for the rice throw to begin. I sat back in my familiar co-pilot's seat, ready to film the endeavor.

Tension mounted as we drew near, with visions of all the scenarios of what could go wrong with this picture dancing through Jim's head: the ramp was moving up and down with the wave action on the water, and if he miscalculated by a fraction of an inch it would all be over, and we and the jam-packed truck would be slowly sinking to the bottom of the river. But thinking about it wasn't getting us off the ferry. There was nothing for Jim to do but gather up all his gusto and floor the accelerator! So in a burst of confidence and glory, we lurched forward and onto the ramp, and were soon on the west bank of the Nile, to the cheering of the people that were waiting! We drove slowly through them, waving and smiling to them all as we went by. It was the triumph of the day!

Lucas, Jim, and Chelsea at Luxor, Egypt

CHAPTER TWELVE

Luxor and the Valley of the Kings

By the time we got through the crowds and out to the main road headed toward the south, it was already early afternoon. Luxor was our destination, and because of all the morning delay awaiting the ferry, it would take us the rest of the day and right up to dark to get there.

The road we had to travel was the famous Nile Road that we'd already spent so much time on. As it snaked its way down from the northern regions of Egypt, this two-lane serpent of a highway had steep banks descending on either side and almost no shoulder; it was a treacherous pathway to travel. Having driven it before to Minya, it was not with great enthusiasm that Jim found himself facing its dangerous pathway for the rest of the afternoon and into early evening. Between the overloaded busses and the tanker trucks speeding around us despite oncoming traffic, and nowhere to go but down the embankments and into the water, I was a nervous wreck and it wasn't getting better as the hours dragged on. I figured out very quickly that it was only the Hand of God that kept us alive on that road.

But we did find ourselves dragging wearily into Luxor at about six o'clock, just as the lavender and purplish hues began to overtake the western sky. We'd made reservations at the Hilton Hotel, and managed to arrive just in time to see a troop of Egyptian dancers performing a traditional dance out in the plaza in front of the hotel. As we neared the entrance I rolled down my window to hear the haunting and mystical notes of classic middle-eastern music wafting through the desert evening. The dancers swayed to the rhythmic beat in a procession that immediately called up Ali Baba and the Arabian Nights. After the long arduous journey we'd just endured, the sounds of the music and the movement of the dancers captivated us and caught us up in a mesmerizing trance. We went almost mindlessly through the motions of checking into a gorgeous room, resplendent, luxurious, and spotlessly clean—wonderful after the hideous death trap we'd just experienced at Minya. After a quick room-service dinner, we fell into a deep and much needed sleep.

The dawning of January 12 found us refreshed and restored! The wonderful room was just what we all needed to recoup our strength and energy. After numerous cups of room-service coffee and lounging about, we got the kids up and ready and headed downstairs to the enormous dining room for breakfast. Almost the entire wall facing the Nile River was glass, and the view was fantastic. Way across the river we could see the pale brown cliffs that rose sharply out of the desert floor at quite a distance from the edge of the Nile, and knew from our Fodor's guide that those were the formations that contained the tombs of, among others, the former Pharaohs of Egypt. We would be making our plans to go there later this day.

Just directly outside the dining room were the landscaped courtyards and swimming pool of the hotel, and just beyond them, the patio area that led by a paved walkway down to the river's edge. Lucas and Chelsea were determined to get down to the water there to skip some of the hundreds of stones we could see that had been on those shores for ageless times, being washed smooth by the waters lapping and receding. But that would have to wait until after we ate, for now food was the pressing detail, and we dove heartily into the splendid array of fruits, pastries, and breakfast delights laid out before us.

After our meal and some quality rock skipping into the water there, we piled back into our faithful Patrol, took off toward the center of town, spending the better part of the morning out in the midst of Luxor. The town was like any other we'd seen so far in Egypt, although much smaller than Cairo. The streets were bustling with shopkeepers hawking their wares and traffic piling up. The horse carriages we'd seen before were in great abundance here, slowly making their way along the streets amid the blowing horns of impatient, modern traffic. They probably survived on money from the enormous number of tourists coming to Luxor to see the Temple of Luxor, the Valley of the Kings, and the Temple of Karnak, which were the main highlights of any visit here.

By early afternoon we were all hungry again and began to look for a local restaurant to have some lunch. Jim found a place called "Marhaba,"which in Arabic is a non-formal greeting such as our "Hi," or "Hello," in English. The building had a lower dining room with tables, but what caught Jim's eye was the upper deck that was open to the elements and appeared to have a great view of the Nile and the opposite shore. We ordered up plates of shwarmas, which we'd come to love after living in Saudi Arabia for the past few years. Shwarmas consisted basically of pita or flat bread wrapped around sliced beef or chicken, with lettuce, tomato, and sometimes even French fries, along with special sauces ranging from Tabasco to tahini. The food was hot and fresh and smelled divine, as we grabbed our individual plates and headed up the stairs to the open-air dining room.

Finding a table with the best view possible, Jim led us over to it and we sat down to eat. About halfway through our meal, a number of blow flies found us and more specifically, our food. They were dive bombing our plates like precision squadrons, and it wasn't long before Jim had taken all he could of their presence. He raised his arm and opened one hand in the air, poised to come crashing down on the unsuspecting creatures, which thoroughly cracked Lucas and Chelsea up. Taking every available opportunity to torment and torture his kids, Jim also advised them that he was going to eat all the flies he caught! Well, that caused a veritable ruckus to erupt at our table, with both kids hurling out comments back at their father in rapid fire succession. In the first place, they agreed that he'd never be able to catch one at all, and secondarily, he'd never, ever, ever really eat one!

Just about the time the arguments reached an all new level of loudness and audacity, Jim's huge hand came crashing down on the table, almost toppling the entirety of the contents sitting thereon. I looked at him out of the corners of my eyes to see if he'd admit to me if he'd really gotten one, and the winking of his eyes back at me told me he had. Now I knew him well enough to know that he'd be doing every trick possible to try and convince those kids that he'd really eat that fly! I held my laughter back and tried to keep a straight face as I watched him turn to the side and open up his mouth wide, ready to fake throwing the unsuspecting insect down his throat. What transpired in the next few seconds lives on in our family history to this day!

As if in slow motion, Jim laid his head back and up went his hand with the entrapped fly inside! His fingers and his mouth opened at exactly the same time, and I gasped in horror along with the kids as we all watched the nasty creature fly directly into his mouth and right down his throat! Jim's face went from that of a teasing trickster to one of horror and repulsion! Of course his original intent had been to throw the fly just behind his head, so that from the side where the kids were, it would look just like he'd really eaten the fly. But something had gone terribly wrong with his plan, and he'd really, truly, actually swallowed that fly! He began to cough and sputter and choke involuntarily, and grasped for his cold drink and guzzled the rest of it right down. Lucas and Chelsea were beside themselves with both laughter and disgust, and all I could do was just sit there and stare, shaking my head. "Serves you right for being such a tease!" was all I could get to come out of my mouth.

We spent what remained of the day touring the Luxor Temple. The ruins there were truly magnificent. I had never seen such huge columns and towering statues, and wondered seriously about how in the world these things were still standing. It seemed that everything in ancient Egypt was made on a grandiose scale, and it was truly amazing that these things remained at all after thousands of years. But what really got to me was the knowledge that the Israelite slaves had been the probable workmen that raised these incredible monuments up to the royalty of Egypt, of which our newly acquired papyrus was a testimony. How many hundreds must have died under this back-breaking labor was crossing my mind at the same time that the fantastic artisanship of their obvious talent was still apparent right before my eyes. It was both a mystery and a paradox.

Jim had the video camera glued to his face for most of the time we spent at the Luxor Temple. This was a once in a lifetime occurrence, and he was determined to record every moment. How strange it was to him, that his father Lyle had so dreamed of seeing Egypt one day, and here he was walking on that very ground that fascinated his dad so very much. I was thinking the same thing about my mother, Nellie Mae. She had always been captivated with the stories of ancient Egypt, just like Jim's dad was, and even had a scarab ring with hieroglyphics etched into the stone. I thought of her as we walked around the vast complex. As Jim worked with the video camera, I worked with the Nikon 35mm still camera. Unbeknownst to us, we were receiving hands-on training that would serve us well in the years that were yet to unfold before us back in Saudi Arabia.

But that would be for another time shortly to begin. We just didn't know it yet.

After we finished at the Luxor Temple, it was getting too late to start any new tours today, so we began making plans to go and visit the Valley of the Kings on the morrow. We ended up meeting a man named Rashid who seemed to know how to arrange tours to the area, beside a whole lot of other things, and decided on his advice to actually ride donkeys all the way up to the monuments! Plans were made to meet him after breakfast in the early morning, cross the Nile on a local ferry, and pick up our donkeys on the other side along with a guide Rashid would have ready. With that set, we carried the children back to the shelter of the Luxor Hilton and the luxurious room we had waiting for us. It wasn't long after a quick dinner that we retired for the evening and sleep overtook our consciousness.

* * *

A far distant sound was beginning to jar my brain and irritate my senses, but I didn't realize just then that it was only the phone in the hotel room announcing the exact time we'd requested to be awakened. Jim recognized it before I did and got to the phone to silence the annoyance before I could get to it first, rip it from the desk, and throw it from the balcony as I had been known to do before. Not one with an overabundance of longsuffering, it was a miracle anything stayed in one piece around me for any length of time. Over the years Jim had tried to calm this destructive tendency down in me and had been graced with some measure of success, but this was not the morning to let me get to that phone before he did. I had been sleeping like a long submerged cypress stump in the bottom of a Louisiana bayou, and the incessant, crisp little "brrrrring-brrrrrring's" coming into sharper and sharper focus in my eardrums were bringing the fury up from my toes to my face quickly. He lowered the receiver back onto the cradle of the phone, and turned back to me and raised himself up on one elbow, looking down at my face just inches away. Across his face spread that million dollar grin of his, and he got right up to my ear to say to me in triumph, "Ha! Beat 'cha to it!"

Well, that was all I had to hear. With a swift move of my leg and arm, I rolled over and pounced squarely on top of him and started pounding him back into the mattress, with him screaming all the while for Lucas and Chelsea to come save him!

The laughter and commotion had them out of their beds in a flash, and before a full minute could pass, the four of us were in a tangled mass of wrestling humanity there on the bed in the Luxor Hilton! Arms and legs were being elbowed mercilessly; cheeks were being pinched and sides were being tickled, and if not for an accidental blow that sent Lucas' glasses sailing right off his face, the spectacle may never have ended. But those glasses were extremely necessary for him, and the ability to get another pair on this trip through Egypt was not a good bet. So, we, the four marauders retreated to our various corners of the bed, exhausted and still giggling between deep breaths. It was the morning of January 13, 1992, and the Valley of the Kings was calling.

* * *

After an enormous breakfast at the hotel buffet, we hurried back to the room to get ourselves ready for the day. In moments we were done, had the cameras in hand, and were on our way to the point on the shore of the Nile where Rashid was to meet us. It was eight-thirty when we saw him, and he spied us. Rashid led us a bit farther on down the shore to the dock where the local ferry was drawing near to pick up people.

Now this ferry was not quite as dilapidated and crusty as the thing that had taken us and our truck across the Nile prior to our arrival in Luxor, but it was close. This one, however, was a people-only ferry, and seemed to have the capability of holding about fifty or so. By the time we followed Rashid down to the dock and he arranged our passage on the ferry, at least one hundred bodies were jammed onto the deck. So what was new? Just like every other method of public transportation, this ferry was no exception to the sure law of Egypt: that being, if fifty was the safe number, 300 would smash themselves onto it in a tight mass of humanity before the thing would leave the shore. And so it was to be this morning. Thankfully, the opposite side was not too far away, and I didn't have time to start the worrying process.

As we steamed across the Nile I found myself gazing ahead in wonder toward the distant rocky escarpment that had been so richly forthcoming in giving to the present world the treasures of the past. That same murky, mystical past that we thought had sent us out on this adventure in the first place was even faintly detectable on the breeze. I looked over at Jim and the video camera as he scanned me, the kids, and the ferry. All seemed perfectly normal until I motioned by a nod of my head forward toward the stone formations in the distance which were becoming more and more prominent. The camera left his right eye and began moving away from his face and down to his side, as if it were in slow motion. Then I knew he sensed it too, ever so slightly maybe, but there nonetheless. He was being drawn as I was, backward in time thousands of years, and we both knew something was still calling to us on the winds. We just couldn't place the origin of the whisper or quite make out the words yet.

The loud braying ahead signaling the discontent of several donkeys snapped us out of the daydreams, and the sudden jarring of the ferry against the dock on our shore of destination almost threw us off our feet. Immediately the crowd of Egyptians, that had been waiting in a swarming mass to board the ferry back to the side we'd just come from, began shouting in their own peculiar dialect of Arabic. I guessed that they wanted us to hurry up and disembark from the shoddy old boat so that they could begin piling on. Moments later as the last of our group descended down the ramp onto the dock, I knew my guess was correct. No sooner had the last individual passed down to the shaky platform and onto the shore than the crowd that was waiting began to rush the ramp and pushed and struggled against each other until they began to squeeze through onto the ferry. Jim and I just looked at each other in amazement. We were starting to use that look quite regularly in Egypt.

One whiff of the air at this dock and even without the loud braying, we knew we were near the stables. Chelsea's nose was in full force disgust, just like it had been at the manure piles preceding Beni Hassan. Rashid shouted orders and moved people out of our way right and left as he shoved his way forward through the last of the crowd headed back across the Nile.

"Isam! Isam!" Rashid yelled into the air. Presently a man broke through the humanity, grinning from ear to ear. Isam was a man of small stature, but obviously without a care about being previously all but crushed in the mad dash to the ferry. He would be our guide through the Valley of the Kings. Rashid greeted him in the usual manner by speaking rapid fire mumbled tones of Arabic at the same time Isam was, and they held each other by the shoulder while kissing opposite cheeks. Jim never did get used to men doing this to one another. He shot me a smirk but straightened his face right back up quickly as the ritual was coming to a close and Rashid turned back toward us.

"This is Caldwell family from USA," Rashid began addressing Isam. "You will take them to Memnon, then Valley of Kings, and back here to me in afternoon." His English was not exact, but we understood him well enough.

Isam looked up at Jim with a huge almost toothless grin, and grabbed his hand to shake it with wild, flailing motions. "Mr. Jim! I am Isam Khaleel Isam, and I take you to Kings tombs!"

His English was not even as good as Rashid's, but his friendliness was contagious. He had dark skin that looked for the world like tanned leather, and appeared far too old for his mere forty or so years, just like the Nile Ferry captain we'd met earlier. He wore the long-sleeved traditional dress called a *thobe* that most men wore in the Arab Middle East, and on his head he had wrapped up a *gutra*, or the classic head scarf. It seemed a hasty wrapping of his own design, as it did not even resemble the crisp folding that marked the Saudi's usual manner of wearing the gutra. But we'd found out early on that Egypt was a very different land than Saudi Arabia, in far more ways than one.

Isam shook all our hands and really was taken by Lucas and Chelsea. He kept trying to pat the top of their heads, which did not thrill them by any stretch of the imagination. But we realized that these two blonde, fair-skinned children stuck out like two white lambs in the midst of a herd of coal black sheep in this country! We found the Egyptians to be a very touch-oriented people, and this need to pat the kids on their heads would follow us throughout our entire trip.

We trailed Isam past the stables to our right and over to a young boy who was holding the reins of five donkeys all together. He handed the boy several Egyptian pounds, and the boy turned over the reigns to Isam who then proceeded to give each one of us a donkey. One of them was notably larger than the others, and he was automatically given to Jim. The rest were about the same size, and Lucas and Chelsea and I were handed the reigns to each of them. Now the kids were excited! The thought of having a donkey to ride all day was far more interesting to them than the old, dank and dusty tombs that we'd already seen quite a few of on this trip. And so we began the donkey journey to the Valley of the Kings.

Immediately ahead of us appeared a small two-lane blacktop road, whose ribbon of asphalt stretched far out in front of us and looked as though it would take us all the way to the distant cliff faces. On each side of this road were small shallow ditches, and behind the ditches trees and shrubbery blocked the views to the side.

Isam guided our little clan onto the road, and right away the donkeys picked up their pace a bit and settled into what must have been their usual gait for carrying tourists. I don't know exactly what we had expected, but what we got was a long way from whatever that was! It didn't take the span of an entire minute before all four of us were laughing uncontrollably at the new sensation we were experiencing on these beasts of burden! As I sat there in the saddle, my donkey began to adjust himself to the speed of the others, which involved him beginning to trot slightly. Just with that small bit of increase, the donkey's back started bumping upward against the saddle, which of course sent me sailing up right along with it. In a moment I was bouncing up and down in a perfect rhythm to the beat of his hooves! And that was a quick enough pace to set my teeth chattering the minute I tried to open my mouth to speak!

As I looked over at Lucas and Chelsea I could see right away that they were having the same experience and were both flashing great, toothy grins at me with various giggles beginning to escape here and there. Because they were so much lighter, they were coming up higher off the saddle than I was, which delighted them even further. But the funniest of all was Jim, whose donkey was directly in front of us and setting the pace for our adventure. I tried to get his attention with my choppy English and broken laughter.

"J-i-i-um. J-i-i-i-i-i-um! C-a-a-a-n y-o-o-o-o-u h-e-e-e-a-a-r m-e-e-e-?"

I could see his head bouncing up and down with the hoof beats of his own donkey, and just when I was sure he hadn't heard me and was about to try to call him again, I saw his head slowly and bumpily begin to move to turn to the right. In his right hand was the video camera as always, and I realized that he was actually attempting to swing it around and video the hilarious sight behind him! His hand was shaking with what looked like an intense palsy, and the lens of the video camera was swinging wildly back and forth. He tried with all his might to hold the viewer against his eye for some sort of control, but it was to no avail. All he managed to do was smack himself in the eyeball over and over again, which sent me into almost uncontrolled laughter. But the laughter itself was broken and choppy because of my own donkey's gait, and that just worked to fuel the giggles even further.

"I-I-I-I-I-I c-a-a-a-n'-t h-o-o-o-l-d t-h-i-i-i-i-s t-h-i-i-n-g s-t-t-i-i-i-i-l-l-l!" Jim yelled in a heroic effort to salvage some footage of this spectacle of insanity. "T-h-i-i-i-s i-i-i-i-s i-m-m-m-p-o-o-o-o-s-i-i-i-b-b-b-u-l-l-l!" It was all he could do to get the words out, and he finally dropped the camera from his battered eye and gave up the attempt. As it would turn out, that little bit of jumpy footage would be some of our favorite from this entire trip!

After about half a mile, the trees and shrubs began to thin out and we could see beyond them to the vast desert plain to the right. Halfway between where we were now and where we were headed, something was rising out of the desert that snapped my attention off the teeth-chattering donkey ride and right out of the hilarity it was causing. What appeared to be two large, free standing statues of some sort were situated next to one another out in the center of the plain. As far away from them as we were still, I wondered how big these monoliths would really be when we got to the base of them.

The Colossi of Memnon, twin statues of Amenhotep III, rose more than seventy feet in height up off the desert floor. They seemed surreal in their current surroundings, most notably because of the lack of anything else around them. Apparently these were statues that once heralded the entrance to a major temple complex, but the yearly rising of the Nile in antiquity had done its damage and totally erased every last trace of it from the desert. These massive stone monuments were all that remained of the complex, but it was clear why the Nile could make no headway against them. Made from enormous blocks of quarried quartzite, it was estimated that they weighed over one thousand tons each. Isam directed us toward them for a momentary off-the-path detour of wonder.

A few minutes later we were back on the road and bouncing again to the incessant trotting of the donkeys. The once far distant rock formations that contained the tombs of the Kings of Egypt were just before us now, and we could see by the steep angles ahead of us that these wonderful little beasts of burden we were riding would have their work cut out for them. Closing in on the edge of the escarpment, we began to see the well worn pathways that had been used by thousands before us who'd taken this same journey to the Valley of the Kings. At first the trail led upward at a very mild angle, and with fair distances before us it seemed that most of the climb would be such. But after several minutes it became clear that we would have to enter into a series of cuts and turn-backs to allow us to get to the higher reaches of the mountain. And by this time, we were getting closer and closer to the edge of the cliff!

The ground beneath us was sturdy enough, I assumed. After all, we were riding up a stone mountain, weren't we? I guess it hadn't yet occurred to me that somewhere along this path we would be nearing the top, and that all things got steep and sharp at the top of a ridge! I had no sooner thought about it than Isam yelled out a few words in Arabic at the donkeys, and we came to a somewhat abrupt halt. He came over to each one of us and explained, much to my chagrin, that the path ahead was a treacherous one and we must not ride the donkeys, but we would have to walk them past that area.

"Jiiiiiiiiiiiimmmmmmmmm!" What else was I supposed to say? Once we had all the donkeys by the reins and began to walk them, we came up to the highest point of the escarpment and it was plain to see why we weren't riding. Not two feet to the right from the pathway we were on, the cliff took on a sheer wall appearance and there was about a thousand foot drop-off straight down! We would have to walk the top of this ridge about three-quarters of a mile before reaching the turn that would allow us to descend again into the Valley of the Kings to view the tombs. I just didn't know if I could take it! But the only response from Jim that I got to my screaming his name was the stony flint face of a man resigned to destiny. He didn't have to say a word. I knew we had to move forward; we were already committed and had come too far to stop now. He was right. But my mind instantly began to try to read that look he gave me, and I couldn't help wondering just what he was resigned to—was it really a determination to see the sight before us? Or was it us plunging to our deaths over the side of this cliff? Only the next few minutes would tell, so I stoically moved onward holding my breath and praying!

Just about the time I felt like I was getting a handle on the fear that was making every attempt to nail me to the wall, I heard the sickly sound of the sliding of rock and turned just in time to see the donkey Chelsea was leading slipping forward. The donkey, who I know must have been that way untold times before this, made a few quick adjustments to his step and was steady almost as soon as he'd slipped. But in that movement to balance himself, he'd managed to mash Chelsea up against the rocks between him and the cliff wall that went up to the left, and she cried out in pain.

I dropped the reins of my donkey in an instant and grabbed her up to me to hold and comfort her and to check her for injury. Isam, Jim, and Lucas were right behind me. She was trembling all over, but it didn't take me long to realize that she was just a bit frightened by the experience, along with being scraped a bit by the rocks. I began to thank God immediately that I'd made both kids stay on the left side of the donkeys while leading them and not the side with the sharp drop-off. The thought of what could have happened was just too horrible to ponder. When Chelsea was all right again, and was sure that the donkey hadn't tried on purpose to hurt her, we took up the path again.

Finally at the end of the upward trail and perched on the top of the ridge, we stopped to look back toward the west at the seemingly vast distance we'd traveled from the river. The sun was almost directly overhead now, and the view was really incredible. In the farthest distance we could see the opposite shore of the Nile, from which we'd come this morning; and about halfway between there and where we were now, the Colossi of Memnon stood out as timeless sentinels in the hazy noonday sun. Once again we were hit with that harsh contrast between the lush greens areas receiving the life-giving waters of the Nile, and the huge expanses of barren sand and rock desert that seemed to gobble up and destroy everything in its path except the Nile. It wasn't hard for me to understand in that moment just why the ancient Egyptians so revered the river. The river was life, and life was the river, and anywhere else, death lurked to destroy.

I gazed over at the captivating face of my husband as he surveyed the horizon. I could tell just by the way his teeth were set that he was far away searching. Just about that time I felt a wisp of a breeze blow a few strands of hair across my face as it moved on toward him. His hair began to lift gently just as mine had, and he gazed over at me with the ocean eyes of both a wild man and a poet, and we exchanged the same glance we had already once before this same morning on the ferry. What was this elusive thing playing with our hearts and minds? Were we both just dreamy, misty-eyed romantics caught up in the moment? Or was there an unseen Hand hovering above us—protecting, providing, and maneuvering us into a place where we'd eventually intersect the highway to our destiny and the fulfillment of Jim's original vision? I took in a long, deep breath of that wind, and held it in for as long as I could.

"Madame. Madame!" Isam's yell snapped us out of it, as he motioned that it was time to lead the donkeys back down the other side of the mountain and into the Valley of the Kings. Almost reluctantly, Jim and I both turned and began to lead the little donkeys away from the ridge. We got about two donkey's lengths ahead when an ear piercing braying started up just behind us. The mood swung in an instant from that of faraway distant visions to the hilarious antics of Lucas's donkey, who must have been enjoying the rest we'd taken at the top. Lucas had both arms stretched out as far as they would go, and was pulling with all his might, but his donkey had firmly planted his front legs and was refusing to move another inch! He remained silent until Lucas tugged on him, and when Lucas pulled, the obnoxious protest would issue forth from his belly. Lucas turned around and flashed Jim and I the look we knew so well: that perfectly knoblike look of incredulity and anger all balled up into one, where the eyes blared and the eyebrows knit together, and the lips pursed and curled! The look that was responsible for one of his nicknames—"the Knob."

There was no doubt in anyone's mind that this was an impasse. The donkey wasn't budging, and the Knob wasn't bending. It was a sheer test of wills, and neither was giving in. If it weren't for the devices and schemes of Isam, who of course held the wisdom of the ages when it came to donkeys, I dare say we'd still be perched on that very same point of rock, watching the geology age on. Isam couldn't help but chuckle at the determined young man in front of the firmly planted donkey. In fact, Jim and I and Chelsea had been giggling now for several minutes. Jim had even brought out the video camera to catch the event on tape! But the hand of Isam prevailed, and it wasn't but a few more seconds before the donkey thought better of remaining seated. The Knob's face of consternation softened into a large victorious grin, soon to be followed by the smugness of a boy vindicated. He'd won, even if not by his own hand. But he'd won, nonetheless.

As we descended over the edge, its difference from the ascent was a welcome sight to see, and I realized that we didn't have very far to go. The ground level in the valley beneath us was not as far down as the cliff edge we'd been riding on the other side, and it appeared that many of the tombs and cutouts in the walls on this side of the escarpment began from about midway up from the valley floor. That, of course, meant that we wouldn't have any cliff edges to walk with these donkeys and suggested that we'd be exploring the tombs of the ancients before long. Isam told us presently that this was about as far and he and his donkeys went, and that they'd be waiting for us after our tours were completed later that afternoon. And so we went on without the donkeys.

We made our way completely down into the valley floor and went inside a large snack bar that sold refreshments and seemed to have the only restroom facilities for the site. We asked around about the tombs and found out that only a handful were open to the public that day, so we chose to see the last resting places of Seti II, Rameses III, and Rameses VI. Jim figured that we would not have the time to see any others if we were to meet with Isam in time and re-collect our donkeys.

Beside that, there was a remote possibility that Rashid had managed to make some arrangements for something special later that afternoon, and it was the sort of appointment one just couldn't miss if in fact it had been agreed upon. Jim had impressed it upon Rashid that he'd like to be able to see some real artifacts from the tombs, not just the plastic and paper mache replicas probably mass produced in China that the locals had been trying to sell to us as "mummia," or mummy parts, since we'd entered the Luxor area. Even as Jim asked, Rashid had shushed him into silence and taken him away from the main crowd and made it very, very clear to Jim that this was always available, but never in the public eye. Rashid had agreed to try and arrange a meeting with the leader of a local village just to the southeast of the Valley of the Kings. Now knowing the delicate nature of what he'd asked for, Jim wasn't about to miss this amazing opportunity should it present itself today by loitering around in the graves of the Pharaohs. These tombs were all starting to look just alike anyhow, he reasoned. So down we went into the last earthly residences of a Seti and two Rameses.

Jim's thought had a great deal of truth to it. The tombs were very similar to what we'd seen before on this trip. The Egyptian Department of Antiquities of course, had to provide the stairs and railings we'd seen earlier to ease the access to the portals of the tombs, and as always one had to climb downward into the dark recesses of the tunneled-out stone faces to experience the treasures of centuries past.

The same musty, dank air I'd sniffed previously inside the pyramids was circulating in full force in these tombs. I decided it must be coming from the rocks, dust, and remains that for thousands of years had been being held captive in these places. All the valuables and idol trinkets, all the gold and jewelry, all the wooden items and tables and chairs had been baking like so many cookies, cakes, and pies in these colossal internal ovens carved right out of the rock. And then some discoverer came along and found the doorways to these graves, only to have the bulk of the ancient air escape with all its closely guarded secrets into the mists of the Egyptian night! Oh, yes, I was traveling at light speed deeper and deeper into my imagination, wondering what it all looked like during the funeral processions of each of these who were once upon a time, considered earthly gods. I was just about to step into the endless line of mourners and devoted followers in the funerary march for the Great Seti II when Chelsea the Nose spoke up with great emphasis and disgust and said, "Woof. It stinks in here like the pyramids!"

What a snap back to reality! She kept right on in her usual way: "Why does everything here stink? And where's Seti II? How do they know it's Seti II? And where's his mummy? I wanna see the mummy! Show me the mummy, Mom! Let's run up ahead to see the mummy. I bet it's the mummy that stinks! Can we see the mummy now? Can we, huh, can we?"

I rolled my head toward Jim, who was for once able to enjoy looking at the sites without the video camera stuck to his head, since they would not let us bring it in at the entrance way without paying a ridiculous fee in Egyptian pounds. Chelsea had already figured out by my expression and the direction I'd turned that she wasn't going to get any satisfaction out of me. That left Jim wide open for attack.

"Dad. Dad, Dad, Dad!" she fired off as she skipped up to where he was and started tugging on the sleeve of his shirt. "Daddy, where's the mummy? Mom won't tell me where's the mummy. Where's Seti II's mummy, huh Daddy? Is it even in here? I'm sure it is because it stinks! Why did we come here if they won't let you see the mummies? Why can't we see the mummies, Daddy? Huh? Why can't we see the mummies?"

Jim shook his head and broke out into a broad grin at the little blonde-haired girl now using his arm as a stabilizer and bouncing up and down in front of him, bubbling over at the mouth. Egypt was planting its own memories into her young brain that were not necessarily those of ancient culture and magnificent structures, but of what she couldn't see and what she could smell. The mummies had all been removed during our time there because of a problem with the Islamic views on burial and the visitation there of. There was no point in going into that arena with her, so Jim just decided to play it up to the full and went into his "I'm going to scare the kids stiff with my horrible stories of the hideous mummy monster" mode. He laid it on thick—how Seti II was really there all along, watching us and sneaking around. The huge blue bug-eyes and suddenly very, very quiet mouth showed quite clearly that his plan had worked, and we continued onward through the beautifully carved and painted walls in silence into the far recesses of the grave. There would be no more questions from Miss Chelsea for the near foreseeable future.

In each of the successive Rameses tombs we found much the same appearance. Although the scenes of the accomplishments of each Pharaoh were represented differently, with each having their own pantheon of favorite gods by their sides, the stories they told were all of a contemporary nature, and stuck to the grand theme of the Egyptian society of that time, which was the preoccupation with the afterworld and the journey of the Pharaoh into the next life. It would be a scene that repeated itself over and over again and seemed in and of itself to have accomplished what it was representative of. Here we were looking at the very stones that had been so carefully chiseled, as literally millions of others over the years had done, and in that way the ancients were living on. But a sad note struck me as I pondered all these things; this enormous effort had been wasted on that which was not living at all. This was cold, hard rock, and those mummies, wherever they'd been taken by the authorities, were nothing more than decayed flesh and bone, bound in lifeless cloth. In a spiritual sense, the stench that Chelsea kept on referring to was there all right, because nothing here was alive. Nothing mystical and supernatural was going on. And I realized that these departed ones had probably never found the answers they searched for so desperately. I knew from that point forward that what we were searching for out on the wind was not to be found in Egypt.

Back up the stairs and out of the tombs, the brilliant sunlight was a welcome sight. There was only so much of what was becoming very familiar to all our eyes that I could stand, and the repetitious nature of the carved reliefs inside all these graves was starting to become monotonous. We made our way down into the bottom of the valley floor, and away towards the southwest corner of the canyon where we found Isam waiting with our donkeys as we had pre-arranged.

Once we got a bite to eat at a local establishment not far ahead that Isam recommended highly, there were but two things remaining on our excursion for the day: the Mortuary Temple of Hatshepsut and the temple complex of Rameses III. As it turned out, Isam was right about the food, and we stuffed ourselves with tabbouleh, hummus and flatbread, seasoned rice, and shwarmas. These were all the staple favorites we'd come to love in Saudi Arabia, and we were really getting to know the minute seasoning differences between the Egyptians and the Saudis.

Soon we were atop our donkeys again; we made our way around the toe of the escarpment we had just that morning traversed from the top and found ourselves on the enormous grounds leading up to the mortuary temple of Hatshepsut. This temple was different from all the rest we had so far seen in that it seemed to be carved right out of the rock face, and the numerous columns were practically straight up and down. It wasn't as deeply carved as most were, but it was certainly huge. It took us about an hour to walk through the columns, and back down the huge and lengthy ramp that led all the way down into the gathering area below. Again I found my mind drifting backward in time, and trying to imagine the power this radical Egyptian queen had once wielded. Legend has it that her nephew, who was also her stepson Thutmose III, tried to erase much of her accomplishments from memory by defacing or obliterating much of her handiwork after her death. I just couldn't keep from wondering why, as I once again rejoined my faithful donkey, and swung my leg up over his back to sit in the saddle.

We trotted onward a bit to the south and entered the Rameses III temple complex zone. This included an area called "The Ramesseum." We would only be taking an outward peek at this one, because the sun was beginning to lower on the western sky, and we were all getting weary. This area was huge and contained so many different representations of the great Pharaoh Rameses that we were beginning to understand completely why he'd been called the Egomaniac of the Century! This temple was much larger than the Hatshepsut Mortuary, but after having seen the Luxor Temple it appeared the only difference was the gigantic statues and representations of Rameses. After a quick peek and cursory video, we mounted the beasts of burden and told Isam it was time to take us back home! In just another moment it was impossible to talk, as the dear little animals broke into a rhythmic trot back toward their stables and the food and water that surely awaited them. Once back there, we said goodbye to Isam and tipped him, and gave our incredible donkeys some well deserved scratching and bid them farewell. One more overloaded ferry ride back across the Nile, and we found ourselves face to face with Rashid, who'd been waiting for us to return to give us the news about the possibility of seeing some real artifacts.

It was not to be for this day, and that was a great relief. Rashid had apparently not been able to arrange this sort of meeting so quickly. We had made plans to drive the next day down to Aswan, spend one night, and then get up and drive to the very edge of Egypt, Abu Simbel. We would have to come through Luxor on the way back, so we opted to catch him and his secretive friend on our return trip. And so our visit to the Valley of the Kings had come to a close.

But as is normal for a crazy family, our own plans for that day were not ended. We'd been watching the horse-drawn carriages jingle their way down the noisy corniche for several days now, and the evening sunset against the Nile was just the beautiful setting we were waiting for. Jim hailed one of them down, and we all climbed up into the seats for a rather hectic trot down the busy street. There were buses full of people swerving around us, honking and blowing; Egyptian madmen in their motor cars sailing around us at just the last moment, and still the horse never missed his gait or spooked! It was thoroughly enjoying, frightening, and relaxing all at the same time. By the time we were finished, dusk had settled over January 13, 1992, and Clan Caldwell headed to the Luxor Hilton for a meal and good night's rest.

View of the Nile River from the Isis Hotel, Aswan, Egypt

CHAPTER THIRTEEN

To Aswan and the Isis Hotel

The morning of the January 14 dawned bright and clear, with just faint wisps of high cirrus clouds to give dimension to the deep azure sky. This day would be a traveling day for the most part, but we had work to do in our hotel room to bring it back into order. As usual, Jim had awakened me with the "Spoffees" song, and the fabulous aroma of the marvelous, dark rich blend he held out to me. We found no problem with the coffee in the Middle East anywhere. Most times it was dark roasted and dripped very strong, which was exactly like the Community Coffee & Chicory we'd been raised on in Louisiana! The Turkish coffee was even better, being strong enough to almost stand a spoon up in the tiny cups it was served in. But this morning, the regular blend was suiting me just fine. The promise of its flavor shot me happily up and out of bed.

The kids were another story. It was never easy to wake Lucas up. The child had a remarkable ability to remain sharp of mind and stay awake until the wee hours of the morning, building with his Lego's or Construx sets, or otherwise pondering great designs of magnificent monstrous machines. It was never easy for him to get to sleep because his mind was always working on something. As a result of all this late night brain activity, when he finally did go to sleep he slept like a rock and did not take kindly to being awakened before at least ten or eleven o'clock. Chelsea, on the other hand, was seasonal with her sleeping late. On most any given day she could fall asleep at any moment if she had five straight minutes with no activity. If we took a road trip anywhere lasting more than thirty minutes, you could count on her to be zonked in the back seat. It was like sunrise and sunset—a given. Here in Egypt, being drug around from early to late, in and out of tombs, temples, and pyramids, the child was exhausted by 7:00 P.M.! She had been falling half-asleep in her food for the last several nights, and as a result had gotten much more sleep than Lucas. This morning in particular, she rose when Jim came in with the coffee and immediately voiced a decree that she was hungry! Another very common announcement from the lips of the Booglet.

And so it was that once we finally got Lucas moving, had all taken our morning showers, eaten our breakfasts, and returned to the room to button up the luggage and brush our teeth, we checked out of the Luxor Hilton and proceeded to the Patrol to travel onward to Aswan.

This trip would be about 140 miles in length, and there were several items of interest along the way we planned to stop and see. Since we'd already been well initiated into the routine of the sights, we knew we should allow at a minimum of one hour per attraction, and we figured we'd be checking into the Isis Hotel by five o'clock, give or take an hour. The thought of entering that Nile Road again with the gasoline tankers flying by (or their passing someone in the opposite lane and heading straight for you and your family vehicle) was not the most pleasant agenda for Jim to accept for the day. But accept it he must if we were to get to our destination.

Aswan held a particular interest for Jim because of the granite quarries just to the south of the city. He'd heard about these huge granite outcroppings where most of the raw material for the statues and obelisks of the temples and shrines of both lower and upper Egypt had been sheered right out of the rock and transported down the Nile to their destinations. It was a colossal feat of engineering and design that intrigued him enormously. To top it all off, his greatest fascination in all of Egypt so far was the obelisks, and this site supposedly held in situ what would have been the most enormous one in all of Egypt. Called the "Unfinished Obelisk," it was something he simply had to see.

With renewed anticipation for what the day would bring, we stuffed the bulging luggage back into the Patrol and took our seats for the journey. We were traveling down the east shore of the Nile within minutes, and with only the road before us, I took out the books of daily devotions I kept on the dashboard and began to read aloud as was our custom. Today the words from *Streams in the Desert, Volume I,* by Mrs. Charles E. Cowman, stood out in a remarkable way: "On, in His name, to green pastures and still waters and mountain heights! He goeth before thee."

"Green pastures, still waters, and mountain heights?" I repeated aloud again and glanced over at Jim. His eyes narrowed to think on those three items, just as mine did. Somehow it was a hint—a tiny portion of what was soon to be. But we couldn't grasp it yet. As I continued reading, the next words stood out as profoundly accurate for this moment: "This is the Blessed Life—not anxious to see far in front, nor careful about the next step, not eager to choose the path, nor weighted with the heavy responsibilities of the future, but quietly following behind the Shepherd, one step at a time."

It was boggling my mind that the Holy Spirit had so orchestrated these words to be penned from a missionary in the 1920s and had delivered them to us for such a time as this. After all we'd seen and been through over the last months, after the amazing and unexplainable things that had begun so suddenly—occurring from the beginning of the planning of this very trip—we knew that we knew that we were being led through this ancient land one day at a time with great design and purpose. It was a blessing that we couldn't understand, more than we could have imagined or handled at that moment.

I closed the book and we sat in silence for a short while, just listening and looking at the land around us. We passed field after field of sugar cane, followed by acres of cabbage and various lettuces, only to rejoin more fields of sugar cane. On the east side there was the same deep ditch, and behind that, mud brick houses with palm frond roofs and dirt floors, teeming with cows, chickens, goats, and sheep that seemed to have free reign to wander in and out of the dwellings. And as always, there were the ever abundant throngs of young children filling in the gaps between the animals—barefoot and dirty, but almost always laughing and happy. It was a sight that burned its way into my psyche and I knew it would stay there forever.

But the reality of Egyptian cultural life was taking a backseat today to the evidence of things not yet seen. The Voice on the wind—calling almost imperceptibly thus far—was getting louder. We had been so certain that Voice would thunder and reveal things hidden from ages past at Mount Sinai in the peninsula almost two weeks ago that we had planned an entire month's vacation around the event. When that had fizzled into nothing more than a gargantuan disappointment, we had made up our minds to keep the spiritual out of this vacation to avoid any future let-downs. But it just kept on coming back, this ethereal feeling that our destiny as human beings was about to come to the fore.

I knew I had to stop thinking like this. It was causing my mind to drift off in too many directions all at once. So I reached for the cassette tapes we'd been playing over and over again since we'd left Ras Tanura. There were three in particular that were the favorites on this trip as far as pop music is concerned: *The Judds' Greatest Hits*, by the Judds; *Time Passes By*, by Kathy Mattea; and *On Every Street*, by Dire Straits. I reached out for *The Judds'* and shoved the tape into the deck. "Give a Little Love" began playing and almost immediately Chelsea started singing along, and I then joined in on the harmony. Chelsea had been determined for about the space of a year now that she and I were going to become the next mother/daughter singing sensation, and I'd obliged her by learning all the songs on the tape so she and I could sing together and pretend. In moments the dreamy mystical state I'd been falling into was replaced by the wild wails of a country guitar and my young daughter's remarkably wonderful voice belting out every word to the beat. Life was good!

About an hour or so down the highway, we could see that a small village of sorts was up ahead of us. Upon drawing closer I noticed the road signals marking a railroad track. I couldn't really tell if this was an actual town or simply a gathering place for the local folks to come up and catch the train. Regardless, almost as soon as I realized it was indeed a set of train tracks, the red warning lights went off and the bells started sounding to signal the oncoming train. With only two vehicles ahead of us before the tracks, we were set to get a good view of the engines as they passed by, and I knew Lucas would be impressed. He had been a train fanatic almost since his birth, and I found myself having a flashback of all the many times I would drive the child all around Baton Rouge searching for one for him to watch! Now here we sat deep in the bowels of Egypt proper, waiting for a train. Just as I suspected, he'd come to life in the backseat, rolling his window down to get the full effect of the whistle as it announced its arrival at the crossing.

I guess I should have known by then that nothing we were prepared to see in our mind's eye would be played out as we expected in Egypt. The scene before us was about to prove that to be correct. As the whistle grew louder and the two big locomotives slowed their movement into town, we were astonished to see that each of them was covered with an enormous crowd of mostly men. The train had not even come to a complete stop at the crossing and did not give us any reason to believe that it would! The throng of humanity on the train seemed to move as a single organism and they must have swarmed right up the sides and onto the top of the engines before they arrived at the crossing. As we sat there in sheer amazement, we watched the train pass slowly in front of us. Just as soon as the engines cleared the highway crossing, we were horrified to notice the train beginning to pick up speed. Surely they were not going to let all these people hang on as they went at regular rail speed down the tracks! Ah, yes! But this was Egypt. Cairo flashed back into my mind—Cairo with its many overstuffed public bus transports with scores of people hanging off the outside of them. Yes, it was apparent that this train had the full intention of accelerating to regular rail speed, even with its cargo of live human beings outside the locomotives! My mouth was hanging wide open as I watched it disappear from sight.

Stupefied at the spectacle, yet beginning to believe that we could see just about anything here in this country, we watched as the crossing lights ceased flashing and the tracks were clear again. I looked over at Jim, who'd been sitting there silent the whole time and noticed his mouth hanging wide open just as mine had been. Yep. He was goggled. Before he started the truck moving again, he looked over into the backseat at Lucas and Chelsea, who were also goggled. Almost in unison, the two of them put their hands to their eyes as though they were about to cover them, but instead began a movement back and forth rapidly to and from the eyes. Accompanying this motion was a gargling, gurgling sound they made by hanging their tongues out of their mouths as they rocked their heads back and forth with the hand motions to and from their eyes. It sounded like someone being strangled. This became known as "The Goggle." It was rightfully born in Egypt and has to this day never been used that much in any other country to which we have traveled. I couldn't contain my laughter. None of us could! We drove off to the sounds of Wynonna Judd singing "swangin' like a slow movin' tra-yain, rockin' with tha rhythm of tha rain...."

It wasn't very long before the road turned away from the Nile and off to the east a bit. The desert was close around us here with the absence of the Nile waters, and Jim saw something up ahead on his left that made him slow the Patrol so that he could focus on what he was seeing. I looked up just in time and a flash of excitement raced through me. A small rocky escarpment was coming into view with a ridge of small mountains between it and the highway, and it actually appeared to have one or more caves cut into its face. Seeing that it was in an area that he could drive the truck right up to, and noting that he couldn't see any Egyptians in the direct vicinity, a smile was beginning to deepen the dimples in Jim's face.

Like a recurring dream that continued to haunt his consciousness, Jim Caldwell's mind forced him to replay the Ark of the Covenant vision he'd had just prior to the beginning of this trip. As soon as he'd seen what looked like caves up ahead, the VCR had played the movie in his brain once more. The quick glance he shot over to me said in no uncertain terms that we'd be out of the truck in moments, and that the kids and I better get our shoes back on.

We pulled off the highway to the left and onto the sand of the desert. It was relatively hard packed. The ground turned rocky very quickly, so we wouldn't have to be concerned about getting stuck. In less than two minutes Jim had the truck positioned where he wanted it, about one hundred yards or so from the object of our interest. Four doors flew open simultaneously, and eight feet were now crunching the desert floor. The ground was littered with a large amount of broken pottery, and as we drew closer we saw clearly what now appeared to be two tomb facades, and not caves as we'd previously hoped, carved right out of the local rock. That in itself was a momentary disappointment, and I saw it right away in the eyes of my precious soul-mate, though it would have been imperceptible to any one else. But he recovered himself almost immediately when we got to what we now knew were doorways and peered in.

We were looking inside a rather rectangular opening and it was very obvious that these were once in fact tombs, long ago robbed of their contents. Above the entrance, ancient hieroglyphics had been carved, but they were in a terrible state of repair and crumbling under the harsh environment. The door had at one time been blocked up by carefully placed rocks, but those had been mostly picked away. The tomb was now open to the elements and the entrance led into a large square room that was also carved directly out of what appeared to be sandstone. Further inside the first square room, another shorter door had been cut which led then to another smaller area behind the first. One wall had a rectangular cavity carved out of it near to the ground, just about the size it would take to lay a human body down. These were just like the ones we'd seen three years earlier inside the tombs in the ancient rose red city of Petra, Jordan, purportedly built by a long vanished people called the Nabateans. As our eyes adjusted to the darkness we could see scattered bits of potsherd lying about, along with some rather unusual looking lumps on the floor.

Just about that time Chelsea exclaimed disgustedly, "Woof! It stinks so bad in here!" I rolled my eyes and looked over at Jim, who was shaking his head and snickering at the now familiar and continual "stink" comments from the Booglet. But something else dawned on him right about that time and he frowned and turned back toward the dark room. Almost in unison, the four of us lifted our eyes slowly to the ceiling of the tomb, and realized suddenly just what the origin of the horrid stench was. Lucas spied them first.

"Whoa, Dad! *Bats!*" he said with a renewed interest in what had seemed to be a room devoid of life. "Look! There's one right there, and a couple over there."

It didn't take me but two seconds to grab up Chelsea by the hand and jerk her away from the door, all the while yelling back at Lucas and Jim as I started back to the truck, "It's time to go! Let's get outta here! Do you know how many diseases bats carry?"

What had started out as a brief wondrous dream that we'd find a hidden chamber and inside it would be the lost Ark had disintegrated into a creepy, crawly habitation filled with these foul creatures of the night and complete with grossly aromatic piles of bat drizzle. It was definitely time to go! Just for good measure, I demanded we all roll our windows down for the first few kilometers down the highway to blow away with the breeze any lingering bat fumes. It should have been a lesson well learned for us not to go poking our noses into every hole in a rock face that looked like a cave. It really should have been.

It didn't seem like we'd been driving for long before we came to the village containing the ruins of Edfu. Here we wanted to stop and make a quick pass through the Temple of Horus, which was recommended as being relatively intact compared to Luxor and Karnak. Just as the *Fodor's '91 Guide to Egypt* had described, we found it to be in remarkable condition. It was a large complex with enormous traditional pylons out in front of the entrance. Just beyond them the colonnades were spectacular, and had managed to retain much of their original painted colors. The massive ceiling had been created by lifting tremendous stone blocks into position to rest flatly on the capitals of the gigantic columns. Most of the ceiling had also retained its original paint and it was truly amazing to see. We wandered around in the temple complex for about an hour or so, fascinated by the deepest inner area, which we soon discovered had a much smaller square room built inside. A room within a room! Faint shafts of light streamed in from small cutouts high above, and were directed downward to a boat of sorts that had been placed in the dead center of the space. The boat had staves on either side, and was about four feet in length.

"Looks like the inner chamber for the Ark in the Holy of Holies, doesn't it?" Jim said in a quiet voice. It was kind of surreal how it felt there at that moment so far inside a stone structure that was so ancient. Even with all the rudimentary destruction of centuries gone by, still this place held an appeal and invited the mind to wonder about the magnificent temple it had once been! But Jim was seeking something much higher than the inner sanctum of an Egyptian temple dedicated to a falcon-headed god. And what he was seeking was certainly not in the darkness of this dead inner sanctum. With a simple head nod to the right, he signaled it was time to leave. We made our way without speaking back out into the bright Egyptian sunshine and shuffled back down the wide and dusty pathway leading to the open air cafeteria we'd passed as we entered the grounds earlier.

Good old Coca-Cola. Ice cold, American Coca-Cola! A rare touch of familiarity to us in this bizarre and wonderful country we were traveling through. And there it was placed right in front of us on the plastic red and white checkered tablecloths. We stopped to sit for a while and quench our thirsts; between gulps we started discussing whether or not to stop at a place called Kom Ombo. It was the last site of interest listed in the Fodor's before arriving in Aswan. Another temple complex, it was purported to be on a hill looking over the Nile and was actually dedicated to two gods to avoid offending either one. The first was Harwar, a hawk-headed god, and the other was Sobek, who took the form of a crocodile. One very unusual feature it was supposed to have was a small sanctuary that contained dozens of mummified crocodiles, obviously offerings to the god Sobek. Just as soon as Lucas and Chelsea heard about the mummified crocodiles, they chirped up and demanded we see them. And so the decision was sealed. But Jim and I vowed to make our way quickly through the temple complex and to go straight to the mummies, for the sun was beginning its circuit toward late afternoon, and we wanted to be off that Nile road and into Aswan before dark.

It took a little less than an hour to reach Kom Ombo. We had to go through another small village, which was the only way out to the ruins, and the locals had set up a large number of outdoor selling booths ahead of the entrance of the temple. They were smart, these Egyptians. They knew just where to make you park ahead of their booths so that you'd have to be on foot to pass in front of them. This allowed each merchant the opportunity to rush out to you and begin a never-ending sales pitch. And you could be certain that they would take every advantage they could! In fact, there were even shouting matches between them when one owner would stray slightly out of his own space and infringe upon the grounds of the next. We learned very quickly to take our own advantage of such situations and all but run to get away from them. Harassment is a fine art in Egypt.

But something caught my eye in the midst of the plethora of mostly Chinese made, brightly colored plastic junk that was for sale: a very small booth that was selling what looked like beautiful, silky shawls.

Much to Jim's chagrin, I deviated from the safety of the middle of the pathway and veered over to the small booth on the left. Almost immediately the owner descended on me and started up. Knowing we didn't have the time to spend in the usual formalities of trading with an Egyptian, I grabbed up a gorgeous large white shawl and held out my pounds in payment. I guess it surprised the guy that he'd not had to fight for this one by the look on his face, but that instantly faded into a broad grin, followed by many "shukrans," or thank you's, and multiple blessings from him upon my children and my grandchildren yet to come! As I wrapped up the shawl under my arm, Jim quickly herded our little group out of harm's way, and set us to walking briskly for the entry gates of Kom Ombo.

Once inside, we could see that it had been described very well to us in the guide book. The remains were indeed up on a hill, and the overlook to the Nile was really beautiful. We made our way past the main sections of the ruins and straightway over to the small temple that housed the crocodile mummies. Encased therein were numerous sarcophagi, with carved representations of the crocodiles that were apparently inside each one. Other mummies were also mixed in with the bunch, enclosed in similar sarcophagi but detailed as cats on the outside. I had to wonder why in the world a people would want to mummify crocodiles and cats; it was still interesting to ponder, realizing how old they really were.

Having seen what we came to see, we headed back out the gates and through the merchant booths which were all now closing down for the evening. The sun was headed for dusk at a rapid pace, and we still had about a twenty-minute drive or so to reach Aswan where we would spend the night at the Isis Hotel. Ever since the Minya experience, I found myself dreading my first view of any hotel where we were to stay in Egypt. And as the countryside began to give way to the buildings and structures of the big city of Aswan, I could feel the apprehension coming on.

The city streets were already bustling with evening life as we drove into the center of town just past dusk. There in the crowded streets, the call to prayer was already sounding in its haunting, familiar way from the multiple imams in multiple mosques. It was a scene reminiscent of the local Saudi Arabian town of Rahima, which was outside the gates of the main company compound we lived on. Strangely comforting it was, to feel just a touch of home out here in the wilds of Egypt. Being a single family driving our own truck and not being a part of any tour group, I could sometimes feel the weirdness of being so far away from all things recognizable. But we continued on and found our way down to the Nile, and without any trouble we located the Isis.

Relief rushed over my mind and body in a much needed wave! The Isis looked to be at least a three-star hotel and was situated directly on the banks of the Nile. It was not a tall tower of death like the Akhenaton was in Minya, but in fact a sprawling one-story building that looked as though great care had been taken to assure a Nile view from every room. The only problem we had was finding a place to park. In fact, because the streets were so crowded, we had to drive about a full block away and leave our excessively over-packed truck locked and unattended, just praying that it would be left alone!

Of course this involved us having to drag our necessary luggage through the hustle and bustle of the night life, all the while standing out tremendously as the only white people within thirty miles. I could tell we were already creating quite a buzz in the community; that much was clear. But that wasn't anything new to me. A flashback of hauling heavy suitcases all the way from a bus stop up to a Steamboat Springs, Colorado, honeymoon condominium, wearing sandals in three feet of snow, tugged at my memory and I just shook my head and laughed out loud. Jim and Penny Caldwell and now their children never followed the conventional or tried and tested way of doing things. It was always some other way, some crazy way, a way no one in their right mind would attempt. But it was our way.

We checked in with no glitches and made our way to our room, which we found to overlook a large patio and pool area that led to a veranda overlooking the Nile. It was quite a lovely view with the sun having just set, and the high cirrus clouds along the western horizon turning random shades of pink, purple, and red. Inside, we found the same three twin beds we'd seen so much of in the Middle East before. It always hacked me off no matter how many of these type rooms I'd been forced to stay in, because not only were the beds narrow, they were shorter than our normal beds in the U.S. as well.

"Oh, here we go again! What, are we all short? Don't any married couples actually sleep in the same bed together in Europe? What's with these little beds?" Hearing my own words was further cultivating my own rising discontent. I was just starting to work my way into a glorious rant when Jim made two simple comments that shut me down.

"I gather, then, that you'd rather be driving the Nile road in the dark? Or perhaps staying at the Akhenaton?" He cocked his head and raised his eyebrows as he watched me ponder the thoughts. That took about a millisecond. Instantaneously, I produced for him a large, toothy grin, which dissolved the murmurings for the rest of the evening.

"Yes, but it's still the ugliest hotel I've ever seen!" The comment from Chelsea surprised Jim and I, having been locked in a battle of the brass-brows as we both had just been. "Yes, it is. It's orange and brown and yuk green, and it's ugly," she continued.

"Well, I don't care too much about the colors. What matters is that it's clean, it's not a death trap, and we don't have to drive anymore today," I told her, reaching to turn her around and head her out the door. "Let's go out for an evening walk, and Daddy'll get some video of this place before it gets too dark!"

Lucas beat us all out the door. Given the slightest opportunity to race down to any water's edge, we could count on him being gone in a flash, searching for fish. From the veranda beyond the pool and patio area, we located a stairway that led all the way down to the river. Below us were large numbers of feluccas, docked alongside other much larger and newer boats that must have been for the tour groups that frequented the area. Unfortunately, darkness was approaching so quickly that we were losing the ability to see any more, and we were forced to head back up to the room to get ready for dinner.

The hotel had within it an Italian restaurant where we'd chosen to eat so as not to have to fight the crowds out in the city. The food was remarkably good, especially after all the time we'd just spent on the road. Once stuffed and back to the room, it was all I could do to get Lucas and Chelsea to brush their teeth and crawl into their beds. I was sure they were asleep the moment their heads hit the pillows.

Jim had already gotten under the covers in the one remaining bed that I'd so profusely griped over earlier. I turned out the remaining light and walked over to it and sat down on the edge. Throwing the gaudy covers back to let me crawl in, Jim leaned over and whispered in my ear, "You know, babe, this really isn't going to be so bad."

Curling up against him and feeling his huge arms wrapped around me, I couldn't have agreed with him more.

The Caldwell's truck on the road to Abu Simbel, Egypt

CHAPTER FOURTEEN

Kitchener's Island to the Edge of Egypt

Something was annoying me. I was being lifted out of the wonderful depths of one of the best nights I had yet spent in Egypt by something I knew was obnoxious, but I wasn't awake enough yet to consciously figure it out. I knew it wasn't a noise bothering me because the room was absolutely silent except for Jim's rhythmic breathing. Becoming more and more aware, I knew I was going to have to finally give in and open my eyes. But no, I decided. Just one eye. That's all I would give this fiendish whatever-it-was. Just one eye.

Raising one lid as slowly as possible, I saw the source of my annoyance immediately. From the window across the room, a single beam of radiant light was splitting the airspace between the curtains and had connected with what once had been my sleeping face. "Aaargh!" I snarled, as I pulled myself upright and rid myself of the brightness. Of course with me out of the way, the beam was now resting squarely on Jim's face.

The growl snapped Jim out of his peaceful dreams, and he squinted hard as he tried to open his eyes in the wicked glare. "What's up? Why the mad?"

I looked back over my shoulder at him struggling to see and pointed straight over to the window at the source of my indignation. "That, dear husband, is why the mad. But I'm fine now, because it's on your face, not mine!" I giggled and pushed myself up off the bed barely in time to dodge the pillow that I knew was coming, and turned back just in time to see it bounce off Lucas's head and come to rest on top of Chelsea.

"Hey!" Chelsea whined. "No fair!"

Not a second later, a very rumpled Lucas with an extreme case of bed head and a seriously mad frown, raised himself halfway up into a sitting position and stared furiously at Jim. I was cracking up with laughter from my safe position which I had run to around the corner from the beds.

Jim sat up on the side of the bed, scratching his head and wondering what had just happened. Chelsea whined words not discernable from underneath the covers she'd pulled up over her head. The Knob continued his deadly stare. And so January 15 greeted us from the inside of our room at the Isis Hotel in Aswan, Egypt.

In the long run, it was probably a good thing that the brilliant beam of light had forced me awake. We needed to get a good early start on this day, because by the end of it we planned to be in Abu Simbel at the Nefertari Hotel, which was all the way to the very border Egypt shared with Sudan. That was about a two and a half hour drive through the far eastern edge of the Great Sahara Desert, and we had things we wanted to do and see here this morning. After breakfast our first adventure would be to cross the Nile behind the hotel on a felucca to visit Kitchener's Island and the Botanical Gardens that were on the other side.

We made our way down to the docks after gathering up our jackets. It was surprisingly cool this morning, though the sky didn't have a cloud in it. Two boys that couldn't have been more than twelve or thirteen years old were already preparing their felucca for a day of tourist activity. Jim called out to one of them and in no time, the kids and I were seated in the wide bodied sailboat, waving to him as he videoed our take off from the landing.

There was no wind to speak of, so we began a series of tacks across the river, which was very wide here. The water was also very clean. This was in sharp contrast to its appearance around Cairo, where it was generally the color of chocolate milk. Unlike Cairo, the terrain at Aswan was largely infused with granite, and as we came around the docked boats, we could begin to see the large granite formations sticking right up in the middle of the water. It was a beautiful sight to see unique rock formations in such clear water! This would be a lovely morning sail to remember!

It took us about an hour to travel down the Nile southward to where the Botanical Gardens were located. It wasn't that they were so far away; it was just that the wind would not cooperate with the sail! But we made it and spent the next hour or so wandering the gardens and videoing and taking pictures of the remarkable and sometimes just plain weird trees and plants. A number of cats also inhabited the island and appeared to be in fine shape and well fed. They were strange looking, however; their ears were folded forward as though someone had pasted them down! I later found out that they were a particular breed whose ears had been altered by natural design.

After our tour we made our way back down the stairs leading to the dock and our felucca. When we got into the boat we noticed that a very nice breeze had begun to blow and figured the trip back to the Isis Hotel was not going to take nearly as long as it had going out. We were right. Just as soon as one of the boys unfurled the sail, the wind filled it with a loud snapping of the canvas and we were off at a marvelous clip! The wonderful old felucca was skimming briskly across the waters, and with the wind in my face, my mind took off backward in time to picture what it must have looked like when a royal entourage made its way down the river in pharaonic times. From the Egyptian princesses with their maids to the servant boys and eunuchs before the Pharaoh himself, I could just imagine the magnificent grandeur. "What a time that must have been." I thought to myself.

Just as I was seeing my vision of the past, the wind really picked up and the boat keeled over sharply which brought me back to reality. Now we were having fun! The kids were giggling away at how fast this old boat could really go, and Jim and I were both remembering suddenly just how very much we loved to sail! So much, in fact, that just before I had become pregnant with Lucas, we were planning to sell our house and build a large sailboat to actually live on! And here we were on the other side of the earth from all we'd ever known, racing down the Nile on a felucca gone wild! It was fantastic!

The only drawback to this exhilarating moment was that because of the increase in wind speed, our trip back to the docks at the Isis was all too short. With a sigh of resignation that signaled the end of our sail, Jim paid the boys and we bid them farewell. It was time to pack up another hotel room. Remembering how far away the Patrol was parked from the Isis made me doubly wistful about having to leave that sailboat! I really didn't cherish the idea of being gawked at as we lugged our heavy suitcases back through the streets of Aswan to our truck like we had been the night before! Right then it dawned on me to wonder if the Patrol had made it through the night unmolested. I knew we were soon to find out.

Jim had a much more decent idea going with regard to the truck. Unbeknownst to me he had already planned ahead to go and get it and drive it right up to the front of the hotel for me so that I wouldn't have to face a repeat of last night. I knew I loved this man for oh-so-many multiple reasons, but this one was on top of the list today. Beside that, I knew right away that we had been extremely blessed as I saw him driving up, for the Patrol had not been touched. Even the roof rack with all its items had been left completely alone. All was well, and we stuffed the luggage back into the rear of the truck and took off. It was time to get out to the south of Aswan where the granite quarries were.

A crowd of tourists marked the spot where the unfinished obelisk lay in situ. Deep inside a granite quarry lay a colossal giant, maybe 120 or more feet in length and estimated to weigh nearly 1,170 tons. Jim was all over it. His fascination was only deepening about these strange towers of ancient Egypt. Just seeing this thing laying there in the rock was amazing enough, but trying to absorb the labor it would take to get the thing out of the quarry and floated down the Nile to lower Egypt was a real brain strain. I imagined that even in this day with the use of modern cranes and machines this would be an enormous undertaking. I had to wonder, as did Jim, just how they really did it. After gazing at the never raised obelisk for a time, Jim gathered us up and headed us back to the truck. We had yet to visit the Aswan High Dam, and then travel the fair distance to Abu Simbel.

Seeing the dam didn't take up too much of our time. It had been built to control the annual Nile flooding, which had been taking place since ancient times. Now because of the technology, the people would no longer be subject to the unpredictable flooding of the great river. Additionally, beautiful Lake Nasser had been created, a direct result of the building of the dam. We read that there was still much controversy over the dam, and we were glad we'd taken the time to include it in the trip.

After all the activities of the morning, we realized we'd better get on the road to Abu Simbel. The guys at the hotel Isis had made it very plain to us that we must fill up with gas, or petrol as they called it, on the south edge of Aswan, because there would be absolutely no stations on the way to or at Abu Simbel. Not even a gas station down there? I wondered if we were headed to the end of the earth? Nearly 170 miles to the south of Aswan, it would be pushing the limits of the Patrol's oversized gas tank to get there and back without needing a refill.

So take the advice Jim did. He topped off the tank with every drop he could squeeze into it, and off we were to Abu Simbel. It wasn't but about two or three miles out of town that the landscape became absolutely desolate and flat as a pancake. The road was a two-lane highway that was in extremely poor condition, with pot holes and crumbling blacktop struggling to last against the harsh elements. The temperature outside was rising rapidly as well, which I hadn't expected because of the wonderful cool breezes we had just been sailing on earlier this morning! But getting hot it was. Not only was it getting hotter, but the glare of the mid-day sun was relentless, and having nothing but the blistering desolation of the Sahara to reflect, was sending a horrible glare into the truck. Jim was already getting a bad case of the afternoon sleepies and asked me to get some coffee going.

I reached into the glove compartment for the coffee supplies, and behind me past the kids and into the kitchen box in the back of the truck, for the coffee maker. In reality it was only a mechanism by which to boil water and not a real coffee maker, but we always referred to it as the coffeepot. I filled it with water and plugged it into the cigarette lighter so that it could start to warm up. This was the same little coffeepot that had been so instrumental in getting us safely across the long drive through Arabia. The same little coffeepot that blew the 10 amp fuse that the Almighty had literally replaced Himself by causing Lucas to find the 20 amp un-blown fuse in the heart of the desert! The same little coffeepot that had labored and given its best to keep Jim Caldwell awake at the wheel. The same little coffeepot that was now beginning to sputter and spit in the truck on the way to Abu Simbel.

"Oh, no!" I said with a greatly worried brow. "I think the little coffeepot's going out!" I spent the next twenty minutes wiggling the wires and the connections every way I possibly could, trying to get it to stay on long enough to boil water, but it was no use. The poor little thing was just dead. There would be no life-saving coffee for Jim Caldwell.

Another ten minutes down the empty highway and Jim slowed the truck down and pulled off the side of the road. It was obviously time for a break; and in the utter wilderness all around, we certainly didn't have to worry about anyone else. Rested and refreshed, one by one we all piled back into the Patrol. Just as we were getting up to road speed, in a move that will live on in Caldwell infamy forever, Jim rolled down his window and in one swift motion, grabbed and flung the poor little coffeepot out onto the barren desert where it bounced a number of times before it lay sadly and silently still. The kids and I shrieked in unison at the atrocity we'd just seen their dad commit! I couldn't believe my eyes. There it lay, watching its family drive swiftly away, leaving it behind to certain demise! There was a stony silence in the vehicle for the space of the next hour and a half as each of us planned and plotted against the hideous and evil monster behind the wheel.

It was late afternoon when we finally pulled up to the Nefertari Hotel at Abu Simbel. The hotel was relatively simple, but the rooms were nice and clean. It was situated back from the edge of a high bluff, with the vast Lake Nasser in the far distance to the south. To the east rose a mound of great height, and we imagined that this must contain the incredible Temple of Abu Simbel which was built by Rameses II. This temple had actually been relocated in its entirety from a position far below on the lower edge of the bluff before the rising waters of Lake Nasser were able to submerge it. Then it was painstakingly reassembled stone by stone on the safety of this higher ground. After our check in, we still had enough time to walk over to it and tour it that evening.

If ever I had entertained a question about the size of the ego of Rameses II, the sight of this temple just blew that to smithereens! As we rounded the corner and the entrance came into view, four colossal statues of the Pharaoh in a sitting position could be seen, gazing smugly out into eternity over the grandeur of the lake in front of them. Each one must have been over sixty feet tall! To the right and left of each of the statues were much, much smaller statues of the members of his royal family, including his favored wife, Nefertari, and one of his mother, Queen Ti. It was truly a breathtaking sight. The details carved into this stone were outstanding, with great specificity given by the artisans to facial features and even such things as knee caps and toenails. They were just all too lifelike. And so, I thought, Rameses II lives on.

The inside of the temple consisted of chamber after chamber of beautifully carved pictorial representations of scenes from the life of Rameses II, including his battles and exploits. We spent the better part of an hour exploring along with the several tour groups that were also inside before moving on into the area that told the whole story of the reclamation and relocation of the temple from the waters. The Egyptian authorities had actually included the engineering feat of the century as a part of the tour, and we all were interested in seeing how it was done. The walls were filled with actual pictures of the endeavor, which was very interesting. Before long we came into an enormous room that had all the appearance of an indoor sports arena with a domed roof, and we recognized that it must be the inside of the mound we'd seen as we drove up to the hotel earlier. What a tremendous undertaking this had been, and what a stunning success!

When we finally made our way back outside, the shadows had become very long and the air was getting quite cool. Away to the west behind the hotel, the sun had already slipped below the horizon and the few clouds against the far edge of the sky were fading to gray. I looked out over the lake to the regions of Sudan beyond and gave Lake Nasser a final farewell. In the wisps of the cool breeze, I suddenly heard the whisper of that same Voice of destiny speaking again, but this time, almost perceptibly. We had been led to *the far edge of Egypt!*

Lucas and Chelsea with Rashid on a felucca on the Nile River,
Luxor, Egypt

CHAPTER FIFTEEN

Rashid's Connection

The bright yellow orb that all of ancient Egypt had once worshipped as *Ra* was already well on its journey across the celestial boundary by the time my eyes finally opened to the new morning. Because of the jam-packed day we'd spent before, having come all the way from Aswan and choosing to go ahead and tour Abu Simbel that evening, we were exhausted at the completion of dusk and by unanimous vote had chosen to go to bed early. Jim had not set an alarm clock, nor chosen to have a wake-up call placed to the room, because we really didn't have any deadlines to meet nor any tours to take; the day set before us was going to entail nothing but driving. We had to get back from the end of Egypt all the way to Luxor about 400 miles to the north, where we hoped a room at the Sheraton would be waiting for us. There was no sense in getting up too soon. It was January 16, 1992, and we had been traveling hard and fast since December 31, 1991, the day this whole amazing journey had originated. We all needed the extra sleep!

Once awake, however, it didn't take us long to do all the morning routine, to include the gobbling down of a short breakfast and packing the truck back out for the return trip to Luxor. We piled in and began the exit from the parking lot when Jim spied something we'd been searching for in vain for days. Just beyond the major parking area for the hotel was a spigot with a water hose attached to it! Our poor truck, which was usually black in color, had been completely covered over in dust and mud from the beginning of the trip when we encountered the unbelievable snowstorm in Arabia! Nowhere that we had been so far in Egypt had even the resemblance of a car wash, much less a usable faucet! This was a bonus find! In moments we were all out of the Patrol, and cleaning up its outsides, albeit scrubbing with just water! By the time we got on the solitary road leading back to Aswan, the truck was gleaming in the brilliant winter sun!

Miles were clicking by as we retraced the same pathway through the far eastern Sahara as we'd come just the day before. The bleakness of this stretch of the highway was like no other place we'd ever seen on the planet. Recalling the fate of our dear little coffee maker lying alone somewhere out in that vast sea of sand and desolation was not leading to warm, fuzzy feelings for my husband at the moment. But for the sake of the arduous length and strain of having to re-enter the Nile road once we got to Aswan, I thought better of bringing the matter up. The notion of having to deal with Chelsea and Lucas feeling sorry for the thing and whining about it for the next six hours in the confines of the truck just wasn't worth reminding them of the tragedy of the previous day.

It would be late afternoon before we finally pulled off the treacherous highway and into the parking area for the Luxor Sheraton Hotel. This one was situated at the far northern end of Luxor, whereas the Hilton we'd stayed at a few days earlier was located at the far southern end of the main road. It was a beautiful and more modern facility than most, allowing our travel-weary bodies to gain just enough encouragement to get out of the Patrol. Although stretching and yawning, we eagerly went inside anticipating a nice room, a hot shower, a good meal, and a fluffy soft bed to collapse into. Within a short few hours, we were given all the desires of our expectations, and sleep came sweet and strong.

* * *

The double "brrrrring-brrrrring" of the telephone's wake-up call stirred me out of the luscious slumber. I hung the receiver back up after listening half-heartedly to the recorded "good morning," and rolled over and up on one elbow to observe the motionless lump lying next to me. Jim was out like a light. The strain of driving the Nile Road had once again taken its toll on the guy. I was caught between two worlds of thought at that very moment: should I go ahead with the hideously devious harassments of waking him up that were dancing in abundance in my head, or be the good and thoughtful wife and quietly phone in for room-service coffee and have it there already before I awakened him? In the end, I found myself whispering the order into the phone and made myself content then just to lie there tracing the lines of his face while I awaited the knock on the door.

Right then it seemed like we'd been on this trip forever. But time was ceasing to be for us, somehow; as though we had been carved out of it and set down into some other dimension.

With all that we'd been through the year before, I found myself being once again astonished and tremendously thankful for the enormity of the miracle that had been delivered into our lives at just the precise moment to save us from total destruction. But right here, right now, lying in bed watching the peace in the face of my husband in the Sheraton Hotel in Luxor, Egypt, all was beautifully and wonderfully right with our world. All that had transpired in the past was not only dead, but had been burned to a crisp in the hot furnace of conviction and repentance, and I knew beyond a shadow of a doubt it would never have the power to resurrect itself again. Coupled with the totally unexplainable signs and wonders that had accompanied us since the beginning of this trip, I also knew that we were headed toward something undeniably huge and out of our scope of control: I just didn't know when it would finally manifest itself.

The rap-tap-tapping entering into my ears snapped me out of the misty, prophetic place I'd escaped to in my mind, and back into my flesh. I eased out from under the covers and tip-toed over to get the marvelous morning drink that made it possible to perpetuate the ritual of the coffee song that I would be singing to Jim this time. And so began Friday, January 17.

Just a few days past we had arranged with Rashid to meet him at the felucca docks on the Nile just down from our hotel at ten-thirty this morning. Because of Jim's desire to see some real artifacts, and Rashid's seemingly endless knowledge of the underground world of Luxor, a meeting had been fixed for that purpose around 11:00, which was just before the time mid-morning prayers would be announced by the calling out of the local religious leaders, or imams. By the time we finished all the morning routines and made it down dockside, we found Rashid had already been there for several minutes waiting for us.

Jim shot a glance over at me and he found my expression to be the same as his. Since we'd met this Egyptian, he'd been very friendly, yet had an air about him that bordered seriously on the shady side. This morning, seeing him with his dark, leathery face enshrouded in his bisht over his flowing thobe, with his head cocked to one side and his eyes squinting against the morning sun, one could have rightly imagined a border thief hiding pistols and bullets across his chest under all those robes. I swallowed hard and wondered as I stepped gingerly down the slope to the felucca if we would return from the other side of the Nile this day, or if some archeologist a thousand years hence would dig up a family of four, Jim with his plastic and metal video camera still in hand. But the brilliance of the water reflecting the sun's rays was promising the joys of another sail across the Nile at the least, and with a quick shove from the shore we were off to parts unknown in the general direction of the Valley of the Kings.

It should have been a sign to us when the other Egyptian, who was apparently the boat owner and captain, failed to even attempt to unfurl the sail. Instead of what we had expected to be another brisk ride, the man reached down for a long, crooked shaft of wood about three inches in diameter and began to pole us slowly across the water. Again Jim and I exchanged nervous glances, wondering if taking these wild jaunts so far off the beaten tourist track with both our young children was at all advisable. But it was too late. We were already on the boat, watching the water slip slowly under the bow and growing edgy in the notable absence of conversation.

After another ten minutes or so, the east bank of the Nile was approaching as well as whatever lay in store for us. We disembarked and followed Rashid, who promptly hailed a small taxi we had to stuff ourselves into at his request. Judging from the small mountains in the background, I surmised that we had to be only slightly south of the Valley of the Kings. In a few short minutes down the dusty track which served as a road, we came upon an area of numerous dwellings which apparently made up the village we were headed for. Nestled in and among the mounds of dirt and rock, the local people had constructed these homes out of what looked like ancient mud brick, as well as the more modern cinder blocks. Most had flat roofs, at least two levels, and were painted in every color imaginable, which would probably have been a nice sight against the barren desert had not the dust and dirt levels accumulating on their outsides been so staggering.

A little way up a hill from where Rashid motioned the taxi to stop stood the focus of his purpose for us today. As we got out of the taxi and looked toward it, all I could do was shake my head and mutter under my breath. Just like the scenarios my mind was ever so capable of conjuring up to torment me, the house fit every description known to man of a place you'd not voluntarily choose to enter as an American in the heart of a Middle Eastern country. This particular house was painted white, with multiple artistic scenes splattered all over the outside. A large 747 aircraft was the first I noticed, followed by a boat, enormous flowers, and a scorpion. The biggest and most notable of them all, however, was a huge rendition of the Kaaba from Mecca, Saudi Arabia, which is the most sacred of all the shrines of Islam. A crescent moon hovered over it, with a large man standing to the right side with his hands raised to the sky. Next to him, verses from the Quran had been scribbled all over the wall. My mind was now virtually screaming for me to grab my kids and run like the wind.

Rashid knocked a very unique knock on the front door of the house, which had to be a secret code of some kind. It seemed like at least five minutes went by before someone came to the door, but I was sure I could hear a tremendous amount of shuffling and arranging inside from the moment that knock went out. The door finally creaked open and inside we went, only a few steps down a short hall to a room on the left that I was now fairly certain we'd all die in. We were led in by a younger man than Rashid who motioned for us to sit on a piece of furniture that I can only describe as being a wood and straw-seated bar stool made extra wide to accommodate three or four people. A makeshift coffee table had been placed in front of it, and it was of substantial size, I supposed to compensate for the height of the thing we were sitting on. The ceiling was much higher than in a normal room, and behind us way up high were two windows with no glass and wooden shutters which were open from the inside.

The air inside the room had been attempting to choke us since we'd entered. The sunlight streaming in through those windows made visible in slowly tumbling clouds the amount of dust and smoke filling the space. The smell was a mingled conglomerate of both stale and fresh cigarette smoke and excessive quantities of strong incense, which at present rose in thick spirals from the opposite corner of the room. The mustiness of it all was taking my breath away. In the center of the ceiling, a metal fan squeaked rhythmically with each passing circle of the single blade that remained attached to it, which seemed caught in a slow death struggle with the density of the air. I watched with inner terror as Rashid and the man who'd led us into this room disappeared down the hall and into the vaporous mists encompassing the rest of the house, giggling and speaking rapidly in Arabic. And then it was just the four of us, sitting motionless and far too afraid to speak a word to each other, watching the foggy air attempting to kill the ceiling fan.

Another long five minutes went by before the man returned without Rashid. "Do you like some mint tea?" He asked in fairly decent English. Jim surveyed his filthy hands and the layers of dirt under his fingernails and didn't even look my way to ask if I wanted any.

"No. No, no thanks. Appreciate it, though...." was all he could muster.

The man disappeared again without expression.

More time went by as we listened to the various Arabic conversations emanating from somewhere in the rear of the house. Just about the time I thought every cell in my body would explode if I didn't get out of that room, the sound of sandals dragging down the hall became audible. All our eyes were riveted to the doorway as they grew louder, and the owner of those shuffling sandals appeared. A plump man, shorter and older than Rashid, he swished forward into the room attended by two servants of Indian descent, who immediately placed a large chair beneath him as he sat without acknowledging their presence. By this time my screaming, internal fear had been transformed into a resigned and rabid hilarity, and it was all I could do to keep from busting out in wild uncontrollable laughter. In a flash from some old mafia movie, the face of Edward G. Robinson decked out as a gangster danced suddenly before my eyes, and this Egyptian kingpin was a dead ringer for him in every way but for his darker complexion! I bit my own lip hard and shot my glance immediately downward to the floor to keep from having to look at him, knowing the weakness of my own nature to hold something like that inside, and realizing the enormous likelihood that if I let loose a laugh of that magnitude at this moment, this guy would take it as an insult and we'd all be goners!

One of the Indian servants quickly exited the room, only to reappear moments later with a towel that had clearly been used to wrap up a number of different items inside. "You see artifacts?" The man finally asked with a horribly thick accent.

"Yes; yes, Sir," Jim responded obligingly. What else could he say?

The man lit up a cigarette and blew a huge cloud of smoke upward, then squinted hard as half of it found his eyes. He grimaced and glared at the Indian servants, who eagerly awaited his every command, then grabbed the wadded towel and yelled much louder than he needed to, "*Emshee! Emshee!*" which we knew from our dear Mr. Mansur to mean, "Get out!" The two servants scrambled out of the room in record time.

Jim watched intently as the filthy fingers of this underworld figure slowly and carefully pulled the edges of the towel back to reveal a number of small bundles of wrapped brown paper. He ran his coal black eyes over the lot of them for a moment, then picked one from the bunch and began to peel the paper away. A tiny figurine appeared at the center of the paper bundle, and he passed it over to Jim for his examination. The kids and I gathered nearer to him so that we could get a look at what we were immediately convinced was a genuine artifact from a real ancient Egyptian burial chamber. The item was a tiny cat no bigger than my little finger, carved from a bluish green stone that sort of resembled turquoise. It was dull and had small points of imperfection, and really looked authentic. My fear turned insanity had now changed again into the awe of what I was holding in my hand.

One by one the paper bundles were unbound, and before long about ten items of great antiquity stood on the oversized coffee table in what we now knew was a bandit's house. A true hush fell upon us as we moved from figurine to figurine, marveling in amazement at the detail on the cats, frogs, and scarab beetles that had been fashioned almost 4,000 years before by an unknown artisan for a famous person of royalty. I could tell that even Lucas and Chelsea were going back in time in their minds, in sheer wonder of what we were being privately shown.

"You choose now." The tomb robber's voice was gruff and to the point.

"Choose?" Jim asked in response.

"Aiwa. Which ones you want to buy?"

"Buy?" Jim jerked his head around and looked at me with an "Oh-no! Now-what-do-I-do!" look on his face. I was frozen in time and could offer him nothing, having had the full brunt of where we were and just what was transpiring hit me in the face.

"Uh, well, uh … do you have anything else?" It was all he could think of to say at the moment.

"Aiwa," came the reply. "Come inside."

Obediently we all got up and followed him down the hall to the next room on the left, where a table stood in the center with a large wooden pharaonic boat sitting on top of it. It was at least four feet long, with wooden figures all over it and around the edges on the table, carved with tremendous skill and truly lifelike expressions. Each figure was clearly made to be an attendant of the Pharaoh for his daily needs as he sailed down the Nile. The exquisite detail of the work took our breath away. It was by far the most fabulous work of art we'd seen since we'd been in Egypt, even surpassing the works of the Cairo Museum!

Playing along, Jim turned to the ring leader and asked him how much. He told us that this item was already sold, and that it was at present being taken piece by piece out of the country. When Jim pressed him further, he finally admitted that the selling price was in the multiple thousands of dollars.

"What happens if the purchaser gets caught at customs with this?" Jim asked next.

"Well, ahhhhh, he will go to the jail, and he will be executed" came the reply. I closed my eyes hard against everything I had seen and my ears against what I was hearing, and let go a quiet whimper in Jim's direction.

"What you want?" the man persisted as he led us back into the first smoke filled room where the small figurines still stood unwrapped.

"I don't have enough money. I can't buy anything, because I don't have enough money." Jim said in a hopeful effort to dissuade this man from going any further than he already had.

With a snort of disgust at the hour he'd just wasted, the Egyptian version of Edward G. Robinson quickly leaned over the coffee table and scooped up all his ill gotten gains into the towel and yelled something in Arabic that sent the Indian servants scurrying back in. Within seconds no trace of the artifacts or the kingpin remained in the room. We could hear the loud shouting in Arabic from the back of the house again, and presently Rashid re-emerged with an unexpected smile on his face and motioned toward the front door. Apparently he and his connection had been in a shout down about the American and how he refused to buy anything from him. By this time the awe I was experiencing at the relics had gone backward, right through the hilarity stage, and was now in full force fear again. When the front door opened and the bright rays of the near noon day sun hit me full in the face, I felt as though I'd been snatched from the gaping jaws of the underworld and delivered back into the safety of the Light! As we scampered at a quick pace behind Rashid toward the already summoned taxi, the first haunting notes of the call to prayer rang out from several small local mosques simultaneously. Now I was absolutely certain we had escaped in the nick of time!

Back down at the Nile River we said our final goodbye's to Rashid, the Egyptian of many arrangements! With no feluccas then available, we opted for the only other choice, which was one of the old diesel, open-aired people ferries we'd ridden before. As we pushed away from the shore, the rhythmic droning of the engines drowned out the buzzing chatter of the other people's conversations, and I drifted away into the relief that now washed over me in waves. Looking back toward the Valley of the Kings and watching it grow smaller in the distance; I knew I was still a very long way from home. Had I just been in the home of a real, living tomb raider? Did I just have in my hands the objects carved thousands of years ago for a deceased noble or even a Pharaoh? What would have happened if we had been caught there by the authorities? It was all too much to think about, so I heaved a great sigh of thankfulness and turned away for the last time from the eastern shore of the Nile River at Luxor. My beautiful children seemed perfectly content and unaffected by what we'd just been through. Child-like trust. It was something I would have to have deeply ingrained inside me for the days coming that I yet had no idea of.

It didn't take us nearly as long to get back across the Nile as it had with the felucca we were poled across on earlier. By the time we arrived it was a bit after noon, and we headed for a local restaurant to get some lunch. The plans for the afternoon were completely filled with touring the Karnak temple of Luxor. After a brief freshening up at the hotel, we gathered up the cameras and the guide book and headed out for the tour.

As we entered the site, it was apparent that we would be seeing much of the same architecture and design as we had already seen in the temple of Luxor, as well as Edfu and Kom Ombo. What was different was the lengthy line of sphinxes that guarded the entire entry walk up to the first huge pylon of the temple. These were ram's head sphinxes, and we stopped to take pictures of Lucas and Chelsea sitting and standing on them.

Further into the temple complex, we came across the most gigantic columns we'd ever seen. It was a tremendous area of nothing but columns, in fact, and each one at the base had to have been about ten feet across! Following the usual style, they had been deeply carved with the gods of ancient Egypt, and away up at the top we could still see faint remnants of the once brightly colored paint. It was plain how the enormity was affecting the droves of tourists visiting the site as we were, as the normal noise of chatter ceased in this great hall of columns. Again we took multiple photographs and video before moving on.

Outside the great hall we found our way into each of the various smaller temple and shrine additions that had been added to the original over the years by the various Pharaohs. The item Jim most wanted to see here was the obelisk of Queen Hatshepsut, which was almost one hundred feet tall and was one of the ones sent up from the granite quarries of Aswan we'd visited a few days previous. It stood as a timeless sentinel, with the deepest cut carvings we'd yet seen still remaining in its surface. Once again, the methodology of how the ancients actually produced and erected these obelisks was all over Jim's imagination. He stopped to use up a good bit of video on this item, and was pleased to see the moon through the viewfinder shining clearly. Although the sun was not yet set, the evening sky was deepening with gorgeous hues and the moon was just bright enough to be captured in the video next to the obelisk. He wondered again why he just couldn't get these obelisks off his mind.

Leaving the area of Hatshepsut's obelisk, we eventually came to what they called the Sacred Lake, in front of which stood a fat granite column of about eight feet in height. On top of it had been carved a huge scarab beetle out of the same granite, and we noticed a rope fence had been established round about it. Various groups of French, German, and Japanese tourists were circumnavigating the beetle, laughing and speaking in their own languages as they did. Just as we were wondering what in the world was going on, we overheard a guide speaking to a group behind us that it was tradition and good luck to walk seven times around the scarab in front of the Sacred Lake. Having heard all they needed to, Lucas and Chelsea grabbed Jim and I by the arms and virtually drug us into the midst of the circling mass, and after seven times around, we broke free and began the long walk out of the temple of Karnak to the lines of sphinxes. The sun was gone and dusk was settling by the time we returned to the Luxor Sheraton. Our journey to the interior regions of ancient Egypt was over.

Morning view of the Nile River from the balcony of the
Luxor Sheraton, Luxor, Egypt

CHAPTER SIXTEEN

Hurghada

The morning of January 18 dawned inside our hotel room in much the same way the days before had done. This time it was Jim who had awakened before I did and having fulfilled all the demanded coffee traditions, he beckoned me out to the balcony for one last goodbye to the gently flowing Nile a few stories beneath us. We spent the next hour speaking in hushed tones, listening to the tremendous roar of what must have been 40,000 sparrows as they chirped and sang and greeted the day. Even though our trip was just at the halfway point, we were already reflecting on how incredible it had been, and wondering what lay ahead.

Today we would actually drive away from interior Egypt and the Nile and head back to the main body of the Red Sea and a port named Hurghada. But that trip would only take us a few hours driving time, and we were content to move slowly this morning. There were a couple of things we needed to do before we actually left Luxor. In the courtyard of this hotel there was a small man-made lake, and several varieties of large birds were kept there. The flamingos were gorgeous but didn't do much except stand on one leg and tuck their heads under their back feathers and sleep. The objects of our delight for the past two days had been two huge pelicans of a variety we'd never seen before. Each time we came and went from the hotel, we'd go out there to see them; and Lucas and Chelsea had grown attached to them quickly. To this point Jim had not taken any video of them, so the first order on the agenda of our departing this place would be to get down there and record the pelicans.

The next item necessary was a return visit to a handwoven carpet dealer we had located inside the Luxor Hilton, where we had stayed the first time. A very large carpet had caught our eyes days before that had been all but yelling at us to purchase it. Almost 8 x 5 feet, it depicted a scene right out of the deserts of Arabia, which was completely unlike all the others being sold which tended to have to do with scenes of Egypt. Camels, tents, and Bedouins, with a sun setting over palm trees and mountains was the theme of the weaving, and it truly captured a scene we had grown so fond of and familiar with. I knew we just weren't going to be able to resist taking it with us on our final exit from Luxor.

Jim and I finished our quiet balcony reflections and got the kids up for breakfast. Once finished, it was a quick pack up inside the hotel room and the now routine smashing of the overstuffed luggage into the overstuffed truck. That having been accomplished with growing finesse, we headed for the pelicans to tell them goodbye for the last time. As the big birds cocked their heads to the side and gazed up at us with what I would swear was a smile, I vowed to never forget the sweetness in their eyes.

Back we went to our faithful Patrol, and four slammed doors later we were on our way to the other end of the main road to the Luxor Hilton's carpet shop. Upon our arrival, we found a new man was working the shop today, and that was a relief. The only reason we hadn't purchased the carpet of note before now was that the salesman had hacked us off by being too pushy. This was a younger man, and obviously full of himself as he began to flirt with me the moment we walked into the shop, right there in front of my husband.

As Jim began the protocols of Arab trading with him, the kids and I just sat down and waited. This ritual was an absolute must if we were to get anything at all, and we'd been living in the Middle East long enough to know that nine times out of ten you couldn't just walk into a shop and buy anything without haggling over price for at least ten or fifteen minutes. It was a tradition as old as time in these parts of the world, and we found it to be especially true in Egypt. After much banter and the shouting of many prices back and forth, Jim's offer of $400.00 was accepted by the merchant, and he made a point of telling Jim that he was only giving him this deal because of the "magic in his wife's eyes." I wasn't so sure if the next thing Jim did would be to shake the guy's hand for a deal well made, or ball up his fist and deck him for flirting with his wife. But in the end, calm prevailed and Jim handed him our credit card and the deal was done. Now all we had to figure out was how to stuff this great big rug into the Patrol, which was bursting already at the seams! But stuff it in we did, and away we went thrilled with our purchase!

As Jim pulled out onto the Nile road for the last time, a relief washed over him as he realized that it would not be but for a short distance and he would never have to face this highway again. He was more than ready for a change of scenery by now and eager to spend a few days doing absolutely nothing except loafing on the beach against the beautiful waters of the Red Sea. As he approached the turnoff to head eastward to Hurghada, it was with great relish and a broad victorious grin that he bid the treacherous ribbon of road adieu.

I had been in awe of all the sights we'd seen from Cairo all the way down to Abu Simbel, both ancient and current as well, but I too was looking forward to getting out of the interior life of Egypt along the Nile River and back to the more rocky desert environs surrounding the Red Sea. The place we were headed for was supposed to have some beautiful diving and snorkeling available, and I figured if we could just get a few warm days on the coast, we would surely take full advantage of that.

The flat, sandy terrain of the desert to the east of the Nile was gradually changing before our eyes. We were burning up kilometers on the asphalt highway headed due east. We could see in the far distance a mountain range that at first just looked like an interruption on the horizon, but now was becoming more and more prominent. The highway was also heading down as we made our way closer to the sea, and by the time we reached the first series of mountain peaks, they seemed much bigger than I imagined they would be. It was about three o'clock in the afternoon in this area when Jim spied something in his rear view mirror that he just had to go back and investigate.

As we were the only people on the highway and had not seen another vehicle for at least an hour, the ever resourceful Jim Caldwell backed up the distance to the item of his interest. To the left of the highway rose a particularly sharp-peaked mountain with a prominent crack that opened just wide enough to be a cave. It looked fairly accessible, and that's all it took to have us marching in single file out of the truck and toward the hole in the mountain.

"Here we go again!" I thought to myself as I felt the rubble of the rocks moving under my feet. I knew that Jim had never once let go of his original vision of the Ark of the Covenant, and he was still looking for a cave that would yield its glory to him. I knew that something entirely supernatural had been leading, following, and guiding us this entire trip; it was something like a mysterious wind I kept hearing—a whispering that I just couldn't decipher. But even experiencing these things, it was difficult for me to keep on being overjoyed at having to stop and explore every mountain crack, crevice, and cave we passed! I was starting to get a vivid picture of the father in the movie *Close Encounters of the Third Kind*, who was obsessed with drawing and building unknown shapes that he didn't even know the origin of, or what they had to do with. Had Jim finally lost it?

But I kept my thoughts to myself and headed with the rest of my family to the now looming crack in the mountain. It was most definitely a cave, and a large one at that, but a quick glance at the entrance proved immediately disappointing. While its size was impressive, the depth was only a few feet, and that left little room for the false walls and hidden chambers Jim was searching for. I looked over at him and caught the momentary let-down expression, just before he picked up his courage again and with a loud command, ordered us all away. "To the Red Seaaaaaaaaaaaaaa!" he yelled, as he chased the kids laughing and hollering all the way back to the truck.

It wasn't but around another bend or two in the highway when we broke through the mountains and got our first glimpse of the crystal clear turquoise waters of the Red Sea! This was the main body of the Red Sea that separated the Arabian continent from Africa, to boot. Up to this moment, the only other time we'd seen it was from the Arabian side at Jeddah. Jim had also seen this great expanse from Yanbu, where he'd first entered Saudi in September of 1987 to work what turned out to only be a three-month job with YANPET, a petrochemical conglomerate in the Western Province. That job having not proven to be what he expected, Jim had reapplied to go to work right away with Aramco in the Eastern Province, and miraculously landed the new position. And a true blue certifiable miracle it was!

By law it was all but impossible to quit one job in the desert Kingdom and get another unless by waiting the allotted two-year period for re-application. We did not have the luxury of that delay as Jim had no stateside job, so he had forged ahead and got what was called a "Letter of No Objection" that had been written by YANPET giving their full permission for him to take another job without the waiting period. He felt like it would be enough. The relocation specialists at Aramco apparently thought so, too; they immediately hired him and sent movers to pack out our house and flew us to Houston for orientation. But the Saudi officials responsible for issuing the visas in our passports did not have the same opinion of the letter from YANPET. By the end of the third day of orientation, Jim had been back to them each day using every possible strategy he knew to get them to change their minds and allow us to enter, but all to no avail.

At the last moment on the last day, as we taxied toward the multistory building in downtown Houston for one last attempt to sway the mind of the consul, I had looked up in desperation, wondering what would happen to us when they said no for the last time. For a brief instant, I thought I had caught a glimpse of something huge on the very top of the building. I'd rubbed my eyes and blinked hard, but I was certain I'd seen it. A wave of goose bumps washed over me, and even as insane and ridiculous as it seemed, I heard my own mouth telling Jim not to worry because I knew we'd get the visas. And I knew it because what I had caught in my eyes for that whisper of a moment on top of that building was an enormous angelic being, who had nodded toward me, as if to say it would be so, and then had vanished into thin air.

Jim looked at me that day like I had totally lost it with all the pressure and stress of the situation; but before the next hour was complete, history would record Jim Caldwell kneeling down in prayer right there in the heart of the offices of the stubborn officials. It would not take but moments more for us to emerge from the place with four freshly inked visas stamped in our passports. Somehow, some way, in the most bizarre case the Aramco relocation employees had ever witnessed, Jim Caldwell had been the single acceptance to the two-year rule by the Saudi Arabian Consulate in Houston, Texas.

I toyed with the memory of that angel on the top of that building for a bit as we headed further down the highway to the intersecting road that ran north and south along the shoreline. We would have to take it to the north and follow it all the way into the city of Hurghada. For some reason it dawned on me right then that maybe, just maybe, there had been a plan to get us to Saudi all along for some purpose that we hadn't understood up to this point. And abruptly the sensation that had been dancing on the winds since just prior to the beginning of the trip was all over me again. What was this thing? I suddenly had the distinct impression that we were being neatly maneuvered in a colossal plan that had begun to work itself out on this trip to Egypt. And when I had that realization, I got scared at the enormity of it all and shook it off before I could think anything further. If I could have jumped out of the truck when we finally reached the juncture of the roads, I would have run like the wind.

The Hurghada Sheraton turned out to be an elusive place to find. After almost an hour of searching round and round the city, we were finally directed almost all the way back to where we'd entered, which didn't thrill Jim one little bit. The kids were tired and getting restless, and we all needed to get out of the truck and to do it soon. Add to that the anxiety of wondering what sort of hotel this one would be—since the fateful experience at Minya—and we were all getting pretty cranked with one another. That is, until we caught the hotel in our sights.

On top of a large jebel of rock stood the object we'd somehow missed on our first go-round through Hurghada. The Sheraton was a circular hotel of about three or four stories, and it appeared that all the rooms had beautiful seaside views. It didn't take us long to check into this one, and upon entering the room I breathed not only a sigh of relief, but a gasp of *Wow!* at just how nice it really was. We'd been given a suite for the night, with two bedrooms and a living room, and each room had an incredible balcony facing eastward that overlooked the Red Sea. From high atop this perch in the landscape, we could see multiple small boats and several larger ones that looked like charter boats anchored in the harbor down below us. A private beach belonging to the hotel was also visible, complete with puffy chaise loungers lining the entire length of it. Jim and I looked at each other with an immediate knowledge that the next few days would be exactly the rest and relaxation we were hoping for.

As dinner time rolled around, we made our way down to the hotel restaurant and found it to be an Italian Feast night. The food was wonderful, and the dining room was situated directly in front of the water for a fabulous view. We ate until we were overstuffed, and then headed back to the room for a few rounds of our now regulation spades games.

Now these games had tradition attached to them already. Lucas would name each player one night, and the next night Chelsea would. This night being Lucas's turn, he promptly dubbed himself "General Norman Schwartzkoft," his mother as "George Bush, Sr.," his father as "Adolph Hitler," and his dreaded little sister as "Saddam Hussein." Chelsea immediately crossed her arms and bowed up into a deeply frowning pout, which caused a monumental delay of game. We had to explain to her that her brother was merely using political and military names common to the recent days of the Gulf War, aside from the glaringly obvious low blow of naming Jim Adolph Hitler!

And so the spades fights of the night finally began. In the middle of one such game, the telephone rang. As Jim picked up the receiver I wondered who in the world it could be. The one thing we had not been plagued with since leaving Ras Tanura on this trip was phone calls. A momentary worry crossed my mind, but Jim's laughter relieved that anxiety before it ever got going. He hung up the phone and shook his head as he made his way back to the spades table.

"You'll never believe it. Remember the guy we bought the carpet from this morning?" Jim asked, still grinning and shaking his head.

"How could I forget that guy," I said rolling my eyes. "Well, as it turns out, his boss doesn't take Diner's Club Card after all. He's coming up here tomorrow afternoon to get the VISA card and run it through. So you'll get to see him again!" Jim snickered and winked at me.

"Oh, what great joys have overtaken me!" I replied in a distinctly Southern drawl. "I shall hardly be able to contain myself until then."

We both burst out laughing at the thought of that playing out, until Lucas and Chelsea started yelling at us to come back and finish the spades game. It wasn't long after that one that we were all yawning too seriously to concentrate and gave up the revelry for a good night of rest. It had been a long day since leaving the Luxor Sheraton, but a good one.

JIM, CHELSEA, AND LUCAS WITH AN ORANGE GROUPER,
RED SEA OFF HURGHADA, EGYPT

CHAPTER SEVENTEEN

Blue Spotted Orange Groupers

Somewhere around 5:00 A.M., I could feel my brain beginning to switch from the arena of my dream sleep and into conscious thought, and as my nose detected the fabulous aroma of coffee in the room, my eyes popped wide open. Jim had already called for and gotten the room service waiters up early and was presently stirring into the glorious, steaming liquid our various blends of sugar substitutes and creams that were always necessary to get the taste just right. And these adjustments to the coffee were especially important this morning because the intensely strong odor of cardamom was permeating the entire room. It was a classically Arabian custom to crush the pods and swirl them into hot coffee just before serving it, and that is exactly what coffee Jim found on the tray from the kitchen. Not his preference, to be sure, but hot coffee was hot coffee—not a chance he'd be turning it down and have to wait for another tray.

All was well and on schedule according to tradition until he caught my eyes opening out of the corner of his eye, and I instantly heard the sound of pressurized air escaping into the room as he threw back his head, pursed his lips together, puffed up his cheeks, and began letting his breath out ever so slowly to get the most perfect sound effect possible. He was "blasting" at me, and I knew I must immediately bow to the prescribed protocols of our own Caldwell Rules of Engagement if I was to salvage the entirety of January 19. It was against all regulation for my eyes to be seen opening prior to the singing of the Coffee Song, and my only way out was to begin feigning a loud snore to alleviate the pressure of the blast. The brief silence let me know my surrender had worked, and my husband had accepted the repentant nature of my fake snoring as a truce. And so the famed Coffee Song rang out at the Sheraton Hotel in Hurghada Egypt for the first time.

I got out of bed quickly after the song, and we tip-toed over to the sliding glass door and opened it so that we could enjoy our first cup of coffee outside before daybreak. Jim had the video camera ready, and I had the Nikon still shot in hand so that we could capture the sunrise on film. We had grown very accustomed in the prior month of December to getting up before daylight and watching the sun come up over the Persian Gulf, and it had been a while since we'd been privy to watching the gleaming orb break itself free from the grips of the horizon in what always looked to us like a nuclear explosion.

It was an absolutely gorgeous morning already, even though we could barely see in the scant light prior to dawn. The sound of the gentle lapping of waves against the shore down below us and the occasional chirping of the little sparrows awakening to the day were the only noises detectable at this hour, and the peace that descended on us was tremendous. We sat there breathing it all in for about the next hour and a half, until the sun was high enough to blaze forth brilliantly, casting a pathway of glistening light across the waters from the east directly over to us. As I finished the last drop of the last cup of coffee, the sliding glass door opened up and a very rumpled Lucas Michael in his long johns, rubbing his eyes and scratching his head, stumbled out onto the balcony.

"Is it time to go fishing yet?" he mumbled as he headed toward me in a dazed stupor.

I laughed out loud. "No, Pie, not yet it isn't. But it won't be long after we get ready and eat breakfast! Come sit with me a while and let's just watch the water."

So he came on over and curled up with me on the chaise lounge for a time. Jim had made our morning plans the night before with the hotel manager and had arranged to charter a boat for reef fishing offshore for the first half of the day. It had only set him back 238 Egyptian pounds, which translated out to about $70.00. A half-day charter back home would have cost five times that amount, and after putting the kids through all the pyramid, temple, and tomb tours, Jim felt like this would be something they'd really get a kick out of. Especially Lucas Michael Fisherman.

"Can't get him up any other time, but mention fishing, and he's up at the crack of dawn, huh, Blat?" Jim said as he walked over to where we sat and further ruffled Lucas's already wild bed hair.

It didn't take him long to awaken fully after getting confirmation that fishing was indeed on the agenda for the day, and he hadn't just dreamed it. That of course, quickly ended our relaxed morning break out on the balcony as Lucas started needling us in no uncertain terms to hurry up and get going down to breakfast so that the trip over the waters could commence. Once he got us moving, he diverted his energies toward his sister, who had been zonked in the bed. He promptly jumped up onto her bed, yelling "Get up! Get up!"

Poor Chelsea had been rudely awakened and was now in the not so enviable position of having to both snap out of sleep and dress to go down to breakfast all at the same time. I took pity on her and helped her with her clothes while Jim tried to keep Lucas off the ceiling in the other room. Before ten more minutes had passed, we were all downstairs milling around the ample buffet that had been spread out in the dining room facing the Red Sea.

At a table across from ours we noticed what looked like a couple of Americans that were almost finished with their breakfast. As they got up to leave, they came over and spoke with us. They turned out to be from Los Angeles and had flown over for an Egyptian vacation for the month of January as well. When we told them of our trip—driving all the way from Saudi Arabia, and touring Egypt in our own vehicle —they thought we had lost our minds and promptly told us so. It was incredulous to them that anyone would be crazy enough to do such a thing, much less do it as a single family alone! But there, sitting at breakfast looking out over the turquoise waters, I felt both strangely at home and at perfect peace. That in itself should have been a sign that something big was up. But a day of simple family fun was ahead, and I was not prone to think of the mystical and unearthly at this hour

SUNRISE OVER THE RED SEA, FROM THE BALCONY OF THE
SHERATON HOTEL, HURGHADA, EGYPT

of the day. We were taking my babies fishing, and that's all I cared to consider.

After a quick jaunt back to the room to clean up and get the cameras, hats, jackets, and sunscreen, we made our way back downstairs to the outer courtyard of the hotel and further on down to the private docks. Large fishing boats were lining the pier, each in their own slips, and it was apparent that charters were a thriving business for this Egyptian resort town. Presently the hotel manager met us and motioned to a beautiful boat that was turning around to back into the empty place on the pier where we stood. Named the "Samba," it would be our seaside get-away for the better part of the next four hours. An older Egyptian and his twelve-year-old son would be our captain and first mate, and as they secured the boat to the docks, we gleefully climbed aboard.

The Samba was a 40-foot-long V-hull boat, with a nice cabin containing a bedroom, a galley, and a head inside along with an inner compartment for just sitting and riding. Above that compartment on the outside was the captain's perch, from whence he and his son would drive us out to the pre-arranged spot for fishing. The back end of the boat was lined with bench seating and offered plenty of room for a number of people to fish. The entry to the inner seating compartment and the other deck below was squarely in the center of this area, and on either side ran a safety railing so that a person could walk down the length of the boat, albeit very carefully, and out onto the long front deck. At the very end of the boat's bow, a small pulpit jutted out from the deck over the water. That was my favorite spot on any boat, and as soon as I saw it, I knew I'd have to get out there onto the point.

The powerful diesel engines came to life presently and after leaving the dock area slowly, the captain cranked them up and we began making some serious knots across the waters. Jim had the video camera out and recorded the amazing blue-green clarity of the sea here. Even though the depth was already nearing about thirty feet, we could still see the bottom in good detail! It was truly remarkable. But up ahead, the color abruptly changed to a deep navy blue, and we knew that the bottom had just fallen out from beneath us. After about a forty-five minute ride out, the drone of the big diesels suddenly stopped, and we knew we must be at the designated place. We were now in deep waters and ready to learn to fish Egyptian style.

The son of the captain let out the anchor to hold us steady, and then proceeded to the rear of the boat to prepare our tackle for us. What was coming for fishing tackle we could not have imagined in our wildest dreams! We were each handed a block of wood approximately ten inches long by six inches wide, and about one inch thick. Wrapped tightly round and round this block of wood was what appeared to be about 60 pound test monofilament fishing line, and at the end of each line, a large lead weight and regular sized steel hook. Lucas looked up at me with a contorted face and one raised eyebrow, as if to say, "What in the world is this?" Just then I would have been in a world of hurt to find an answer for him.

But it wasn't as kooky as it looked. In fact, it couldn't have been any simpler. All we had to do was loose the hook from where it was tied, bait it, and unwind the line end-over-end from the wood block while lowering it into the water. The fishing procedure was equally simple: just hold the line over the forefinger, keep it in place with the thumb and the rest of the fingers, and bob it up and down until a fish strikes. At least this was the best we could understand from watching the captain and his son, because neither of them could speak a word of English.

Within about two minutes of the bait going into the water, Lucas exclaimed, "I've got one! I've got one!" The captain came right over to show him how to pull the line hand-over-hand backward into the boat, and up came the most incredible looking fish we'd ever seen! It was obviously a juvenile grouper from its size and shape, but the color scheme was absolutely eye popping. The fish was a brilliant, dark neon orange, and the entire length of its body was covered in round spots of royal blue that were just as dazzling.

Lucas and Chelsea were filling the air with *Wow's* and *Whoa, baby's* in rapid fire succession. I raced into the inside compartment for the cameras immediately to capture this unusual fish on film before we would throw it back because of its smaller size. While Jim held it up, I shooed Lucas and Chelsea together to get them into the picture. The joy and excitement surrounding the catching of this first fish was thick in the air as I snapped away with the camera to try to get a permanent record of this event. Before the next few hours had passed, twelve more of these incredibly beautiful fish would be brought up from the crystalline depths, and I knew the preservation of this memory was sealed in stone. Out here, I felt as though I had been whisked away from the entire world, floating on the most beautiful sea on planet Earth. I would never, ever forget the blue spotted orange groupers of Hurghada, Egypt.

Regrettably, our time on the boat had expired. After all our lines had been pulled in and rewound around the wooden blocks, the first mate pulled in the anchor and the engines started up once again. The ride back was almost ethereal as I stood soaking up the sensations from the pulpit of the vessel. I thought to myself what a family of true water fanatics we really were. We currently lived just a block from the blue-green waters of the Persian Gulf and had been Florida beach bums every summer prior to our moving to the Middle East! Raised near the Louisiana and Mississippi Gulf Coasts, the sea was no stranger to any of us, even the kids, and we all agreed that this trip had been a great time of refreshing from the dusty, dank corridors of the pyramids and the tombs. The landing appeared way too soon for my liking, and before I knew it, we were walking back up the pier toward our hotel room.

We figured to head down to the hotel's beach area to do a lot of nothing and relax the afternoon away, and that decision was final when we realized that there was an active open café down on the same beach where we could get some lunch. When we'd gotten settled in four empty beach loungers, Jim called over one of the waiters and ordered us each hamburgers and French fries, which turned out to be delicious! After we ate, I felt myself getting very sleepy as did Jim, and we napped intermittently for the next couple of hours. Lucas and Chelsea were perfectly content to be beachside and spent the afternoon digging and playing in the sand nearby.

Along about four o'clock a very brisk wind blew in, along with some high, wispy clouds and it turned sharply colder. The kids were too cold to stay down on the beach any longer, so we all went up to the cozy confines of the beautiful suite that was our room. Jim ordered up more room service coffee and turned the television on just in time to catch the beginning of the movie *Home Alone*. We laughed the remainder of the late afternoon away, and then cleaned ourselves up to go down to dinner. There was not much of a choice for food this evening, and between the gritty spinach and the watery squid thermidor, none of us had much of an appetite. Right back to the room we marched after eating a lot of bread, crackers, and butter for supper.

As tired as we were, we still had to get in several spades games for the evening. It was Chelsea's turn to name the players tonight, and she crowned herself "Nefertiti" first, Lucas "Tutankhamen" second, me "Cleopatra" third, and her daddy, "Marc Antony" last. A fight broke out among us over the pronunciation of Jim's new name. Was it *Anthony* or was it *Antony*? After it was clear that none of us could make a final decision, we turned to the game and only played a few rounds before calling it quits and heading to bed.

After Jim and I tucked each of the kids in and returned to our room, we noticed that the moonlight must be very bright outside because of the light that was coming in under the curtains. That lured us out there like moths to a flame. Jim grabbed the video camera, and for the next several minutes shot some of the most beautiful footage he'd yet taken. The moon looked almost full. Its radiance was laying a sparkling pathway across the water to us and had the appearance of glittering gemstones, randomly scattered, along the entire length of it.

I looked over at Jim to tell him how utterly beautiful this was only to find that he'd already put the camera down and had been steadily and silently gazing at me. The moon was casting a soft yet vibrant light that was dancing in the breeze onto our faces, and the scene was utterly surreal. It was ultimately clear as we stood there, a thousand miles away from all the desolations we had been through the year before, that not even hell itself could break the eternal bond our souls had forged with one another so long ago. As he reached down and cradled my face in his hands, he whispered deep, secret things into my ear that only he and I could share, and the night was unforgettable.

* * *

It was nearly nine-thirty before I knew it was even morning. In fact, if Chelsea's stomach had not been growling, the lot of us could have probably slept for another couple of hours! But the Booglet could not go far without her breakfast, and therein lay the problem. I felt a hand grab my exposed shoulder and start shaking it back and forth.

"Mom! Mom, it's morning! ! Wake up! I'm starving! Mom!"

Not willing to give in so easily, I pulled the covers quickly over my head and waited for the next volley of verbal abuse. What I didn't realize was that Jim was already awake, but faking sleep beside me. Chelsea leaned way over me to where her face was directly above my own under the covers and started up her protest again.

"Mom! Come on, Mom! My stomach's soooooo empty and I'm ready for breakfast!"

Before I could even think up a retort, the bed gave a lurch and out from under the covers came the mighty monster arms of her Daddy, grabbing Chelsea by surprise, picking her right off the floor, and crashing her down on her back in the middle of the bed! Jim was snapping and biting and mashing his daughter mercilessly, and she could barely breathe between her giggles. Suddenly her whines of hunger turned to pleas for deliverance!

"Mommyyy! Heeeeeelp meeeee!" was about all she could get out. But it was to no avail. Jim's leg had me pinned down and I couldn't move. All I could do was wait for the Daddy carnage to finish its course. And it wasn't long before Jim knew if he didn't quit, Chelsea wouldn't be able to breathe any longer from the laughter, so he finally let her go and fell back down next to me in the bed, promptly pulling the covers right back over the both of us. I looked over at the grinning wild-eyed father of my daughter.

"Happy with ya bad self?" I inquired with a half-cocked grin of my own aimed at his million dollar dimples.

"Ohhh, yeah!" Jim smoothly replied. "Are you hearing any more complaints about breakfast? Is your shoulder being pounded? Didn't I get her off your case rather nicely?"

It was the truth. With him, it was always that way. He'd do something totally unexpected and get a result that I could never argue with. Chelsea had escaped into the far recesses of the other room the moment Jim's grip had loosened on her, and she wasn't in my face any more about food. I just closed my eyes and smiled large, shaking my head from side to side on the pillow. What could I say?

"We don't have a thing we have to do today," he whispered, "except get Chelsea her breakfast and get ourselves to that beach down there and loaf all day soaking up the sun. I didn't order a wake-up call on purpose."

Without a real agenda planned for the day, I was completely content just to lie there until the certain return of Chelsea would break the peaceful quiet again. And sure enough, about five minutes later here she came, but this time with reinforcements. She'd managed to get Lucas out of bed somehow and both of them charged in together, jumped up onto the bed, and shattered our morning cuddle. After a brief wrestling match, we gave in and let them win and were forced out of the bed and into January 20.

Once we were all dressed, we headed downstairs and gobbled up a beautiful breakfast buffet that had been set in the dining room. Another hour and Chelsea was stuffed sufficiently to let us leave, and right back to the room we went. My first objective was to determine just how cold it was going to be on that beach for the day so I'd know how much extra clothing to take with us. As before, we were feeling the strong urge to get out into that glorious blue-green water and at least snorkel, but the temperatures had just been too low to handle it. As I opened the door to the balcony and the sharply cool breeze hit me in the face, I was fairly certain I'd be needing my sweat suit over my two piece swimsuit! So I stuffed all our sweat suits into the beach bag and about noon time we headed on down.

We found four loungers that were not already in use because the chill in the air even had our usually robust European bathers hanging out on the inside of the hotel. Lucas and Chelsea set out immediately for the water's edge and proceeded to build a massive complex of sand castles for an hour or so Then we rented a paddleboat for them to use, cruising the waters close to the beach. They were in their element and in their glory, having a ball.

Jim pulled his lounger over as close as he could get it to mine, and we curled up together and just took in the atmosphere, listening to the lapping of the waves the stiff wind was beating against the shore, and gazing intently from time to time into each other's eyes. Life was good. No, life was phenomenal! It just couldn't get any better than this, or so we thought at the time. We had no way of knowing the tremendous adventure that had been gift wrapped from on High that was awaiting us not many days hence. And for the moment, that was just fine.

Along about three o'clock, we roused ourselves out of our dreamy daze and Jim ordered some food from the outdoor beach café. He wouldn't tell me what he'd ordered, but a few minutes later when the waiter arrived, the surprise on my face must have been what he was after in the first place. As the waiter lowered the tray to my lounger, I felt my own eyes bugging out of my head when I saw a fabulous lobster dinner looking back up at me. "Lobster?" I asked him, not believing my own eyes.

"Only the best from now on for you, my dear!" And he bowed low against the lounger. I just looked at him in amazement, and said, "I *knew* I loved you!" And with that, we dug in heartily and licked the platters clean.

It was early evening by the time we gathered up the kids and gear and called it a day, heading back inside to clean up for a light supper. The schedule we were keeping had us traveling all the way to Suez the next day, and we would have to have a wake-up call set for early in the morning. It had been a beautiful day in every way, and sleep came swift and easy.

MINE FIELD WARNING SIGN ON THE GULF OF SUEZ,
SOUTH OF SUEZ, EGYPT

Chapter Eighteen

Mine Fields and Old Insulators

It seemed like the phone started ringing right after my head hit the pillow. I had slept so soundly that I didn't sense any time had passed since I'd crawled into bed, even though the night was over. But then again, this wake-up call was an unusually early one, and I grudgingly reached for the receiver to hear the pre-recorded "Good Morning" before replacing it onto the cradle. Jim rolled over and looked at me with just one eye, way too close for me to focus on his face.

"Time to rise and shine!" he chirped. It never ceased to amaze me how much of a morning bird he really was. I closed my eyes back quickly again and thought of a way to snooze a bit longer, capturing him in a catch-22 of his own rules and regulations.

"I can't rise and shine, because I'm not supposed to open my eyes until I hear the Coffee Song!"

Not hearing a response at all, I knew I'd cornered him, and presently I felt his body leave the bed and shuffle around to my side where the phone was.

"Room service? Yes, I'd like four American coffees … yes, cream and sugar. Thank you." Even with my eyes shut tightly I could tell he was smirking when he added, "Somebody's a wise guy this morning, eh?" I just grinned big enough to show him all my teeth.

But we really did have to get going early, and I knew it. I stayed put until I heard the knock on the door and the Coffee Song rang out, then immediately crawled out of bed. Jim and I shared the first cup just between us on the balcony to catch that all- important sunrise one last time, then quickly set about waking up the kids and gathering all our things to pack up and head for Suez. It would take us about four hours to get there, and we did not have a clue about how to find the hotel we had secured for the evening. We would have to find it once we got there, and we needed the time in the afternoon to look.

We ate a rushed breakfast and then set about the usual procedure of stuffing the truck with luggage.

I was not looking forward to telling the Hurghada Sheraton goodbye but was definitely going to enjoy the privilege of the drive up the coast of the Red Sea. It was over 200 miles north to the town of Suez, but the entire drive was within sight of the water. About a third of it would be along the main body of the Red Sea, and then the Sinai Peninsula would appear on the eastern horizon and we would know we were traveling right up against the Gulf of Suez.

As soon as we cleared the edges of Hurghada, the real beauty of the landscape began to blaze forth. With so many hotels having been built against the water's edge, it was not so easy to view an uninterrupted horizon in the city. But here, away from all the buildings, the stark contrasts were magnificent to behold. To the west of the highway, the mountains rose sharply into the crisp blue sky, against which their multiple shades of brown stood out in beautiful distinction from one another. To the right, the camel-colored sand from the edge of the highway all the way to the sea painted a dramatic pathway to the fantastically blue-green waters. The entire panorama was a palate of the many shades from light tan and dark brown to blue and green. Only the occasional passing truck or car momentarily lent any other hue to the scenery. It was truly magnificent.

The air outside was cool and clean, so we decided to roll the front windows down for a while to enjoy the breezes. I once again felt the total freedom of spirit consume my body and lift me up into the wonder of this magical vacation I was sharing with the three people who meant the most to me on the planet. It seemed unreal—the beauty, the wind blowing my hair all around, the smooth progress of the Patrol as it flew down the desolate highway toward Suez.

By the calendar, it had only been one year since the U. S. led coalition had started the ground war in Iraq against Saddam Hussein. I drifted back in time to the beach house in Bay St. Louis, Mississippi, where Lucas and Chelsea and I had been safely evacuated; I remembered how horribly worried I was at the time for my precious Jim, who was still in harm's way in Ras Tanura. How phenomenal it was that I was now sitting next to him having the trip of a lifetime.

We were one tiny little family all alone against the wilderness of the Red Sea, and I was loving every minute of it. At that very second I was overwhelmed with the peace and the Presence of God, and I spent the next hour lifting praise and adoration to the One who had saved us so completely from the grasp of the enemy.

I reached for the dash and grabbed *Streams in the Desert* and read again the daily words from the morning's devotion for January 21, 1992. "The moment we get anything from the Lord worth contending for, then the devil comes to seek us." Boy, did that ring true to all we'd witnessed! One of the nights prior to this trip, Jim and I had been lying in bed awake and had even actually seen with our physical eyes several dark, shadowy figures hanging in the air near the ceiling of our room. There was no doubt in either of our minds that we had been targeted for total annihilation.

And now, it seemed every fiber of my being was saturated with the sure knowledge that something was trying to be delivered to us from Heaven—and that all hell had broken loose to stop it from getting down to us! The book continued on with words of truth I was only now beginning to understand: "Tribulation is the way to triumph. Crowns are cast in crucibles. Our crowns will be wrested from the giants we conquer!" Right then I felt invincible, knowing of a certainty that I had been given a mighty Sword to wield in one hand and held the head of Goliath in the other.

"Mo-om! Chelsea's touching meeee!" The sound of my son's twenty-eighth complaint against his sister sent me crashing back down to earth out of the realms of the Spirit.

"Chelsea won't stop poking me with her finger, and she keeps looking out my window. Make her look out of her own window!"

Lucas grumped indignantly and turned toward Chelsea, sticking his tongue out in triumph that he'd finally told on her.

"I'm not touching you, and I can look out any window I want to, so there," she shot right back at him, sticking her tongue out the same as he had.

I rolled my eyes and replaced the book of devotions onto the dash and readied myself to turn around and deal with what I knew was coming. This fight was going to escalate to a point where I would have to unbuckle my seatbelt, turn around to face the back of the truck, wedge my body between the two front bucket seats with my behind in the air, and threaten to beat the fire out of both of them before they'd leave each other alone. It had come to be quite a usual position for me as we traveled through the desert in the years since 1988 when we first began to take long, cross-country camping trips with the kids. So many hours crunched into a jam-packed four-wheel drive had a way of bringing out the worst in a kid's character, and this morning had been no exception to that cardinal rule. But if there was one thing I couldn't tolerate in my kids, it was them being obnoxious to one another. And sure enough, the sound level was rising in both of their voices, as various threats and accusations began to fly more abundantly. I stealthily began to reach for the latch of my seatbelt, so my unsuspected quick action would have the greatest amount of shock value.

I waited until the argument turned into a full fledged fist fight, then snapped myself free of the harness and whirled around in a fit of fury, screaming at the top of my lungs, "Both of you quit fightingggggg! I'm gonna make your dad stop this truck and I'll put you both out and leave you here if you don't quit it now!" There was no ambiguity in either my fiercely livid face or the commanding tone of my voice. I meant exactly what I'd said, and was just right on the verge of doing it. The challenge was always getting them to believe that I would. This time I must have scared them senseless, because in a flash it had worked like a charm. Dead silence was the only thing I could hear coming from the back seat.

I turned around and once again, tried to regain the wonderful unearthly feeling I'd been enjoying before the reality check had hit. I closed my eyes and leaned back against the headrest, only to hear Jim trying to muffle a snicker. "What?" I asked, looking over at him with feigned big-eyed innocence.

"You're such a wild child, that's what! One minute you're off in that dreamy world you fly away to all the time, and the next minute you're back down here tearing the heads off lions! What am I gonna do with you?" His smile melted me down in a heartbeat.

"Whatever you wanna do, Baby, but you best not make me mad," was what I heard my own mouth answer before I could even think up a clever retort. We both broke out into wide grins and looked forward at the road ahead of us.

A bit further down the road I started noticing some small red signs posted here and there on either side of the road at varying intervals. At first I couldn't make out what was on them because we were moving too fast and because some were too rusted to be legible, but when Jim slowed down for us all to take a break, I could finally focus well enough on what I was seeing to understand. Each of these little signs had the skull and crossbones symbol on them, and I wondered what in the world could be so dangerous out here in the middle of nowhere.

The thought occurred to me to look in the new book we'd purchased in Hurghada which was a how-to for tourists when driving in Egypt. I opened up the book to the section on driving in the Sinai Peninsula and much to my surprise, found them almost immediately. Apparently the skull and crossbones signs had been placed there many years previous as a result of the Six-Day War with Israel and were warnings that land mines could still be present in the areas where the signs were. I felt a chill run through me when I thought of what could have happened to us if we had stopped earlier before we knew what these meant! I thanked God we'd been informed!

As we got a little nearer to Suez, the mountains on the west were getting closer and closer to the road, and the myriad colors in the layers of rock were just fantastic to behold. Pinks and roses and mauves were all mingled in with the varied browns, and the lines of demarcation were extra crisp and clean. The nearness of the peaks made them look all the higher as well, and I just had to have some still camera shots of their majesty.

Jim was all too glad to stop the truck to stretch his legs, so just this side of a ramshackled set of railroad tracks that crossed the highway, he pulled the Patrol over to the right side to oblige me. He swung his long legs over and out of the truck and stood there with both arms above his head, closing his eyes and letting loose with a huge, loud yawn. He raised both his eyebrows and looked skyward to stretch his neck as well, before shaking his head and settling his sights back on me; but just then, something beside me and my camera caught his full attention. His eyes narrowed against the glare of the sun, and he put both his hands up to shield them from the brightness so that he could focus on the objects he thought his brain had noticed.

A long line of dilapidated telephone poles stretched as far down the tracks as he could see, and here and there a pole had fallen down to the sand and rocks below. What had caught his eye were the items still attached to the top of each one: items that were, to one soul he knew all the way back in Waveland, Mississippi, of enormous importance. Though the old line had ceased to function for some length of years, the insulators were still there! And to a collector such as the one he now had pictured in his mind, Jim Caldwell had just struck gold!

A broad grin escaped from the edge of his lips, and he knew what he had to do. In spite of the remnants of a barbed wire fence that would bar his forward progress and in spite of the menacing little red signs with the skull and crossbones vividly screaming out to him the warning of unexploded land mines, Jim girded up his courage and fortitude and started out across the road to where I stood still snapping photographs of the colored mountain.

"Isn't this just beautif …," was as far as I got before I knew he was up to something beside me and my mountain. "What are you doing? Where are you going?" I asked in a state of almost immediate dread.

Jim yelled out as he passed by me and leapt down from the highway's edge right over the remnants of the fence with the little red signs. "Look at what's sitting on top of those downed telephone poles over there! I'm going grab your Mom some insulators from the Sinai Peninsula for her collection!"

I almost froze in stark terror at the gravity of his words. It was true enough. I flashed my eyes over to what he'd seen and was amazed to notice the insulators, hanging out like ripe oranges ready to be plucked from a tree. It was rare to find any that were this easy to grab, and we'd been on plenty enough missions back in the States over the years looking for them to know. And I also knew what an enormous specialty item this would in fact be to my mother, who would be extra thrilled to add foreign soil insulators to her collection! Jim's status with her was already tremendous, but this feat would catapult him right to the stars in her eyes! But to have him traverse a mine field to get to them? It just wasn't worth the risk to me. I weighed all the pros and cons for the length of about five seconds before I screamed out, "Have you lost your mind?"

He didn't answer and never looked back once. Straight to the downed poles he went and started unscrewing the juicy prizes from their positions on the crossbars. I knew all too well that there wasn't a thing I could do now except pray. And pray I did!

"Oh, God, have mercy on my husband, Your insane servant Jim, who in spite of the brilliant mind You've given him, seeks to tempt Your goodness and place himself in harm's way, anyhow, like he had no sense at all! Please forgive his trespassing inside this fence and keep his feet from the land mines, in Jesus Name!"

I waited in total silence after that, holding my breath and completely immobile as I sweated it out—until I saw him safely cross back over the fallen fence, with numerous insulators in tow. I had no idea as I watched him lift the back gate of the truck and slip each insulator down into any crook or cranny it would fit into, that this was just a taste, a tiny little morsel of an appetizer, of the days that were to come. This tiptoeing through the mine field was nothing compared to the feats I would witness this man accomplish in the next several years behind other fences much more dangerous than this one—and guarded by living men with AK-47 assault rifles, a much more current threat than thirty-year-old land mines. But I didn't know that today. All I knew was that I was married to an extraordinarily brave man who could look danger right squarely in the eyes and laugh at it to get at his objective. I was both tantalized with the excited thrill of him at that instant, and filled with the monstrous desire to strangle the life out of him for taking such a colossal chance. Lucky for him today, the goose-bumps won.

Within a half hour the city of Suez was in our sights. At first glance Suez reminded us of a smaller Cairo. Traffic was barely creeping, crowds of people littered the streets, and the noise of the honking of horns was pretty much constant. The dust of many years seemed to cover the buildings, and I felt myself already wishing that we didn't have to stay in this area at all. For the drive up here to have been as beautiful as it was, the entry into Suez felt like finding a garbage dump at the end of the rainbow. The only thing that was different about Suez was its being situated on the Red Sea, and the evidence of that was clear each time I looked out my window to see the outline of the huge cargo ships just beyond the multi-story apartment buildings. It was time to start the search for the Summer Palace, the hotel Jim had booked for this night's stay.

The nagging uneasiness I felt was not the least bit lessened when after three or four consecutive passes around the main city center we could not locate the hotel, which meant that Jim was going to have to stop somewhere and ask directions. Having spent almost three weeks in Egypt thus far, we had learned the hard way that this process usually involved either a ridiculous sum of bribe money, or *baksheesh*, and a favor for the individual offering his assistance. And today would prove to be no different. Much to his dismay, Jim was forced to roll down his window and ask how to find the Summer Palace.

The Egyptian who came over to the window was a man maybe thirty years old, with a pleasant face and a seemingly friendly outlook. His demeanor was steady as Jim mentioned the Summer Palace, and in fairly understandable English, he got it through to us that he thought he knew where it was. When he didn't ask for *baksheesh*, we knew we'd been sent another angel. The only thing he seemed to want from us was a ride, which he was perfectly content to take from the running boards of the Patrol! So away we went in the thick traffic, slowly navigating the congested highway with an Egyptian hanging off Jim's window, shouting directions as we drove. It scared me that I was getting used to this.

In about a half hour, we made the final right turn and saw the Summer Palace Hotel for the first time. It was situated on a back bay connected to the Red Sea, and could have been a really nice place if it had been kept up at all. Most of the rooms were at ground level and opened up to a vast patio and pool section that bordered the bay, and I was sure it must have been beautiful at one time. The pool itself was a perfect circle and enormous, but full of filthy water with a layer of scum on the top. Rusted playground equipment was all over the place, and wooden bench swings that were strategically placed throughout the area had been over run by tall grass. Weeds were growing up out of every crack in the concrete. As we hauled our luggage toward our room, I thought it was a shame that it hadn't been looked after. Jim believed that the reason it was in such disorder was simply because this was January, and the likelihood of many people coming to this site to enjoy the outdoor facilities were slim to none. I had to concur that maybe he was right.

The room itself was at best, adequate. It was small, and there were only three single beds that would fit inside, leaving us to have to arrange ourselves wisely to be able to accommodate four. It was clean, however, and almost the entire wall next to the door was a plate glass window overlooking the patio area. We dumped our belongings inside decided to get a bite to eat in the restaurant. With great courage I decided, as did Lucas, to order fried shrimp, which was usually a real risky venture in a place such as this, but it turned out to be delicious! One vote of confidence for the place, I noted to myself.

Because it was still early enough in the day, we decided to go ahead and drive out to the Suez Canal to watch the big ships pass through. There we found a sort-of park had been attempted along the canal, with a few concrete benches here and there for viewing. After an hour or so of seeing one huge vessel after another creep slowly by, Lucas and Chelsea decided to jump down onto the sandy bank below the paved area and poke around. They found a large, dried palm frond and started playing baseball with the rocks and the frond as a bat. I wondered at the time why we always spent so much money on toys for them, when they had such a good time on trips like this one with simple ordinary things! And just as soon as the thought crossed my mind, I realized that there were no other trips like this one, and ordinary was not a word I should have been using in my vocabulary. As I watched them having a blast playing a blatantly American game with make-do equipment, in full view of the ships in the Suez Canal on their way out to the Mediterranean Sea, I was once again flushed with the knowledge that I was a long, long way from home!

JIM, CHELSEA, AND LUCAS TAKING VIDEO AT THE SUEZ CANAL

CHAPTER NINETEEN

Return to the Sinai Peninsula

January 22 dawned cool and hazy. We had gone to bed early the night before as all of us were exhausted from traveling all the way from Hurghada and going nonstop until dark. The sleep was remarkably peaceful for having had the uneasiness I'd felt about the Summer Palace at first, but I awakened happy that we would soon be on our way back into the Sinai Peninsula as fast as we could get ready. The thing that had particularly bothered me about this place was the crows that seemed to be present in every tree, on every pole, and hanging on the wires like black and grey beads on a necklace. I'd never seen so many crows in one place before, and all of them were so continuously squawking that I swore I was beginning to make out understandable words in their language. I felt like they were watching every move we made, and that had given me a bad case of the creeps. But now another day had dawned, and I didn't have to face nightfall again in this place.

After stuffing the truck as we had become accustomed to doing time and time again, we took off toward the Suez Canal for one last view of the big ships. As if to give us a hint that we should be going ahead and making tracks out of there, only one vessel, the *Cape America*, was in sight in the Canal. Not another ship on either horizon was to be found. Jim shot a little more video of the area and off we went into the desert.

The road trip today would take us right down to the very tip of the Sinai to a place called Sharm el Sheikh, where we were hoping to find our reservations still intact at a place called the Hilton Fayrouz Village. Unlike the drive up to Suez from Hurghada, the near scenery was that of a mostly flat sandy desert, with mountains off to the southeast in the distance. We were actually traveling down the eastern edge of the same Gulf of Suez as we had the day before, but the highway had been constructed quite a distance from the water's edge, and the sea was not visible to us for the better part of the journey.

There were a couple of places, however, that we were cautiously optimistic about locating on the way down. Still hoping against hope that we were re-entering the land of the wandering of the Israelites, and that we had some heavenly purpose for being here, we had circled them as points of interest on our map and planned to at least stop momentarily to see what we could find. We were just about to come upon the first of those two places.

Ayn Musa, which translated means "well or spring of Moses," was just off to our right. As Jim slowed the truck down, we searched diligently for any resemblance to the biblical record we had studied so thoroughly in the weeks before we began this trip and found nothing that would lead us to believe that the text had ever spoken of the place we now beheld.

These waters were nothing more than a salty marsh, common along the shores of the Gulf of Suez. Immediately we were met with the same disillusionment that hit us so hard at the beginning of our trip at the traditional Mount Sinai. First, we were disappointed at the traditional mountain. *Strike one.* Now it was the springs of Moses. *Strike two.* We had one last place to go. I looked over at Jim and read the growing sadness in his spirit, which was now written all over him in large, bold type.

Further to the south, the Wadi Feiran we were told was the traditional location where Moses struck a rock and miraculous waters came forth for the thirsty Israelites after their escape from Egypt. A rock there was said to have holes produced from the actual waters as they poured forth out of it. It was our last holdout of hope. When we passed by there and realized that the rock they spoke of was nothing more than sandstone with round fissures typically found in many of the indigenous formations, it was like a deathblow to our dreams. The traditional rock Moses struck: *Strike three*. Egypt was out!

Just before we pulled away from Feiran, Jim glanced over to me and gave me a look of resigned acceptance when he saw me biting down hard on my lip to stop the tears forming in my eyes. He spoke softly.

"Whatever's His will, Babe. Even if my overactive imagination produced that vision in the beginning, we've still had an awesome trip. And if it really was something sent to me out of Heaven, it ain't over yet."

I knew his words were true, but I couldn't help wondering what it had all meant. I began to fire off at the mouth, no longer trying to hold back my disappointment.

"But what about the rainbows? What about the snowflakes? What about Lucas finding the 20 amp fuse, and all the lights going out all over Egypt!"

I was especially puzzled about the lights business and paused to consider it before continuing my frustrated rant. Throughout out trip thus far, street lights continuously went out as we passed by them. Funny thing was they'd pop back on just as soon as we got out from under them. This had happened over and over again. It had escalated, when during an evening stroll through the shopping districts, we'd turned onto a city block and ALL the lights on the entire block went out at once! Egyptians were shouting and wondering what happened all over the street. But just like before, when we cleared the block and turned onto the next, ALL the lights came back on. I was fairly certain in my mind it must be the angelic guard above us whose power was shorting out the electric lights just over our heads! And now, trying to make me believe that was mere coincidence was just about impossible. So I continued.

"What about this feeling we've both had all along that we were being guided into something bigger than ourselves? Were *all* those things just *coincidence*?"

Jim cocked his head to one side and reached over and gently touched my face with the back of his hand. "I don't know what to think about any of that right now, my dear. All I know is that as a family vacation, this has been the most incredible thing we've ever done; we're a family again, and the time you and I have spent together has just been phenomenal! Beyond that, I have to leave it in His hands. That's all I can do."

We rode in hushed silence for a good while down the highway, lost in the multiple questions of our souls and coming up with no answers. With not much to look at, both kids were sound asleep in the back seat of the Patrol, which added to the strangely poignant serenity. The sound of the tires on the pavement and the wind blowing into our open front windows was hypnotic, and before long I felt my eyes growing heavy with sleep. Some time went by before I heard Jim speaking.

"Babe. Babe! Wake up!" The tone of Jim's voice was back to the normal optimistic man I knew so well. "Look up ahead!"

I rubbed my eyes against the glare until they adjusted and looked down the road to where we were headed. While I had been napping, the terrain had become quite mountainous, and off in the distance between the sharp peaks, the actual land tip of the Sinai Peninsula was clearly visible! Beyond that, the fabulous waters of the northern-most end of the main body of the Red Sea shone like gleaming jewels in the sunshine. I felt a surge of refreshing blast through my entire being as I drew in a deep breath of the now moist seaside air and shot a huge grin over at my husband. The cloud of despair had totally lifted, and the beach was calling out my name.

"*Yeeeeeee-hah!*" I screamed, thrusting my entire head out of my window into the airspace of the Sinai. "Man, is that *fine* or *what?*"

Jim just kept on looking straight ahead at the road in front of him, smiling and shaking his head from side to side. He knew me better than I knew myself and had full knowledge that the minute I saw the waters again, my spirit would soar up out of the murky depths of uncertainty. He had first witnessed the exhilarating effect the ocean had on my soul on the first trip we ever made together to Panama City Beach, Florida, some fourteen years ago, and he'd never, ever forgotten it: even after our wearisome seven-hour drive through the night, he'd watched with utter amazement when my eyes first glimpsed the morning waves and I suddenly threw open the door of his '61 Corvette and took off running for the water with sheer abandon. I knew he was silently wondering at this very moment just how long it would take me this time.

"Calm yourself!" He said, knowing it was pointless. "We've got to find the hotel and check in before you can fling yourself into the sea."

I knew that already. But it didn't faze the elation I felt in my heart. I knew I had to wait to get to the hotel, get everything unloaded, and settle the kids in before I could make a break for the beach. But I also knew that we had almost a whole week to do nothing but hang at the water's edge, and whatever was trying to bring me down was going to have to wait for another time.

The hotel was a series of bungalow type cottages strung out perpendicular to the beach, with all the comforts of a Caribbean resort. Although it was far too cold with the stiff wind blowing for me to actually throw myself into the water this afternoon, I determined to race down to the beach anyway and get a quick look at what we were in for.

The place had been built up against a boardwalk of sorts that ran east and west for quite a distance past this particular hotel, and both were set back from the water's edge. Numerous shops and other hotels were also built along the north side of the same pathway. Just south of the boardwalk section, the Fayrouz Village was situated on its own private beach area. It was beautifully landscaped and tastefully decorated with palm trees, patio furniture here and there, and several great sets of playground equipment for the kids. Even a mini-golf course had been built into the park! Down close to the water's edge, big puffy chaise loungers were placed in pairs, each boasting its own blue and white metal beach umbrella. Next to the loungers, Plexiglas wind screens had been placed to shield the sun bathers from the beach breezes. And last but certainly not least, a circular outdoor café and bar stood in the center of the area, with waiters scurrying out to bring drinks and food to the guests relaxing outside. I thought I had died and gone to Heaven!

Although it was getting to be late afternoon by the time we had everything settled in our room, we decided to take a stroll down the boardwalk and just let the sea breezes unwind the day's travel stress from off our shoulders. This was truly a beautiful place to be, and we were already plotting how we could come back in a warmer month and haul our good friends from Ras Tanura with us. After finding out that Sharm el Sheikh actually had an airport and that flights came and went from Cairo on a daily basis, we figured it would be a snap to come back sometime during the late spring or early summer. With snorkeling, diving, sailing, jet skiing, windsurfing, and even glass bottom boat rides available year round, we believed we'd found a paradise that would only require about a four-hour plane ride from home.

About the time we ended our walk, the sun was sinking below the mountains in the west, and it was time to find the restaurant and get something to eat for dinner. If it was anything like what we had seen thus far, we knew we were in for a real treat. And we were absolutely right. The restaurant had been built near the boardwalk as well, with huge plate glass windows looking out over the entire private beach. Inside, the whole place was set up with a tropical theme, complete with artificial palm trees and vividly colored macaws, all surrounding an enormous buffet hosting every sort of food imaginable. After a most enjoyable supper, we waddled back to our bungalow and quickly fell asleep.

CHAPTER TWENTY

Astonishing Revelations

Without the need to rise early, no wake-up call would be forthcoming to annoy my ears this morning. Even so, my brain remembered all the lovely sights I'd seen the afternoon before and was nudging me slowly but surely into conscious thought. I peeked to see if Jim was yet awake, only to find that he was not only missing from the bed, he was gone from the room. I knew that could only mean one thing, so I quickly pulled the covers up and faked sleep, and I did so just in the nick of time before he returned with the coffee!

The door creaked slowly open, and the oh-so-familiar sonnet came wafting into the room along with the delicious scent of strong, Egyptian coffee. "Coffee in the morning, coffee in the evening, coffee at breakfast time! Be my little sugar, have coffee all the tiiiiimmmmeee!" The sound of Jim's daily refrain that was so deeply ingrained in my heart worked its magical powers one more time, and I threw back the covers and stretched out my arms to give a huge good morning bear hug to the mate of my soul.

Right then it didn't matter where we were or why we were there; the only thing that mattered was that I was in his arms and my coffee was fresh and steaming on the nightstand! These simple yet precious rituals were satisfying treasures that coursed through the blood in my body. The wholeness I was beginning to feel was settling the former nightmares that had once shredded my heart. Egypt had been a safe harbor for us; a secret hiding place from the pursuit of the enemy, and this morning I knew a brand new page had turned for good.

Fortunately, even Lucas and Chelsea got up earlier than usual, ready to get down to the beach. Our eagerness was almost strong enough to push breakfast right out of our thinking, until we remembered just how good the buffet restaurant had been the night before! Last evening we had sampled every kind of German food possible, and if the cooks were that good, we were betting on a fabulous breakfast. We were shortly to confirm those suspicions.

Along about ten-thirty we were full and finally ready to make the leap out to the beach. With great anticipation off we went, arms loaded down with the things we would need to spend the day outdoors. Of course we had been hoping against hope all along that the weather at the tip of the Sinai would be a tad warmer than the more northern interior regions of Egypt, and as a result had brought all our snorkeling gear with us just in case. It made up the bulk of the items we were dragging this morning. We found a pair of empty loungers behind a windscreen just to the right of the center café and claimed them as our spot for the day.

In less than a minute, Lucas and Chelsea were at the water's edge with all their equipment. Jim and I settled down into the loungers to relax and try to let a little more of our breakfast go down. A little time went by before I reached under my chaise for my bag to extract my notebook and pen to catch up on the current trip happenings. Since the moment we pulled out from the corner of Surfboard and Seashore Drives on December 31, I had been chronicling this expedition to Egypt in great detail in my journal. It was not an uncommon thing for me to feel the need to write about such things. In fact, I'd actually been writing on my own since the age of about fourteen, when Laurie Landry, my very best girlfriend from high school and I would sit for hours and hours writing poetry and prose to phantom heartbreakers and love-makers as yet unknown. Laurie had an uncanny way of being able to convert the things she was feeling with great ease onto the written page. It always flowed out of her so freely that it was a great inspiration to me. Before we were seniors, she and I both had amassed volumes of spiral notebooks of one kind or another, filled from beginning to end with every emotion either of us had experienced or wished to. For a brief moment I let myself drift back in thought to the level of intensity

I'd been through this past year and had to laugh out loud at any other time I felt I'd been through anything at all.

But that was then. This was now. And drinking in the atmosphere at the edge of the Red Sea had me smiling.

"Mom! Mom, mom, mom! Come see! Come see the crab we caught!"

The familiar sound of Chelsea's usual rapid-fire "Mom's" was carried loudly into my ears on the brisk wind. "Come see quick! We named him Yellow Eyes. And Lucas made him a giganturous house!"

I grinned and shook my head at her choice of words, which of course she had invented in her own little head. But I couldn't blame her for her constructions of the English language. She'd been born into that equally from her Daddy's side and mine, and trying to delete that tendency from her system would just not be possible. So without any corrections, I set my journal down on the chaise and reached over to shake Jim's shoulder and try to pull him out of the deep sleep he'd fallen into.

"Huhrmpph?" He muttered as he grimaced and rolled over toward me, squinting hard in the near noonday sun. "What's up?"

"Your daughter's yelling for us to go down to the water and see a crab they just caught. She say's Lucas has built something or another. You know what that could mean. Better get the camera."

I knew from nine years of experience with this boy that his creativity had ascended heights unknown to humankind, and what we were probably about to witness on this beach would be something we'd want to have on record. And I was right.

Jim and I strolled down to where they were to find a huge sculpture rising out of the wetter sand near the water. A large pylon of sorts had been constructed on the south side next to the water to keep the tide from coming in and ruining the work; it was eerily reminiscent of the Edfu Temple we'd toured the week before. A moat had been fashioned beyond the pylon as a barrier to protect the central core structure, which turned out to be a conical rampart enclosing what looked like a window glass. Upon closer inspection, the glass was the face of Lucas's dive mask turned upward to face the sky, and running in circles below the glass we could make out the body of a tiny crab. Oh, there just wasn't a doubt in the world that *these two kids belonged to us!*

LUCAS AND HIS CRABESSEUM, SHARM EL SHEIKH, EGYPT

Lucas started explaining everything. "Dad! See all the detail? Here's the pylon—I call it the Crabesseum!"

Of course Lucas was building his work upon the stones of the ancient and aptly named Ramesseum, another mega-monument erected to the ego of Pharaoh Rameses that we had toured earlier in the trip. I don't know why this name boggled Jim's mind at all. This was bone of his own bone and flesh of his own flesh. Why in the world would this be a surprise?

After the required amount of video tape had been spent, Jim and I turned around and began to walk back toward our loungers. For a brief moment I thought I caught something flash in front of my eyes from the direction of my chaise, but I shook it off as nothing in favor of taking a short walk around the café to see what was brewing for lunch. Just as I had suspected, most anything that was fast food was available out here at the grill. Hamburgers and hot dogs, with sides of onion rings or French fries—that was all I needed to see; if the kids did get hungry, they'd be perfectly happy with this. Good thing. It was all they would be getting!

As we started back to lie in the sun, a sudden gust of wind hit the back of my head sending my long hair flailing wildly forward into my face. It was strong enough to have almost knocked me off balance, and it took me a moment to pull the hair out of my eyes so that I could once again see. And what I saw ran a cold chill up my spine.

My notebook had been caught full force by the same hard rush of wind and was presently splayed open with page after page whipping from one side over to the other. To my sheer horror I realized that just that morning I had torn out three pages of written text from the previous week that was barely decipherable so that I could replace each entry with legible text, and had left them folded inside the closed notebook. If this wind had been strong enough to open the thing and turn page after page, I feared for those torn out pages. I took off in a sprint and snatched up the notebook, praying that my careful record had not been lost. But it was no use. As I thumbed through the pages, I realized all too quickly that all my silent begging was to no avail. The pages were gone!

I screamed out to Jim; he had been following a number of steps behind me in the direction the wind had blown and was helping me search. We combed that beach for the entire next hour looking for any sign of them, but it just wasn't to be. There was nothing to do but sit back down and try with all my might to recall the details of those last few days and jot them down to the best of my memory. I was in a sad, aggravated frump now.

By the time I had finished, it was two-thirty in the afternoon and I didn't have a good feeling that I'd been able to recapture what I had previously penned on those pages. In total disgust I decided that my only recourse to cleanse myself from this evil thing was to throw myself headlong into the sea. I grabbed up my dive mask, snorkel and fins, and turned toward Jim who was already in a deep snore and said to him, frowning hard, "Hey. Hey! Wake up! I'm going down to get in the water. Since I've managed to lose everything on those three pages I may as well *drown* myself! *Bye!*"

"Hey! it's not worth this much upset! Get over it!" He had pushed himself up on one elbow now to challenge me with an aggravated retort, tempting his fate. With a sudden self-righteous indignation at having been so rudely disturbed, he shouted a zinger over the wind right back at me.

"Did I hear you say something?" I could feel my own nostrils flaring in and out, waiting for his reply. I drew back my right hand and sent my snorkel sailing end over end through the air in his direction and it clipped him squarely in his upraised shoulder. The snorkel bounced off and hit the sand hard enough to stand upright.

Jim lay back flat again, as still as a stone. The only sound he dare attempt came out as a pitiful effort to fake a snore.

"I thought you better be asleep!" I snorted in victory. But as I stomped away toward the water, I had to smile at my own self, knowing good and well he was muffling his laughter with the towel he now held tightly over his face. He just knew me oh, so well.

As soon as my big toe touched the water I knew I was in big trouble. Even though it was early afternoon, and probably the warmest temperature I could expect from late January, the water was absolutely freezing! But the fact of the matter was that I had just put on a command performance of bluster and bravado, and whimping out because of cold water was not an option I would even consider. Nonetheless, this would be no easy task. I strapped my mask on and donned my fins, and gingerly began walking backward into the icy domain.

By the time my knees were underwater I was gasping hard to catch my breath from the jolts of cold shock firing through my system like electricity along a grid. I turned, gulped in a huge breath of air, and dove straight out and under to the bottom of the sea in front of me, which had dropped off rather quickly to a depth of about eight feet. The only thing that I knew would give me an advantage in this situation would be to kick and paddle as fast as I could to work up some body heat against the drastic thermo clines. And little by little, I began to catch my breath.

Near to the beach there were two actual reefs, with an abundance of multi-colored corals and equally exotic fish. Within five minutes I had seen two huge parrot fish, two hilarious puffers, and a wide variety of wrasses, butterflies, and emperor angel fishes. The clarity of the water was the best I'd seen since our trip to the Cayman Islands in the early 1980s, and I just had to share the goods with Jim. Besides that, he had my snorkel!

"Jim! *Jiiiiiiimmmm!*" I knew I'd really have to yell from where I swam for him to hear me. I also feared that he would completely ignore me for hitting him with my snorkel. But it was a chance I would have to take.

"*Jiiiiiimmmmmmyyyyyy!*" He wasn't moving, either way. Plan B went into action, and I managed to get Lucas's attention and sent him up there to shake his Dad awake. As soon as he did, I waved wildly with my arms to get him out of his lounger and motioned that I wanted him to get in the water with me.

"The water's really not that bad once you get in!" That was the lie part; I continued on with the truth: "And you should see the corals and the fish! it looks just like Grand Cayman out here!

I knew I had him when he stopped walking to think, so I continued hopefully onward: "And when you come, bring me my snorkel, will ya?" I was praying he hadn't heard how hard my teeth were chattering.

"All right, all right. I'm coming. But it better be worth this. And I'm not bringing your evil weapon back to you just so you can hit me with it again!"

I knew better. By the time he got to the water's edge I could see the hot pink color of my snorkel, dangling out of the back pocket of his swim trunks where he'd tried to hide it. It was with supreme delight and delicious revenge for my lost journal pages that I watched him stiffen and gasp for breath as the frigid waters closed in over his shoulders.

* * *

It was nearing four-thirty before my lips began to change from royal blue back to their normal shade of rose, and I realized I was terribly thirsty. As it was getting late anyway, we decided to head on up to the room, but not before stopping at the hotel's little gift shop for a few soft drinks to take with us.

What I was about to find in that place would change our entire lives forever!

The shop was only a single room and was somewhat of a cross between a convenience store and a tourist gift shop. Even though it was small, it was jam-packed with Egyptian novelties, much as we had seen all over the rest of the country. Finally my eyes caught the cooler where the soft drinks were, right next to a rack full of chips, cookies, candy bars, and gum. "Bingo," I thought to myself, and made my way over to it. I put my choice of drink on the counter, and looked back over my shoulder to ask Jim and the kids what they wanted, only to notice a single book rack I hadn't seen upon entering that was back by the door. Jim was already standing in front of it, and I knew what he was looking for. He was still determined to find out all he possibly could about the obelisks of Egypt, and all the ways the ancients could have constructed and lifted the huge monuments into place.

"What do you want to drink?" I asked him across the room.

"Just get me whatever you get," he answered without looking up. "I think I finally found a book about obelisks!"

I put another drink on the counter for him as well as the choices for the kids, and told the clerk I would come back to pay when Jim decided whether or not he would buy the book he was looking at. My feet then moved my body across the floor to the bookshelf where I figured I'd view the same titles I'd seen a hundred times already on the Pharaohs, their Queens, and the Pyramids of Egypt. There were the exact books I had suspected, several of which we had already purchased up in Cairo. Just as I was about to divert my gaze away from the bottom shelf in disinterest, a pale orange volume much smaller in height than the rest of the books caught my eye, and I felt my entire body suddenly flush in a *tidal wave of goose bumps.*

I couldn't move at all for the space of a minute, so I just stood there gazing intently at the title that seemed so out of place among the rest of the books. *The Gold-Mines of Midian,* by R. F. Burton. Suddenly it garnered my full and complete attention. I was at a loss to understand why. There was just something about that word *Midian* that triggered a reaction deep inside my spirit—something so very familiar yet so elusive, that I couldn't quite grasp the significance of it. I reached over to pick up the book and before I could even stand up straight again, I felt myself being drawn up and out of the Hilton Fayrouz Village gift shop and backward in time to the winter of 1991 and the Happy Church of Waveland, Mississippi. As the first few fuzzy images began to clear, I saw myself sitting on a pew listening to the preacher's sermon on a Sunday night, taking notes in my notebook as I always did. As I sat there, a unexpected phrase was spoken in an audible voice into my ears only: "Harass the Midianites." The Voice was one of authority, speaking loudly and clearly, though its words were not related to the sermon.

As the remembrance tape continued in my head, I watched the puzzled look on my own face when I heard the phrase, and I remembered not knowing what in the world it meant; only that it was important enough that I should write it down.

Then, as if the fast forward button had been pressed on this spiritual VCR, I saw myself again but in a different setting. I was in the beach house of Joy Cyrulik, an ordained Assembly of God pastor with whom I had been knit together in an inseparable, eternal friendship, and who had become forever my spiritual mother in the Lord. I was asking her about the phrase and what it could possibly mean when I heard her begin to speak; her voice reached right out of that memory playing in my head and all the way to Sharm el Sheikh, Egypt, where I still stood frozen in time, staring into the book in my hands.

"Penny, Midian is the land where Moses fled when he feared that Pharaoh would take his life after he killed the Egyptian. It's the land where God appeared to him in the burning bush, darlin'—the land of Mount Sinai!"

I knew the second I heard her voice in my memory why my soul had been pre-programmed from on High with the words "Harass the Midianites." It was because this little book was a key to something far bigger than I could imagine, and had not that phrase been given from Above to puzzle my understanding, I would have never even picked *The Gold Mines of Midian* off the shelf. No! It was for such a time as this, when thousands of miles away from their point of origin, and months after they were initially spoken, the words would be brought back to my remembrance by the familiar voice I loved and trusted and would always follow. I snapped out of my inner movie, still covered in wave after wave of goose bumps, and alerted Jim.

"Jim!" I yelled out loud right there in the gift shop, though he was standing right next to me. "Look what I found!"

I thrust the book right over the top of the obelisk book he had been scanning. "*The Gold Mines of Midian*?" he wondered out loud.

I just stood there, staring up at him with a huge grin on my face and wildly excited eyes.

"Midian, Midian ..." he repeated slowly. And then it hit him. It hit him just as hard as it did me, and I looked down barely in time to see the hair on his forearms stand to attention as the same goose bumps I had been experiencing raced over him as well.

"Harass the Midianites!" he said in triumphant recall. "You heard that at church all during the war, didn't you?"

"You better know I did! We gotta get this book quick and get out of here so we can see what's in it! It has to mean something!"

I was charged with the sure realization that I really hadn't conjured in my head all the goings-on that had been, and were, taking place—even right here, and right now—with impossible precision. The odds of this being a coincidence were already becoming astronomical. A window had truly opened somehow above us in the heavenlies, and *clues* were beginning to fall out of the sky just as the impossibly identical little Star of David snowflakes had at the beginning of this trip!

We raced over to the clerk—who was surely concerned about our sanity by now with all the excited chatter coming from us at the book rack—to pay for our things and get back to the room to examine our new find. Once inside, I threw all of the items we'd drug down to the beach into a messy pile by the door, not caring a whit what it looked like, and plopped down onto the bed with the book. I discovered at the beginning that it had been written by Sir Richard Burton, the great English explorer who had set off to the land of Midian in 1877 to search for the fabled ancient gold mines that were purported to be there. As I flipped through the pages quickly, I discovered that in the back of the book was the reprint of a map that Burton himself had penned about his travels. As I began to unfold the map, the location of three little words jumped off the page at me and nearly stopped the very beating of my heart. It took me a second to catch my breath, and when I did, all I could get out was "Oh, *unbelievable*, Jim!"

My husband, hearing my cry from the bathroom where he was showering, stuck just his head out of the door and said, "What's the matter? Are you okay?"

"I'm fine, I'm fine. Get out here. You have to see this for yourself. You won't believe this!" I was trying my best to keep my act together, but my voice was coming out in wild bursts of excitement, and I couldn't control how it sounded.

Jim wrapped himself in a towel and came out and plopped down onto the bed where I was bouncing up and down. He frowned at me with one eyebrow raised and said, "Calm yourself! Calm yourself down! *What?*"

I didn't say a word, but slowly unfolded the map from the back of the book and pointed at the words "Shoreland of Midian," which were boldly emblazoned on the eastern shore of the Gulf of Aqaba, which translated in current times to *northwest Saudi Arabia*! I waited, holding my breath, to see just how long it would take him to come to the same conclusion I had. "One thousand five, one thousand six, one thousand sev ..." I counted in my head, when his own scream stopped me cold.

"Oh, NO, Penny! We've been looking in the wrong place. Mount Sinai's over there! *In Saudi Arabia!* It's really over there!"

In an instant, the room became electrified with the Presence of all things holy. We had in fact been sent on a journey of purpose; a mission yet to be fulfilled; a search we had yet to fully embark upon! Our tour had just been a tour, yet with stunning clarity and comprehension we both knew instinctively at the same moment that every little whisper we thought that we had heard on the wind had indeed been speaking to us! Every supernatural occurrence had been intricately woven by the fiery messengers of God into the days since we began to plan this trip, to prick our intrigue and plant us firmly on this pathway with a singularity of heart and soul that we would need for the enormous task that lay ahead of us! It was all real! *It was all true!* And most mind-boggling and inconceivable of all, *Jim's vision was not dead.* It was suddenly very, very much alive.

The date was January 23, 1992, *exactly four years to the very day* since our four sets of footprints touched Arabian soil together for the first time.

Lucas, Penny, and Chelsea on horseback in the Sinai Peninsula,
Sharm el Sheikh, Egypt

CHAPTER TWENTY-ONE

The Return of Signs and Wonders

How either one of us got any sleep was a mystery to me. Perhaps it was the enormity of the revelation we found ourselves sitting on. Perhaps it was just the fact that we'd been out all day on the beach and in the cold water and we were truly physically exhausted. But one thing was for certain: we had slept as though we'd been deprived of the nightly ritual of rest for days on end. It was with great effort that I forced one eye open, sensing it must surely be daylight outside, to gaze over in Jim's direction to see if the coffee-meister was up to his daily morning business.

Much to my surprise, there remained a large lump next to me in the bed, and only a minimal wandering of my right foot in his direction confirmed the fact that he'd slept every bit as hard as I had, and was in fact, still flying in the midst of what I guessed to be the exhilarating dreams of our new found knowledge. I grabbed for what appeared to be a shoulder from the top of the covers and shook it back and forth gently.

"Hey, Babe. Jim. Wake up." I didn't want to talk too loud because the lack of any other noise in the room assured me that the kids were still sleeping soundly, and for the moment, I wanted to keep it that way. "Wake up."

The covers slowly began inching their way down from the place they'd occupied over his head and stopped moving only after one big eye could peer in a Cyclops-like fashion out from under their domain. The eye slowly panned the room, purposely looking everywhere but at me, and within about five seconds I promptly pulled the pillow out from under my own head, sat up in a swift motion, and bopped Jim right in the head with it! The war was on! It didn't take him but a flashing moment to swing his entire body out from under the sheets, pinning me under the covers and rendering me instantly immobile.

"Smack me upside the head with a pillow, will you?" He asked through grinning teeth. "Now whatcha gonna do, hummmm?"

"Hide my Midian book and the map in the back so you can't find the mountain," I answered with a cool and calmly collected voice.

"Too late, Baby! I memorized it already." He said with the sneer in his voice of a five-year-old, smugly defeating an enemy.

I really had no further comeback. I knew good and well this man had already calculated, probably to the very kilometer and GPS reading, the pathway in and the pathway out of the area we were already determined to go to in northwest Saudi Arabia. And of course, it was a hollow threat to begin with. We were about to set out on the greatest adventure of our lives, and we all had to be involved for it to work.

"All right, all right, all right! You win," I said, closing my eyes and throwing my head back against the pillow with an exasperated sigh. When I felt no release from the leg lock that was holding me pinned under the covers, I opened my eyes to find his right hand balled into a fist, jammed up against his mouth and nose, and I could hear him drawing in deep breaths and letting them out again. His eyes were darting back and forth around the room without really looking at anything, and I knew I'd lost him and the morning frolic to the devious plotting of our upcoming exploration. I lay there for another minute before I broke his concentration.

"Ahem! I said, *ahem!*" This time I broke through, and he snapped out of his planning phase long enough to pay attention. "You wanna stop plotting your path long enough to let me move now?"

Like a boy caught red-handed with his hand in the cookie jar, he said, "Am I that easy to read?"

"Like a flashing neon sign, Baby. Like a flashing neon sign!"

He swung his other leg over the edge of the bed, and sat there on the side so I could then be freed to do the same. For a few minutes we just remained there silent, taking in the new morning and all the fresh revelations that seemed to be firing off one after the next.

I broke the silence gingerly. "Hey, haven't we forgotten something?" I held an invisible mug up to my empty mouth and feigned a fast series of sips.

"Whoa! I've never forgotten the coffee before!" He was astonished at himself. In less than two minutes he was dressed and out the door to the hotel lobby to retrieve the necessary elixir.

Yes, I'd say that we were just not ourselves this morning. Nor would we really ever be ourselves, that is, our former selves, again. What had connected over our heads in the Heavens would solidify into a roadmap before our very eyes, and the rest of our entire future on Earth had been established. We just didn't know it quite yet.

But it was still only January 24. We absolutely could not cross the border back into Saudi Arabia until at least January 30 to meet the required days out-of country, and it was already weighing heavily on my mind that we'd just have to be patient and wait to begin this incredible journey home. Six more days. And patience was not a virtue I possessed in any quantity measurable to modern man. I decided to ponder the situation deeper.

This was such a paradox, really. To have been so thoroughly convinced just one month ago that we would cross into Egypt and find the keys to the relics of ages there, and now, to be fully aware with a new depth of understanding, that we would have to return to the land from which we'd come to fulfill this profound destiny, was truly astonishing. I was drifting further and further into the mystique of the whole thing when the loud thumping of Jim's foot on the room door snapped me back to reality. I jumped off the bed and ran to the door to let him in with the coffee.

"So what do we do now? And how are we going to stand not leaving this moment? Don't you realize that everything we do here now is going to pale in comparison with what's up the road ahead of us? Who wants to dive the reef now? Who wants to go horseback riding in the mountains when I could be looking for the real Mount Sinai? And why is it always this way, that I have to wait?" I was overflowing at the mouth nonstop, but I couldn't help it. All I wanted to do was sling all our belongings back into that truck and drive like the wind back to Arabia.

Jim just sat quietly drinking his coffee, watching me and my tirade around the room. When I finally did stop, and disgustedly set my coffee on the table and flung myself backwards onto the bed, he then began to speak.

"The first thing we're going to do is enjoy this coffee. Then we're going to reserve those horses and ride out into the Sinai Peninsula just like we planned to do for today before all this came up. And you, my dear, are going to enjoy it, in spite of yourself! And we will with *patience*, eagerly await the next sign from Heaven that we're on the right track! Now get off the bed and pick your mug back up and snap out of it!"

He was the only person in the world who could calm me down enough to realize that we may not have all the pieces to this now rapidly forming puzzle in our hands yet. If all these things had taken place already, completely without our personal planning, then the unfolding of the remainder of the mystery would surely come right on schedule without my hurrying it up. It was truly out of our hands to control or dictate what would come next. It was our job to just stay on course—and watch.

The next hour or so was spent getting Lucas and Chelsea moving, and marching them over to the restaurant buffet and the omelet station we'd already become fond of. Although it was a chilly morning, it was still really awesome to be able to eat outside on the patio in front of the establishment, which of course overlooked the beach and the gorgeous Red Sea. The sun was sending out brilliant early morning rays across the waters already, and the peaks of the waves were sparkling profusely in that trail of sunlight. The sky was a spectacular deep blue with a sprinkling of high, wispy cirrus clouds along the far western horizon. It was going to be a beautiful day.

The stables of interest were located just across the street from the hotel entrance, and Jim had figured that it would not take long to make the necessary arrangements with the attendant of the horses. As usual, he was correct. By 11:00 A.M., we were exiting the truck and standing before the stable personnel, inquiring about the horses and the options we had available.

The stables themselves were nothing more than a ramshackle conglomeration of corrugated tin, steel, and two-by-four planks, being held together by who knew what. At various places throughout the structures, pieces of fabric, from large to small, were woven into the mix, and were presently flapping with great gusto in the stiff breeze. As far as I could tell, there were five or six separate units within the complex, which I figured must contain the horses. Almost as soon as we got out, four Egyptians emerged from one of them and came to greet us heartily, as we had come to expect them to do

"*Salaam alay-kum!*" rang out from the mouth of the one who must have been the owner or manager, as did a broad smile with precious few teeth. At almost the same time, a large and weathered hand stretched out in Jim's direction

Jim took his hand and began the vigorous shaking necessary to establish an air of trust between them, and responded with his best "*Alay-kum Salaam!* How much to ride the horses?" He asked, gesturing to the stables beyond us.

And so ensued again the time-honored tradition of bargaining back and forth that the sons of the Arabs were so adept at and enjoyed so greatly. It would not be but another few moments when their two right hands were again shaking robustly; the deal sealed and done.

While Jim had been discussing the event with the owner, I had been standing apart with Lucas and Chelsea, describing to each of them what one must do and not do concerning a horse. This would be the first time either of them had ever mounted one before, and I didn't want them to think that kicking a horse in the flanks was a good idea, as they may have seen on television. Just about the time I was finishing all my motherly warnings, Jim came over and told me the deal was done. We would have about a two-hour ride up to the mountains and back, and one of the younger Egyptians would ride with Lucas and Chelsea on his own horse to keep theirs under control. He and I would be on our own with our horses, which was perfect. This was shaping up to be a great time, and I was truly looking forward to it, even in spite of my eagerness to get back to Arabia.

It took about ten more minutes for the stable hands to saddle up the horses and get them ready. The owner then motioned for us to come on back over and nodded to the left, where five beautiful Arabian horses were being walked toward us. The younger Egyptian got Chelsea and Lucas seated high up in their saddles first, then mounted his own horse and took the reins of both theirs and his. He looked back to signal to Jim and me that it was time for each of us to swing up into the saddle. As soon as we did, he uttered a quick burst of Arabic commands and we were off.

The hooves of the horses began a rhythmic beat as they marched in unison, and the crunching sound of the crushed granite they were walking on would become a sound that I would hear beneath my own feet for years to come But I didn't know that at present. I could not even imagine what it would entail in the long run. All I knew was that it was a gorgeous day, and the wind was in my hair as I rode through a region where the ancient desert met the sea on the other side of the world from home! Just as I was about to drift into a magnificent odyssey in my mind, I heard Jim's voice coming closer rapidly, and I looked over in his direction to see what was up.

"Whoa. Whoa, *whoa*! His expression was that of a wild-eyed man who didn't quite know what to do next. He was holding the reins with one hand, and the video camera with the other, trying to steady his horse and film at the same time. In only a matter of seconds, the horse I was on turned around and raced over to Jim's, and the two began snorting and whinnying, and bucking at each other! I grabbed the reins of my horse even tighter, and clamped my legs tightly around its back, just in the nick of time to avoid being flung backward onto the ground. By this time both Jim's horse and mine were actively rearing up on their hind legs at one another, and all he and I could do was hold on for dear life!

The guide that was leading Lucas and Chelsea's horses heard the commotion and turned back at a full gallop to where we were struggling, leapt off his horse in one smooth move, and began shouting loudly in Arabic at our two horses. In moments he had both their reins and had them calmed down, and a broad smile broke over his face as he turned to Jim and I. "Madame's horse; girl horse. Mr.'s horse; boy horse. *Wajid Mishkula!*" Jim and I knew enough Arabic to understand that this was a big problem, and that it's not so good to mix a stallion and a mare on a joy ride. From that point forward, Jim had to ride up ahead of our entire group to keep the scent of my mare out of the stallion's nostrils. For the rest of the journey, that problem did not arise again.

The scenery around me was nothing short of spectacular. We were riding in a northerly direction, heading toward the high mountains in the distance that made up the first in the massive ranges that rose eventually to over 8,000 feet in the southern heart of the Sinai. The same range that we had visited at the beginning of this journey from the north side looking south: the same range that was supposed to hold the real Mount Sinai and as we were now coming to believe, didn't.

The color palate in front of me was striking to say the least, with the stark contrasts between the pinkish tan of the loose granite beneath us, the pure dark brown of the mountains ahead of us, and the deepest blue sky above the entire scene. But for us and our horses, the scene was totally devoid of any other thing, either living or man-made. There was not a bush or a shrub, a house or a vehicle to clutter the pure desolation of the picture in front of me. It was almost indescribably beautiful!

I turned around to see the view behind me and was just as taken with what I saw there. We were already ascending as if on a long, steady ramp to a higher place on the foot of the peninsula, which now afforded me a fabulous view of the electric blue-green waves of the waters to the south. I found my mind tracing a geographical map of this marvelous place on the planet, where the huge main body of the Red Sea met the tip of the relatively tiny triangular bit of land we call the Sinai Peninsula of Egypt.

Time was slowing down. In another moment, I felt it grinding to a certain halt. As the wind began to lift long strands of my hair gently around my face, all I could hear was the sound of the horse's hooves in the granite gravel again, and I succumbed to the daydreams of destiny that had been whispering in the ears of my heart since the month before this trip began. I had the sensation of being lifted in slow motion completely from my body, and taken away up to a vantage point high above the scene I was just observing, to see it all from high above, but somehow closing in fast. Right then it didn't matter that I couldn't figure it all out. The peace and contentment laced with the tingling excitement of being in a wild land on an even wilder adventure was all that mattered. I wanted to keep this frame of time frozen forever so that it could not end. I had no idea it was only just about to begin!

The horse's belly beneath me began to vibrate and I was suddenly brought back to the present when I heard the low whinny that caused the shaking. I looked up ahead of me to see that we had reached the mountains, and Jim and his horse were already up on a ridge that was readily attainable by these sure footed creatures. We all made our way up to where he was, being careful not to get our horses too close to his. When we turned around to gaze to the south, that map I'd envisioned previously was almost laid out before us! From this height, you could even see the triangle that the land made where it hit the sea! It was an exhilarating feeling, and we sat there for several minutes just taking it all in.

But the mundane and earthly has a way of making its way back into even the fondest of delightful daydreams. As the kids, their guide, and I turned our horses back down from the little ridge we'd ascended, I heard Jim calling out to me.

"Hey, Penny. Penny! I lost my lotus! My earring's missing!"

Jim had one pierced ear, and had just the day before purchased a tiny dangling Egyptian lotus of gold from the hotel jewelry shop that he was already quite fond of. A great souvenir—as prominently as the lotus flower was represented in ancient Egyptian life—and now it was not in his ear!

"You guys go ahead and start back! I'm going to get off the horse and look around a little up here on these rocks," he continued to yell.

And so it was that we began walking back toward the stables, which now appeared only as a tiny batch of dots in the distance. We covered about the space of a hundred yards when I could hear Jim's horse neighing loudly in the distance. I turned around to look up to where they were still, atop the ridge, and had to laugh right out loud! The spectacle in front of my eyes was turning into a full blown war of wills, and Jim's horse had the upper hand at present Jim had the video camera in one hand and the horse's reins in the other, and he was trying to lead the horse back in the direction we'd come from to look for the lost earring. The horse, however, had already seen that his group was heading back to the stables for food and water after the journey and was insisting on going back with us. All Jim was managing to do was turn him in circles. The horse was not going to go backward! I was beginning to hear Jim's voice shouting at the horse between the whinnies.

Inevitably, Jim was only able to make minimal progress back down the path we'd come up. We were almost back to the stables when I looked back toward the mountains and saw him finally allowing his horse to turn toward home. I dismounted as did Lucas and Chelsea, and we handed our fine steeds back to their handlers who led them to their water troughs for a much needed drink. About that time I heard a voice from the midst of the distant desert yelling, "Whoooooaaaaa!" I turned around just in time to see that Jim's horse had broken into a wild gallop and was blasting back at record speed to the stable Jim's hands were holding onto the reins for dear life, and his hair was being plastered backward by the force of the wind as the horse galloped!

"Hang on!" I yelled, hoping he could hear me. It seemed like it only took a minute for that horse to cover the ground it had taken an hour for us to cover before! Soon he roared up with gravel flying to the place where we were all standing with our mouths gaping open in awe, and Jim said with final, out-of-breath authority, "I said, *whoa!*" I knew him well enough to know that he would have to get in the last word, even if it was in an argument with a horse!

Jim jumped down from the big stallion and handed him over to the guide. "You saw what he was doing up there, huh? He wanted to go back with the rest of you. He didn't want to go the other way at all. I tried to lead him, but he kept pushing me with his neck! He actually leaned on me and pushed me! I even got it on video!"

"Well, did you find the earring?" I asked between my muffled snorts of laughter.

"No! And what's so funny?"

"I just got a picture in my head of that old movie where Conan the Barbarian punched either a horse or a camel in the face and knocked it out," I said, now beginning to giggle. "I was expecting to see you punch the horse in the nose any minute!"

By this time we were all cracking up, even Jim "I guess we can't even take a simple horse ride without some kind of event going on, huh?"

"Apparently." I answered, shaking my head and trying to get myself back under control. "You know we're going to watch that video some day and roar ..."

It was almost two o'clock by the time we got back to our hotel bungalow all dusty and thirsty from the morning's escapade. After a quick cleanup, we decided to go on down to the beach to spend the afternoon loafing in the sun and reading the *Gold Mines of Midian*. As we walked toward the boardwalk that lead down to the beach, we decided to make a quick jaunt back into the little hotel store to get some snacks and cokes for the afternoon. We entered in and I went straight to the refrigerator where the soft drinks were. I had no sooner pulled out the drinks and turned toward the potato chip rack when I heard Jim yell out my name.

"Penny. Get over here!" Jim had gone directly to the one small bookshelf where we'd found the Midian book only the day before. I put the drinks onto the counter, and bolted over to where he stood holding open an enormous book. He looked down at me with a dumbfounded look on his face, and said quietly, "It's happening again ..."

Jim slowly closed the huge volume and lowered it to where I could see the cover. *The Mountain of God*, by Immanuel Inati," I read aloud. "*The Mountain of God*? The goose-bumps were starting to run up and down my arms and legs. Does that mean what I think it means?"

"Yeah." Jim was now speaking in a hushed tone, as though spies were about that were listening to his every word. "That's *exactly* what this means. This wasn't here yesterday, Penny. I swear to you, I would never have missed this big a book with this title! We've got to get this immediately and get out of here where I can see what this is all about. But I think its further proof that Mount Sinai is *not* in the Sinai Peninsula of *Egypt*. And this is some famous archeologist saying this! Not some amateur like we are! Good grief, what in the world is going on here!"

Jim was as boggled as I was. Here it was, starting all over again. Where did this book come from? It wasn't even on an Egyptian topic! It was as out of place in this little store as the Midian book had been yesterday. And *how* did it just happen to be placed on the shelf today? Something big was going on, all right. *It was as though some giant hand was setting these things right in our path, one piece at a time, and making it impossible for us to miss.* It was almost frightening, the way these things were falling into place. I had a flash in my brain to run, and run like the wind right at that moment. But I knew that I never could. I knew that Destiny was bearing down upon us with a load that we had been created to carry, and somehow would. I turned toward the checkout, after nabbing four bags of chips, and paid for it all. Then, in overwhelmed silence, we headed down to the beach.

We spent the entire rest of the afternoon, and well into late evening, pouring over the treasures we had found in the little store. We also engineered our route into the highest mountains of northwest Saudi Arabia as Lucas and Chelsea played contentedly on the beach.

The new book Jim had found was a wealth of information about *what one should look for and expect to find* if one found the real Mount Sinai! Within the pages of this new book was an "identikit" as it were, which we would be using to help in our search once we got into those mountains.

It was also made ever so plain in this book *that the real Mount Sinai had not been truly found*, though tradition had squarely placed it in the Sinai Peninsula of Egypt. It was becoming ever more obvious to us that we were not on some personally contrived wild goose chase after all: *we were in fact, being maneuvered by the Unseen Creator of Heaven and Earth.* It was a heavy idea to grasp, and yet, felt so very, very right.

We ate an early supper at the buffet, which happened to be serving what they called "Italian night," and went to the room relatively early in the evening. With all the tremendous possibilities dancing around in our heads, we just had to shut it all down and be normal for a few minutes. Incredibly, on the television we found an old episode of *I Love Lucy* and laughed until we were worn out. The night would be a night of deep, deep sleep, and remarkable dreams.

Lucas free-diving at Ras Mohammed, Sharm el Sheikh, Egypt

CHAPTER TWENTY-TWO

The Reef at Ras Mohammed

I knew it must have been well before dawn when my eyes opened wide and the room was still pitch black. I lay there momentarily staring up at the ceiling, gathering my bearings and trying in that fuzzy morning mist in my mind to determine what day it was. Something inside me was determined that if I could just contemplate the calendar hard enough, I could speed up time and the sunrise would bring forth the momentous event of the day of our crossing back over the border into Saudi Arabia. Within less than a minute, I found my senses acutely sharp and awake, and I sat up in the bed and looked around the room as my eyes adjusted to seeing in the darkness.

Lucas and Chelsea were both still sound asleep, mostly under the covers, with only bits of tussled hair poking out from beneath the edges of each of their pillows. My eyes scanned the room as I sat there in the silence, looking over all our scattered belongings we had been living off of for almost the last month. Could this all really be happening? Could we, this little family from south Louisiana really be sitting in a bungalow on the real Red Sea, waiting to go traipsing off into the wild, untamed deserts of Arabia, seeking an elusive mountain that history had as yet, been unable to find? I shuddered at the enormity of it all and looked down at Jim, who as if by command, opened his eyes at that instant and looked directly at me.

"You been awake long?" He asked in a soft voice.

"No. I just sat up, actually. But I'm very, very alert and totally awake. It's kind of weird." I still couldn't place a reason on why I was so instantly and vibrantly awake. That usually didn't occur until after the first cup of coffee.

"Yeah, me too." Jim sat up and reached up with one hand to try and smooth his hair, which at present was angled toward me in a perfect triangle.

"Don't bother," I said quietly, breaking into a smile and reaching over to kiss him on the cheek. "The hair's hopeless until you wet it in the shower!"

"That bad, huh? Oh, well, its cold outside. I'll pull my knit cap over it." Still he tried, now with both hands, to plaster the hair down, all to no avail. He continued on in a hushed tone. "I think it's time to break out the Coleman stove and make some coffee. It's sunrise at beach time, love."

I got up and began hunting for clothes in the dark, as Jim did the same. Once he was dressed, he headed out the door and to the truck, and in a few minutes returned with the faithful camp stove and the coffee, the coffeepot, and all the fixings. The bungalow had a small patio out the back sliding glass door, and we quietly slipped out there to brew up the hot refreshment.

The patio was actually on the east side, affording us a good view of the morning sky. The icy wind hit us almost immediately, and I knew a cold front must have passed though in the night. In fact, I actually had to go back inside and find our heavier jackets. It was a while yet before dawn, as the stars were still brilliant above us against an ebony sky and the far eastern horizon was just beginning to change to a paler shade of black. There was a larger than average number of clouds spun out where we figured the sun would eventually rise, as though an artist's gray-tipped brush had floated along the line where the sea and the sky met. It was going to be a spectacular sunrise.

Once the coffee was made, we decided to go on down to where the boardwalk traced the beach, to get the best view of the upcoming dawn. Jim grabbed the video camera to capture the moment, and he narrated as we walked slowly along the path. The Big Dipper was still looming large in the sky, and oddly enough, seemed to point in the direction of Arabia. It was an item of note to us, because every morning in December we had made the journey down to the beach of the Persian Gulf and watched the sun rise, noting the position of the Big Dipper each time. It was a sort of a signpost to us, this constellation, and here it seemed to be pointing us back in the direction from whence we'd come. I noted the event in my journal, which I was now carrying with me wherever I went.

As we walked, the eastern sky began to change rapidly from pale black to deep blue, and then quickly from deep blue to a warm glowing orange. The clouds began to take on a deep gray color, with fringes of fiery brilliance around the edges. It would only be seconds before the blazing sun broke the horizon where the sea met the sky. And suddenly, there it was. It seemed somehow larger than usual, and we could actually see the huge waves of the far distant sea shadowed against the bright yellow center of the sun. The wind was now almost howling, and it was really bone chilling cold! But the sun's entry was just too magnificent to miss, and we stayed there on the boardwalk huddled together until its distorted shape that resembled the cloud of a nuclear explosion lifted off the base of the horizon and reformed itself into a perfect circle in the early morning sky.

Almost the instant it did, Jim and I looked at each other and all but raced back to the patio and the warmth of the coffee and the stove. We sat there cuddled up together on the patio chairs, sipping our second cup through chattering teeth. "Great," I finally broke the shivering silence. "And today's the day we're supposed to dive the reef?"

"Aw, come on now. It's gonna be *great!*" Jim leaned in and rubbed his nose against mine. "You know you're going to love it!"

All I could do was hold out my empty mug, which was now, with the absence of the warm coffee, frozen cold to the touch. "Feel this, I said through teeth that were now clanking loudly together. "Now if I take all these clothes off and jump in the water, this is what my skin is going to feel like. Oh, yeah, baby! I'm *really* gonna enjoy that."

"As soon as you see how fine it is underwater, you're gonna forget about how cold it is! You just wait and see." And with that final word of self-satisfied confidence, he put his coffee cup down and grabbed me up into a huge bear hug, burying my whole upper body into his chest. I closed my eyes and smiled, enveloped in the warmth of his embrace. Life was good. No, life was incredible And we hadn't seen anything yet!

But today would bring a variety of visual delicacies that would truly make an impact on all of us; sights seen from a point on the planet that was protected and left intact for all to see: the coral reefs of Ras Mohammed. This place was right at the tip of the southernmost part of the Sinai Peninsula, and was a national park of sorts for Egypt. Divers from all over the world sought to explore this underwater garden, known for its incredibly well-preserved corals and marine life. I knew that no matter how cold it was outside, we would be insane not to at least make an attempt to see what was so very close to our vicinity here. And so the plan was sealed.

We got the kids up and made it out to an earlier breakfast than the previous day, and I was determined not to eat as much as I had before. Swimming on a full stomach just never set well with me, so I restrained myself from overdoing it. Once we ate, we went back to the room and got all of our swim gear on. We completed the preparation by stepping into our sweat suits and jackets, which felt like a weird thing to be doing, to say the least! But it was entirely necessary to bundle up in such a manner with the wind whipping up a chill that could cut right though you at any moment!

From Sharm el Sheikh where our hotel was, we would follow the beach highway back toward the west for about thirty or so miles. We were now out in the wilds of the coastal plain of the Sinai again, without so much as a single building to mark the presence of mankind. That was probably a good thing, and part of the reason this underwater park remained in such pristine condition. Only the high mountains in the distance to the north and the Red Sea to the south were visible to the naked eye. It washed over me again, just how incredible this trip to Egypt had been already. The starkness of the untamed environment all but screamed out to every part of my being, and I gulped down the thrill of it in deep drafts. Here before me was the truest representation in nature that I had crossed over the very edge of civilization. And here I sat in my front row seat, just plain Penny from Baton Rouge, wife of one man and mother of two, an entire world away from all I once knew or ever dreamed I'd see. I was filled with wonder and amazement!

A little bit further down the road and I could begin to make out what appeared to be some very tall, inverted cone-like structures made out of stone in the distance on the right. As we drew closer, we found them to be the man-made markers at the entrance to the park at Ras Mohammed. Jim slowed the truck down and made the left turn that would take us right between them, and then lead us down to the very edge of the sea. A number of coves and small bays were accessible to us as visitors, and Jim drove to the very first one he saw and parked the truck as close to the water as he could.

From the moment I got out, the exquisite beauty of the place enveloped me and carried me right back into the state of profound wonder I was starting to experience quite regularly as this vacation of ours progressed. To my left, or eastward, was a wall of water-gouged rock that appeared to be about twenty feet tall, set at the edge of the flat area where we had parked. The flat area was about the size of a baseball diamond, and both it and the rock wall extended far enough out to be able to reach the edge of the water. To my right, the rest of the western edge of the Sinai was visible, and the vista took my breath away. As far as my eyes could see, the waters sparkled brilliantly against the mid-morning sun, and the coastal landscape remained uncultivated and unspoiled. The waves were breaking in a timeless, rhythmic beat on the seemingly endless shore, and coupled with the song I heard whistling on the now steady sea-breeze, I was completely enraptured.

I made my way down to the edge of the water directly in front of me, and found it to be crystal clear, with a bottom of white sand and relatively little coral or rock. One glance outward and it was obvious where the coral reef began by the difference in the shading of the waters, as well as the huge waves that were crashing on the edge of the deepest blue color. White caps and foam were being further whipped up off the crest of the breakers by the wind and were in some places actually going airborne in the strength of the gusts. But that was a hundred yards or more from the tranquility of the little cove where I stood. Only little rivulets were cascading across the surface of the water here, and I decided to park myself on the rocks and contemplate this total sensory overload.

Lucas and Jim had almost immediately opened up the back of the truck and gathered up their masks, fins, and snorkels for the inevitable plunge into what would certainly be icy water. They knew as did I that those big waves out against the horizon not only signified the edge of the reef, but represented the sure presence of an enormous drop off underwater—depths that could both thrill and terrify at the same moment! It drew them like a magnet, despite the howling, chilly wind. That prospect was calling to me as well as I watched them don their gear and slowly begin to walk backward with their fins into the water. But it was then quickly squelched by their loud *Ah-ahhhh's* as their naked skin began to feel the bitter temperature of the water. Ultimately Jim gave up the slow and steady approach, and with gritted teeth and sheer determination, made one final plunge into the sea, frantically paddling with his arms and legs in an effort to generate body heat. Lucas, who was directly beside him in the water when he made his escape, was drenched inadvertently by the strength of Jim's kicking and threw himself on into the water to get out of the wind! And so they were off.

I watched until I could barely see their heads and the kicking of their feet any longer, and knew they must have reached the reef breakers. With that, I turned my attention back to the gentle lapping of the water at my feet. I decided to pick up the video camera and record the beauty around me. Chelsea decided, upon her first glimpse of Lucas freezing as he entered the water, that a dip in the sea was not on her agenda this day. She came near to where I stood filming to wander around and search for treasures by the shore. As we meandered around, we didn't have a clue that a major drama was playing itself out just beyond our eyesight on the reef.

It wouldn't be until after I filmed the return of Lucas first, and then Jim from the far waters to those at my feet, and both were folded up in warm, dry towels and I had bandaged the torn skin on Jim's knee from the coral battering, that he began to unfold the story of their adventure. He told of their swim out there, of the pure white sandy bottom in the shallow that soon gave way to various groupings of colorful coral as the water dropped to about ten-feet deep. As he went on, he described their being over the thickest part of the reef and the profusion of marine life that inhabited this vibrantly living ecosystem.

Apparently the sheer numbers of fish and living corals were so impressive that he and Lucas were caught up in the glory of the whole event. As they worked their way down the inner edge where they could see the depth racing out from under them, they neglected to notice how far they were drifting apart from one another. But before long, the father in Jim cautioned him to put an eye on his firstborn, to keep track of his distance away from him. Jim knew that Lucas was an expert swimmer, but the great thundering of the six-to eight-foot high waves as they crashed against the reef wall was getting closer and closer, and he knew that the currents and undertows at that point would be too strong for even him to overcome. He did not want Lucas to get caught up in them, and then carried out over the outer edge where the sea bottom plummeted away from the reef wall hundreds of feet downward into the inky blackness below. As Jim surfaced and blew the air out of his snorkel to scan the horizon, a horror seized his entire being when he could not find a trace of Lucas anywhere. In fact, the horizon was lost to him completely between the enormous waves as they crested and crashed down on the reef.

In a rush of sheer adrenaline, he gulped in a tremendous volume of air until he felt as though his lungs would burst, and then plunged himself head long underwater, kicking with all his might to get far enough down to have a view of the calmer waters below the surface. Over the edge of the coral wall that stretched downward into unknown depths, he began to search desperately for Lucas. He made a rapid 360 degree scan of the area, and just as he was beginning to feel the last of the air he'd filled his lungs with recede, caught a motion out of the corner of his eye that gave him hope. A quick blast to the surface, down again he went in the direction he had detected the shadowy movement. As he drew near, he knew that the frantic prayer he had just moments ago sent up for the safety of his son had been answered. At a depth of about thirty feet, out from the edge of the wall, and directly over the great deep, there was Lucas swimming nonchalantly along with a school of large tuna, having achieved neutral buoyancy and appearing for the world as if he had no need of oxygen at all!

Jim's heart was flooded with thanksgiving and relief to see that his son was not only fine, but thoroughly enjoying himself in his favorite element on the earth. In a way, he had to marvel at the skill and expertise this mere nine-year-old boy had underwater, and the grace and fluidity he exhibited as he swam along. But out over the edge of this chasm was not the place that either of them should remain, and he was forced to get Lucas's attention to motion to him that it was time to start heading back toward the shore.

Just as Jim turned to begin the swim back in, he felt something slip from the third finger of his left hand, and watched in disbelief as his wedding ring began a shimmering dance downward toward the darkness of the deep. His mind reeled at the thought of losing that simple coral, turquoise, and sterling silver band that had been blessed by the hands of Monsignor Lester Lacassagne as he married us January 1, 1979. It was irreplaceable. Instinct drove him underwater in a flash as he tried to keep the ring in his sight, able to see it only because the surface light continued to sparkle off of it at regular intervals. Much to his despair, he watched as it began to pick up speed, faster than he could kick down toward it. It would only be moments before it would glint right out of his sight and be lost forever, or so it would seem.

His heart sank like a stone in the same waters as he looked on helplessly. What could he do when the ring was sinking faster than he could swim? But then suddenly, as though out of nowhere, an antler coral appeared on the wall in the path of the ring, and with great, wide eyes Jim Caldwell watched as it slipped right onto one of the branches and came to a halt! It was a miracle! It was an absolute miracle! Although his lungs were screaming loudly at him from lack of air, Jim felt a burst of strength that allowed him to reach the antler coral that held his ring, and he retrieved it and placed it firmly back on his own finger. He balled his hand up into a fist to keep it from falling off again, and proceeded back to where we were on the shore. And thus was the tale he told us of the drama of the morning snorkel!

I was speechless at the sequence of events he had been describing to me. First, he loses sight of Lucas, and then he finds him again. Then his wedding ring flies off and almost sinks out of sight, just to be caught by a single finger of antler coral! I shuddered for a moment at the intense battle that was still being waged against us at every turn, but I had to acknowledge that the rescues from potential disasters were coming faster than I had ever seen.

Without a doubt, we were being watched over and guarded jealously against destruction of any kind. Instead of leaving me with a breathless fright, as things of this nature would have done in the past, I felt a strange and wonderful peace overshadowing me. Psalm 91:11 came to my mind, and I spoke it out loud: *"He will give His angels charge over us, to keep us in all our ways."*

Jim looked over at me and I knew he felt the overshadowing of the same Presence I did. We sat silently in the sun for the next few minutes, absorbing the notion that Heaven was up to something big, and that we were going to find ourselves at the very center of that whirlwind.

I couldn't think on it for very long. It was just too much of an overload. Lucas and Chelsea were already beginning to get restless from sitting still in this one place, so Jim decided to load us all up and head for a more sheltered cove, where the big breakers would not be a factor. Just a kilometer or so further west and we found what appeared to be a nice spot with very calm waters. A jetty built from old concrete and broken up pavement stretched a long way out into the water, and not another living soul save us was in the vicinity. Jim pulled in as close to the shore as he could safely drive the truck and parked it again.

I don't know what finally spurred my decision to go into the water—whether it was that an hour had passed and the sun seemed to have warmed the temperature up ever so slightly, or whether it was the descriptions Jim and Lucas had been yapping about nonstop since they came up from their morning outing. Whatever it was, I found myself opening up the back of the truck and searching for my own mask, fins, and snorkel. This time it would be just Jim and me.

This beach was composed mostly of water-washed granite rock, with hardly any sand visible at the water's edge. Lucas had spied a plethora of hermit crabs moving across the crooks and crannies therein and was intent to catch them for the moment. Chelsea was still far too cold to attempt the plunge and decided to opt for the hermit crab roundup. As I made my way with my gear toward the water, I muttered a silent warning to the crabs. "Run, run! Run for your lives!" I already had a clear picture in my head of what I was surely going to find when I finished my snorkeling and came back to this shore.

But feeling sorry for the soon-to-be captive crabs was only a momentary thought. With the first step backward into the water, I let out a scream at the frigid wave that passed immediately through my foot and all the way up to my brain!

"Oh, you've got to be kidding!" I screeched out at Jim, who was a good way further into the sea than I was.

"Come on, it's not that bad," he spoke out of a sly, wicked grin. "You know you'll be mad if I see all this twice and you don't even see it once! Now come on or I'll splash you!" By this time he'd turned around to face me, and I knew by the devilish smile and the way he was looking at me that I was about to be dunked!

"Oh, no, you don't!" I managed to squeak out through chattering teeth, just before I held my breath and sat myself straight down in the water up to my neck. Even though the move nearly took my breath away, it was a better scenario than having that icy water broadcast all over my skin where the still brisk wind could hit me!

Jim just laughed and turned back toward the open sea. "Okay, then. Let's go, let's go, let's go!" I fixed my mask firmly against my face, bit down onto my snorkel, and we were off. Right away, my eyes were treated to the vast and incredible coral field just beyond my present location. As cold as my body was, the spectacle before me actually exceeded what Jim had described just this morning. I wasn't even in deep water yet, and the colors and varieties of the living corals were simply phenomenal. At first, a sandy bottom was about four feet below me as I floated along the surface. But then the impenetrable fortress of coral began to rise up from the bottom, and there was barely enough room for my body to pass above their heads without getting scraped up as I went by. For the space of about fifteen to twenty linear feet, my forward motion was severely impeded as I sought to circumnavigate the higher ones. Once past that area, however, the sea floor began to fall away sharply as did the top level of the corals, and I was free to float again and not worry about being injured. And, wow! What a paradise I found myself in the middle of!

I was soon hovering over a sea bottom depth of about twenty feet, and the profusion of fish in and around this spot was nothing short of spectacular. Though I had been scuba diving in the Cayman Islands and thought I'd seen some underwater beauty before, nothing could compare to this. In the first place, these corals were not damaged in any way. There were no broken off pieces and no pale corals that lay dying—a sure testimony to the remoteness of this area and the lack of droves of divers. Every single one was a brilliant, vivid color that looked for the world as though someone had switched on a giant black light and stuck it underwater. Interspersed throughout the corals, enormous

THE GLORIOUS UNDERWATER REEF AT RAS MOHAMMED,
SHARM EL SHEIKH, EGYPT

clams of electric blue and hot magenta were stirring up the water for passing food as I looked on. The huge sea fans closer to the bottom were waving gently with the currents as if signaling me to come on a little bit farther out, which is exactly what I did.

As I kicked my way onward, the bottom suddenly disappeared out from under my view, and I had an immediate sensation of freefalling before my brain reminded my body that I was bobbing around in the ocean, not sailing out of a skyscraper! The rush of adrenaline was intense, and the thrill that washed over me was even greater! The floral garden of corals and sea fans that I'd been focused on stretched itself further and further downward with the bottom, and the colors faded first to pale blue, then to azure, then to cobalt, sapphire and indigo. It was a rainbow of blues that culminated in a place where eyesight fails and light is absorbed into the darkness of the hidden depths. I was totally mesmerized by the scene below me.

I made several dives down to get a closer look at some of the fish, which were literally swarming about this incredibly healthy reef. I could hear the loud crunching of the massive parrot fish as they ate away at the coral beneath. Blue-green with intense red facial markings, they were one of my favorite reef fish. But by no means were they alone. Sergeant majors, angelfish, butterfly fish, emperor fish and gobies were all in abundance. Puffers and boxfish, lionfish and morays I spotted with but little effort. And beyond in the deeper waters, barracuda circled in slow, deliberate paths, flanked on occasion by the gleaming flashes of the swift darting tuna. I even had the honor of seeing a huge sea turtle slowly paddling his way across the far bottom! It was a cornucopia of life teeming underneath me, and looking back up as I began to ascend, it was as if a mirror of quicksilver had been strewn across the surface of the waters. I could feel the intensity of the living sea pulsing like an intoxicant in my veins, and I knew I would not ever have to worry that this memory would fade in my mind's eye through time.

I cleared my snorkel and poked my head back up through the water and for the first time remembered that Jim was out here somewhere with me. At first I couldn't find him, but then his head surfaced and I was able to get a bead on his location. I hung there treading water until I finally got his attention by waving my right arm wildly in the air. In moments he was headed my way. But in the brief time it took him to swim the fifty or so yards that separated us, I realized that my entire body was beginning to shake and my teeth were beginning to chatter uncontrollably. It was most unfortunate, considering what I had just seen, but I was going to have to get out of this water. It felt as though it had just run down from a glacier. As Jim came up alongside me, I told him I was going to have to go in.

He decided to stay on a little while longer to take some underwater photographs, so he sent me back with a message for Lucas to come on out and see the sights at this location. Lucas was by this time bored with his hermit crab chase, and as I neared the shore, I could see him gearing up to go into the water all on his own. I didn't have to tell him anything.

I knew that getting out of the water was going to be dreadfully cold, especially when the wind hit my now wet and shivering body, but there was no avoiding it. With one radical move I ripped off my fins, threw them onto the shore with my mask and snorkel, and took off running for the truck where I knew a large beach towel awaited me. It was only after I was safely wrapped up in it and sheltered from the wind that I made my way over to a spot on the beach where Chelsea sat with her swimsuit bottoms on and a sweatshirt on top. I knew already what I would see when I got there, just like I did before I got into the water.

"Whatcha got there," I asked in feigned wonder as I gazed down at her.

"Hermit crabs. Lucas has been catching them all this time. He's making me guard them and not let them escape!" Her voice had just the slightest hint of imposition laced in it, as she reached over to grab one of the crustaceans that was trying in vain to exit the rock pit Lucas had them all cornered in. I bit my lip to keep from laughing and searched her beautiful little face intently. Her gigantic blue eyes looked right back up at me, and within a minute's time, her face screwed itself up into full blown indignation, the same tone I thought I'd heard in her voice before.

"No fair!" She wailed through her frown. "Why do I have to watch these stupid crabs?"

It was all I could do to keep from roaring right then and there, but I knew her well enough to know that doing so would stoke up that furnace of injustice cooking inside her, and then she'd fold up her arms, snort, and be in a mad stew at me for the rest of the day. It was a far better idea for me to just take over the dreaded crab duty from her and set her free to do other things.

"Okay, Boogie. I'll watch over the hermit crabs for you. You can go play!" I smiled at her and watched as the mad melted right off her face, and she jumped up from where she'd been stationed by her tyrannical brother and began to sing as she skipped along the water's edge away from me. It never ceased to amaze me just how quick she could go from all bent-out-of-shape-mad to glad-again, as long as she got her way. Over the years, I would see that with her, some things would never, ever change.

It wasn't long before I realized why this job had been so aggravating to her. Lucas had about thirty hermit crabs stashed in a natural depression in the rock, and at least every twenty to thirty seconds, another one would make a run for the edge and try to escape. I didn't know hermit crabs could scurry so quickly, but they sure could! I was also well aware that my son would be intensely hacked off if he came back up from his snorkeling session and all his hard caught crabs were missing! But luck would be on my side this day, for he and Jim could not take but a few more minutes in the cold water, and were soon kicking their way back in. After greeting them with towels at the shore, I marched him over to the crab pit and stationed him there to watch his own prisoners! And because hunger and cold had just about taken their toll on us all, it wasn't long before we were all packed up and ready to leave. Our final video taken of the spot would mark a parade of hermit crabs staging a revolt and escaping in a single, massive jailbreak from the grips of the dictator king, Lucas.

By the time we got back to the bungalow, Lucas and Chelsea had already fallen asleep in the back of the truck. It had been a very physically active day so far, and they didn't even put up a fight when I told them they should lie down for a while once we were inside. Jim and I piled into the other bed and turned on the television, hoping to find anything that wasn't an Arabic channel playing at this time of the afternoon. As Jim panned through the eight or so channels available, his mouth and mine fell open at just about the same time as we heard the ever-so-recognizable "Soi-tun-lee" of Curly Joe from the Three Stooges!

I couldn't believe my eyes! One of my all-time favorites just happened to be playing right then! Now that was lucky! While the kids slept on for the next two hours, Jim and I laughed our heads off at the bungling comics. It was great! And it lasted just long enough for the kids to be refreshed, and the time for the evening meals to begin at the hotel buffet. The night had been advertised as "India" night, and we were really looking forward to that.

As it turned out, the food was just as good as we had expected. We stuffed ourselves again far too much and had a very hard time staying awake until the 9:00 P.M. deadline when the underwater photographs Jim had taken earlier in the day were. developed and ready to be picked up. As soon as the clock struck nine, we headed over to the little photo shop and paid for our pictures, then brought them back to the room. After a very quick look through each packet, we all but dove headlong into the bed. Jim began snoring almost immediately, and I felt myself drifting quickly off, levitating somewhere out there over multi-colored corals and deep blue seas.

CHAPTER TWENTY-THREE

The Battle Intensifies

I could sense a tugging at my consciousness coming from somewhere, but my brain just wasn't awake enough to register whatever it was that was trying to tear me out of the dream-sea I'd been sailing upon. I closed my eyes harder against the onslaught, but years of repetition had doomed that resistance to failure, as my ears now sent the signal racing to my mind that what I was hearing was in fact, the coffee song: "Beee my little sugar, have spoffees all the timmmmmmmmmmme!" It was all my mind could catch, as I forced my eyes open and groped for the mug I knew was somewhere in my general vicinity. Jim must have had mercy on my ever-so-groggy condition and grabbed my searching hand and placed the cup securely in it. My eyes had already closed again by the time I got it to my mouth and downed a huge gulp, which I knew for sure I'd need plenty more of this morning. It was all I could do to keep myself from falling back over in the bed, coffee and all, and I wondered what in the world about snorkeling in ice water could have this big an effect on me!

"I can't wake uuuup!" I whined as I struggled to keep from spilling the coffee all over the bed.

"Just drink up, my dear," Jim replied to my pitiful outburst. "Drink up, and you'll be waking up directly."

I managed to get one eye partially open, and looked over at him questioningly. "Why in the world am I so out of it this morning?"

"Because we not only spent half the day in the freezing cold water, which intensifies your exertion level; but then we snorked out on all the Indian food and put ourselves into a virtual coma! That's why."

I knew he was exactly right. I'd forgotten about all the Indian food. A long lost memory of late nights spent pigging out at a Mexican restaurant called "El Palacio's" in Baton Rouge crept back into my fuzzy head at that moment, and I remembered how vivid my dreams would be and how much of a fog I'd be in the morning after we ate there. "Palacio-syndrome" was all I had to say.

Jim grinned and nodded in absolute agreement. "Now you get it," he said, lifting his own mug up to his lips.

It would take three huge mugs of coffee to even give me the energy necessary to get out of the bed at all. I was really moving like my blood had been replaced by molasses. As I slowly lifted one leg and then the other over the side of the bed to get up and head for the bathroom, a thought hit me that opened my eyes up wide, if only for a moment.

"What's today?" I turned around and asked Jim.

"The twenty-sixth. Why?"

"Yay!" A brief rush of adrenaline hit my brain as I thought for sure it was the day we could leave to return to Nuweiba and begin our trip back to Saudi Arabia. "We get to leave today!"

"Not so fast, babe. I'm not sure of that. I have to count up my L-days on the calendar." Jim did not project nearly the enthusiasm I thought he should, and I frowned at him without saying a word as I continued on into the bathroom to brush my teeth. When I emerged a few minutes later, the look on his face told me everything I didn't want to hear.

"Oh, come on! Have you lost your mind? We have to stay another day before we can even head back up to the El Sayadin? You've got to be joking, right?"

I had gone from groggy, to exhilarated, to thoroughly outraged in a matter of ten minutes. (And I wondered where Chelsea got it from!)

"Look, I can't help this, Penny. Go see for yourself! I have to stay out of the country until I use up my L-days to be legal, and there's nothing I can do about it. We can't leave until tomorrow!"

I felt the hair beginning to stand up on the back of my neck as I heard his words. Oh, I knew what he was saying was accurate, all right; but what microscopic patience I'd had before had been burned long ago up in my eagerness to get on with this expedition back home. I stood entirely still as the first waves of a perfectly nasty mood came crashing over my bow, and I did absolutely nothing to even attempt to prevent them.

"Well, fine!" I said as I spun around and marched back into the bathroom. "I'm taking my shower!" I slammed the door behind me hard enough to make my point exceptionally clear. I turned the water on as hot as I could stand it, partly for my own comfort, and mostly to try and use it all up so that Jim would have none for his own shower. I spat out the items of my discontent all over the bathroom as I scrubbed down, and then it hit me that something else must be at play inside this bungalow. Why in the world had I so quickly and easily turned on Jim, as though it was his fault that the calendar said what it did? I toyed with the thought for only a second before the anger crept back in and over-ruled the mini-revelation.

"No!" I said out loud, still in the shower. "We could leave and at least go back as far as Nuweiba! But nooooo! You just want to stay here another day. And of course we have to do what youuuu want!" I continued my snide remarks as though Jim could hear me in there, chewing off his head.

I finished up in the bathroom after some time and ripped open the door, gruffly brushing past him as he sat on a chair next to the bed. He had all of our road maps spread out there, along with some of the NOAA maps we'd been carrying with us as well. "Hey, babe, look at this," he said without taking his eyes off the map. "This is a current day map. Get a load of what this reads."

Not wanting to appear interested at all, yet unavoidably pricked by the thought of another new piece to the puzzle, I grudgingly looked over his shoulder without saying a word.

"Look at this," he continued. "See this area of northwest Arabia? They still call it Midian!" The chill bumps started running up and down my arms as my eyes found the spot he was referring to on the map. There, in rather large type, intentionally covering quite a big chunk of the northwest were the letters M-a-d-y-a-n! Madyan! Spelled just slightly differently, but pronounced in Arabic in exactly the same

PENNY WRITING IN HER JOURNAL ON THE BEACH AT
SHARM EL SHEIKH, EGYPT

manner, Jim had found yet another absolute fact that had been staring us in the face all this time, yet not uncovered until just now!

It was fascinating to continue to find these clues to the mystery unfolding right before our eyes, but this new bit of information just made me all the more anxious to get out of the place we were presently staying. And it served to frustrate me all the more that Jim was not willing to leave Sharm el Sheikh and get on back to Nuweiba. He had tried to reason with me that this place offered so much more for the kids to do, and so much better restaurants and shops than did our next stop down the highway. But I would hear none of it, even though he was right on those details. I wanted to go, and that was that, and I was getting more aggravated by the minute that he wouldn't budge.

"Well, I'm hungry, Penny, and so are the kids. Let's go on down to breakfast. I know you want to leave, and so do I. But we can't, and I'm not, so that's it. Now get over it, and let's have a good day. We'll do some shopping." His words were meant to tempt me with the thought of buying some Sinai souvenirs, and while that did spark a way to salvage my already ruined day, I sure wasn't going to let him know that. I sulked along behind the whole crew as we walked from the room to the buffet.

But it was hard to stay in a bad mood in this environment. The day had dawned gorgeous, and not quite as chilly as the previous one. A few white wisps of high clouds danced along the jet stream above, and the crisp breeze was already flirting with my hair. I shoved it out of my eyes and tried to maintain my huff, but it was not working. The rush of the wind and the clean, clear air had already settled down over me, along with the sounds of the water lapping at the shore. After living all these years, I still didn't have a clue as to what magical thing the seashore really did to me,. All I knew was that it was playing with the very primal nature of my being as it always did, and a wide smile broke out across my face in spite of myself. I felt the tension physically lifting right off of my shoulders, and by the time we entered the restaurant, I was a changed person.

The breakfast was just as good and plenteous as it had been on the days before this one, and once again I left the place feeling like I'd eaten way too much. But with no reef to swim and no horses to ride today, I was not nearly so concerned as I was just plain stuffed. As we rounded the turn walking back to the bungalow, the guilt of my morning actions overcame me and I held Jim back a moment to apologize.

"Hey, I don't know what got into me this morning. I'm sorry for acting like such a brat. I am just having such a hard time waiting this thing out, you know?"

Jim smiled down at me and grabbed me up into his arms in a monster hug, squeezed me tightly, then released me again. "Accepted. Now let's go buy stuff."

After a brief room visit, we headed out with Egyptian pounds in hand to visit the shops up and down the boardwalk once more, but this time with intent. I had been eyeballing an adorable skirt that I'd seen another of the hotel guests wearing all that week so far, and really wanted one for myself. It was a short skirt with two layers of sassy ruffles, and it had not escaped my recognition that it had turned Jim's head a few times already since we'd been there. I walked straight into the store where I'd seen it, and promptly bought two of them; a red one and a lavender one. Each was imprinted with the Hilton Sharm el Sheikh logo, and they would remain an excellent reminder of this time spent here for years to come.

In another shop not far from this one, we both had laid our eyes on some huge beach towels that were embroidered with only the word, "SINAI." That already meant to us our quest for the real mountain and not the peninsula, so we grabbed two in a hot chartreuse color and paid the owner for them.

One more shop full of beach gear beckoned me in, where I found two pair of Roman-like lace up sandals that came all the way up to the knee. It was a must for me, and I knew they'd look adorable with my new skirts! Into my shopping bag they went, and back out onto the boardwalk we marched.

By the time we were finished it was noon, and we grabbed a lunch snack from one of the fast food eateries along the way. This whole strip of hotels, restaurants, and shops was so absolutely inviting that we decided to go back to the room, grab the video camera, and make every sales pitch possible to our friends back in Ras Tanura to all come back here together when the weather turned warm again, and we could spend more time in that spectacular water. Eventually, we just about videoed the entire area, including several of the hotels, until the shadows grew long and the sun began to sink low in the west. The onset of evening was fast approaching, and a little girl and her stomach were beginning to get restless.

"Mom ... Mom, Mom, Mom! I'm starving! It's been *hours* since I ate! When are we going to the other hotel for supper? Can't we go now, huh? Can't we?" As fast as she was whining she was tugging on my jacket. "When can we go? *Please* let's go now!"

Already having anticipated this familiar ritual, Jim had made plans to take us back out of the shoreline town of Sharm el Sheikh, and up to a sister hotel of ours called the Residence. It was back to the west and up on a high cliff overlooking the sea, but at a much greater distance than our coastal resort was. Just as the sun was beginning to disappear completely from our view, we drove up into the parking lot of the establishment, and headed straight for the evening buffet.

This dining room was even larger than the one at the Hilton Fayrouz Village, though we could not have imagined that to be possible before seeing this one! On a number of extended tables was laid out before us the most sumptuous buffet we had yet seen to date! Instead of having a theme night with a particular country's food featured, as our own hotel had been doing, this one was large enough to have an entire table filled with the delicacies of each different country all in one night! There was a table filled with French food, one with Italian food, one with German food, one with American food, and of course one filled with Middle Eastern dishes. And then there were the dessert tables! Attached to each of the theme tables was a smaller one, covered with the main desserts of each country. It was almost ridiculous, in a way, to see so much food in once place at one time. But it was also a marvelous opportunity to sample a great many things we'd never tried before. I knew before it was over with that I'd be waddling out of this place too!

We spent nearly the next two hours leisurely consuming the feast, as it were, fit for a king! We couldn't have enjoyed ourselves any more, save for the one item that at first we saw as efficiency, but rapidly turned into a major irritation. The wait staff was abundant and excessively eager to remove each plate we were eating off of the moment we scooped up our last forkful into our mouths. It was as though they sprang forth out of nowhere to snatch the china right out from under our noses, almost before we were finished! After a while, as my plate became less and less full, I would search the room over to be sure there was no one hovering over me like a buzzard, waiting to descend upon road kill. I could feel the mood I'd started the morning out with beginning to knock at my consciousness again, and I was very soon more than ready to get up and walk out. Even Jim was becoming ruffled as the plates whizzed out from under his hands, and he finally motioned for the dinner bill so that we could be on our way.

As we left, darkness had set in and the floodlights from the hotel were blazing forth. We chose to walk down a different pathway back to the truck and found ourselves entering a playground we had not noticed on coming in earlier. Right away, Lucas spied a most unusual and creative outdoor activity. An enormous checkerboard in white and black had been painted on the concrete, and chess pieces the size of my kids were scattered about on the squares! For the next half hour we had a ball trying to move these huge game pieces about the board, marveling at the genius somebody had to envision such an activity out of doors! Another memory was made that was unique to our Egyptian adventure.

By the time we pulled up to the bungalow back at our own Hilton, it was nearly ten o'clock, and my head was beginning to hurt really badly. It was long past time for me to turn myself in and try to sleep off this gnawing feeling that was beginning to creep over me that something somewhere was very much out of whack. I pulled the covers over my head and fell into a deep, dark sleep.

Much of the night I spent tossing and turning in a fitful attempt to rest. It was most unusual for me to be so troubled that I couldn't sleep, especially on this vacation. But when morning came, all I could feel was worn out and upset, both mentally and physically. I had hoped to awaken thrilled that today was the day we would head back to Nuweiba, and I could really plan our visit to the highest mountain of northwest Arabia, which Jim had already determined was a mountain called Jebel al Lawz. But what I felt as I opened my eyes was not the least bit exciting. In fact, it was an intense sensation of dread that I could feel washing over me.

Lucas and Chelsea were still asleep, and Jim was missing from the bed, so I figured he would be back momentarily with the coffee. As if on cue, the door swung open and in he came, cheerily singing the coffee song. One look at the joy in his morning face and I decided, at least for the moment, to keep this weird mood of mine to myself. We drank down two cups, read our daily devotional, and tried to ready ourselves for what lay ahead.

Jim began to tell me of all his plans for the secret jaunt into the Jebel Lawz region of Arabia. He had already decided to approach the area from the south, and just travel the mountain range until we got up to the highest peak, which is where the book *The Mountain of God* had shown this particular mountain to be. The more he unfolded his ideas, the more unstable I felt my stomach becoming. I couldn't hide my face from him any longer, as he noticed the lines forming across my forehead and finally stopped and asked, "What's wrong?"

I looked down at the floor and said nothing for a moment, but then raised my head and looked him directly in the eyes and said, "I don't know, but something sure seems to be. I didn't sleep a wink last night, and to top that off I had bad dreams when I did! I'm just really, really uneasy, and I don't know why! I've been waiting to leave here all week!"

Jim's eyes narrowed and his face got very serious. "You can't even put a direction on it? Do you think something's happened to your Dad or something like that?" We always thought of my Daddy first, because he had been fighting heart trouble since a major heart attack almost killed him in 1989.

"No, I don't think its coming from back home—but I really can't be sure. I just can't figure it out, but it's growing stronger by the minute, and I don't like it at all!" It seemed like the more I spoke it out, the worse it got. "Look, let's just get the kids up and go eat breakfast. Maybe it'll subside."

And so we did. But sitting at the buffet, which had become a favorite morning routine already, was making me all the more anxious, so much so that I couldn't even eat. Jim finally put his fork down and told me to go on back to the room and call Saudi Arabia to see if something had happened. We had given our friends all our itinerary for this trip we were on, and our families in the U.S. knew to call them if they needed to contact us. It was a great relief to me that Jim was allowing this long distance call, because we both were well aware that it was going to cost us a fortune from Egypt. We'd already been told that it sometimes took four or more hours just to get a phone call connected back to the U.S. I was hoping since Saudi Arabia was much closer, that it would not take that long.

I took the key from Jim and with heart racing, headed back to the room. I really didn't realize just how upset I was until I tried to get the key into the lock and my hand was shaking so badly I couldn't get it into the keyhole! I actually had to take my left hand and steady my right with it to get the key to go in! This was a signal to me that I was really, really out of whack. I was not at all the nervous type, nor did I become upset for just any little thing. No, this was definitely not me!

Once I got into the room, I raced over to the phone between the beds and called the operator for instructions on how to dial out to Saudi. I was relieved to hear that it was usually a rather immediate connection there, as opposed to a call all the way back to the states. So I punched in the numbers to my girlfriend's home, and within about two minutes, had her on the phone. I had braced myself to hear that she'd received a call from my parents or Jim's mom, and that something disastrous had taken place; even to the point of someone having died. When she cheerily told me she'd received no such call, and that all was perfectly well with our home in Arabia, I was completely baffled. Greatly comforted, mind you, just totally baffled. I hung up the phone with her and sat on the bed shaking my head in bewilderment.

What was this feeling that I just couldn't shake? What was the anxiety I feeling at every angle? It was as though I myself had become a conduit antenna, and I was picking up signals of deeply disturbed spiritual energy from somewhere. I just could not for the life of me place it. But the butterflies in my stomach were settling down ever so slightly at the reassurance that no one had called in from the states with bad news. I determined in my mind to try and enjoy the day anyway, for it was January 27 at last, and our final day in Sharm el Sheikh, Egypt.

I rejoined my family at the restaurant and was actually able to eat a bit, which I had not been able to do at all before. Jim was extremely happy that I was doing somewhat better, and he decided that we should stay on until about three or four o'clock to enjoy the last vestiges of this wonderful place. I was not immediately happy about that, because everything inside me was screaming to get out of there and head back to Nuweiba as soon as possible, but I was too tired from the lack of sleep and the anxiety to argue any more. After hearing that nothing was wrong back in the U.S. or in Arabia, I was beginning to think I was just losing my mind. I could no longer trust my instincts to leave and leave quickly, even though I still felt we should go. The battle raging inside me had not subsided in the spirit realm one iota, but in the long run, it was Jim's plan that stood.

THE STARK MOUNTAINS OF THE SINAI PENINSULA
ON THE WAY TO NUWEIBA, EGYPT

CHAPTER TWENTY-FOUR

One Last Way Mark

I t was four o'clock in the afternoon when we pulled away from Sharm el Sheikh and finally began making our way back up the Sinai Peninsula to the same city we'd first entered in Egypt some twenty-five days ago. A hush of unreality was hanging over me like a thick fog that rolls into a coastal town, stifling the ability to see clearly and making any definite assessment of the road ahead impossible. And yet, just as soon as we pulled away from the civilized areas that marked the edge of the town, I found my spirit soaring to be out in the wild, mountainous desert climate once again. It was such a paradox, this tug of war going on inside me!

The landscape was the same beautiful combination of stark contrasts that the drive down the western shore of the Sinai against the Gulf of Suez had been, and I rolled down my window to breathe in the sounds of the wind and the highway as we sped along northward toward Nuweiba. It would only take us about two hours to get there, and I would have to start telling this final frontier of Egypt goodbye. My mind was so flooded with emotion that I couldn't stop the tears from rolling down my cheeks, and as before, I purposely turned my head away toward my window to keep Jim from seeing me cry. There were no words I could utter that could describe what Egypt had meant to us; no words written that could capture the enchantment this ancient land had been used of God to produce. I was suddenly filled with the sadness of having to leave it behind me, and the surety that I would have to now face whatever lay in store ahead. After all the past days of impatience to leave Egypt, now that I was, I didn't want to at all. Once again, I felt the war raging inside me.

Watching the gorgeous colors on the mountains dissolve in the deepening shadows of late afternoon, it occurred to me that this piece of land called the Sinai Peninsula was not nearly big enough for a million-plus Hebrew people to wander around in for forty long years! It was a sudden revelation—a moment of clarity—where so much emotion had been choking off all common sense. If we could drive this land in just a matter of a few short hours from bottom to top, how in the world could the many children of Israel have been lost in it for so long? It seemed to me that the front end of the line of people would of a necessity be touching the back end before they could cover the entire place! I filed it as one more vivid reality proving that we were *not* in the land of Midian where the mountain of the Lord was supposed to be.

By six o'clock that evening, we were on the last leg of the journey toward Nuweiba, and I saw the big curve to the right coming up on the highway. This right curve would begin a long, gradual drop in elevation back down to sea level, and would take us back through Wadi Watir and directly through the huge gorge that led to the Gulf of Aqaba. The mountains were looking higher and higher as the road went down, and they became closer and closer to the edge of the asphalt the nearer we got to the gorge. It was a unique landscape unlike any other we'd seen up and down the peninsula, because strangely enough, the gorge opened out onto a rather large beach head, upon which Nuweiba was built. The geological formation of the region made it almost impossible for a beach to be found anywhere along the western shore of the Gulf of Aqaba, because the high mountains literally touched the sea. All except right there at Nuweiba!

As we continued through the gorge, we could now see the waters of the Gulf of Aqaba gleaming out in front of us, and knew we'd made it all the way back to the place this Egyptian adventure had actually begun. All the initial trouble we had in customs that had threatened to ruin our trip at the onset seemed but a trifle now compared to the rich glory of all the things we'd seen and what had happened to us all along the way. It had been well, well worth everything we endured at the beginning, to have experienced everything since that time. I felt the tears welling up in my eyes again.

Just a few more minutes and we were turning in to the El Sayadin Village, just as we had before at the start of this trip. But we would find out seconds later that this would not be the same as that first entry at all. In fact, nothing in our lives would ever be the same again.

Ziyad Taleeb, the same Egyptian hotel manager and blessed soul that had helped us in the beginning to get our truck out of impound at customs, was pacing the ground back and forth in front of the hotel. Just as we made the turn through the gates of the establishment, he dropped what I was sure were two cigarettes down to the dirt below, stamped them out, and literally ran over to where we were with an enormous smile on his face. As we disembarked from the vehicle, Taleeb all but swarmed each of us with greetings and hugs, and what I soon sensed was intensely nervous chatter. I sent a glance over the hood of the truck to Jim, who caught my drift right away and put his spiritual antennas on. As we headed for the lobby of the hotel, I noticed that Taleeb pulled Jim aside and I could just barely make out the words, "… must speak privately with you!"

A chill raced through my being, and I wondered what in the world could possibly happen now. Had our paperwork been rejected? Were all the original problems we had with the tryp-tyche going to come back to haunt us now? Worse yet, would we even be allowed to leave Egypt? I was almost hyperventilating at the possible scenarios of doom that peppered my brain right then. Taleeb led us into the lobby, where he continued his ear-to-ear grins in front of me and the children, and sat us all down. He got the kids Cokes, and Jim and I our favored Turkish coffee. He had remembered what we all wanted from our first trip through here and that impressed me. But that little item was not at all strong enough to replace the tension that had my stomach tied up in knots right then. I knew something was going on, and it was creeping over me slowly that the weirdness I had started picking up on at Sharm el Sheikh could have been pointing to what was happening here in front of me now.

I noticed that Taleeb kept looking over to Jim, waiting for a moment where he could get him separated from the rest of us and outside the lobby. I also was not at all eased by the steady stream of cigarettes that

Taleeb was lighting, one right off of another. I nearly dropped my teeth when he disappeared from the room for a brief time and re-emerged with a cigarette in his mouth, a cigarette in one hand and a half empty bottle of Vodka in the other! I shot a desperate look over at Jim, who could stand the tension no longer and motioned for Taleeb to head outside with him.

Fortunately for us, the place seemed almost as deserted as it had the first time we'd been through here, and I didn't have another soul save Lucas and Chelsea to have to entertain in the lobby. The two long sofas were positioned in an L-shape, and I sat down on the edge of the one facing the large picture window looking outside so that I could see what was going on with Taleeb and Jim. I had a perfect view of them as they walked over to our truck and Taleeb began to speak. His back was directly toward me, and I could see Jim's face easily because of how much taller he was than Taleeb. It seemed that he had not been speaking for more than a minute when I noticed Jim gulp visibly, and I thought for the life of me that I could actually see the color draining right out of his face. In just another second, I could have sworn I saw his knees buckle, and he literally swung his hands backward against the truck to keep himself from falling down.

I felt as though my heart had just stopped beating inside my chest. I gasped in a breath and realized I must have been holding it for the length of time this had been going on. I just knew something awful had taken place, or that we were in deep, deep trouble with the Egyptian government because of our tremendous problems with paperwork at the beginning of this trip!

Jim steadied himself and shook his head hard, as if to knock whatever this newfound information was off him. Taleeb was looking around now to see if anyone else had heard what he'd been saying, and promptly lit the fifth cigarette I'd seen him light since he took Jim outside. He turned the bottle of Vodka upside down at his lips, took a long swig, and then turned back toward us and the door to the lobby, with Jim staggering right behind him. I could see Taleeb purposefully change his facial expression as he entered the room, and once again the big smiles were all we were allowed to see.

Jim, on the other hand, was looking right over Taleeb's head behind him as he walked, and shot a face over at me that I would never in a million years forget! He greatly exaggerated his facial muscles as he mouthed the words, "YOU WON'T BELIEVE THIS!" When Taleeb turned and Jim thought he may be able to see him out of the corner of his eye, he straightened up his face instantly and replaced the contortions with a broad, calm smile.

I was about to have a fit to know what was going on. The plot would thicken substantially as I got up and walked with them to the counter, and Taleeb handed us the key to their best suite, only charging us for the amount of their smallest room. I could barely contain myself, but Jim's expression let me know in no uncertain terms that I was not to know anything—at least until we got into the room in private. By now I was smiling and playing completely along.

As though on cue, the dread I'd been feeling unexpectedly broke and it felt like a physical hand actually touched my neck and grabbed the fog of fear off my heart and soul! I was overcome with gigantic goose bumps all over my body! Up and down and up and down, my emotions and feelings had been on a roller coaster for the last two days, and I was about to see clearly why. I was acutely aware now that a massive clash of both gleaming angelic warriors sent from Heaven and hideous, twisted demonic figures sent from the depths of the black abyss must have been battling it out in the airspaces above our heads for the past year! But whatever resistance the dark side had put up to destroy us and keep us out of this tremendous plan of God had just been severed for good by the final, fatal swing of the glittering, unconquerable sword of an Archangel! These events were about to reveal the very reason Jim and I had been created and joined together in the first place, and why every force in hell below had tried to take us out before such a time as we could understand it.

We gave a quick "see ya later" to Taleeb, and headed down to the suite we'd been given for the next two nights, while we awaited the calendar to hit January 30 so that we could cross back into Arabia. Jim had no sooner turned the key than I shoved the door in, and all of us with it.

"What? What, what, what!" I screamed out at him, unable to contain myself any longer.

"Whoa, Babe! You won't believe it!" He all but fell down on the sofa as he spoke. "Taleeb's sitting on a huge secret! Apparently there was a guy here, who's trying to get into Saudi Arabia. Taleeb didn't really give me the details very clearly, but get this: the guy says Mount Sinai's in Arabia, just like we think! And, we just missed him by about four hours! He's been here for days trying to get a visa into Saudi, but he can't, and he had to leave already."

My face was numb and expressionless. All I could do was sit there, staring into Jim's face with my mouth wide open. Here we had been pre-programmed all these weeks and months to get to the real Mount Sinai, and had even plotted our course up to a mountain called Jebel al Lawz just last week, and we get back to Nuweiba to find out that someone else believed the mountain was there as well! I was searching for any words to speak when Jim began again: I told Taleeb I had to get y'all into the room, so let's go get all the luggage and stuff you need. Then I'm going back to talk to him again. He says he has something to show me." Jim got up and started to walk toward the door, but swung around and looked directly at me with a warning. "By the way, he made me swear and promise I wouldn't tell even you about this. I don't know why it's got to be so secretive, but he's really, really nervous about it all. You know nothing, got that?"

I instantaneously put on a zombie-like stare, and bleared my eyes at Jim while extending both my arms straight out in front of me and repeated after him like a parrot, "I know nothing!" But it couldn't have been a bigger lie.

Abruptly, like the sudden and catastrophic breaking of a dam or the un-predicted eruption of a once sleeping volcano, I felt like I knew everything! I knew now why the past year had been so difficult! I knew now why so much evil had broken loose against us! I knew now why Jim had the vision he did, and why we saw all the signs we did coming over here! It was actually, literally true! We were being sent by God Almighty to the real Mount Sinai, and hell had just lost its greatest bid to keep us out!

I hurriedly followed Jim out the door and back around to the front of the hotel where the truck still held all our belongings. We were able to snatch up in one trip the things I needed for each of us for that night in the room. The adrenaline was pumping in my veins and Jim's as we thought about the possibilities, yet all we would allow ourselves to do was pass wild-eyed looks back and forth until we were safely back inside the room again. Once there, Jim dropped the suitcases and all but flew out the door.

I found myself jabbering incessantly to Lucas and Chelsea about nothing and about everything as I sought out the pajamas and the toothbrushes we would all need later that evening. The excitement was just too great inside me, and I was staggering with the reality of the connections that were hitting me one by one, like enormous oceanic waves rolling in a steady and rhythmic procession as they crashed upon my mind's shore. It was just too much to comprehend, yet it felt as natural as breathing. I shook my head quickly back and forth to disperse some of the intense energy I was feeling at that moment, just before Jim came sailing back through the door.

His eyes did not meet mine; not even for a second, and for a fleeting moment the fear I'd experienced before tried to squirm back inside my head. But it vanished in an instant when I heard him say, "Pen! Pencil! Anything to write with! Paper! Don't say anything!"

I scrambled to my notebook that I'd been journaling in for this entire trip and ripped out a page, grabbing up a pen that was nearby and threw them over to Jim. He grabbed them both out of mid-air, slammed the paper down onto the coffee table, and immediately began to sketch something he'd apparently just been shown. I watched as though spellbound, the picture that began to form in front of my eyes.

The rough sketch was done in a matter of seconds. Jim had concentrated all his efforts on memorizing something Taleeb had apparently shown him minutes before now had just reproduced it again. From what I could make out, the picture showed a mountain that stood in the background, with a stick tree between two slabs of rock located at its peak. Somewhere below that formation was a circle that must have represented a cave of some sort. Toward the bottom of the drawing there were several stacks of what appeared to be stone piles that were sort of circular in nature, and similar in size and shape to one another. There was also what looked like two long, cylindrical columns lying across one another, just behind the stacks of stones. Noted on the far bottom left were the words, "twelve cows." And finally, a lone, winding line that seemed like it must be a track of sorts, coming into this picture to the right of the mountain with the tree on top. I sat there all but breathless as I awaited Jim's explanation!

I could tell Jim was studying this reproduction with great detail to make certain it matched the item he must have just seen. As for me, I was trying to get a grip on just what I was looking at. Was it a map? Was it a picture? I puzzled for a minute or so to weigh both ideas in my mind before I finally decided that it really wasn't a map, but a collection of ruins and geographical features as to what should be at the mountain. The only line that could be considered a road was the single one that went from the mountain off to the right side of the page. As I continued looking, Jim began to speak in a very determined yet very soft whisper.

"When I was with Taleeb, he pulled out what looked like a napkin with this drawn on it. He told me that it had been left for him by the guy that was here. When I reached over to hold it so I could bring it closer to see it better, he immediately snatched it out of my reach, and told me I couldn't touch it! So I'm a little bit worried. Dear Lord, I hope I've remembered it all!" He sighed heavily, and frowned.

"Hey, don't stop now! What else?" I was already on pins and needles, and I couldn't wait for the whole story!

"Well, he said the guy wanted him to go into Arabia and shoot some photographs of these things for him! The reason Taleeb is going on and on, and gave us this room and everything else, is that he wants me to get him into Saudi Arabia!"

I had to interrupt him right then. "You? How on earth could you get him into the country? They barely let us get back in every time we leave, much less if we're hauling an Egyptian with us!"

"Like I could do that anyway! I'm not sure he understands that I can't get him a visa! Only the government issues visas! Anyhow, I told him that, and so then he comes up with this other plan. He wants me to go into this place, get the pictures for him, and then bring them developed to his brother in Tabuk. Then his brother can get them to him, and he can get them back to this guy. Oh, and by the way, he won't tell me who this man is!"

By this time, the enormity of this thing that had settled upon us earlier had reached the depths of our innermost understanding, and what had been before just a dreamy, wild vision suddenly took upon itself a living, breathing reality! This little scene that Jim had painstakingly tried to remember and re-sketch from a napkin that Taleeb had not even let him touch was like a *way mark* of old from a somehow familiar ancestral boundary! It was the final sign in a supernatural sequence that had been unfolding in perfect order since Jim had decided to safeguard his little family away in Egypt over a month before! Our charge now stood out like a lighthouse beacon, crisp and clear, and we knew a stamp of approval had been forever sealed on the decision we'd made back at Sharm el Sheikh to get ourselves as fast as we could to the mountain in Saudi Arabia called Jebel al Lawz!

A single verse of the Bible from the prophet Jeremiah was now flowing incessantly through my consciousness: "Set thee up way marks, make thee high heaps: set thine heart toward the highway, even the way which thou wentest: turn again, O virgin of Israel, turn again to these thy cities" (Jeremiah 31:21). We would indeed be returning again to the land from whence we had come!

JIM WITH THE COLEMAN STOVE ON THE PATIO OF THE EL SAYADIN VILLAGE,
NUWEIBA BEACH, EGYPT

CHAPTER TWENTY-FIVE

T-Minus 48 Hours and Counting

My eyes opened to almost complete darkness. I lay there just staring in the direction of the ceiling for a moment, trying to get my bearings. As my eyes began to adjust, conscious thought began a faint knocking somewhere in the background of my mind, and it occurred to me that I was lying in a bed in a hotel. That much established, I rolled my head over to the right to see if Jim was awake yet, but I couldn't quite see well enough to tell. Figuring that it would take just a minute to focus, like it had with the rest of the room, I just held the stare, waiting for clarity to set in. The sudden flash of his pearly white teeth in a wide grin confirmed that sleep had fled the premises.

"Good morning," he whispered, as his smile deepened.

"Mornin'," I whispered back, but I wasn't smiling. "Now I'm worried."

"What? Already? Before daylight? What's wrong?"

"We just woke up. That means we've been asleep. And that means that this wild unimaginable adventure that's coming back full force into my brain right now must have just been a dream!" I rolled over onto my right side got within inches of his face, and said, "Tell me it's not a dream. Go on, tell me. And mean it!"

Out from under the covers came his big hands and he placed one on each side of my face and held them there, looking directly into my

277

eyes. "Penny, this is not a dream. Listen to me, Babe. I'm serious. And here's the proof. Not even you and I can concoct something this big and interconnected! And you know that!"

I let the words sink in and stick, pondered them but for a second, and broke into a smile to match his own. "You're right, you know. Not even we could have conjured this up!"

"See? Logic dictates that this is all totally supernatural and miraculous."

I leaned back from him against the pillow, stupefied. "*Logic* says this is miraculous? In whose world does logic claim that miracles even exist?"

"In the world we'll wind up sharing all-that's-happened-to-us with, that's whose world."

That was a sudden revelation that brought the serious back into the bedroom. Share it with? Now that was a brand new concept. We had no idea that, with the passage of time, we would be quite literally broadcasting all this around the globe! But lying there in that bed in the darkness, we just weren't capable of handling that yet. I wasn't all too sure we ever would be. I ran quickly back in my mind to the familiar and the traditional for safety.

"Where's my spoffees?" It was a mere whisper, but one powerful enough to shoot Jim straight up off the bed and send him scrambling to find his clothes. He found his pants and managed to get one leg into one side of them before he stopped and turned back toward me, now sitting upright in the bed with the covers pulled up to my shoulders.

"What?" I asked.

"There's no place to go get any here until seven o'clock when the restaurant opens." He puzzled for a moment, and then I was absolutely certain I actually saw the light bulb appear over his head and turn on as the idea hit him. "The Coleman stove! Of course! Get your clothes on! We're going outside to make the spoffees, and watch the sun come up over the mountains of Midian."

He didn't have to tell me twice. I threw off the covers, slid off the bed, and began to feel around for a lumpy pile on the floor, which was what I was remembering had happened to my clothes the night before. I found them without any trouble at all and was actually finished dressing before Jim was. But I knew that it was going to be very chilly outside, and we would probably face a pretty stiff wind coming off the Gulf of Aqaba, which would necessitate our sneaking around in the next room where Lucas and Chelsea were asleep to find our coats and caps. I really didn't want to go there, but we had no choice. Fortunately, we had not unpacked the bag with the cold weather gear in it, and I motioned to Jim to just bring the whole thing into the bedroom and we could deal with finding the stuff in there without disturbing the kids.

The battle plan for the spoffees was already written in Jim's mind. He sat me down and relayed the step-by-step procedure like a good drill sergeant, and then beckoned me to the back door of the suite, and out we went! The first blast of the wind, which was even stronger than I imagined it would be, nearly caused us both to lose our breath! It was cold, and I mean icy cold, and I immediately wondered if a cold front boundary had passed through here during the night. This was the kind of cold we'd first felt weeks ago when we spent the night in the desert and were surprised and astonished to witness the snow the next day! I shot a glance upward to scan the horizon for clouds, but it was as sharp and crystal clear as any pre-dawn sky I'd ever seen. The stars were just beginning to fade slightly from view, but what planets were visible were blazing forth brilliantly with a steady light. The sky's twinkle factor was tremendous this morning, and I just stood still in my tracks, stunned by the magnificent view.

Jim snapped me out of my stare skyward by grabbing my coat at the elbow and dragging me forward. "It ain't gonna make itself, my dear," he said, speaking of the dark liquid I was now starting to twitch for.

"Yeah, yeah, but do you see how sparkly they all are this morning? I couldn't help myself."

"They'll look even more spectacular when I am looking out at them from behind a steaming hot cup of spoffees! Come on."

I knew he was right, and dutifully followed him down the sidewalk that skirted the back of all the rooms and led eventually out to the parking lot where our faithful old truck sat resting in the cold. As I walked along, I still couldn't quite believe what was happening to us. I allowed my mind the luxury of thinking of it only for the space of time it would take to get to the truck. Then I snapped it off and went into prep mode, lest the drill sergeant return to Jim Caldwell's body.

In no time we had gathered up the old green Coleman stove, the pot for the water, the cups and the coffee, the sweetener and the powdered creamer, and were making the long trek back down the sidewalk, now beginning to visibly shake in the biting wind. But it wouldn't take long for the water to boil, and soon we'd be relishing the fantastic aroma of our sure addiction!

Out the back door of the suite, a small patio was situated with about a three-foot high wall that had been constructed to enclose the area. It was here we decided to set up the stove and await the sunrise. From this spot we had a perfect and unobstructed view of the Gulf of Aqaba as well as the mountains to our south, and then east across the waters to Arabia. Jim fired up the burner, and we settled back in the chairs to take it all in.

The sky was changing moment to moment as it always does when the dawn is imminent. The outline of the high ridge on the far shore was becoming more apparent now, as the first few bits of color began to filter through the atmosphere and the night sky started losing its grip to the dawn. I looked over at Jim to see him staring intently away to the east, and by the flint set of his jaw, knew in his mind he was already driving up to the foot of the mountain that had managed to elude us thus far. I held my eyes there on his face, trying to pick his thoughts.

The sound of the burner on the stove was the only thing audible, save for the rushing and ebbing of the wind that was oh, so cold! It seemed that it would play around that patio in a swirling circular motion, like a sprinkling of mini-whirlwinds dancing on a tiny stage; and when it did, the pitch of the blue flame would rise and fall as though seeking a voice with which to speak. It was another of the long list of memories I filed away and vowed to never, ever forget, for it seemed to me that once more, time was slowing down and perhaps even headed to a point of cessation altogether. I still just couldn't wrap my logical brain around any of this. So I shook my head quickly from side to side, shook off the dreamy and the mystical, and said, "Burrrrrrrr," as loudly as I dared with respect for the time of day.

Jim whirled around and shook his head back and forth just like I'd done! I laughed aloud at how scarily alike our thinking was becoming.

"Had to shake it off, huh!" I said with a grin. "I know what you were thinking. So don't say a word. Just get that spoffee poured, and start singing. I'm turning purple over here!"

Jim reached over with trembling hands and filled both our cups with the wonderful liquid, then went through his personal routine of blending sugar substitutes and creamers to his own satisfaction. He finally stirred the mixtures until a rapid whirlpool could be seen from the top of each mug, and motioned for me to come quickly and stand over the cups for a surprise.

"What?" I asked with true curiosity.

"Watch and you'll see. Any second now, a little boat of creamer's gonna pop up and go sailing round and round the top!"

I looked at him like he had lost his mind and was just about to accuse him of being insane, when suddenly, just as he had predicted, a teaspoon-sized blob of creamer popped up like a bobbing cork, and followed the current round and round the mug! My mouth fell open, and I just stood there, amazed. One glance back at Jim and his smug, toothy grin was about all I could take.

"Aren't you supposed to be singing me something about now!" I protested in defeat. And immediately, the sweet strands of the spoffee song began wafting through the crisp, morning air.

We sat there enjoying several refills as we watched the sun break the barrier of the Arabian mountains, and rise like a round, smoldering furnace over the face of the Sinai. We squeezed every moment we could out of this dawn, knowing that just the day beyond the morrow, our trip to Egypt would be an item of history. Somehow, as eager as I was to get back into Arabia and onto the original adventure again, I was feeling a reluctance to leave this Egyptian sanctuary. Something wonderful had taken place inside us on these ancient sands, and I knew instinctively such a time as this comes once in a person's lifetime.

But there was no time to spend being misty-eyed today. There were too many preparations to be made with what lay ahead of us. Now that the sun was up, and three cups of coffee had filled our insides, it was time to clean up the mess and get ready for whatever was next. And for the immediate future, that probably meant heading back to the room to wake up the kids and readying ourselves to be at the hotel's kitchen when it opened for breakfast on this day, January 28, 1992.

When we all finally sat down at the table, a heavy sense of *deja vu* came over me as I looked out of the windows facing the Gulf of Aqaba. Had it already been a month since we'd been seated here before and watched with wonder and amazement as that crazy funnel cloud had dipped down out of the clouds three times in succession in exactly the same place? I was just about to remind Jim of that strange phenomenon when it hit me like a runaway freight locomotive, roaring down the tracks at ninety miles an hour!

"Jim! The funnel cloud! Remember? The one that came down three times, in the same place, hovered, and went back up? Look! *That's what it was over!*" I pointed at the Saudi shore, to a specific series of peaks that were the highest there that we could see. "Could it have been pointing to the place we were supposed to be going? Could it have been trying to tell us something before we ever even got to the traditional Mount Sinai at St. Katherine's?"

I was beside myself in astonished realization, and every hair on my arms was standing straight up as though they'd been combed that way with super glue! Jim's eyes got bigger and bigger as he gazed out across the expanse of waters, then back at me.

"Whoa, Babe. You're right! That's exactly what it was pointing to! That biggest one, just there," and he pointed toward the mountains. "The one with the two big dips on the top—kind of like two gigantic feet stood there and left an imprint. Let's just call it Foot Mountain, so we'll know which one we mean when we talk about it. Oh, it's true!"

Even after the food was brought out to us; even after we'd completely annihilated every morsel and every crumb from every plate; even after we'd complimented the staff and the workers extensively for their great food and service, we could not tear ourselves away from the row of windows that had once again revealed the answer to a puzzle, a mystery that had been set before us. It was as though the finger of God in those crazy funnel clouds had tried to tell us in the beginning where he was trying to lead us, where the real Mount Sinai was to be found! The real mountain of God, as it was called, had been there *in Saudi Arabia* all along—a sacred monument, concealed, the truth veiled behind centuries of incorrect or lying assumptions about another vacuous location. But the time for the Lord of Glory to expose that deception was upon us, now!

As the time of concealment slipped away, something new had begun to count down on another prophetic timepiece—in a perfect progression of events in the unseen world above our heads. We had entered the season of revelation of the hidden; truth would soon come to the light. And we knew that we knew that somehow the secrets of the past would all be made manifest as a *foundation for the future*.

The revelation had purpose.

The vision that had started this whole trip, the purpose of the supernatural manifestations that had led us, were all becoming more accessible and real. This was no cleverly devised tale of our own imagination! This was all genuine and true.

The heavenly maneuverings of the past month had been both extreme and remarkable, but at long last the purpose of God had arrived at its launching pad. Like a colossal Saturn V rocket, it was fueled to its limits and securely locked into place. The rocket, staffed and on ready, awaited the ticking down of seconds on the clock at Mission Control.

Tensely the world awaited the lift-off.

It was T-minus 48 hours and counting.

Chelsea and Lucas on the paddleboat at the El Sayadin,
Nuweiba, Egypt

CHAPTER TWENTY-SIX

On the Beach at Nuweiba

After breakfast we continued to sit there at the cleared table in almost complete silence, still too awestruck to carry on any worthwhile conversation. But the quiet was about to be shattered by the sounds of a young boy and a young girl, arguing loudly with an adult male in Arabic, getting closer and closer to our vicinity. I looked up to see who was coming and was greeted by the tremendous smiles of Taleeb, who had both of his kids in tow. Jalal and Jameela were just about the same age as Lucas and Chelsea and dropped all hint of discontent with Taleeb when they saw that other children were about! It didn't take them long to scamper off to one of the other empty tables and begin their attempts at communication with one another.

Taleeb treated us with warm friendship, and wanted to know how our sleep had been, as well as our morning meal. We told him we were perfectly satisfied, much to his contentment. And then, as if another personality took him over completely, he leaned over the table near to our faces, became extraordinarily serious, and began to whisper.

"This guy who was here. I will tell you now. This one is called Ron Wyatt. He has the white hair and beard. And he talks about the big boat a lot, too."

Jim and I looked at each other. "Boat? What boat?" I asked Taleeb.

"You know this one. The story—the two and two animals, and the old guy, he builds the big boat. Noo-eh, I think. Yes, Noo-eh."

"Noah's Ark? Is this what you mean?" Jim blurted out.

"Aiwa! Yes, yes! This one! This man, he say he find Noo-eh boat, too."

Something began to prick away at the memory banks in the back of my mind. Jim had been given a gift of a VHS taped copy of a television program he became very interested in and studied closely back in November of 1990. On the show a man was talking about the possible finding of Noah's Ark and even showed a replica of what he thought the thing would have looked like. But I couldn't remember exactly what he looked like, nor could I recall his name.

About that time, one of the wait staff came into the dining room looking for Taleeb to inform him that he had a telephone call at the desk. He excused himself from us and went away to take the call.

"Hey, do you remember that tape about Noah's Ark you got last November?" I kept my voice low enough so as not to allow anyone but Jim to hear. "Didn't that guy have white hair and a white beard? I'm having a hard time remembering it clearly, but I think he did. But I can't remember his name at all."

Jim puzzled for a moment before saying, "Yeah, I remember that guy. He did have the white hair and beard. But I don't remember his name either. You think that could be the guy that was here just yesterday?"

"I don't know. But Taleeb says he was going on about Noah's Ark. It could be, I guess. Man, alive, would that just be too bizarre."

Jim looked at me with a very strange look on his face. "Wait a minute! You do realize that I downloaded the VHS copy of that show onto one of my Hi-8 tapes to get it back into Saudi Arabia, don't you? I might still have that copy, and it could be here with us."

As a way to save money, Jim had made it a practice to re-use the expensive Hi-8 tapes the camera required over and over again, after downloading whatever the current event was onto VHS format. He would then simply film over the old event with the new. He'd been doing that very thing the entire time we were in Egypt.

"Are you telling me that after almost a month in this place that you still have tape left that you haven't written over with Egypt trip footage?"

"I think there's just one left. But I know I've copied over part of it already. I just wonder if that's the single that had the show on it, or if I've already overwritten that one."

Both of us shoved our chairs out from under the table at the same time, and it made such a loud racket that it startled the table full of kids, still trying to make their tiny bits of mutually understood English and Arabic understandable to one another.

Jim turned toward them and said, "Hey guys, we're just going back to the room to get the camera. Y'all wait for us here. We'll be right back."

We blasted back to the room as fast as our legs could carry us. Jim grabbed up the video camera bag there, and back out the door we flew, back to the same table in the dining room where we'd been sitting just a couple of minutes ago. The only tape that Jim had not rewritten over completely was inside the camera. He took it out and examined it to find, much to his dismay, that only about half of the tape had not yet been re-used. The odds that this half of the last remaining tape would contain that old program he'd placed on it over a year ago were astronomical. After all, he'd been choosing them at random from the bag. But this had already proven to be a vacation unlike any other we'd ever experienced, and the seemingly impossible was just not so far out of reach any longer.

Taleeb came walking back toward us just as Jim was telling me he needed to see if the hotel had a TV with video outputs so that he could hook up the camera's cable and view what remained on the tape. Taleeb heard him and led us into a side room off the dining area, where a big screen TV was sitting across from a couple of sofas. It seemed to have the hook ups Jim needed, but after about an hour of futile labor, he gave it up.

We gathered up all the camera gear and headed back to the room. Jim decided that if he had to look through the eyepiece as the tape played to view it, it would be far better in our room where we could pull the heavy curtains and block out the bright sunshine completely. Even though he wouldn't be able to have any audio this way and would not be able to hear the man's name, if he did happen to find a shot of the guy we could show it to Taleeb to see if he recognized him. And that would work.

By this time the kids were all getting restless and wanted to get out to the beach to play. I spent the next few minutes getting Lucas and Chelsea dressed warmly enough for playing on the beach, which lay just beyond the patio. I went with them, sucking in a deep breath of the clear, clean air and enjoying the scent of the sea I loved so much. I just had to linger there for a short time, taking in the gentle lapping of the waves against the shore. But once I saw that the kids were happily walking down the edge of the water, kicking rocks and picking up shells, I turned my attention back to my husband and the task he presently had at hand. I had only to open the door and look over at his face for the affirmative answer I'd hoped and prayed for. It was written all over the dimples and grins glaring back at me.

"No!" I said with disbelief.

"Oh yeah, baby! We got it!" Jim was beside himself at our good fortune.

"Are you going to sit there with your grinnin' self and tell me that the show with that guy on it survived and just happened to be on the one remaining tape you hadn't reused? Are you kidding me?"

"Here. Come see for yourself." Jim turned the camera around so that the eyepiece was facing me and punched the play button while handing it over.

The first few seconds of video I saw was from the day before, from our trip back up to Nuweiba from Sharm el Sheikh. But then the screen flickered, and changed abruptly to a scene where two men were sitting across from one another, and the model of a large boat sat on a table between them. The camera then zoomed in on a white-haired gentleman with a white beard, and I knew we had him, just as Jim had said! I felt the smile break out wide on my face!

"This has to be the guy," I said to Jim as I handed the camera back to him.

"Yeah, I bet it is." Jim just sat there, staring a hole in the camera. "Shall we locate Taleeb?" And back out the door again we went, evidence in hand, looking for a match to a mystery we had no idea was just beginning.

Taleeb was occupied as we found him at the hotel desk and could not come just then to see what we were so eager to show him. So we went back into the dining room where the wonderful windows faced both the eastern beach and the southern beach where the kids were, and waited for Taleeb to finish. It didn't take him very long, and as he made the turn from the lobby into the dining room, Jalal and Jameela joined him again. By the time he reached the table, Jim had the camera turned toward him and he handed it over in anticipation of just what we would learn.

Taleeb closed one eye shut to view what the tiny screen would show him, and all at once began speaking rapid-fire Arabic to Jalal and Jameela. His one free hand began to wave wildly in the air, and then he held the camera down to each of them, one at a time, and they too began to speak the same. After about one full minute of watching the tape run, he sat down in the chair next to Jim and fired off at the mouth nonstop, but at least in English this time.

"How do you know this man? *This is him!* This is the man. He was just here, and how is he on your camera?"

Taleeb was becoming more and more excited, and lit up a cigarette and began to take long, deep drags on it. He continued asking us questions, but wouldn't give us a chance to get in a word of reply! Finally, he stopped, and Jim tried to explain to him how we had come into possession of the tape. How much of it he actually understood, we did not know. But the one thing Jim was determined to make him comprehend was that we did *not* know this man named Ron Wyatt; that we had never met him before, and that which was happening here around us was very, very unusual!

And apparently Taleeb did understand that part. He jumped up and left us sitting at the table and headed back up to the front of the hotel, only to return in less than a minute—with another cigarette he had just lit off the other one in one hand, and a new bottle of Vodka in the other. All this and it was only eleven o'clock in the morning! What was going on?

Now Taleeb was visibly nervous again, just as he had been the day before. We were sure he knew much more than he was telling us, but there was no point in trying to get anything else out of him before he was ready. I was certain I could see the cogs turning in his head as he fought with himself internally, trying to determine what he would say next. Apparently, the secretive side of him won the battle, because the next words out of his mouth had nothing whatsoever to do with the wild revelations of the morning. He put the cigarette down that he had smoked to the very filter and a most friendly and hospitable smile spread across his face.

"Let's go outside," he remarked in a much more normal tone of voice. "It's a beautiful day, and it's warmed up a lot, and the kids are all on the beach. We should be with them, and I'll have the cook prepare us all a feast for the lunch time. I will have made for you more special foods of Egypt!" And with that he stood, motioning for us to go before him to the cabanas on the beach. As we rose and headed toward the door, I made a mental note that he'd left the Vodka bottle on the table.

True to his word, Taleeb had a feast prepared for us out on the beach. As a dish would be prepared, he had instructed the kitchen to send it out hot and fresh as opposed to waiting for all the food to come out at one time. With each arrival, Taleeb would tell us what we were eating along with the history of the dish. It was a wonderful learning experience, taught first hand by this Egyptian who seemed to be an expert at cuisine! I was ever so happy that hardly any other guests were visiting the hotel at this time of the year, because Taleeb had the ability to spend so much time with us as a result. We adults and the four kids sat out on that beach, eating and visiting for the remainder of the entire day. It was not until sundown that we said our good-nights and made our way back across the sand to the room.

Although we were mentally overwhelmed at the events that seemed to be breaking, we had been completely relaxed for the majority of the day and been treated like royalty. The sea breezes had indeed warmed as the day progressed, and we had been lulled into a state of marvelous content. After tucking Lucas and Chelsea into their beds, we headed back to our room to do the same.

Just as I closed my eyes, and was about to drift off into that heavenly dream state, I thought I sensed something tangible above our heads. It was nothing visible, yet it was so very perceptible to my spirit. I leaned back against Jim and asked, "Do you sense something up there?" motioning toward the ceiling.

"Uh-huh. I do. And it's something good, Babe. It's something to cover us and prepare us for what's about to happen." If only we could have seen into the Spirit realm just then, we would have known that a *mantle of authority* was being draped down upon the two of us. And we would have known that we were certainly going to need it.

* * *

I guess I was so tired that I didn't even remember falling asleep. The first cognizant thought I recognized as I opened my eyes to the new morning was that I could actually see inside the room, which meant we had slept right through the dawn and into the early morning. This in itself was an unusual thing; most of this trip we'd been awake to catch the sunrise regularly. Jim was still snoring lightly with each breath, so I knew he was still asleep. And there was not a sound coming from the other room, so Lucas and Chelsea were also both still dozing. I decided to close my eyes again, and just let the rhythm of Jim's breathing send me back into dreamland. It would be another hour before we woke up for good, and by that time it was already late enough to get coffee from the hotel's kitchen!

As it turned out, we would spend almost the entire day and early evening on the beach. Taleeb saw to it that our meals were brought out to us to enjoy on the outdoor tables, just as he'd done the day before. Lucas and Chelsea, along with Jalal and Jameela, spent their time alternating between the paddle boats in the water and various sand castle activities. The weather had been picture perfect all day, with the temperature rising a bit from the cold we'd experienced the past several days, and the sky as clear as crystal.

But as the late afternoon progressed, a stiff wind arose from the west, and long lines of steel gray clouds began swiftly moving across the sky from northwest to southeast, over toward the mountains of Saudi Arabia. The sea began to form white caps on the crest of the waves, and before an hour had passed, they had risen to a height of six to eight feet.

We found ourselves in the midst of a full blown gale. Not even a tiny patch of the formerly glorious blue sky could hold its own against the onslaught of this storm front. My heart began to pound as I remembered that tomorrow I would have to face another trip across the Gulf of Aqaba on the Jimy Z Arab Bridge Ferry. I could feel the fear trying to creep into my brain almost immediately, and I shook hard against the wind to try and dislodge it from whispering its nightmarish scenarios in my ears. It was ultimately only the sound of the laughter of children that snatched me out of its terrifying threats of death.

Lucas and Chelsea, along with Jalal and Jameela, had taken several large beach umbrellas and turned them over sideways against the wind, lodging them against the bench of one of the picnic tables. This formed a marvelous wind block for them under the table, and they had a full blown fortress in the making. They were each smiling and working together to build their shelter against the elements.

As I looked at them, a revelation hit my brain and my spirit at the same time, and sent the creepy sensation that evil had been trying to plant deep within me sailing out into the water. Here was a perfect picture of how I should be, just as these dear children were. The storm was gathering strength, and yet in the midst of the howling wind and rising seas, the children were playing contentedly against all odds. No worries, no fears, and no gnashing of teeth. Just simple trust. They knew of a certainty that nothing would happen to them, because we were there to protect them and preserve them through whatever may come their way.

I sat myself down on the opposite bench from where they had the umbrellas stationed and leaned over to peek under the table from a close angle. I peered over at Lucas, who was having the time of his life!

"Hey, Lucas! Son! Aren't you cold?" I asked him, knowing for sure that he must be with no shirt on and only his swim trunks. "Don't you want to come inside?"

Lucas looked up from his work stabilizing the umbrella shaft, frowned hard and said, "Mom! No! I'm not cold at all. And this is the best fun! It's great out here now! Why would I want to go in?"

I turned to Chelsea, who was scooping shovelfuls of sand into a mountainous pile under the table. "Boogie, how about you? Do you want to go in now?"

Chelsea just kept right on shoveling sand, and said, "Nope! I'm not going in! I like it under here."

I felt a smile breaking out across my face. The lesson was simple, yet profound. I just knew it would become the central core, the ever-holding anchor of everything my family would experience in the years to come. In the midst of a howling maelstrom, I would learn to retain an inner calm. I would learn that there was always either a way of escape from the danger provided, or a shelter through the storm. That was a promise of God! And I would somehow be given the strength I needed to stand up tall again and march with my head held high, even right up a rickety old ferry plank and back onto the Jimy Z for a second time! Hurricane, or not, my ship was *not* going down!

"Well, okay then." I said to the kids. "You guys can stay out here until dark, and then we'll go inside and get us something to eat."

"Yayyyyyyyy!" Came the immediate cheers from under the picnic table.

And with that, I got up from the table and turned headlong into the wind, letting it hit me full blast right in the face! My hair streamed out behind me, whipping about in the chaotic gusts like so many individual tornadoes. It felt magnificent! In a moment I was invigorated and refreshed with a tremendous sense of excitement! I felt a strange and wonderful power coursing from my innermost being out to the very tips of my toes and my fingers, and I knew I was back!

I began to search the beach for Jim, who had walked down to look over at the foreign shore with his binoculars prior to my investigations of the kids and their fortress. The dusk had settled in enough to make it hard to see in the distance, and I couldn't spot him in either direction. Just as I was about to turn again and head out to find him, I felt two hands from behind me descend on my shoulders, and the warmth of a face against my right ear.

"You're always best on a beach with the wind in your hair, aren't you?" He turned me around and looked me full in the face.

"Well, yes, now that I'm me again!" I answered him with a big smile.

"You know tomorrow is the day! Tomorrow we leave to go back to the land we left to come here to find what we should have been looking for where we came from."

"What did you just say?" I asked in disbelief.

"We left Arabia to go to Egypt to find my vision in a cave at Mount Sinai. Turns out now we have to leave Egypt to go back to Arabia to search for what we first came to Egypt for! Does that make better sense?"

"No! But I know what you're saying. The question is will anybody else ever believe it?

"Babe, the world will one day. The world will!"

His words sunk deeply down into my heart, and I turned to look back out over the rolling sea in front of us. Somewhere out across that vast expanse, in the very center of those towering peaks, lay the object of our burning desire. The thing we'd been searching for since we'd left our home on the Persian Gulf almost a month before. And now it was within our grasp for the first time. I couldn't find the words to speak as we stood there against the wind, but I knew that a holy defiance was being birthed into the core of our beings that would enable us to accomplish the impossible task that lay beyond us.

"We need to eat good tonight, and then turn in early. I want to be out there to get all the processing done when the docks open for the ferry." Jim had found the words we needed for the moment. And that is exactly what we did.

CHAPTER TWENTY-SEVEN

A Farewell to Egypt

The ring was loud.. I shot straight upright in the bed and started shaking Jim's shoulder, saying, "Get it! Get it!"

Jim stretched one arm out from under the covers and reached out to the nightstand where the phone sat, lifted the receiver into his hand, and put it right back down on the cradle of the phone.

"What did you do that for?" I asked in disbelief, fully expecting that he'd hung up on some emergency call we'd been finally tracked down to receive.

"It's just the wake-up call, Babe. Nobody's calling us in Egypt!" He mumbled back at me, pulling the covers back up and over his head.

I fell backward down onto my pillow feeling like a moron. Of course it was a wake-up call! I'd been present when Jim had requested it the night before! What a bozo! I briefly made an attempt to fall back asleep, but the call had worked its purpose on me, and I could not keep my eyes closed. I looked over at the clock next to the phone and it read 7:02. I shook Jim again.

"Hey, Babies? Time to get up."

"I'm not asleep under here," came the groggy reply. "Just thinking of what I've got to do first."

"That should be easy enough," I replied as he pulled back the covers from his head and turned it over to look at me. The exaggerated smile I gave him overruled the necessity of any further conversation, and he dutifully swung his feet over the side of the bed, slipped on his pants

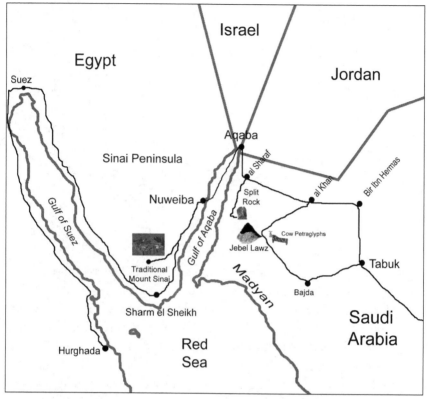

THE CALDWELL'S ROUTE BACK FROM NUWEIBA, EGYPT, TO TABUK, SAUDI
ARABIA, AND OUT TO JEBEL LAWZ AND THE SPLIT ROCK.

and his shirt, and walked around to my side of the bed where I still
lay prone.

"I'll be back," he said, grinning as he leaned over and kissed
my forehead.

As the door closed behind him, a thousand thoughts lined up
inside my brain, vying for positional authority. The first was that we
had finally arrived at the day we could leave! It was January 30, 1992,
and our Arabian adventure was on the cusp of its birth. The incredible
thrill of what was waiting on the other side of the Gulf of Aqaba was
simply too great to be imagined, and the possibilities too endless to be
comprehended. The culmination of all we'd been to Egypt to find was
waiting for us on the far shore, and the deepest most primal part of me

was itching to connect with what I'd been put on this earth to be a part of. It was statistically absurd to think that all the things that had led us to this point were just random acts. In fact, it was more ridiculous and unscientific to even entertain the concept that these events taken *all together* were coincidence. I settled the thoughts by just accepting that it was too marvelous a thing for me to consider too heavily, and that I should just concentrate on the task that lay before me this day. That would involve repacking the items into our suitcases that were strewn out across these two rooms as though a grenade had been thrown in the window. And it would be no easy undertaking.

And then it hit me. The weather! The rising wind the night before! The mounting height of the waves in the gale! Was it still stormy outside? Did I have to face that giant ramshackle, metal bucket of a ferry again, but this time in a tempest?

I grabbed the covers with both hands and pulled them over my head, squeezing my eyes as tightly together as I could and gritting my teeth. I was determined in my heart that I had to squelch this fear that was headed toward me or I would never be able to hold myself together enough to do what I had to do. I pressed mentally against it with all I had and suddenly felt the same sensation I'd felt the day before on the beach when the fear had first hit me: I could feel the strength and warmth of it flowing out to my extremities: the fear was bowing before it! I knew beyond a shadow of a doubt that the Lord was giving a gift, a necessity for the exact purpose of this calling—a bold invincibility!

Just as I was smiling to myself, and thanking God for the wonderful gift of strength He'd bestowed upon me, the door rattled momentarily, then swung open with Jim's voice singing the coffee song right on schedule! I sat up in the bed with an outstretched hand, into which the steaming mug was placed by the husband of my delight. And just about the time I was thinking how sweet and thoughtful he was, his entire countenance was altered, and the drill sergeant returned.

"We have to hurry up and guzzle this down, then wake up the kids and start packing. We all need to get showers, and we can do that between individual suitcase jamming. You know we have to get breakfast still, then check out, and then we get to go through the paperwork of customs, which could take hours. And all that before we even get to the boat for processing out at the border. As much trouble as we had getting in here, I don't want to chance missing that ferry because we're not out there in time! Oh, yeah. It's not nearly as windy as it was. The clouds are higher, and not so ragged. Looks like better weather's afoot, but it's colder!"

He knew me. Man, alive, he knew me so well! I looked heavenward and thanked the Almighty for calming the storm, then focused on Jim's rant. His orders were crystal clear with me. I gulped down the coffee and sprang out of bed and into the shower.

By eight-thirty the Caldwell clan had mobilized, showered, packed, and stood awaiting the signal from Sergeant Dad to head out for morning rations. By nine-thirty we had finished eating and saying our goodbyes to Ziyad Taleeb and his kids, and had piled our over-burdened luggage and ourselves into the truck. And with the start of the engine, we were off.

We didn't have far to go to get to the first stop, which Jim was not excited to revisit. This would be the same disgusting office of the chief of immigration that almost a month prior to now he'd had to endure hours and hours of argument in. The same dark, dank hut of cinder blocks and mortar, complete with long strands of bent, rusted rebar sticking out from the four corners of the flat roof. The same bug-infested walls and floors; the same filthy desk with paperwork strewn about that was covered with dust and dirt; the same broken down chairs that were sticky beneath a tar-like substance that was most certainly the residue of the multiple thousands of cigarettes smoked over the years inside; the same semi-functional ceiling fan whose motor whined and struggled to move the blades around, which were also encrusted with grunge and discolored. Worse yet, it would be the same official who, by virtue of his uniform and the ridiculous amount of metals, bars, stripes, and emblems attached thereon, must have considered himself to be their equivalent of our five-star general.

We pulled up to the front of the building, and Jim reached for the two yellow Egyptian auto plates that we had been using over our Saudi plates since the first deal to allow us to have our truck inside the country had been struck right here. He opened the door and got out, then leaned back down into the opening, looking right at me, and said, "Well, here I go. Pray with everything you've got in you that they let us leave!"

And so I did. And I continued to do so for the next forty-five minutes, getting more and more worried as the seconds clicked by on the clock that something was going wrong inside that room! But it wasn't going wrong at all. In fact, before an hour had been completed, Jim came through the door with a big smile on his face, and I knew we'd been set free to return to Arabia.

We drove around to the right and on out to the enormous docking facilities over against the Gulf, and continued on through boarding procedures without any paperwork problems whatsoever. With the passing of another hour, our truck, our belongings, and all of us were onboard the old ferry, and the clock was counting down for departure.

From the lowest deck, we made our way again to the uppermost forward deck, where I had managed to convince myself on the first trip that I would be safe. The weather was exactly as Jim had described to me before: intermittent cloud cover and breezy, but cold. I buttoned my coat up around my neck and jammed both of my hands into my pockets, and made my way over to the starboard side where I could look back on the Sayadin Village in the distance. From this high vantage point, it was easy to locate it, and I said a silent goodbye to the place where it had all begun here. Oh, all the troubles, and all the finagling we'd had to do just to be allowed to leave this port in the first place! One thought kept circling my brain over and over again: oh, what we would have missed if we had been stopped at this border!

The ear-piercing scream of the Jimy's mega horns blowing the departure signals to the docks below us tore me away presently from my ponderings. I had forgotten how loud they were from the first trip, and the sound jolted me so much that I jumped. Lucas and Chelsea grabbed at their ears, all the while grinning ear-to-ear at the experience of riding on the big boat again. I was so filled with love for them. I had to fight back tears of joy, and I couldn't help but be tremendously proud of these two hearty little troopers who had seen in their few short years more than most adults see in a lifetime. They had been dragged by their obsessive-compulsive, over-adventurous parents through every imaginable, and some completely unimaginable, scenarios! And here they stood on this grimy old boat deck, bundled up against the wind in their coats, hats, and gloves, ready for the new day's escapades!

VIEW FROM THE JIMYZ LEAVING NUWEIBA, EGYPT

How many kids, I wondered, could have endured what they had been forced to endure?

With a tremendous lurch and a loud clanking and rattling of metal against metal, the engines that drove the huge anchor winch clattered into action. It was located on the below deck, which jutted out farther than ours to the very bow point of the boat, and we all moved to the center railings to witness the sight. The massive links of the anchor chain came one by one back aboard as the motors struggled and whined against the heavy load. Before I knew it, the ship was in motion, carrying the Caldwells out of Egypt.

The Jimy steamed ahead through the quiet bay, around the corner point of land jutting out into the sea as a natural jetty holding back the rough waters. It finally made the turn toward the north-northeast and out into the outrageously deep waters of the Gulf of Aqaba. I suddenly realized something surprising: ever since the day on the beach at Sharm el Sheikh, when we bought Sir Richard Burton's book, *The Gold Mines of Midian*, and had determined to make a beeline straight to Jebel al Lawz as soon as we were back in Arabia, I had been chomping at the bit to make fast tracks out of Egypt! I had even thrown fits about it to Jim! But now—now that it was actually happening—what was this gnawing sensation of bittersweet emotion that was washing over me on the deck of this ferry? Why was I suddenly overwhelmed with a deep sadness to be leaving this country of priceless, historical antiquity and loud, obnoxious, overcrowded insanity?

I made my way to the port side of the ship and leaned hard against the railing, gazing in perplexed wonder out toward the jagged shores of ancient Mizraim. Once again, I thought it strange that the only place where the feet of the mountains did not plunge downward at extreme angles directly into the cavernous sea was there at Nuweiba. The large, pale sandy beach from which we had just departed stood out like a neon sign against the only two strong colors the landscape had to offer; the dark browns of the bare, rocky mountains and the aquamarine to navy blue of the Gulf of Aqaba. I marveled at the experiences we'd had in the land as it grew farther away from where my feet stood on the Jimy with each passing moment. This time I could not stop the silent, steady flow of warm tears that streamed down my face and onto the rail in front of me. I would never, ever forget the land of the pharaohs that had been our shelter since the year had begun, nor the invisible hand of the living God that had led us so caringly there. I managed a hoarse and broken whisper between my muffled sobs and bid farewell to Egypt.

THE HIGHWAY FROM JORDAN INTO SAUDI ARABIA AT AL KHAN

CHAPTER TWENTY-EIGHT

Home to Arabia

It was a while before I could tear myself from the railing and turn away from my brooding thoughts. When I was finally able to, I looked across the sprawling deck toward the bow of the boat and zeroed in directly upon Jim. He had apparently gone inside for the duration of my private goodbye, knowing by his precise reading of my heart that my countenance had taken a tumble. It would be incumbent upon him to lift my spirits. I had been born that way: prone to drift out over the sea of thoughts and emotions triggered by special events. He had perceived a nudge saying, "Go, and carry her back from the precipice!" It was at this sharp command that he'd gone inside to buy what would surely snap me back to task immediately!

I stopped walking to let him come over to where I stood not far from the edge of the vessel, and as he got closer, realized that he carried delicately in each of his hands, the tiny demitasse china cups in which Turkish coffee was traditionally served. Finally he stood directly before me and offered the steaming liquid to me, like a priceless jewel brought before a princess. "I know it's not morning, but you looked like you could use some spoffees!"

It was the very thing I needed. Something that would bring me back to any semblance of normalcy. A tiny gesture that carried with it the tremendous power of both who we were, and who we had been, since that fateful day in June of 1978 when he'd chased me down a white, sandy shore in Panama City Beach, Florida, and informed me that I was, in fact, going to marry him! I reached out and took the fragile cup, and looked directly up into the sweet face of the mate of my soul. "Yeah. I sure could use some spoffees."

We made our way over to a seating area that would allow us to look forward as we went along, and sat down close to one another against the wind that had picked up substantially since we'd left Nuweiba's port. The Jimy's massive engines were locked in an intense battle with the ferocious headwinds that were now howling out of the north, and voluminous swells in the center of the Gulf had become crowned with angry white caps, foaming rabidly as they crashed one after another into the hull of the ship.

But the fear that should have had me frozen in terror because of the change in the weather had been replaced with a perfect sense of inner calm. And that calm carried with it two tantalizing companions: pure anticipation and prickling excitement!

If only we could have seen from a higher viewpoint the courage and determined purpose that was being poured out on us from above as we steamed steadily up the Gulf of Aqaba toward Jordan, sipping our Turkish coffee! But seeing it with our physical eyes could not have made it any more of a reality: the mantle was now firmly in place, and the mission had been determined long before. A tangible strength was now residing within us like a raging fire, stoked by the breath of God, and it had taken the experiences we'd had in Egypt to accomplish that. It was time to go back. It was time for the real Mount Sinai.

Suddenly, the bellowing blasts of the Jimy's horns were sounding again. The great wenches had been loosed, and as the huge chains began peeling off to lower the anchor down into the depths, their loud clanking was keeping up the rhythm between the sounding horns. We were already preparing to tie up to the docking platform on the shore in Aqaba, Jordan, by the time we realized what was happening! And in less than an hour, we were back inside our faithful black truck, rolling down the highway toward Haql, just over the border.

Because there was an extraordinarily high number of ferry passengers that were apparently headed back to Saudi just as we were, the procedures at customs were backed up and tedious. We found ourselves in a long line of vehicles, which were, unfortunately, loaded to the roof racks with luggage and goods. Of course that meant more time spent on each vehicle by the agents, as they sought contraband from each passenger. I could feel the frustration rising inside me, as I recalled the first time we re-entered Saudi Arabia from Jordan in 1989 at this very same facility. That time we had driven all the way up to the Syrian border, taking in such places as Jerash, with all its Roman ruins in the north and Petra, the beautiful rose red city in the south. It had been a fantastic journey up to the point we'd reached this place. And then it had all gone straight to hell.

We had been pulled out of the truck, and Chelsea and I were sent off into a room alone, where a Saudi woman appeared and all but tore our clothes off trying to detect if we were hiding anything. All the while we were inside, Jim and Lucas had been roughly frisked in the same manner. By the time Chelsea and I were finally allowed to proceed back outside to the pavilion under which the truck sat, what I saw was an absolute disaster! Jim and Lucas had been ushered over to the side of the vehicle, but not within such a distance as they could reach it. I remember watching in revulsion as the team of Pakistani and Indian workers descended upon our things, throwing suitcases, camping gear, and sleeping bags alike onto the black, oily concrete below. Each bag was opened ahead of a supervisor of customs, who would then proceed through the strewn piles of our things, rifling through them randomly but thoroughly and tossing whatever was in his way onto the grimy floor. They even went so far as to unzip every single sleeping bag, as well as digging their grossly dirty fingers through all of the ice in our ice chests!

That other time, when the guy had finished his inspection of what had already been placed outside the truck, he then waved the workers over to the inside of the truck itself, which I thought to be empty. But it hadn't been empty enough for this supervisor, apparently, as he motioned for the opening of the glove box and the center console, which contained nothing more than cassette music tapes and paperwork and the like. I just could not believe my eyes when this agent had forced the workers to open every single cassette tape and take it out of its case, as though we could have hidden anything inside them!

I recalled vividly the way my face felt as white hot anger rose up inside me to the bursting point. I was a pressure cooker ready to blow after the cassette incident, and Jim saw me jump down off the concrete block I'd been seated on, headed for the supervisor's throat! He grabbed my coat from behind, and intervened just in the nick of time to keep me from nailing the guy squarely in the jaw for such an extreme violation of our things! It was probably a really good thing for him to have done, because my actions would have most certainly secured us each a prominent position in the local prison that very evening.

But the nightmare was far from over. When it had been officially declared empty of searchable items, it was time for the integrity of the truck to be severely violated. From behind a cinder block building underneath the pavilion came another Pakistani worker with an air tool in his hand, connected to a long hose. He pulled the trigger on the tool slightly as he walked toward the truck, and the "brrrrrrrh-brrrrrrh" sound it made was ominous. Jim had looked over at me with a face of utter disbelief as he watched the other workers float a jack underneath the truck and lift it from the pavement. Air tool man then proceeded to remove all four tires from the truck, and rolled them away to the x-ray machine a bit further down the line! As if that wasn't enough, two other workers then got inside and began removing the door panels and the wheel panels one by one. Jim's truck was disintegrating right before his very eyes!

At the final end of that hideous episode that was being permanently etched into my brain, the workers did replace the tires and the truck panels fairly effectively. But then, as the supervisor came by for the final inspection, holding the clipboard which contained our pertinent paperwork and stamping it about fifty times, he simply walked away and on to the next poor victim of his harassment, leaving everything we owned still taken completely apart and scattered all over the grimy floor! I was fit to be tied, and so was Jim! We shoved everything, as disheveled as it was, into the back of the truck and onto the roof rack, spitting poxes upon all of them under our breath as we went, and all but leaving skid marks as we made fast tracks away from there!

These were the former memories that I found myself rehearsing as we continued to sit, waiting for such atrocities to be performed on all the poor souls ahead of us, and watching for an open station to pull into. This particular facility had the capability of searching about four cars at the same time, and I looked over at Jim to ask him if he remembered the last time we'd been sitting in this very place. All he answered me was, "Don't go there!" as he nervously twitched, awaiting our fate. Just about the time he said it, horns began to blow and the agent ahead of us was motioning Jim into one of the slots to the right. And that's when we saw the Mercedes.

It appeared to be almost new. A beautiful, pearlescent ivory-colored, four-door model, or so we had to guess. It was hard to tell now that the doors had been removed! This luxury vehicle had already been poked, prodded, and pounced upon with power tools and border agents, up to the removal of its tires and fender wells! The trunk was open and the hood was up, and the owner just stood there with his mouth agape, looking for all the world like he was in a true state of trauma-induced shock. He too had been taken away to such a distance that all he could do was watch and cry as his car was methodically stripped of its dignity.

Two hours had passed before we had even gotten to this point, and the emotions of the day coupled with the now pulsing memory of what had happened to us here before, as well as the Mercedes massacre, were beginning to take a toll on all of our personalities and levels of patience. It was never easy for Jim to step away from his vehicle and let it be descended upon by men with filthy, greasy hands and feet, knowing full well that the objects of their seeking would require the systematic disassembly of his truck! I, on the other hand, resented their dirty hands that I knew already would find their way inside all of my personal items of clothing and the like. I was also beginning to fume ahead of the search because I knew that they would never put back a single thing they took out, and I would have to get it all repacked and reorganized at this late hour for us to continue our travels on to Tabuk this evening! And Jim was all but certain after seeing the destruction of the Mercedes that we were in for another dismantling of the truck.

But in the end, only half of the former scenario was played out. Every removable item was, in fact, taken out of the truck as it had been before, and thrown down on the now wet, black, greasy pavement. Every zipper was opened, every latch was unlatched, and every item was gone through by those gross hands just as before. But this time, after the truck had been emptied out, the inspector whistled for another man to come out, who brought with him a drug sniffing dog. The dog was walked over to make a round inside and outside our truck, and when he made no discoveries, the supervisor returned with his familiar clipboard and our paperwork, and waved us onward to freedom! We had escaped the taking apart of the truck!

Even so, Jim and I were both ready to scream. It had been such a long, long day, and the kids were tired and hungry. Our belongings had been violated by strangers, and we had a long drive ahead of us to Tabuk, where we thought the first possibility of a hotel would manifest itself. Although we had been given the excessive stampings of approval that would allow us legal passage back into the country, we drove away from customs as frazzled as we had ever been at a border before. It was almost ten o'clock, and we were both fried.

Just past customs, and several blocks into the little town called Haql, we found a tiny hole-in-the-wall restaurant on the right hand side of the street selling one of our favorites: broasted chicken. This chicken had the appearance of fried chicken on the outside but had additionally been pressure-cooked for tenderization on the inside. No matter where you got it, it was usually delicious! Jim immediately veered over and parked, and we bounded out of the vehicle as fast as we could before the place could close up for the evening. The smells of the hot, fresh food revived our weary, aggravated souls, and in no time, four orders with French fries were placed in front of us to eat. I was certain that food had never tasted as good as it did this chilly night in Haql, after what we'd been through at the border! A certain freedom was beginning to wash over us, now that the episode at customs was over.

Back on the highway, Lucas and Chelsea fell asleep almost immediately. We figured it would take us about two hours to drive into Tabuk and seek out a local hotel where we could all get a much needed night's rest. I noted that we were the sole vehicle on this vast stretch of highway traversing northwest Arabia and turned to watch the sky out of my window as we drove along in the darkness. I could see that the clouds were beginning to thicken and lower as we went. We had only been on the road for about a half an hour when a light rain began to fall, enough to turn the wipers on. For a moment, their rhythm and the noise of the truck's engine were the only sounds we could perceive as we made our way across the desert wasteland toward the east. Just as I was about to drift off to sleep against the window glass, a low thumping sound began to repeat in my ear.

Jim looked over at me and asked if I could hear it. By the time I answered him, it was already making itself louder and louder. And Jim knew instinctively just exactly what it was, as he sought a place to pull over to the right side of the road. He shut off the engine and stared blankly out into the night.

"Flat tire," he said in monotone. It was all he could muster.

I felt my whole being slump in disbelief. In my mind, I had just been pleasantly counting the minutes before my head could fall gently onto a puffy pillow at the upcoming hotel, and now my entire, peaceful scenario had been blasted into oblivion.

But one glance over toward my Jim softened my heart with compassion for him. His forehead was resting on the top of the steering wheel, arms up with his elbows bent, and his hands clasped together against the back of his head. This worn out buccaneer was every bit as fatigued as I was, both mentally and physically. And he was the one who'd have to get out and fix the miserable tire in the cold, drizzling rain! My attitude had been given a quick, stiff kick to its backside, and I made up my mind to do whatever I could to help him get the job done as quickly as possible. We'd get to the hotel soon enough. So as he sighed, raised his head slowly from the steering wheel, and turned around behind him to reach for his jacket, I turned around and reached for mine as well, drawing his immediate attention.

"What do you think you're doing?" he asked in quiet resignation.

"How're you gonna hold the flashlight and get the lug nuts off at the same time?" I whispered back with a grin. "You gonna use that third arm growing out of your back?"

He managed a sweet smile back at me, cocking his head to one side and holding me in his gaze for a few seconds before saying softly, "Let's do it!"

About thirty to forty-five minutes later we were back in the truck, peeling off our wet overcoats. We had unknowingly passed the first test of our ability to work together to overcome difficulties in this desert. But that truth would become manifest on another day at another time. Right now we were just two shivering spirits blowing fog as we breathed inside a frosty truck, seeking shelter for ourselves and our young, against the ebony darkness of the night.

With the heater fan on high and the spare tire now securely in place, Jim proceeded to follow the road again to the east as the blacktop rose steadily against a long, gently sloping hill. As soon as we crested that hill, the headlights shone a beam across a couple of now familiar road signs; Al Zetah, and Al Khan. This was the very place where the snow had begun to fall on us for the second time on January second, and we'd stopped to play in it again with the kids earlier this month. For that matter, it was very near to the place where we'd camped out in the desert on that former trip to Jordan in 1989, when in the middle of the night, a whirlwind had decidedly altered its path and made a bee-line for us, all but lifting our tent with us in it right off the ground! For a split second I wondered what it all meant, and why these three notable events had taken place with us within this two-mile stretch of highway! But my head was now aching and my brain was on overload, and I was just too tired to ponder the possibilities. I leaned against the window glass once again, and closed my eyes to sleep.

The sensation of bright lights in my eyes woke me with a sudden, startled jolt. I sat straight up in the seat, my heart pounding in my temples and noticed that the engine was not running. I whirled my head around in panic, realizing that Jim was not in the truck, and we were sitting in a half-empty parking lot where the pale orange glow of the overhead halogens was streaming down into my window! I spun my head back around to check on the kids and was much relieved when I found them both still sleeping soundly in the back seat. My head snapped back to the front again to try and ascertain where we were. A foggy voice from the back of my brain somewhere started speaking, "Tabuk, Tabuk...." Of course! We were in Tabuk! Just about that time, Jim reappeared at his door and opened it, leaned inside, and said, "We're here! Wake up, everybody, and grab what we need. I've already got our room key!"

It was wonderful news. No, it was heavenly news! Five minutes was about all it took to gather up our necessities, and the four of us trudged in weary procession like so many worn out slaves of the Pharaoh, up the steps leading to the lobby and over to the awaiting elevator. I can't truly say that I even recall what the room looked like that night, only that there was a bed and it had my name on it. Four heads soon hit four pillows, and we were out cold in mere seconds.

We had done it! We had been led safely to the farthest frontiers of the land of Egypt and had been carried safely back out again. Tomorrow would bring our long awaited trek into the mountains of *northwest Saudi Arabia*!

Jim's Face Mountain south of Jebel Lawz, Saudi Arabia

CHAPTER TWENTY-NINE

The Mountain of YAHWEH Beckons

"Mom? Dad?" A small noise was growing louder as though it was coming from across a vast, empty convention hall.

"Mom?" I recognized Lucas' voice. The next thing I heard was in harmonic stereo.

"Mom! Dad!" As I opened one eye, I saw him coming from way across the room, with Chelsea close behind him. By the time I had my eyes open they were already on us and managed a mid-air sproing that landed them both squarely on top of myself and Jim! Chelsea took over the loud complaints.

"Mommy! I'm starving! When are we gonna get breakfast? Why are you still in the bed? Get up!"

Lucas took the opportunity to take revenge on the father that was always shaking him awake in the mornings and started rolling Jim from side to side mercilessly. "Dad! Dad! Rise and shine! Let's go, let's go, let's go!"

"All right, all right! Stop it! I'm up! I'm up," shouted Jim.

By this time, I was giggling along with Chelsea.

Our joy was underlined with the high expectations of our planned trip to the mountains! This was the day we would be off! We were ready to start the journey to the mountain of God. Although we had traveled the length and breadth of Egypt searching for it since Jim had felt the burning desire to get to Mount Sinai in early December of 1991, it was now that we knew we were on the right track. The time had finally, *finally* come.

But my musings and observations were trumped by the growling of my stomach, and it was past time to get dressed and out the door to breakfast! It was nearly nine o'clock, and neither Jim nor I had even had our morning coffee .

This was going to be a very busy day! We would have to find a garage to have the flat tire we'd changed last night fixed, so as not to head out into the desert with no spare, and then find a place to buy the necessary supplies to be alone out in the wilderness for the next several days to boot! So we hurried to ready ourselves and went downstairs to the hotel's single restaurant for coffee and fuel for our bodies to start the day.

Though the restaurant was small, absolutely wonderful smells were emanating from the kitchen. And the coffee that was brought out to our table on a fancy little round tray would become the most favored of any we would ever have in all our years in the Middle East.

Much to our mutual delight, the breakfast food was just as good as the kitchen smells had made it out to be. Hot flat bread with a variety of soft cheeses, jams, and jellies was served first, with eggs to follow.

Just as soon as our plates were empty we headed back up to the room to pack up to head out into the desert for the next few days. The anticipation of what could lay ahead of us out there was trying its best to break out of me. But we still had much to take care of logistically. The tire had to be first on the agenda. So, with suitcases and backpacks in tow, we headed out and down the hall to the elevator, where the four of us did our best to smash ourselves and our things inside it all at once. Then it was into the lobby, out the door, and back into the waiting Patrol. We piled ourselves inside, in what seemed like the thousandth time since we'd departed from our Arabian home a month previously.

Jim pulled out of the parking lot of the Al Adel Hotel, and began searching for a tire dealership, or at least an automotive mechanic shop where a flat tire could be repaired. He found exactly what he was looking for, and within thirty minutes time, we were back on the move again with a repaired tire and now searching for a supermarket. Out toward the edge of town we came across a large one called the Astra Supermarket.

In all the days and all the miles we had traveled throughout Egypt, including the enormous sprawling, breathing organism of a city named Cairo, we had not run across a single supermarket! Plagued by tiny corner vendors with extremely limited supplies, Egypt was not the place to go if one was looking for the variety and quality we had become accustomed to in the U.S., and in fact, in Arabia! The Astra represented our first foot back into what we remembered to be modern society, and even Lucas and Chelsea were excited to go inside.

In the end, the Astra had everything we needed, plus! In the space of about a half an hour, we were loaded up and restocked with water, food, and all the camping necessities we required, with a few special treats from the checkout counter.

In the Patrol Jim pulled out all the maps we by now knew so well and had been plotting on since we'd found Burton's book at Sharm el Sheikh. Studying them, he mentally filed the turns he would need to make inside Tabuk to get us out to the main north-south highway out of town. Just as he had planned to do before we'd ever gotten back to Nuweiba, Jim set a course to approach the high mountains from the south, even though the only thing on the napkin that Ziyad Taleeb had shown him that resembled a road, showed an approach from the north. It was a gut instinct he just couldn't shake.

So, once underway, we followed the road southward from Tabuk, and searched for a road sign that would indicate a turn toward the west and a town called Duba. Duba was actually on the coastline of the Red Sea, and we would not be going that far. But it was off of this road that we would soon find a desert track leading northward again, somewhere near a tiny settlement called Bajda. As soon as Jim saw the sign, he pulled off the road and stopped the truck momentarily to switch from two-wheel to four-wheel drive.

"Well, Babe, this is it!" He cocked his head toward me and continued. "This is what we've been waiting for. This is what I went to Egypt for! *Somewhere out there is the Mountain of Yahweh, the God who called out to Moses from the burning bush. You know He called Moses by name, and I'm telling you, that mountain is calling me, Penny!*

It's calling my name just like God called Moses name! And it's drawing me like a giant magnet!"

I knew the truth of what he was saying. Moses had been grazing the flocks of his father-in-law Jethro, in the land of Midian, when he'd seen a phenomenon a short distance away from him. He's spied a bush out of the corner of his eye that seemed to be on fire, and yet it was not being consumed. He turned aside and went to see what this sight was, and a Voice spoke to him out of the midst of the bush, telling him he'd been chosen to deliver his Hebrew brethren who were in slavery in Egypt. When Moses asked God what to say when the people would ask him who sent him to deliver them, He told him His name was Yahweh, meaning "I AM WHO I AM."

As I pondered the wonder of such an encounter with the Living God, all I could do was grin from ear to ear. It was time for the anticipation to find its outlet. Electricity was darting rapidly through the air inside the truck, and even the kids were affected by it. We all knew the words we would next hear coming out of Jim's mouth: "Let's go, let's go, let's goooooooo!"

Jim smashed the clutch to the floor in one swift move, and jammed the Patrol into first gear, slamming his foot down on the accelerator a nanosecond later, which sent the truck lurching forward and sand and gravel sailing into the air behind the back tires. I grabbed for the handle on the dash and the one over my door, and looked back at Lucas and Chelsea, yelling, "Hold on, kids!"

"Yippee!" was all I could make out from the screams and squeals coming out of their mouths. As the tires all began to pull at the same time, the truck got a solid grip on the sands beneath us, and we began to accelerate quickly. In less than a minute we were sailing along the desert floor at almost eighty kilometers an hour, searching for a turn in the track that would take us due west again toward the mountains. And in about ten minutes, we found it.

Once we were facing west again, we found ourselves in a vast, broad plain, flanked on the south side by large sand dunes and sandstone formations shaped like giant, rounded blobs. To the north, the dunes were absent, but the sandstone continued on. Away in the far off distance, I could just make out the bare outline of a range of mountains, but the wind had been steadily increasing as we traveled, and there was a good deal of sand particulate in the air, making distant sightings fuzzy at best. We would travel onward for about the space of another hour before they became clearer in our sight, and before the track would make another turn, back again to almost due north. It was then, out in the distance, that we saw a peak that we actually recognized. I felt the chill bumps raising the hair on my arms as I looked off toward the west at the very mountain we'd named "Foot Mountain" from the other side of the Gulf of Aqaba, at Nuweiba. Jim and the kids both recognized it as well, and we knew now for certain that Jim's choice to come in from the south had been the right path after all!

The terrain around us was beginning to change significantly the further north we drove. The vast plain we had traveled so deeply into had been left behind, and the sandy ground was becoming more and more infused with pebbles and stones. Rocky hills had replaced the blobular sandstone formations on both sides of us, and the farther north we went, the taller and more jagged they were becoming. By about four o'clock, their height to our left was sufficient to block the sun as it traversed the sky toward its setting in the west, and it would soon also be able to keep us from being able to see the heights of the much larger range in the distance.

Jim's eye caught something there along the very southern end of that range that caused him to slow the Patrol down a bit so that he could gaze out of his window at the far away peaks. One seemed to stand out from the rest, and he cocked his head to the side to gain a proper perspective on what he thought he was seeing. Sure enough, especially from this vantage point, he was certain he was looking at the perfect representation of a man's face pointing skyward on the top of this mountain. He spoke up to get my attention.

"Hey, look at that mountain over there, Babe. Don't you think it looks just like a man's face? See the nose, and the lips? I mean, it's a perfect outline."

I strained my eyes at the mountain in view as he continued driving slowly along. I could see that the ridge on the very top of the mountain looked like something familiar all right, but I couldn't figure out which end was what. My problem was that I could make out a pair of lips and a nose from either end!

And so the question remained for me, because Jim was too intent on observing everything to be serious about the face on the top of the mountain. Beside that, as we continued to slowly creep along, a few other items of interest were coming into view that were so very plain in our sight that they would garner no playful argument from either of us. In fact, we were about to stumble upon the first in a series of archeological remnants that would lead us even deeper into the mysterious and wonderful land we were now skirting.

In the immediate vicinity, the slopes of the smaller mountains were beginning to show some interesting circular formations that Jim was intrigued enough to stop the truck to investigate. Formed by the gathering of local rock, it was blatantly apparent that they were both manmade and ancient. This was just the beginning of what we would soon discover to be numerous stone circles, placed all throughout the valleys between the mountains by a people as yet undetermined a long, long time ago.

We got out of the truck to wander around an area where several of these circles were located and immediately discovered that the howling wind that had kicked up so much sand and dust into the air all day had also brought along with it an extremely cold air mass! I scrambled back inside the truck to grab the heavy coats, gloves, and knit caps for Lucas and Chelsea, as well as for myself and Jim, so that we wouldn't freeze in the gale. Once bundled up, it was a far more comfortable venture.

The four of us spread out across the area, each scouring the ground for would-be artifacts, hoping to at least be given some clues as to the possible meaning of these stone circles. As I walked along, I could see several larger rocks against one of the circles, and began to make my way over towards them. When I got within about five feet of the rocks, I could see that there was writing all over them, etched directly into the face of the stone. The writing appeared to be very, very old, and included what looked like both symbols and alpha characters. I called Jim over to see them, and swung the camera I had hanging around my neck up to my face to snap a few photographs.

Lucas and Chelsea had been exploring the region to the east of where Jim and I now stood, and as we began to walk back toward them, the noise of the fluttering of wings filled the air between us. We got close enough just in the nick of time to see a number of birds a bit smaller than pigeons scurrying along the ground, then attaining the optimum speed for flight and lifting off right in front of us. As Jim had been videoing the entire region since he'd stepped from the truck, he managed to capture the event on tape that was taking place before us now. And once again, as I studied the last of the now airborne bodies of the fleeing flock, I became awash in chill bumps!

"Jim! Lucas and Chelsea! Do you realize what those birds are?" I asked them with stunned wonder. "Those are *quail*! Remember what the Lord sent down to the children of Israel when they were in the wilderness by Mount Sinai? *Quail!*"

Jim looked at me and I looked back at him, and we knew it was happening to us all over again. The air was popping again with electricity, and we knew it was high time to start recording and memorizing everything our eyes would witness in this land from this time forth.

Lucas and Chelsea began skipping through the area in and around the desert shrubs and scant brush here and there, seeking to flush out more of the ever so curious fowl. Lucas had been the one to jump them up in the first place, as he had followed what he'd called "a little peeping sound" to the main flock, which was now nowhere to be seen. But even though they were gone, a few stragglers remained behind, and the kids were successful in chasing them into the sky just as they had done moments before. Once again, Jim was ready with the video camera and caught the whole episode on camera. But we were starting to get a little bit cold to continue the exploration of this one spot, knowing that we had yet to find a secure campsite for the evening and setting up camp in the dark was not in the least a pleasant undertaking. Beside that, there appeared to be something out of the ordinary way up ahead of us and just off the track to the right that bore investigation. We packed back into the truck without removing any of our cold weather gear and drove down approximately a kilometer to the place where the object stood.

When we got out again, it was clear that what we'd seen from a distance was a very ancient deep, circular, water well. In recent times, concrete had been placed around the edges to keep anyone from falling in, and the remnant rebar still stood uncut out of the top of the reinforcements. Upon closer inspection, the well was surprisingly deep, and a water level was still visible all the way down, at least thirty feet. The ancient structure had been dug and lined with jagged rocks, carefully placed against the circle of the well, and I instinctively grabbed both of my kids to keep them from leaning too close to the edge, even though it would have been hard to fall into with the concrete wall about the top.

Lucas was thrilled to have stumbled upon such a potential opportunity, and blasted off to find just the perfect rocks to cast down into the water. Chelsea was on his heels, struck with the same idea as he had. As Jim recorded the spectacle, the kids dropped the biggest rocks they could carry one by one and sent them plummeting down into the depths of the well, waiting each time for the sound of the massive sploosh, and the inevitable reverberations that would echo rapidly back up the sides and into our waiting ears. The joy and laughter of children was rising from the floor of the desert again, reminiscent of a time ages ago, when a people and their children had been lifted from enslavement at the hands of a harsh taskmaster to the wild freedom of the wilderness. What had been but faint whisperings on the wind in Egypt had become a freshly blowing breeze of clear understanding to me as I stood there, watching the delight of my children. I knew the revelation was making itself known to us now, and that the days to come would only make it more and more apparent just what we were doing here at this place and this time. It was inevitable.

Dusk was beginning to fall around us, however, and the revelry had to end in favor of locating a campsite. Not much farther ahead of us, the track turned right to go around a large boulder that was protruding out into the desert floor, and just before it the level of the ground sloped gently downward against the edge of a small ridge, affording a place to get off the main road. The height of the ridge would not only be sufficient to hide the vehicle from the northern view, but it would shield the campsite from the wind that still maintained its strength, carrying the cold air along with it. Jim pulled the Patrol into a nice sandy spot against the rock wall and parked for the evening.

We quickly went into "make camp" mode, each with our various responsibilities learned over the past few years of living in the desert. Jim began by opening up the back of the truck and pulling out the heavier items for us, setting them on the ground and allowing us free access from there. Once the truck had been unloaded, the first order was to get the tent set up and ready. We carried with us a large mat made of plastic that folded up into a square not much larger than a bed blanket. When open, however, it had quite a large footprint, and made a great foundation upon which to set the tent. As the tent was not so large as to cover the entire mat, this allowed the space in front of the doorway to be shielded from the ground, and kept our feet from tracking sand and rock into the insides of the tent.

It was primarily Jim and I that always set the tent up once the mat was down, while Lucas and Chelsea would forage around the camp vicinity for stones of a similar size with which to form a protective circle that would enclose the campfire. This evening would be no different. As they set about to perform this part of their job detail, Jim reached for the tent bag, untied the cords at the end holding the tent and the bag containing the poles inside it, and dumped the contents onto the mat. I grabbed up the bag containing the tent poles, loosed the cord holding it closed, and dumped it onto the mat in exactly the same manner. I then went for the poles, which were each folded up accordion-like with elastic cord inside, and began unfolding each into their full lengths, thus making them ready to be threaded through the outer loops of the tent. While I did this, Jim was busy unfurling the tent and setting the base of it exactly as he wanted it on the mat for the evening. Once he'd made up his mind, we each began passing the poles through the loops until all were set, and we could bend the first one into final position. This motion would actually lift the top of the tent from its base, and the structure would rise from the desert floor, a shelter from the night and the wind. As many times as we'd done it before, it never ceased to amaze me how the thing went up the way it did.

With the tent now in place, Jim moved on to oversee the making of the fire. By this time Lucas and Chelsea had all the rocks they needed and had them neatly placed in a circle a safe distance from the tent. They had already begun the hunt for small pieces of dried desert shrubs which would serve as kindling for the fire and had started piling them up in the shape of a teepee in the center of the fire pit. They'd even located a few larger ones that looked like small tree branches, which would burn for a lot longer than the ones we usually had at our disposal when we'd camped in the Eastern Province where we lived. These they had stacked outside the stones of the pit, for easy access once a good, strong flame had been established within. They were doing a great job in the wilderness this late winter's eve, and without a doubt, they knew it!

With Jim's attention now directed at them, they both sounded off with great pride of workmanship, making sure he didn't miss a thing they'd accomplished. And of course, he didn't. He was all too proud of these two little warriors for who they were and what they were capable of! They were already becoming great adventurers, just like their parents were wont to be, and it did not escape my mind at that very moment that someday they would be dragging their own children off into some wild, unexplored regions of the earth, requiring of them the same tasks they were now being trained to do.

But with the darkness growing by leaps and bounds, I had no time for the luxury of such a sentimental interlude. I had to get the inside of the tent set up for the night, which was falling fast like a mist around us. I grabbed up the four sleeping mats, which thankfully were auto-inflating, unrolled them, and unscrewed the tiny silver caps on the end of each to begin the process. Once the air had been sucked inside by these little miracle mechanisms, all I had to do was screw them back on tight and the mats would be ready to provide about an inch and a half's barrier between us and the cold, hard ground.

Now that I had the mats filled with air and had them placed inside the tent where I wanted them, all I had to do was pull the down-filled sleeping bags from their stuff-sacks and let them fluff out to their full size. These bags were rated for extremely cold weather and had already been an integral part of why we hadn't frozen to death on the frigid night we'd spent in the desert on our way to Egypt. As icy as the wind felt against my face now, I was very thankful we had them at our disposal to sleep in once again. I laid each one out on top of each mat, and left the final step concerning mine and Jim's to be completed by him.

It was the one thing in all the camping gear that Jim would never allow me to touch. In fact, it suited me just fine not to have to deal with the matter at all. And I had no animosity whatsoever for him or his rule concerning the stupid things, because I knew of a certainty that he was absolutely correct in his final assessment that Penny Caldwell should never be allowed to go near the zipper of a sleeping bag. Never! Part of what had drawn him to purchase these specific ones was that they could be zipped together to form a double, allowing us to snuggle up inside one, big bag. Upon my first attempt to perform this task, I'd lost my patience and zipped up half the nylon of the outer bag into the heart of the zipper track, and Jim had come upon me wildly thrashing the bag from wall to wall trying to get it unstuck! After an hour of painstaking effort, he'd finally freed the bag and its zipper from my evil grasp and threatened me within an inch of my life if I ever went near the things again. And so I left the tent prepared for the night's sleep, except for the zipping together of his bag and mine. I crawled out of the open door flap of the tent, leaving it wide open behind me, knowing I was also banned from touching its zipper because of a similar incident as well.

By this time, darkness had enveloped us and the night air was sharp and cold. Lucas and Chelsea had been moved on to their other job which Jim required of them at each campsite. That task was to set up the little fold-out table, complete with seating benches on each side, that he'd been lucky enough to find at a store within Arabia. It was relatively easy to set up. The only potential problem was that you really had to watch while unfolding it that you did not pinch your fingers between the plastic and the hinges. Once fully extended, however, it made a perfect little table with four seats! In the dead center of the table, a circle had been cut out for the placement of a large beach umbrella on a pole. This was perfect for daytime eating while camping in the desert. But Jim had rigged a way to use the unopened umbrella at night as a lamp pole on which to hang our classic old time Coleman lantern, and the moment the kids had secured the final hinge lock, Jim was right there with the pole and the lantern. With the strike of a match and the turning of the valve that allowed the gas to enter the firing chamber, the lantern blazed into action, casting a bluish-white light suddenly all over the immediate campsite! Jim's last task was to open up the two-burner Coleman stove and attach it to the gas, and then place it on the table so that I could get our dinner prepared for the evening. And now that the campfire was blazing away, the bulk of the work was completed.

Jim opened up the two compact lawn chairs he'd taken out earlier and sat down to relax for a moment. I went over to my kitchen supply box and took out a pot and the can opener. After dropping them off on the table, I went back to the food box and withdrew a huge can of beef stew and a can of corn to go with it, and brought them back to the table as well. Once I had the two cans combined and in the pot over a medium flame, I covered them and went back for the tin and enamel painted bowls we carried with us to eat out of, along with four spoons. It would only take a few minutes to heat the stew and corn to boiling, and as cold as it was, the taste of a steaming, hearty meal had us all salivating!

I served us each up a heaping bowlful and we sat down together at the little yellow plastic table to eat. After Jim had asked a blessing on the meal, we dug in like people who hadn't been fed for days. There was just something about being out in the wild that made food taste better than at any other time! And there was something about this setting that made me realize what a strange dichotomy this whole scene truly was—for it was just as fragile as it was fantastic. Here we sat in the true middle of nowhere, chowing down our meal as though we were still at our own dining table in our own home. Yet all I had to do was look around me to realize our complete vulnerability and to know of a certainty that we were a long, long way from anything that even resembled home! The camp light flickered in the wind, causing the rise and fall of remote shadows against the rock faces around us, just barely keeping at bay the deep, velvet darkness of the night. Above my head, the dense canopy of the sky was sparkling with the refracted light of a million glittering stars, and I was filled with a hushed wonder I could not for the life of me comprehend. I was bouncing rapid-fire back and forth between two worlds, the earthly and the celestial, and I was being drawn further out each time. But the mundane came to rule with the tiredness I was beginning to feel, and things still had to be done before I could crawl into that tent and sleep.

After the dishes had been cleaned and everything had been put away for the night, Jim and I tucked Lucas and Chelsea into their sleeping bags and Jim, of course, zipped them up to their eyeballs to keep them warm. Chelsea was out like a light before a true minute had passed, and Lucas was not far behind her. All we had left to do was to extinguish the lantern outside and bed ourselves down for the night. Jim reached up and turned off the valve to the lantern, and the glow grew more and more dim, and finally winked out after a brief, final burst of light.

Jim beckoned me over to him in the last moments of visibility, and we stood there in a mutual hug, both gazing intently skyward at the indescribable beauty of the heavens above us. It occurred to me at that moment that this was the last day of January, 1992, and the same date some fourteen years previous, that the soul and spirit of my precious grandmother, whom we all called Mama B., rose up out of her frail little body and flew on the wings of the angels to her heavenly home! I couldn't help but wonder if somehow, from the midst of that starry heaven above me, she knew of the plans that had been so carefully laid out and initiated by our Father! The plans that at present had her granddaughter and her husband standing watch over her two great grandchildren in the total darkness, perfectly alone in the center of the great and terrible wilderness!

I felt a warm tear spill over the lid of one eye, and roll down the side of my cheek at the memory of one so very, very dear. There was so much that I didn't understand about all that had taken place in our lives already, and how we'd come to this place at this time. But right now it didn't matter. There was a sense of the reality of eternal life that was washing over me in great waves out there under the stars, and the sensation of the protective covering of the mantle of our God was all around us! It was no surprise when the brilliant flash of a shooting star lit up the eastern sky, streaking at breakneck speed across the firmament towards the west. "Wow!" Jim said softly against my ear. And in quiet awe, we made our way into the tent and crawled into our double sleeping bag, Jim zipping us in for shelter against the cold and the night. I didn't have to try to feel safe and secure at all; I just knew in my heart of hearts that we were!

PENNY, CHELSEA, AND LUCAS AT THE CAMPSITE
SOUTH OF JEBEL LAWZ, SAUDI ARABIA

CHAPTER THIRTY

I awoke to the sound of the gentle movement of the tent fly against the inner fabric over us. I could tell that the sun was up for certain and had been for quite some time, but it was apparently still behind the mountain peak across the valley to the east from where we were camped, leaving us in the shadows of its rising. I felt it was later than we normally awakened when we camped, but I had no idea what time of morning it was.

Almost as soon as I opened my eyes I became conscious of just how cold it was, even inside the tent! I guessed that we had been so exhausted that we hadn't noticed it much in the night, but now I found myself shivering against it and decided that if I was frozen, Jim had to be as well! His back was turned toward me, so I reached for his shoulder and shook him slightly. Not surprisingly he was awake already but had determined not to budge from the warmth of our double sleeping bag until he absolutely had to. "Brrrrrh!" was all I was going to get out of him for the moment.

And he had the best idea, actually. Both kids were still very much asleep, and with no one screaming in my ear to feed them yet, I still had the luxury of lying there for a while longer. I had no idea that closing my eyes and curling up against the warm hulk next to me would cause me in mere moments to fall deeply asleep again!

Jim must have silently unzipped the tent and slipped outside at some point after I had gone back to sleep. He had built a campfire and fired up the camp stove for the coffee that we couldn't start our day without. I knew that was the case because of the very familiar words of the traditional morning song, wafting through the thin film of the tent and finding its way into my ear! Knowing that the song would be accompanied by a hot steaming mug of strong coffee, already stirred in an especially perfected blend that only my husband could concoct, I gladly crawled out from under the downy bag and donned my shoes and coat to join him.

Once outside, the sharpness of the air stung. The sky above us was crystalline, devoid of any clouds whatsoever, and stood absolute in the brilliance of its blue. There was a tangible depth in its clarity, and I had a difficult time trying to determine just what color of blue it was. The closest, I determined at last, was sapphire. Deep, rich, sapphire. It was a very rare occasion to see such a clear sky and such vivid color in Arabia because of the strong prevailing winds and the airborne dust and sand that usually marred the horizon. But when it did happen, it was spectacular.

Such dawned the morning of the first day of February, 1992, and such was the sky on what I would come to know was a pivotal day of great discovery and destiny. But the smell of the coffee was overwhelming all my senses and having it was all I could think of presently.

Upon the pouring of the second cup of morning ritual, I heard the tent material being strained against and rolled my eyes in that direction to get Jim to look with me at what I knew was about to take place. The tent zipper began to slowly move up and around, and two rumpled little heads with eyes that were already squinting against the brightness of the morning began to slowly emerge. But just as soon as they did, the chilly air hit them full force in the face, and both heads disappeared right back into the tent from whence they had come!

"It's *freezing* out there!" The loud whines came in a stereophonic blast toward us.

"Well, put your coats on!" I yelled right back at them. "And don't forget your gloves and your hats too! I've got hot chocolate out here for you both!"

After much loud rustling and stirring from within the confines of the tent, our offspring materialized again, but this time almost unrecognizable for the abundance of their covering. Chelsea had her coat on, zipped to the top as far as it would go. The hood of the coat was pulled as far forward down on her face as it would go, and she had tucked her mouth and nose in under the collar so that only her eyes were showing. Lucas had chosen to don his bisht, ever being the rugged individualist that had to stand out from the crowd, and had pulled on a bright red, full head and face ski mask, such that only his eyes were showing as well. On top of the ski mask he'd added a pair of brown fuzzy ear muffs that stuck out from the sides of his head like tennis balls. Jim and I just looked at each other in amazement.

"What's this? Is there an alien running around in my campsite?" Jim asked as he made his way over to poke and mash on Lucas as he usually did in the morning.

"And what about this creature?" He continued, grabbing Chelsea by the shoulders and moving her side to side.

The scowl that arose from her face at her daddy made him back up instantly and run back across the campsite toward Lucas, where he took up the mashing of his son again.

"Ooooooh! Is it mad and stewing this morning?" he asked, but from a safe distance away this time.

Chelsea folded up her arms and frowned all the more at him, and through the hood of her coat, managed to muffle out a flurry of complaints. Jim knew that accusing her of "stewing" was always a button that, when pushed at the right time, would set his daughter off like a rocket. These were the kind of things that Jim used to bring forth the great satisfaction that only aggravating your kids could provide.

"I'm frozen, I'm hungry, and I'm thirsty! You better leave me alone!" The consternation on what little of her face he could see made him think better of continuing his onslaught.

Jim was now hiding behind Lucas instead of harassing him and began begging me to get his Booglet some hot chocolate and breakfast before she hurt him. And that's exactly what I did. By the time an hour had transpired, we were all filled with nourishment and hot drink and able to move about without our teeth chattering too badly on this beautiful winter morning. It was time to break the camp down and pack everything back into the Patrol as it seemed now that we had done a million times. Another half-hour and we found ourselves safely tucked back into the truck with all our belongings, rolling slowly across the desert floor to the north, looking for signs and archeological remains.

The mountain range to the west that we had been following the day before was becoming increasingly higher and more rugged as we went, and it seemed to me that the desert beneath us was in a downward slope toward the north. Out my window to the east a vast plain was beginning to open up, broken only here and there with singular mountains not seemingly connected to any range. Stone circles dotted not only the hills on either side, but were becoming more and more scattered about in the plain as we continued northward. It was obvious that at some time in the ancient past, a large amount of people had passed through this way. *A very large amount of people.* Jim and I passed a glance, and the chills that ran up and down my arms had nothing to do with the crisp air outside. He leaned toward me and all but whispered, "We're getting close, Penny. I can feel it. There's just something about this place."

It was close to two-thirty before any of us was hungry enough to search for a place to stop the truck and take a lunch break. As we looked, the sky began to undergo a complete transformation before our very eyes. From its former heavenly blue and crystal clear expanse, a multitude of stratus cloud layers, pale gray to almost charcoal in hue began rolling in from the northwest. I was puzzled by the complete and total about-face in the atmosphere, and the tremendous stillness that was draping itself now like a blanket across our pathway.

Jim noticed a small track veering to the east that encompassed a huge pile of boulders, and decided to take it. It was right then that we both, at the same moment, noticed the white fence that completely encompassed the rock formation. Although we could not see anything unusual as of yet, Jim decided it was well worth our parking the truck for at least a little while to investigate why in the world this rock pile in the middle of nowhere had a substantial fence around it, including barbed wire in three threatening strands at the top. The truck came to rest on the far eastern side of the formation, and we all stepped out to see what we could. With the video camera glued to his face as it had been on this entire trip thus far, Jim Caldwell began a slow and deliberate walk around the outside of the fence, with Chelsea in tow directly behind him. And then, suddenly, the entire atmosphere was charged with electricity! In the air that was now so silent and so still, I heard a precious little voice whisper excitedly: "Dad! Dad, it's the twelve cows!"

ONE OF THE MANY CATTLE PETROGLYPHS FOUND TO THE EAST OF
JEBEL LAWZ, SAUDI ARABIA

Jim was on it as fast as she was, and stood there completely enthralled at what he could now see coming into sharp focus through the lens of the video camera. There, right there on the rocks in front of him were the cattle we had been searching for since Ziyad Taleeb had shown Jim the napkin drawing in Nuweiba! They were larger that we had initially imagined, with one being nearly four feet long. Carved right into the stone by unknown hands thousands of years before, these petroglyphs stood out and rang as clarion bells internally inside our spirits! This had all the possible components necessary to become a very real and tangible candidate for the altar to the golden calf that the Children of Israel dedicated their molten idol on!

Jim was now motioning all of us to be as quiet as possible, as he quickly moved around the entire formation grabbing up as much video as he dared take. I was snapping photographs with the Nikon camera as fast as I could fire off the shutter and had somehow caught the same warnings in the air that he had. While this was exhilarating, it was also becoming very clear to our senses that the forces of darkness would

THE GUARD OUTPOST BUILDING AND FENCE ENCOMPASSING
JEBEL LAWZ, SAUDI ARABIA

just as soon not have us there recording the proof of this stunning witness to the truth—the reality of the biblical account of the exodus and Mount Sinai for anyone else to see. When Jim finished his initial video, he thought it best to move a moderate distance away from the site to eat our lunch. If anyone had come by, he reasoned, they could become upset about the cameras. We were in the deep desert here, and westerners were not often seen, much less photographic equipment, which always had a tendency to cause trouble.

As a result, we got back into the truck and went on past the formation and continued for about a kilometer into the vast plain behind the cows, where Jim parked the Patrol and we all got out in preparation for lunch. We could still plainly see the fence in the distance, but we were not so close as to be accused of mischief should we attract any local company. And once we stopped, I realized just how hungry I really was. I had the hot dogs made and fresh and warm in our hands in no time at all, and we sat in the back of the truck on our camp chairs to eat and try to decipher what we had just seen with our own eyes. The day had gone from normal to dreamlike in just a matter of a few hours, and the sensation was beginning to overtake me that the fate of our lives was about to be initiated. I gazed off into the distant high mountain peaks behind the cows, noticing that the upper peaks of some of these mountains were enshrouded in the lowering clouds. These mountains looked much higher, I reckoned, than the ones around the traditional Mount Sinai in the Egyptian Sinai Peninsula. It was just then that I noticed the areas of white dotting the upper slopes of the same mountains. Were my eyes deceiving me, or was I seeing snow again in Saudi Arabia?

Not being able to sit still after seeing something so profound, Jim and I gobbled down our dogs and began to wander still further away from the cows, searching the ground to the east. Stone circles were all around us and seemed to continue on as far as we could see to the horizon. *Was this the plain of the camp of Israel?* We looked at each other again in stunned silence. This was it! It had to be it! And the very stones of the circles before us had been lying there for thousands of years, waiting to tell their story. The words of Jesus came thundering into my ears: "If these should hold their peace, the stones would immediately cry out...." Well, these rocks were screaming into the envelope of air surrounding us—screaming aloud to every fiber of our beings that we were finally in the right place after the thousands of kilometers we had driven in search of Sinai—screaming aloud their testimony that *the exodus really did take place,* and the mountain we sought really was *in Saudi Arabia*! But if these cows chiseled into these rocks did represent the altar to the golden calf idol, and the plain we now stood in surveying the hundreds of stone circles was the camp of the Israelites, then *where was the mountain*?

Jim turned the truck around to face the cows again and began driving slowly toward the west. When we got back to the north side of the formation, still facing due west, we could see something we had not noticed before. Another vast plain ran north and south in front of the cows, and just beyond it in the distance we could see the outline of

WHITE MARBLE PILLARS NEAR THE BASE OF JEBEL LAWZ, SAUDI ARABIA

another white fence of the same make as the one that enclosed them. But this fence looked like it went on for a mile in either direction! Jim peeled off into the desert on a track leading to the north and followed it until he came to a set of gates that was apparently the only way in or out of this fence. Just beyond the gates, a white building made entirely of cinder blocks stood, but was seemingly uninhabited. We got out and began peering through the fence to see if we could notice anything that would explain why this area was cordoned off. Nothing at all was visible from where we were standing at the gate.

Puzzled and a bit concerned, Jim scanned the heights diligently for any sign of what he'd remembered from the napkin Taleeb had shown him in Nuweiba: the cows were there, all right, but where was the cave? Where was the tree between two stones that had so captivated his mind since the first time he'd seen it? Where were these supposed columns that had been drawn out in front of the cows? As he stood there pondering, the noise of a truck engine at some distance came drifting up into his ears and he turned to me with a nauseated look on his face. "Well, babe. They've found us." It was all he had to say.

The little white truck was next to ours in a matter of minutes. A Bedouin man and what must have been his teenage son stepped out of it and came walking over to us with great suspicion written all over their faces. Hoping that it would in some way ease the already mounting tension, Jim offered up the first greeting.

"Salaam Alay-kum!" He said in his best Arabic dialect.

"Alay-kum as Salaam," came the proper greeting back toward him in an uneasy monotone, with a definite undercurrent of mistrust filling the air between them.

For the next several minutes, as this uncomfortable exchange continued between them, the children and I smiled as brightly and innocently as we could muster the strength to do, hoping our family persona would somehow help to divert the attention away from the blatant questioning of what we were doing there. Because of the lack of understanding due to the language barrier, and perhaps the added friendliness we were exuding in our desperation, the Bedouin man became undecided as to whether we were there on a mission of devious intent, or if we were simply a small family of idiot Americans, lost in a place far too far away from home, and ignorant of what any good son of the desert would realize was a rapidly approaching winter's dusk. We felt this momentary breakthrough was genuine when he seemed to be asking Jim if we wanted to stay in the white building for the night, motioning to the children and then making every attempt in sign language to inform us of just how cold it was going to get in a few short hours.

But Jim was insistent, as was I, that we wanted to get inside that fence, and that was all we wanted to do. We tried our best to show him that we just wanted to go inside, look around, and then leave again out through the gates. The longer this dance continued, the more frustrated we could plainly see that the man was getting. He finally stopped speaking to us, turned to his son, and rattled off a sentence or two in Arabic. The boy answered in a few short words, and suddenly the man was in his truck and gone. We knew right away we had a brief respite of time to plead with Heaven for favor, because when that little white truck came back again, it would not be the only one. Jim and I zeroed in on the son and smiled wide and hopeful.

Astonishingly enough, within about five short minutes of our attempts to communicate with this boy, his hand reached into an unseen pocket and brought out a set of keys. Jim's eyes met mine and I swore I could actually hear his heart beating as we watched to see just what he was about to do with those keys. In stunned amazement, we stood still as stones as he seemed to motion us over to the large, double linked chain that had been wrapped in and out of the solid piping of the two huge gates, and raised the lock with his left hand to open it. I know I was holding my breath as the key, seemingly in slow motion, was raised and driven straightway into the lock. In the stillness the sound of the key turning in that device and the click of it opening the lock reverberated through the air as though a gleaming, mighty sword had sliced the lock off clean!

I was immediately certain—by the way the hair was standing up on my arms again and by the electricity that was all but visibly arcing through the atmosphere—that something tremendously earth shattering had just taken place right in front of me! I was so sure that something monumental had just occurred that I shot a glance upward to see if I could actually glimpse the supernatural radiations I knew must be emanating from some fixed point in the heavens directly over that gate. However, all I saw was the same sky that was now a uniform, bright pale grey, with clouds surrounding the higher peaks of the mountains ahead of us, completely and mysteriously hiding them from view. In the natural that was all I could see, but on the other side of this reality, all hell was shrieking and reeling backward at the death blow it had just been delivered. There was no way I could even begin to ponder the relevance of what lay beyond us as we entered that gate and began walking that specific plot of ground. In fact, it would be years before all the pieces of the massive puzzle would begin to fall into place in just the perfect and prescribed timing. But today was a day of wonder and discovery. I didn't need to understand it all and felt sudden fear sweep over me, fear that if I even had a clue of what was to come because of this day, I would run like the wind away from this chosen destiny. So I shut down my mind's wanderings and snapped myself back to the present. We followed the boy as he led us directly over to the white, cinder block building, where he proceeded to open the door and show us inside. The building was primarily empty, except for a few sacks of what must have been some sort of food for the sheep and goat herds they owned. It was now noted as fact that we were right in assuming that the Bedouin man had been offering for us to spend the coming night inside this building. It was obvious that this is what the boy was trying to show us and get us to understand.

But inside this building was not where we wanted to be. Jim made one circle of the interior, and walked straight back outside. He began to speak to the boy in English, though he knew he could not understand it and tried to get it across to him that we wanted a tour of the ground upon which we stood. As he continued to try to communicate, we continued to walk on, deeper and deeper inside the previously concealed territory. The further we walked, the more white stone we began to see scattered about on the ground, including what looked like short, fat pillars of some sort. I was just about to attempt to enter into a dialogue of my own with the boy when suddenly, out loud, in a not so quiet manner, I heard Jim's voice utter a proclamation as he raised his hand and pointed toward the rocky mountain face to our right.

"The tree! The tree! It's the tree!"

Just below the cloud deck, and at the very top of the ridge of the mountain that stuck out like a finger into the valley, I could see the outline of a tree between two very huge rectangular-shaped blocks of granite. Below it some distance, yet still on the rocky face of the outcropping, was almost certainly a large cave. I knew in an instant why it was impossible for Jim to contain himself.

I felt the ground beneath me all but giving way as I turned toward him with my mouth gaping open in silence, and witnessed the oh-so-sturdy legs of my Jim buckle out from under him. He crumpled like a rag doll down onto his knees, sensing the enormity of the holy place in which he now found himself on the ground. For over a month now he had been chasing what he had sometimes deemed no more than the wind; a vision so weighty and glorious that it was almost impossible to grasp. For thousands of kilometers he had carried us along, searching under every rock and inside every cave for something that had seemed to be no more than a brief, illusionary thought; a dream so unattainable and so far-fetched that was always just beyond his grasp. But suddenly, in a swift and charted event, planned by Providence before he had ever been born, he had been brought forth and placed by Him in the very

CLOSEUP OF THE ALMOND TREE BETWEEN THE GIANT STONES AT
JEBEL LAWZ, SAUDI ARABIA

spot where he was destined to be—and every fiber of his being had been made glaringly aware of it. *He had found the place he'd been searching for, and he knew beyond any shadow of any doubt that the whole vision had been reality. Jim Caldwell was home!*

I stood there in the hushed and holy, reverent silence, just staring in a fixed sense of awe at the mountain before me. I was totally unprepared and caught by complete surprise by the sense of wonder I was experiencing.

And then I heard it! I heard the Voice! I heard the sound—not of many rushing waters but of steady power, strength, and complete Authority! It coursed through my entire being as a shock wave of sound, down to the souls of my feet and back again, and up into my ears with such magnitude I nearly lost my footing and almost fell to the ground! Just a statement of utter simplicity, but spoken with such command

I knew it would be the mandate of our lives, for the rest of our lives. *"Take this to my people, Israel!"* I could not help but utter the words aloud, and Jim whipped around and looked me squarely in the eyes.

He couldn't utter another word, and neither did he have to. I knew it as well as he knew it. And we both realized that a flood of information was pouring into us right then through the visuals all around us. Though the boy had not allowed us to take a camera inside those gates, these scenes were being permanently imprinted on our hearts and minds, and we would never forget what we were viewing at this profoundly powerful moment in time. It was only the far distant sound of vehicle engines that got the attention of the son of the Bedouin, who then immediately began to push us back toward the direction of the gate that could drag us away from this experience. But the mystery was now revelation. The mountain that we had been called out to seek had been revealed in blazing clarity before us. Whatever would happen back on the outside of those gates was irrelevant. This was ground zero, and to this place we would return!

We could see the father of the boy returning in his white truck from a good distance, and beside him the army-green color of a Frontier Forces official desert police truck. Judging from the clouds of dust that were billowing skyward from behind their tires, we knew this was not going to be a pleasant encounter. While we awaited their arrival, the boy began to make a campfire to try to shield us all against the icy wind that had just begun to blow. It had started almost on cue as the gates closed behind us, and I could sense tiny little ice needles beginning to form in the sky. Before the trucks ever reached us, the snowflakes were beginning to blanket the ground.

Sure enough, just as we had suspected, the trucks roared up to the gate and the Frontier Forces police were upon us. They jumped out of their truck while it was still running, leaving the doors open, and raced over to us with AK-47's pointed and began waving them at us and at Lucas and Chelsea. They reminded me of the bandoleers I used to see in old western movies with their sashes of bullets strapped across their chests in an X pattern. It was abundantly clear that they were radically unhappy that we were there at all. They began to point at the shovel Jim kept attached to the front of our truck with sand boards, and accused him of digging for things in the vicinity right away. In reality, the sole purpose for the shovel was to help us dig the truck out if we had become stuck in the desert sand, but there was no convincing them of that. And this time, it would not have mattered if they would have understood English. We were not locals, and they wanted us out of there. No *ifs, ands,* or *buts* about it.

The shouting was becoming louder and louder as the Bedouin screamed at his son, and the Frontier Forces police screamed at us and continued to wave their weapons. Finally, one of them pointed his gun in the direction of the track to the north leading out of the valley in front of the mountain, and yelled, "Tabuk! Tabuk! Tabuk!" With another wave of that gun I grabbed both the kids and shoved them back into the back seat of the Patrol and headed for the front passenger's door.

Two more minutes of shouting, and Jim was back inside, starting up the truck and moving along the track to the north that the weapons had forced us onto. He was furious! Dusk was falling, and these desert police were forcing him onto a track he'd never driven before and demanding he get out of the whole region and back to Tabuk! He had not calculated having to leave this place via the northern track and had therefore not studied it on the maps. It would be a miracle if he could do it in the daytime, much less with night fast approaching. But it was a day for miracles. It had been a journey of miracles. And those thoughts gently settled back over him and calmed him down completely. The boldness of a conqueror rose up inside him, and in a final act of defiance, he stopped the truck after about a kilometer or two, reached for the Nikon camera, and snapped off a few photos of the darker mountain we could now see parts of from the north looking south. "We'll be back!" he declared with absolute assurance into the frosty air.

Three-odd hours later, we pulled into Tabuk and headed straight for the Al-Adel Hotel. Emotions and exhaustion and the aftereffects of prolonged adrenaline release had taken their toll on our worn out bodies. Yet there was a great sense of power and strength internally that had crept in, almost unawares. It had been made abundantly clear to us that nothing we'd experienced in the last month's journey in Egypt was by happenstance. *It had all been not only real, but planned!* And the culmination of all those way marks along the path had led us right to Mount Sinai, which we'd been in hot pursuit of since we left Ras Tanura. The search was over!

THE DARK TOP OF THE MOUNTAIN FROM THE NORTH LOOKING SOUTH

Just after we got Lucas and Chelsea tucked into the now familiar Al-Adel beds, and just before we turned in ourselves, it occurred to me that we'd not read our daily reading from our devotional book that morning. It had been so cold, and so many things had taken place one after another, that I'd forgotten to read it as we had been doing almost every day since we'd left home for Egypt. I wearily reached out for the book, which lay just beyond my reach on the table next to the bed, and found February 1, and began to read. The words were precious and true, as we always found them to be, but it was the Scripture quotation that really blew us away! "This thing is of Me" (I Kings 12:24)! And there was no doubt in our minds or our hearts that it really, truly was!

THE SPLIT ROCK AT HOREB

Chapter Thirty-One

The Discovery of the Split Rock

March, 1992 – Ras Tanura, Saudi Arabia

The end of March; *it is already the end of March*, Jim was thinking silently to himself as he gazed at the cluster before him. How in the world could so many days have gone by so quickly? I could almost hear his thoughts as he surveyed the preparations in the living room of our home, which appeared as though some great tempest had cut a swath of destruction in its midst. There, over near the sofa, stood the tent bags we'd gotten since our last trip, the second one. Here, underneath his feet, well within tripping distance and threatening, were the provisions: the light jackets, the Thermax long johns, the flashlights, the extra clothing, and the medical supplies he and I would need. This third trip would not include the children.

Our backpacks stood next to the stereo cabinet, ready and waiting to be loaded with the items now strewn across the floor. Sleeping bags and bedrolls were poised in the center of the room, awaiting their cue. And, most important of all, the cameras were in their own nightmarish tangle behind him. Jim knew he needed the extra batteries, the volumes of film, the backup gear—but somehow all he could think of at this moment was how much it all would weigh once on his back.

This trip would be an all-out first for us, as neither of us had ever climbed a mountain before. Climbing was exactly what we planned to do on our six-day trip. We were going to attempt to climb up the western side of Jebel Lawz. Jim felt a knot of apprehension trying its best to wear a fray in his usually steely constitution. "Oh, well," he sighed out loud, "I'd better get to it."

"Stop it right now!" I ordered him from the balcony at the top of our stairs where I'd been hanging over and watching him, anticipating his next move. "Did you hear me, Jim Caldwell? Don't you touch a single thing! Just as sure as you do, I'll never find it again, and I won't know where anything is! I've got it all laid out just like I want it, and we're leaving tomorrow with what you see! Now get outta my stuff!"

This would be our third trip into the Jebel Lawz area since the beginning of February, when we had first passed through on our way home from Egypt. Three weeks later, we had flown back over again, unable to ignore the calling of the mountain. At present, it was hard to imagine a divine call in the midst of such clutter. It was a real challenge to be certain we carried with us all we would need for each of our growing number of excursions.

Preparations had a tendency to drive Jim mad. Perhaps in a way, it was a good thing that I had figured him out long ago and had memorized everything we needed. After all, I was the housewife with all the hours at home, and I really didn't mind at all. It gave me a good feeling to be able to help by doing this part, which always prompted a broad smile on his face, and a beaming glow he'd get when he saw all of our gear was ready and awaiting his inspection. But things weren't to that stage yet this morning, and there he was, "diggy-dooing" as his mom was fond of calling it, all through my well-placed preparations. I'd already had to get him out of it once before, and I knew good and well I'd have to do it again. When I got down the stairs far enough, I could see he wasn't listening to a word I'd said, as usual. The smirky giggle slipping from his lips told me what I suspected anyway: he was pulling my strings on purpose by poking around. I glared up into his impish face and squinted my eyes at him.

"I mean it, Jimmy! Go away! You know I can't stand it when you hover and mess up my piles." This trip was too important for me to be sent spiraling off-track by a missing item he'd just happened to squirrel away in his pocket or some other room in the house, which he was entirely all too capable of doing.

I was having my own battles of intensity during the past two weeks anyhow, and I didn't need the added worry of forgetting gear. My dear friend Leslie Osborn was due to make this trip with us, and nothing had fallen into place to allow her the opportunity. Oh, she had been able to find a sitter to keep her three girls, and she had gone through the hassle of all the paperwork Aramco required: she'd even gotten the travel letter stamped *Jebel Lawz*—yet we weren't discerning an all clear signal for her to go with us.

She and I prayed, and even fasted, and still no firm yes had arrived to confirm our plans, nor to ease the growing sense of doom and darkness that had crept in like a fog in the night. That was last week.

These past few days had been so confused, and thoughts of disaster and corruption filled the air. It was as though an invasion had been launched by the enemy into the atmosphere above our homes, and a vaporous cloud of fear hung thickly between us and peace about the whole trip. I was having enough of a struggle—flying off and leaving my children behind for six days—without having to deal with all this pressure. It felt like my mind would explode with the hideous scenes of "what if" that played like some horror movie inside my head. At times it sounded in my ears so loudly that it was as though a literal voice was speaking to me. One particularly gruesome monotone kept whispering insidiously in my ear that we'd be killed in a plane crash and pay dearly for being so irresponsible with our kids. I'd rebuke it and it would leave, but always, always, it would come right back, as if on cue, when my mind was occupied with something else. The consistency of the attack had begun to seriously effect my stability.

Jim had been observing me closely and had seen the anxiety increasing and intensifying. It was not at all unlike me to be nervous about flying anywhere, anytime, and I had been known to get pretty upset in days past before a flight, but what he was witnessing now was beyond anything he'd ever seen within that normal scope of apprehension. And he thought he knew exactly what the problem was—Leslie wasn't supposed to be with us. No, he had no qualms about her being there. Quite the contrary. He felt deep gratitude to her for her prayers a year back when all hell was stirred up against me and

345

his kids. Thus he was actually looking forward to her being along. But something just wasn't right somewhere. He had watched vacation days he didn't have supernaturally appear for him to use. He had seen money all but materialize into our bank account for us right when we needed to purchase airline tickets to fly out west to the mountain. These trips had been so carefully and precisely arranged by the heavenly Father thus far, with great and miraculous openings being made where none should be found, and he knew we were supposed to make this one a go. What had he missed?

Then it occurred to him in a quiet, subtle manner: maybe since our work was not completed yet, we should still go after it *alone*. He hoped our desire to share the unbelievable glory of it all had not caused us to overstep our place by inviting another. But he was not sure. All he did know, as he looked toward me, his unraveling wife, was that he had to set his foot down for the sake of the trip's purpose; and if that meant only the two of us, that's what it would have to mean.

Phenomenally, the clearing of the air was almost instantaneous, once the difficult decision had been made. The three of us regained our respective peace without further hassle. When we talked with Leslie, she understood perfectly and was almost relieved herself at not having to leave her own children alone while her husband was out of Kingdom. She had been concerned about his feelings in the matter, unbeknownst to us. Jim had heard right and made the rearrangements, and I was released from the hideous scenes of calamity that had been plaguing me so fiercely. Harmony had been restored, and we, the two adventurers, were reunited with our Godly audacity and fervency of mission. The forces of evil would have to retreat for now.

The first day of April dawned basically clear, but a few small clouds against the horizon had multiplied into quite a covering by the time I hitched myself up into the driver's seat of our ever faithful Patrol and drove out to the refinery to pick Jim up early from work. I was proud of my packing job and was anxious for him to see all that I'd done. It had been more work than I'd imagined, preparing for the children to be home while we'd be gone, and I'd barely allowed myself enough time to do it. Now on the other side of ready, however, the adrenalin pumping in my temples told me we were off again, and I could allow myself the luxury being excited. As I turned the corner toward the gates of the refinery, I looked down the street and saw that Jim was already out, standing on the curb waiting for my arrival. At the sight of him my smile broadened over my face, so big I felt my teeth showing. It was unavoidable. The great secrecy and excitement of what we were about to go off and attempt, totally alone, was just too fantastic not to grin!

"Going my way?" Jim asked, as he leaned over into the window and wrenched open the door so forcefully I thought he was going to rip it right off its hinges. His enthusiasm coupled with my excitement kept us at a standstill right there in the middle of the road for a while, as we laughed and gave each other the gaping-mouthed, goggle-eyed faces that seemed to just pop out automatically in moments of extreme glee. If any passerby had peradventure glanced into the windows, the rumors that would spread about us could have forced us to leave the country, I was certain! Fortunately for us and the local community, we had not the time to waste here on dramatics and silly antics. It was a four and one-half hour drive to our first plane in the capital of Arabia—Riyadh—and we'd only make it if we left immediately. Right then is when it hit us both—we had yet to tell the kids goodbye.

Lucas and Chelsea were both waiting for us when we got back from the refinery. Amy, the daughter of my best friend Renea Morrison, would be staying with them for the duration of our absence, and they were all inside, waiting for us to leave. My instinct had caused me some serious doubts and fears about leaving my kids for so many days, and I was afraid that they'd be really upset at our leaving them behind this time. Thankfully, however, I was saved from the pain of that scene. In fact, after the first series of *I'm-going-to-miss-you's* and *I-love-you's*, the kids were getting disgusted with all the gushy emotions and were entirely ready to go swimming. I knew that they'd have a blast with Amy, and my ever faithful Renea would take care of anything and everything they would need, even if something happened to us. She and I had been virtually inseparable since we met in the late summer of 1991, and I trusted her with my very life! My kids were in the best of hands!

"Mom, we're gonna to be fine! Would you please leave now so we can go to the pool?" Lucas drawled out disgustedly. "I have to get to the pool to play with my friends! They're waiting!"

"Yeah, Mom," chimed in Chelsea. "You already told us you love us fifty-hundred times! Bye!"

Chelsea had her own way with words that none of us could quite define yet—but her being her usual self made my heart rest at ease. We boarded the Patrol and slowly drove around the corner of Seashore and Surfboard where our house stood, waving and blowing kisses at our offspring, and then turned our voices skyward in unison to ask protection for them while we were away. As we went through the gate separating our compound from the Arabian city of Rahima, the vastness of the desert lay before us and a single strand of highway led the way. And so it began again.

* * *

We were probably only about fifty kilometers out of town when I glanced over at Jim, and found he had already moved into *calculus roboticus* mode. In his mind, lists were being checked off and scenarios were being played out at an alarming rate of speed. He was totally absorbed in one of those mind games where he was being chased by our old friend, the gatekeeper Bedouin. In this act, the guy had caught him with his camera inside the fenced off area that we now knew was closed to all but the locals. Just as Jim was about to make the hero's move that would give the old dude the slip, my sudden shrieking loudly inside the truck snapped his head around to glare at me and ruined his triumphant victory.

"Look!" I exclaimed in sheer disbelief, staring down the road in amazement. "It's pouring down rain just up the highway!"

Right about the same time as my shriek, a loud clap of thunder rattled the other half of his daydream to an abrupt halt, and Jim was forced back down to reality for the moment. I could tell as soon as he saw the phenomenon ahead of us that he wasn't going to attack me for spoiling his heroic mind game, though. Rain at any time in Arabia was an occurrence to get excited about—unless, of course, you had to catch a plane and fly through it! He glanced over at me again, this time with a semi-worried look in his eyes, to see if it had hit me yet. And it hadn't. I was still smiling and enjoying the elements.

The rain was torrential for this part of the world. Arabia had some of the finest superhighway systems we had seen anywhere, and Jim and

I were utterly amazed as we watched this one beginning to go under. The desert just couldn't handle much water without a flash flood. It was a simple matter of science. We were only about an hour out of Riyadh before it finally subsided a bit, but not before we passed a place in the road that was completely submerged. The Frontier Forces had the highway blocked off, and waved us through a service station parking lot to get around the deep pool of water! Flashbacks of living in Louisiana went through both our minds. Today too much was going on to be homesick, though.

It wasn't too much longer before we saw up ahead of us the exit for the airport coming into view. It was 7:15 P.M., and our plane for Tabuk was scheduled to leave in forty-five minutes. We knew we were cutting it close. Real close. But if this trip was ordained, we'd make it. Simple enough. Except for one, tiny little thing: when I looked over at the gas gauge, we were coasting on fumes! Jim had been driving at breakneck speeds to get us to the airport, and now, with it in sight, the old Patrol was heaving and puffing her last drops of energy into the night! I got his attention and just pointed at the gauge.

Jim froze inside himself. "We'll make it, we'll make it, we'll make it! We've gotta make it!" he muttered to himself. He didn't realize he was mumbling out loud. Time was ticking away from us, and so was his ability to get us there. He could waste no precious minutes. The plan was forming in his head.

"Babe, I hate to tell you this, but you're gonna have to jump out and go grab our boarding passes while I park the truck, if we make it up there. Then I can park without having to circle around and waste fuel." Had this been any normal airport anywhere else in the world besides where we were, that would not have been a problem. But a western woman, with her face showing, diving into a sea of Arab men was not the best possible scenario for me to act out on purpose.

Despite that, when he said it I felt a burst of energy flare up inside my spirit. I had to try and make him feel it, too. "Hey, what's the matter with you? Of course we'll make it!" I shot back at him. By this time, though, I was working with all the fake confidence I could muster. My eyes had seen the gas gauge, and it was the very least of my worries at that point in time. What did have my rapt attention was the ring of storms that flashed brilliant zigzags of lightning at regular intervals now, all around in every direction of the horizon. I closed my eyes, hearing Jim's instructions yet not really hearing them, and crunched up my nose to resist the onslaught of fear I knew was on its way. I'd been able to quell it all the way up to now, but here, at the last minute, these storms had popped up and thrown me off course a bit, and I felt myself having to struggle to maintain my cool about getting on that plane. This time it was me who was startled by the insistent voice of my husband.

"Get *out*, Penny! Go up there and get our boarding passes! Hurry up, before the flight fills up!" Jim's booming vocal chords brought me back to the importance of the moment. There was only one thing capable of making me shut down and get on a plane anyway; that was him. This was a race indeed, because our flight had not been confirmed, and with the Islamic Ramadan holiday beginning, there was a real chance if I didn't get there first, we could be bumped from the flight. And we had to be on that flight!

I grabbed up all I could carry and flew through the entrance doors to the King Khalid International Airport. The ocean of men, dressed in their traditional white thobes and red-checkered gutras swaying in unison as if to the beat of some unknown and unheard lyric, told me I'd better find that counter for the flight to Tabuk fast! Dread was beginning to fray the edges of my conscious thought in a very serious manner. I went up to an empty end of the ticket counter to see if I could ask someone where I should go. The man I found myself speaking to appeared to me to be cleaning up that end and didn't look like he even held a position with Saudia Airlines. But before the words had time to leave my lips, the very same man reached under the counter and pulled out a big sign that he proceeded to hold up high into the air. "Tabuk" was the next word out of his mouth. And there I stood, maneuvered by the Unseen, first in line, flabbergasted! I still couldn't believe it, as I watched two hundred Saudis pushing and shoving their way in behind me! If I had lingered one more moment in fear at the truck, we'd have never made that plane. All I could do was look up and smile. And I heard the words coming out of my mouth out loud before I could stop them! "Jimmy ain't never gonna believe this here!" And then I couldn't help laughing out loud at what the locals must be wondering about me talking to myself.

Back in the parking garage Jim had found his spot to leave the Patrol, and though it was a long way off, he was quite satisfied and thankful he'd made it at all with what little drops of gas, or benzene as they called it here, must be remaining in his truck. One crisis averted, he now focused on whether or not I'd been able to get us seats on this plane. As he came up to the level of the entrance to the terminal, his heart sank down to his knees. Before him was a crowd unparalleled to any he'd witnessed in this huge airport before, all pushing and hollering in the usual manner. They tended to form horizontal lines rather than normal ones, and whoever's arm was long enough to wave tickets at the clerk behind the counter usually got to be next. I know he was thinking to himself that we'd never get on the flight, and subsequently that I must have been absorbed by the tumultuous uproar of this unruly crowd and vanished into the blur of humanity. But his real concern was not as much where his poor wife was, but indeed, did I get those boarding passes?

I looked back down from my skyward glance and saw him come in at a fast clip across the terminal from where I'd gone to wait for him. He was too far away for me to yell at, and with the noise inside there, he wouldn't have heard me anyway. So I gathered my things and proceeded to follow him from a distance. I knew I'd catch up to him when his forward motion was stopped by the crowd. As I drew closer, I couldn't resist the temptation to tease him a little.

"Hey! You lookin' for me?" I casually and coolly inquired.

Jim wheeled around and looked at me incredulously. "What in the world are you doing way back here? We'll never get on this plane now! Why aren't you in line?" The flurry of questions and disappointment in his voice made me stop the game before I went any further.

"Jim. Jim! Calm down! I've got them! I've got the boarding passes!"

"Wait—what? You've got them already? How? What? When?" The bewilderment on his face made me laugh in spite of trying to hold it in.

"I was looking for someone to ask where the Tabuk counter would be, and the man I was about to ask *was* the Tabuk counter! Can you believe it?" I was giggling out loud to him by this time. "I was the very first one to get boarding passes, and I didn't even have to fight any of these guys," I said, motioning to the racket and goings-on just beyond us.

Jim closed his eyes, bowed his head, and brightened my heart with his laughter. Oh yes! This trip was definitely meant to be! We waltzed over to our gate, just in time to hear the clerk open our plane for boarding for the first time. It was just like what had happened with the Tabuk ticket clerk. And now we were first in line to board the plane. This never happened in a Saudi airport! Not *ever*! We stopped just short of the gate and gave each other a ridiculous look of disbelief. This was beyond us. Not even any waiting to board the plane. Absolutely unheard of! A ripping of passes, and a few steps forward, and our feet were inside the Lockheed L1011 Tri-Star, hunting for our seats. Fifteen minutes later, the landing gear clanked and clattered its way up inside the big jet, and we saw the lights of Riyadh disappearing below us. "Incredible!" Jim leaned over and whispered in my ear. And, for a while, we relaxed and unwound.

The first few bumps of turbulence brought me back to immediate attention, as it always did when I was flying. The pilot's voice was suddenly on the intercom, and he was calling our attention to the lightning slashing the sky below us and to the right. I leaned over to look out my window and quickly back again, as the brilliance lit up my face. "Great, Jim," I said loud enough for several rows of people to hear. It was my own fight, again, inside of me; one that I knew so well, and had never quite disposed of completely. But this evening was already going so well, and I had so many blessings and miracles to remember, it was not all that difficult to calm myself back down. I closed my eyes and began thanking my Father for keeping us through so much. I felt His calming Spirit envelop my fears and quiet me, and lost track of both the turbulence and the storm. I got absorbed enough in it that I lost all track of time, even in the bumping and grinding turbulence. The next thing I knew, the voice of the stewardess was calling for seatbelts and upright seats, and we were cleared for landing in Tabuk. I sat up and sighed a great sigh of relief, and leaned back to look out the window into the lights of the city beneath me.

Jim was grabbing all our stuff for arrival when he heard me make a funny little noise that sounded like a whimper from next to him. I hadn't wanted it to come out, but it had, in spite of my trying. He gave me a strange look, and when I turned to face him, he caught the beginnings of the tears shining brightly in my eyes. But there was a smile on my face, which caused him to puzzle to himself. That was until I reached over and pulled his face to the window from which I'd been looking out, and he knew the same fullness I'd just experienced: there, filling the window we'd been seated next to was the crystal clear radiance of the Big Dipper, just as it had been positioned and looked down on us the past December, before we'd left for Egypt. It welled up inside him; he heard the Voice say again, *"I will open you the windows of heaven, and pour you out a blessing"*(Malachi 3:10). It was another moment we'd never forget.

Currently, however, the plane was landing and the quaint little airport at Tabuk was beckoning, so we moved on. Tired though we were, there was much to do before the bed at the Al Adel Hotel would cradle our sleep. First was to secure our four-wheel drive rental truck from the Al-Rehily Rent-A-Car booth inside the airport. Because we'd been there twice before, the Egyptian behind the counter considered us his new friends, and greeted us warmly. As promised the truck was ready, and after signing all the pertinent documents and gathering our luggage, off we went down the highway leading into the heart of the city. This time we got a white two-door Toyota Land Cruiser, the same model as the one we had back in February when we first attempted to get the pictures we needed out on the mountain. The truck we'd rented in February had a tape deck that had given out on us after a brief period of usage, so this time we made sure the cassette tape player worked. And, to our delight, it did. It was already our habit to blast praise and worship music into the desert airspace as we traversed it, and so now we were set!

Next was the gas fill-up, and then on to the Astra Supermarket for the case of water we needed to pack with us. Another few odds and ends and we were off to the Dairy Queen beside the supermarket for a hamburger and fries. These inter-Kingdom flights were notorious for not feeding us anything, and as a result, we were starved! We sat down and buzzed for a while, not even noticing it was already eleven o'clock.

Not more than an hour later at the Al-Adel Hotel's Room 505, we grabbed hold of two of the twin beds inside and shoved them both together for us to sleep on a bit later. We still had to get our backpacks packed properly, as excess baggage would encumber us too severely once on the climb. We decided to leave extra clothes and particulars here at the hotel while out on the mountain, just as we had the time before. Then we could pick them up on our way back to the airport on April 6. Presently we curled up for the few hours of rest we could grab. Four o'clock was only a short snooze away.

* * *

Brrrrrrrrrrrrrring! Jim shot straight up in the bed at the sound. For that brief moment, he had no earthly idea where he was, or what he was doing there. In fact, he didn't even recognize the hulk of crumpled covers, nor the dead give-away of my mangled mop of hair that poofed out of the top of those bed sheets. But when he glanced through the one squinty eye he held open by sheer force and saw the backpacks ready and waiting by the door, his mind focused and delivered the data necessary to determine his whereabouts and his mission. That's when the excitement hit.

"Riiiiiiiise and shine!" I'd already groaned at the sound of the alarm, knowing this was next in line to harass my ears. I was so exhausted that I preferred to remain a lump that as yet had not been seen in motion. But I knew it was futile. And again it came at me from across the room: "Time to rise and shine! It's four o'clock! Let's go! Let's go! Let's go! Eh-he-he-he-he-he-he-he! Erench." Now he was cackling like a devious old man. It was a crazy language only I could understand.

The same voice, the same lyrics, the same tunes had been waking me up for all these years. Why would an adventurous, death-defying mission cause today to be any different? Jim was Jim. As I lay there, purposely frozen to prod more of his choruses out of my other half, I knew I would not be disappointed.

"Come on, now. Get those bones out of bed! Today's the big day! E-rench-a-bles! I've gotta take my shower, and you have to call in the spoffees. Time to rise and shine!" Jim was in rare form this morning, bleary-eyed as he was. It was all he could do to contain himself from screaming to the sleeping town what he was about to go off and do right behind their backs. And the more he sang out his traditional routine melodies to me, the worse he got beside himself.

I, on the other hand, was none too energetic. The tension of the flight itself had worn me out last night, much less all the preparatory work involved in gathering all the gear we needed for mountain survival. "What in the world are two Cajuns from south Louisiana like us doing here climbing mountains? What are we doing here at all?" I muttered out loud but really, to myself. I leaned my head from side to side to get the creaks out of my neck and chuckled at the thought. Fishing I was well versed at. Hunting, well, I'd been a time or two. But this? I wondered at the insanity of the plan unfolding before me.

Meanwhile, I didn't hear the flow of the shower any more, and Jim came bouncing out from the bathroom still dripping with his eyes bugging out and his mouth flapping nonstop. "Can you believe it? We're baaa-aaack! Oh, man I love this. I love it, love it, love it! We're going back to the mountain!"

I sat there, motionless, except for my eyes following his insanity around the hotel room. Right on cue, seeing my facial expressions judging him to be an idiot, he abruptly stopped sproinging and warbling, and said, "Oh—sorry," and proceeded to walk and talk like any normal human being. I felt my eyes close in familiar disbelief as I tried not to be too amazed at him. It was shower time.

The coffee arrived and Jim had it ready for me when I got out. He also ordered room service breakfast, which consisted of eggs in the shape of omelets and Arabic bread, freshly baked. Small packets of cheese and jelly came with them, and, with the little pots of hot milk and hot water for stirring up the Nescafe coffee, we were set. It didn't take long for Jim's joy to turn into a push to get out of there and on the road. He was a patient man for the most part, but he absolutely could not abide staying any longer than necessary inside a hotel room when the wide open frontiers lay before him. I barely got my teeth brushed after the meal before his deep voice bellowed out, "Come on! Let's go, let's go, let's go!"

"Jim, I am coming. Watch me. See me walking toward my backpack? See me strapping it on? See me gathering all my other stuff? I *am* ready! Now shut up already," I retorted back to his barrage of impatience.

But there was no tension between us at all. We both grinned ear to ear and heart to heart in an eye-lock, knowing the enormous secrecy of what we were about to go off and do. And that was exhilarating!

Out we walked through the door, down the hall, down the stairs, and to the waiting truck.

The air outside was crisp and clear. It was nearing six o'clock by the time we turned into the gas station just on the outskirts of Tabuk to fill up while we had the chance. The highway leading out was a beautiful six-lane job, typical of the layout of other Arabian cities. It circled the main parts of the town so that you did not have to go through the city center unless you wanted to. Lining the median were the plantings of shrubs and trees, which survived only via the labor from third world nations that had been placed there to water them. Tabuk was actually a pleasant, clean town, and there seemed to be a semblance of care for cosmetic areas that was sometimes absent from other such places we'd been in Kingdom. But this morning, with an empty highway before us and the time we needed to really root around in the mountains, the last thing on our minds was the landscaping job completed by the hired help of the architects of Tabuk.

After we prayed for protection and guidance that morning, I snapped the tape into the cassette deck. *Army of God* was the title; it was one verse after another from the Bible that had been put to melody, and the lyrics repeatedly rang out of the glory and power of the Almighty. Not only that, it spoke of deliverance and safety, which was paramount on my mind this day. I thought back over the wild series of events that had led us to this point, and a phrase popped back into my mind I hadn't heard since I was reminded of it in Sharm el Sheikh in January. *Harass the Midianites.*

"Harass the Midianites." I let the words roll smoothly off my tongue.

Today, as I watched the road narrowing to two lanes and the first fingers of light poking their way through the eastern sky to the right, several other instances came to mind that had occurred during those difficult days of the war. Jim had come home for a visit during November of 1990 and had to return alone to Arabia for work by the first part of December. He and I had gone in to see the pastor at the church for special prayers of protection for him before he left. As we sat there in his office chatting, the pastor suddenly began to speak in a forceful tone over Jim, and said "You are to go forth to Arabia from this place! These orders are coming directly from the throne of God! You have a mission to accomplish there! When you speak to people, they will be reminded of what their parents taught them as children about the Bible and its message, especially the stories of the Old Testament! As a pastor, I thereby ordain you to go!"

We had sat there stunned. Neither of us knew how to react or what to say. Nothing like this had quite ever happened to us before, and it wasn't over yet. The pastor continued on: "Write your name out on a slip of paper. I'm going to place it in my study Bible and it will be a reminder to me to pray for you while you are there. You will come again and remove this from where I will place it, and that will be a reminder to your wife that you will indeed return safely. I feel these words very strongly, Jim."

With that, he grabbed the paper Jim had written on and quickly shoved it into his Bible, without looking where it had gone. A few minutes later, just before we left, he said to us, "Well, now let's just see where that paper fell."

The pastor's Bible was one of the older versions, and had the very old artist's renditions of important happenings in the Scriptures in painted pictures from place to place. When he opened up to where Jim's name sheet had been randomly placed, it was right on the same page as the picture of Moses looking at the Burning Bush! At that time, we had seen no significance in that. But now, in remembering, it stood out as though a ten-foot tall, flaming winged angel had appeared physically before us and spoken the words himself!

Just the week before this incident happened, another strong word had come from the same pastor. We had been particularly moved to go down to the altar after a service for prayer, as had many others. The atmosphere inside the church was charged with a Holy Presence you could actually feel, and the altar was crowded with those people who wanted a touch of that Presence. Jim was looking to find God's perfect will for him and our lives together and intended to ask for prayers accordingly. But when the pastor got to us, he abruptly stopped, saying "Just a minute—just a minute." He stood there over us praying for a moment, and then said very directly: "You've got to turn your will to His will, Jim. You've got to turn your will to His. The Lord has some very specific plans for your life, and He's been pulling strings unbeknownst to you to arrange it all. It involves a financial zenith.

But you have got to let go of your will and seek His will first in your life!"

Looking back at that moment, I could now see exactly where those words fell into place. I could mark the day on my calendar when Jim had done just that and seen the miraculous that followed. It was almost too much for my brain to assimilate. God had been so good to us that He'd even told us beforehand what would happen in the days to come, the days we found ourselves in now! At the time, we just didn't know what to think of it. But now all the words spoken over us were blazingly clear in their content and purpose. Now we knew perfectly what they meant.

Jim had turned his will back over to God. He'd been led to Egypt and out again, to the actual land of Midian; he had seen the Holy Mountain of God—the same mountain Moses was looking at in the pastor's Bible. I had surely harassed the Midianites this year, invading their fenced territory. And here we were again, trying to get pictures. Pictures would show the world that the stories of the Bible—the ones children had been taught for centuries by their parents—were actual truths. And what the pastor said was true. Everything was happening just as God said it would. I would never again doubt that there were true prophets of God still active in the world. All this was ridiculously beyond coincidence!

Probably the most amazing prophetic word had been given to us on Jim's second visit home, when we were sitting in the same church for a Wednesday evening service. Jim had not yet settled down from his trip and was just entering the sanctuary when a woman who didn't even know him came up to me. She asked me if I minded if she spoke something out to Jim, something that she felt she heard the Lord say. I hated to admit that it sounded pretty strange, but being polite, I said "Of course. It's fine with me."

This lady then pointed her finger quickly in Jim's face, and turned to the other people seated nearby, and said in a loud, booming voice: *"HEAR YE THIS MAN, FOR HIS FEET SHALL TREAD HOLY GROUND!"*

The power of the statement knocked us both backward, literally, and it was another case of not knowing what to think. The way Jim's life was going at the time, holy ground was the last place his feet were planted. After a while, we sort of dismissed it as being eccentric and a little off the wall.

But today, watching the white lines on the highway zipping by, I pondered the statement and how *true* it was. Yes, actual truth had been prophesied: holy ground was our destination this morning. Frighteningly holy ground—the very ground upon which Almighty God had once descended in flames and fire to meet with Moses. The same ground that meant certain death to anyone touching the mountain when God's Presence was upon it! It was here at Sinai that God spoke to Moses, declaring His law for the sake of all mankind.

"Penny. *Penny*!" Jim's voice crashed and tumbled my stroll down memory lane, and I had to shake my head to regain my whereabouts.

"What?" I asked nonchalantly, trying to convince him I'd been paying attention.

"Check out the maps and see how far it is to Al Sharf from Bir Ibn Hermas." Jim had shifted from drill sergeant to chief navigator.

He was good at this, I thought to myself. Really good. Outrageously unafraid, and totally willing to attempt the impossible. But that's how he always had been to me. I had never known him to be anything but that.

"Bir Ibn Hermas, huh?" I asked him. Okay." I found the data he needed and looked away out my window toward the now rising sun. There in the east, the bright early light had silhouetted a fairly large mountain range. Out Jim's window, far against the western horizon, the foothills of the big ranges we were headed for were barely visible. And everywhere, and on both sides of these far off peaks, nestled the broad, flat land that the Arabians tilled and planted in. Tabuk region was filled with these farms, and the brilliant green of the irrigated spots was an astounding contrast to the earth tones of the natural desert landscape. It had been interesting from the airplane to view these agricultural areas, because they were all huge circles of green, formed by the life-giving waters of the irrigation sprinklers that went round and round the fields. From above, it looked like the hand of some unseen giant had stamped them out with a cookie cutter. And they went on for miles and miles; great, green circles in the sand.

I felt Jim let up on the gas pedal, and asked, "Whatcha doing?"

"The land of Midian was bordered by two mountain ranges according to what I've read. I want to get a shot of this at this time of day on video."

We stopped and pulled off to the right, and Jim got the footage he wanted. The turnoff toward the west was only a few kilometers ahead of us, so we were making good time: time enough for him to consent to a leg stretch, anyway. We walked around a bit before getting back on the road. It was lovely to breathe the cool clean air.

Soon we came to the familiar sign that pointed left over a bridge of sorts, and down another two-lane highway much like the one we were on, was another that read "Bir Ibn Hermas." The old building that was situated right on the corner between the two highways came into view with it, and we knew exactly where we were. That was a good feeling. I remembered the first time we'd been on that highway, coming home from Jordan four years previously, and how I had felt so lost and all alone. Now I'd traversed these roads so much, I thought out loud, "How vulnerable and unaware we were back then."

"What was that?" Jim asked me.

"Oh, I was just thinking of how familiar this territory is all becoming. We thought we were lost when we came back from Jordan this way, remember? And now we know these highways so well."

"Boy, do I remember!" Jim answered.

"Yep. Those are the kind of things I've been thinking about all morning." I emphasized my words, and Jim got the point. Ever since we decided to make that crazy trip through Egypt, our whole lives had revolved around the miraculous and the incredible.

The next hour went by just watching the desert. Bir Ibn Hermas came and went. The mountains were coming closer and closer, and eventually swallowed us up, as we passed through Al Zetah and Al Khan, then onward to Al Sharf. By the time we got there, the truck was getting lower than Jim wanted it to on fuel, and we pulled into the corner station, which appeared to make up most of the tiny town. The road we'd have to take turned south at that point, and after filling up the tank, that's just the direction we went.

The mountains were huge sentinels on both sides now, and we got our first glimpse of the backside of the range that would eventually include Jebel Lawz. Since we had turned, Jim had the vantage point, which secretly thrilled him to no end. His mountain was out there. And he was going to plant his feet where so few others had since the time of Moses! The daydreams were starting already, and he could feel the adrenalin beginning to flow.

The road was built up from the wadi bed we were on, which gave us the capability of seeing down into the valley. It was criss-crossed with tire tracks, which was a bit distasteful already. That meant the locals would be out in force. Jim calculated we would have to go about twenty-five kilometers before making our turnoff toward the east, and as the number approached, he began looking for a major path to follow. As this was all new territory, he was a bit more cautious than usual. We needed to get to climbing early enough not to waste the precious few days we'd been given. Find it he did, though.

"Mark this down, Babe."

I took the compass and kilometer readings and looked up to see that we were entering the expanse of the north/south wadi upon which the highway had been blasted through. In front of us now stood a cinder block fence, which was having a hard time containing a huge gum or eucalyptus tree. Its green foliage was a stark contrast to the barren landscape before us. It appeared to be directly in front of one of several huge water tanks supplied by a nearby well, which explained its ability to survive perfectly. The track led up to it, then turned left around it and right again. I could see we were headed for another wadi, which must be running from up in the higher mountains somewhere, as it appeared to empty into the larger one we were presently crossing. Sure enough, it ran east/west, and the deep rutted tracks dead in its center told us it must be the major one for heading back up to the highlands.

Jim went down a bit until the track turned sufficiently for our truck not to be seen from the highway. This wadi was not unlike the terrain we had seen in Arabia before. It was dotted here and there with acacia trees, which were rather large, and scattered evidence of abandoned Bedouin dwellings. The track seemed to be filled with crushed granite, not sand, which was a new driving trial for Jim to have to deal with. With his usual adaptability, however, he mastered it in no time. As we were driving along, we noticed several large granite knobs of rock that were crumbling away from the elements, and decided to take a break to stretch our legs. Glad to be able to change positions, I joined him in a brief climb to the one closest to us on the right.

The roundish jebel was not but about thirty feet or so high, but it was enough altitude to give us an advance view of the network of wadi systems we now found ourselves involved in. We would be following the one we were in, but Jim could see clearly that there were many possibilities to come back to if it suddenly dead-ended. The small mountains in front of us were a hodge-podge grouping that followed no particular lines at all. Their only consistency was in the fact that their size and number increased as they got closer to the monster range in the far background, which was, at present, enshrouded in haze.

"Let's head 'um up and mooooooooooove 'em out!" Here came the order from the Boss. "I can't wait another second!" So down the jebel and into the truck we went in eager anticipation of what lay ahead of us. I could feel the adrenaline starting to course through my own veins!

We followed the track just north of due east for another twenty or so kilometers and entered into an area where the main track had a curve off to the right that was almost as well used. Jim pulled up to the fork and stopped, looking down the turn to see where it would lead. The big mountains were not far off now, and this could be the track we'd been looking for.

Just the moment I gazed down the wadi, a feature in the landscape at the far end of the valley leaped out with commanding prominence. "Look at that big rock up on top of that jebel!" I was captivated immediately. "Do you see that down there, babe?"

"Yeah, that's pretty strange," Jim agreed with me while he puzzled over it. "It sure sticks out like a sore thumb!"

A good way away from where we sat, a rather large jebel stood out from the wadi basin. It was just about the same as all the others we had seen thus far: more like a huge pile of massive boulders than a shaped mountain. But this one was different in another way. At the very top was a huge slab of rock that stuck up into the air like a candle sitting on top of a birthday cake. It leaned slightly forward and to the right from our vantage point, and even from as far away as we were, caught the eye at once. It was the most obvious thing in the wadi.

"Let's go on down and check it out," Jim decided out loud. "I think I might be able to follow this track around to the left and up into the big peaks back there once we pass by that thing," he said, motioning with his hand toward the monumental rock on top of the jebel.

So we started off again. It wasn't but a few kilometers before we noticed great piles of small stones were collected in what resembled dwellings all around us. The closer we got to the big rock, the more the stone piles. The track under us was also changing. It was giving way to solid, smooth granite, which rose and fell like an earthquake had once caused a great undulation of the bedrock to take place here. These rises and valleys boasted upwards of twenty-foot swings, and provided an excellent opportunity for us to hide the vehicle and get out for pictures and exploration. Jim headed for the valley ahead of us and saw quickly that the driving was about to get very interesting. In front of us lay a hairpin curve at a very steep angle to climb. He put the Toyota into 4 wheel drive low, though, and slowly crept up and over the spot. Seeing its performance did his confidence in the little jeep a lot of good. After all, he didn't know this truck, and it sure wasn't our Patrol! Once over the hump, the other side dove down into what almost looked like a river channel, but for it being rock instead of earth. Into this slip he pulled, and out we popped instantaneously from the jeep: the pair of would be archeologists.

We began walking around poking through the stacks of rocks we'd seen all along the way. One thing was sure; these were definite placements of stone. Some were relatively intact at their bases, and revealed both circular and square patterns. Most all the tops had caved in, and that explained the look they had of being mere piles of rubble from the track. We noticed that as the wadi size narrowed to pass in front of the jebel with the huge rock at its apex, the frequency of these sites increased. Jim began to video all these things we were looking at, while I manned the still photography camera.

We were making steady progress toward the big rock now and decided it was time to begin climbing up toward its base. We started upward to the left and compassed the ridge that would connect us behind and just slightly to the left of it. As we drew closer, one thing was glaringly obvious. It was one hundred times bigger than it appeared from the end of the wadi where we had first seen it. This rock was *huge*! It was not apparent right then what the most amazing characteristic of this colossus was, for our angle of vision had not yet changed. It would only be after we turned back again to the right, and were even with it, that the rock would reveal its wonderful secret to us. For the present moment, we had stopped to argue over something much more mundane; the brownish black markings on the side of a rock we were standing in front of.

"It's a bee. A bee, I'm telling you! Can't you see those wings?" Jim cackled out at me. He could not understand why I couldn't see it.

"You've lost your eyes, man!" I shouted back at him from the boulder where I'd perched myself. "It's a moose as plain as a moose can be!"

"Ha!" Jim's laughter filled the airspace. "A moose?" His face crinkled up and he roared. It was bad enough I couldn't see the very obvious bee there, but to envision a moose? That was the most ridiculous thing he'd ever heard.

"All right, smart-alec!" I yelled back. "Let's just get over there to it and examine it closer!" I was as convinced of my moose as he was of his bee. Neither one of us realized that this very argument would still be continuing fifteen years later.

Even now, at the spot we moved to which was directly in front of the markings, both of us were still just as sure of our own foregone conclusions. Both of us shook our heads in dismay at each other's ignorance and lack of vision. We sat there laughing and flipping each other hand signs, not at all unlike Curly and Moe of the Three Stooges. But we didn't have long to play like this; we had to move on and not relish this moment. We decided to drop it and bring it up again at our campfire later that evening.

It was only a matter of steps now before we reached the big rock, and we decided to climb on up there to see how in the world it was standing. When we got alongside of it, though, our thoughts of the bee flew off with the moose, and our laughter faded into unbridled awe at what we were seeing.

"It's impossible!" Jim's face froze as did his forward motion.

"I can't believe it!" I was not at all prepared for what I was suddenly standing directly below.

There, running from the very bottom of the immense structure to the very top, was a crack; a cleanly sliced, gargantuan gash wide enough for a man to walk through! This gigantic rock had been split clean in two, right down the middle by what must have been a terrifyingly tremendous force! We looked at each other and swallowed hard. And there was something else that ran chills up and down our bodies. From our angle, this split rock looked so much like something we'd seen on the east side of the range on our first two trips into the region: the two great blocks of granite with the almond tree between them!

From the backside, we scrambled up toward the huge, towering stones, and realized quickly that this must be a representation of something. A verse kept floating around in my head. Just now I couldn't remember where it was exactly located in the Bible; only that it was in the Psalms somewhere. *"He clave the rocks in the wilderness, and gave them drink as out of the great depths, He brought streams also out of the rock, and caused waters to run down like rivers"* (Psalms 78:15,16). I knew the word "clave" meant to divide, or split evenly. Searching the Hebrew would later confirm that. And then it hit me! This was one very healthy candidate for the rock Moses struck with his rod at the command of the Almighty, where waters gushed forth for the children of Israel to drink!

I was up ahead of Jim, because he had stopped momentarily to get his video going. I couldn't wait a moment longer to touch that rock and get in between those two huge slabs of granite. My impatience and excited wonder was propelling me forward like a thirsty desert traveler who'd finally seen the springs of an oasis on the horizon! Of course I reached the split in the rock first and saw that it was so big I wouldn't even have to squeeze my shoulders through. Normal walking would suffice. And all at once *I found myself standing in the cleft of the rock.*

The scale of God's greatness was beginning to overwhelm me. All my life, I'd thought that the rock at Horeb, which is the name given by the Bible for that location, was probably just any ordinary rock on the ground Moses walked himself up to and struck. This mammoth thing seemed like it was at least a hundred if not two hundred feet off the ground, and I imagined it would have taken the very hand of God to have the power necessary to cleave it cleanly apart like this! The closer I examined it, the more convinced I became of its authenticity: and the more I understood the significance of standing still in the heart

THE SPLIT ROCK AT THE FAR END OF THE VALLEY

of that Rock, where the wind ceased to blow and I was sheltered from the brilliant rays of the sun.

I just stood still there in the hush for a brief interlude, soaking up the revelation. But more was in front of me, and I didn't stay motionless very long. I continued my search through the midst of the actual split itself and found that it ran cleanly from top to bottom, and no fissures or other evidences of natural wear were visible. However, in several places, what appeared to be huge flakes of granite maybe a quarter of an inch thick were torn from the bottom of each side of the split upward. This was no tiny crack in a rock, but a widened gap that fit none of the properties of erosion that I was aware of.

"Penny! *Penny!*" The insistent voice was hollering my name again. I was so deep into what I was thinking that I was actually ignoring

Jim's voice at first. It took a lot to make me ignore this man's voice! "Hey! Where are you going? What are you doing?" Jim yelled out a second time.

I hesitated and stabilized my foot against the right wall of the split, then answered between my breaths, "What do you mean, what am I doing? I'm exploring!" I knew good and well he was just trying to slow me down so he could get into that crack with me, before I found something interesting first. I shook my head and as I looked right, I found a cavity within the wall that had a round black stone inside that caught my eye. It too, had been split in half. I fingered it for a while then put it back, not seeing any significant reason to drag it along, knowing without a shadow of a doubt that I would have to add it to the already insanely heavy pack I'd be lugging up the mountain on my back in just a few short hours. After all, we had only been climbing around for an hour, and with five days ahead of us, I knew the weight of all I'd have to carry home would crush me if I started collecting specimens now.

As I walked on through to the other side, I found that at the base of the rock itself, a channel had been cut out of the granite exactly in line with the split. That channel then branched to the right and to the left and continued down the boulderous jebel that the massive rock was sitting on and into the valley below. This I thought was a real find, because the amount of rainfall in that portion of Arabia would have not been substantial enough in twenty thousand years to wear such a deep cut into the granite via natural runoff. Indeed, odds were beginning to stack up in favor of the scriptures: "He clave the rocks in the wilderness, and gave them drink as out of the great depths. He brought steams also out of the rock, and *caused waters to run down like rivers* (Ps. 78:15,16). I sat there transfixed in time at the headspring: the place where the waters must have gushed up out of the center of that rock and flowed in torrents down the sides of the rock hill and into the valley below. It was clear from my vantage point just how perfect this spot was for the pooling up of waters below me. The ground surface in all the areas we had been traveling through so far consisted of the same crushed granite gravel that Jim was learning to drive in; and it occurred to me as I sat there high above the valley floor that if that had been the same here, the waters would have been swallowed up as rapidly as they hit the surface of the ground. But in this place, the whole perimeter way below the

BARE ROCK FLOOR BELOW THE SPLIT ROCK WHERE
WATER WOULD HAVE POOLED

rock was uniform, smooth granite, which would have caused the waters to collect and pool instead of being absorbed into the gravel.

It dawned on me that there must have been hundreds of thousands of people and their animals, and one little trickle of water flowing from a little rock would have taken days and days to quench their thirsts. Somehow all of a sudden, I just couldn't picture the typical Sunday school remembrance of this event as being that little stream of tradition! But being here in this place I found myself surveying the topographical features; I realized that any waters coming out of this rock and flowing into the valley below would have formed great, deep basins of the life-giving liquid, easily allowing the crowds and the flocks to drink in many places all at the same time. This scenario would have worked!

By the time I'd figured all this out in my head, Jim had come up behind me and we had to move on. We decided to go on down the front side of the jebel upon which the split rock sat and walk around several of the stone piles that were scattered at its base. In doing so, Jim kept the video camera rolling, and I began snapping photographs again. For a while we wandered independently of one another, doing our best to cover distances that were far larger than we ever imagined they would be. It had been that way ever since Egypt: *everything* was bigger than we imagined!

Jim had become intrigued by a monstrous flat, smooth boulder that had a strangely perfect looking hole about two feet wide in its top. He stood up on it, and then beside it, noticing that on one end, these same small stones that were the building blocks of all the other dwellings in the vicinity were piled up as if on purpose. One of them in particular caught his eye. It was typical of the other stones but for its surface, which was a deep rusty color on one side, and very smooth, as though glazed with a finish. He was just about to video it closely when a great rumble shook the air and the ground around all around him!

"Whoa!" he yelled out in my direction. I had been investigating one of the square groupings of stones out in front of the base of the split rock. "Did you hear that?"

"Wow, did I hear it! It sounded just like thunder!" I yelled back at him, looking skyward in curious bewilderment at the crystal blue canopy above my head.

"Jim, how could that have been thunder?" My mind raced back to the day we'd been high atop Karak Castle in Jordan, close enough to the Israeli border to hear the military shelling that was then going on in that region. I remembered the booming sounds it had produced, and the vibrations. This had been a similar sound, but not identical. This sounded exactly like thunder! But here? There was nothing in the sky at all save endless blue, and we had just heard an earth shaking concussion of thunder. Nothing we could see could have produced that sound. Nothing, that is, except the Voice of God! Psalm 81:7 says, *"Thou calledst in trouble, and I delivered thee: I answered thee in the secret place of thunder: I proved thee at the waters of Meribah. Selah!"* Apparently where Moses struck the rock was called the waters of Meribah, and Massah, by the Bible; it was associated with a secret thunder! Was this truly the Voice of God we had just heard?

We continued wandering around the base of the split rock for the next hour before moving on. We had yet to find the track that led up to the high peaks in the distance, and it was getting close to noon. So we returned to the truck and backed out into the same track we had first been on to enter this place. Jim followed it for another kilometer or so and continued on as it progressed around a bend to the right. Curious jebels were perched on either side of us this whole course, and the bend took us into a very wide wadi that looked like the major runoff from the main heights behind us. Just as soon as we entered the turn, another phenomenon sprung into our view. It was a vast outcropping of white quartz that just stood alone in the midst of the gravel. It looked ridiculous sitting there, so pristine and out of place. It gave me the impression that it had suddenly just burst forth from the depths of the earth below.

"That's a weird sight!" I commented to Jim. "I thought quartz was typically found in vein structure! I've never seen it in a huge clump just lying around in the middle of a gravel bed!"

"I haven't either. Let's go on over and see." Jim's interest was pricking him big time, considering some rare facts he knew about the white stone.

We rolled up beside it and walked all over the outcropping for a few minutes. Of course we'd have to take a few of these stones, I rationalized. And within a moment, Jim had a prize piece. About six by four inches, it had all the earmarks of having been sawn on by some instrument. Regular grooves covered one side of the chunk, and I could sense the smugness of a first find settling over him. I screwed up my face and frowned it into a blatant pout, delivering it to him so as to be certain he noticed. But there was no time to waste. As we continued on, we saw a large Bedouin tent that had been rolled up and was semi-hidden against the far side of this formation. We stayed clear of it out of respect for the owners, whom we were afraid could surface any time and end our little excursion.

Looking up and around, just in case, we discovered some other stone groupings in the background, up against the jebels. We decided not to move the truck, but to just walk on over to them. Upon arrival, we got

STONE CIRCLES WITH THRESHOLDS NEAR THE SPLIT ROCK

the feeling immediately that these sites were far more ancient than the piles of stones we had seen back around the corner by the split rock. The stones were larger, and very rounded in design. These were then placed to form large circles on the ground, and several had a feature that caused us to really stop and pay attention. In fact, it boggled our minds right away! These few circles actually had thresholds!

Two rectangular stones of much larger size had been placed standing up next to one another, with about a man's breadth in between, as though representing a doorway. So then each circle, which ranged in circumference from eight to twenty feet, had an entrance. One of the very large circles had a smaller one attached to it via one of these doorways of stone, which gave Jim the impression that this had once been some kind of a worship site, as inner "holy places" were often represented in such a manner. As he stood inside this circle and looked straight in front of him, his gaze fell right across the white quartz, then onward across the wadi and right up to the tops of the high peaks in the background. It had to mean something.

"Significant. This one is really different, Penny! Come see this." Jim ordered me over and explained it all to me, and I witnessed with his conclusions immediately. I had been reading a book about how ancient peoples put great store in precious stones, and how different formations in any landscape were often used as holy sites for their rituals. This place had all those properties and then some, I thought.

But that was a short lived thought. "Oh, great! Take a look over there!" I grimaced in agitation, and motioned with a wild waving of my right arm toward the objects of my immediate discontent.

"Argh! Back to the truck!" Jim snarled through gritted teeth. There against the foothills were several young camels, which could only mean nomads in the vicinity. Jim didn't want to be there that far away from the truck if we ended up in an encounter. So we took off at a fast clip and jumped in before we could be seen. It was very fortunate that we were not, because the day would have most certainly turned out far differently.

Jim turned the jeep back toward the range now, and we went around another bend back to the left, which pointed us back in the same direction we'd come from before, toward the split rock. But this time we were on the backside and another track, so it was unfamiliar territory. Jim had planned to do a quick exploration, only to look for the track that would get us the closest to the mountains so our distance to walk before the climb began would be diminished. By taking this track though, we ran across a series of rocks with ancient writing all over them, much the same as the ones we'd seen on the other side of the range in February when Lucas and Chelsea had been along. A unique design became our immediate focal point here, however.

These rocks were full of not only what appeared to be lettering of some ancient form, but footprints had been etched all over the boulders which lay strewn across the entire perimeter. But these were not mere footprints. On either side of the foot drawing, lines had been etched to clearly mark out the straps of a sandal. Even the toe had such a mark! I knew we didn't have much time to linger, but these really, really

SANDALED FOOTPRINTS NEAR THE SPLIT ROCK

intrigued me no end. Why would so many people stop to trace the outline of their sandaled feet in this place? I had no way of knowing at that moment that these petroglyphs would become one of the most important discoveries we would ever make; a mark placed by an ancient people of extreme prophetic destiny! But for now, all I really wanted to do was to stuff a few of these in my backpack, or at least in the truck. I reached out to try and get one of the smaller rocks on which a particularly nice pair of sandals had been carved, but I couldn't even begin to lift it from the ground, much less carry it. So, unfortunately, we only had time to snap a few photos and off we were again. It was already one o'clock, and we were behind schedule. We had not expected to find what we had found already this morning!

We drove on down back into the same wadi where we started, where the white quartz was, but this time turned to the right and toward the mountains instead of to the left back to the split rock. Jim came over a ridge, and followed the track down further, as it dove off into the deepest part of the dry watercourse. Here, he found what he had been searching for. In front of him, the desert tracks branched off in several directions. Each disappeared back toward the mountains, hidden from the sight of each other by the deep gorges that had been formed between them. He continued on as far back as he could drive in one of them, and parked the jeep. He looked over at me, and grinned.

"I'm going to climb up that ridge and see if this is where we want to start."

"Okay, I think I'll just stay here and look around a bit," I answered back. I really had no desire to walk all the way over there to where he'd pointed and then have to come all the way back. That huge mountain was glaring at me already, and my feet and back were starting to hurt before I ever got started.

Once up on the top, Jim saw that there were several identical ridges to the one he'd just mounted between him and the mountains behind us. Not exactly close parking, he thought. He estimated it would take us several hours walking from this spot just to get to the bottom of the place he wanted to begin our climb. We'd be worn out by the time the climb began if he started us from here. He kept going a little farther, though, just to see what lay ahead in the valley between his ridge and the next one.

"Come on, Jim!" I started grumping out loud, though no one was there to hear me. I had been waiting for what seemed like an eternity for him to get back, and I was not content to just sit there any longer. My patience, or the grand lack thereof, was an established given, and the end of its short fuse was approaching. I walked around the truck a few more times, and stopped to listen for a moment when I got to the front bumper. "Yes!" I exclaimed through my teeth, with a smile back on my face again. I could hear the crunch of the granite gravel behind me and when I turned again, there he was.

"What'd ya see, big boy?" I asked in my best Mae West impression.

"Well, I did see something, but I want you to see it before I say anything. That way you can make up your own mind."

I hated it when he did things like this to me, especially knowing my lack of patience to be what it was. "No, tell me now!" I pleaded, looking up at him, blaring my eyes as big and wide as I could make them.

"No can do, my dear," he said, relishing his position.

"Oh, all right, all right! Let's go then!" I retorted, realizing my eye batting had done nothing at all to persuade him. I kicked the beady gravel up with my feet and began to charge forth to climb up the slope.

He grabbed me by the arm and arrested my forward motion, which made matters even worse. "No, no; we're not climbing up to see. We're going to drive over to where it is." His toothy grin just hacked me off all the more. I guess he couldn't help laughing when he saw the look I gave him, though. "Yes, my Penny, who wants everything now! You will just have to wait!

"But that's not fair. You saw something, and now you won't show me? Or even give me a hint?"

"Nope. Come on, get in the truck."

I had no choice. He was bigger than I was. So off we went to try and find a closer place to get to whatever it was Jim had seen. I puzzled and pondered, but had no clue as to what it could be.

But I didn't have to wait long. Just up ahead was as far as the truck could go, as the ridges and boulders were getting thick and blocked the way.

"Grab the camera, and follow me," Jim said as he gathered his video. "I want to see your face when you see it."

It took about five minutes to get to the edge of the valley that fell off sharply from beneath our feet. This was a deep channel that had been carved out over the years as a natural drainage from the mountains. When I got to the edge, I felt my breath catch in my throat when I saw the same thing Jim had seen from the other ridge.

"Whoa, Jim! Palm trees! It's a whole grove of palm trees!" I was astonished to see the majestic fronds swaying in the breeze, hidden away completely from anyone passing through the major wadi.

"I wanted to see if you got the same reaction as me, and I guess you did," Jim said, enjoying my enthusiasm. He'd seen the palms from up above, and Elim—the biblically noted area containing seventy palms—had crossed his mind.

"These are the only palms I've seen out here on this side of Jebel Lawz at all! The only trees I've seen were those big acacias we passed earlier. This whole west side seems so harsh and arid compared to the east!" I was speaking in hushed tones of amazement. "What do you think it is? Elim?"

"It could be, I guess. I don't know. For sure there has to be a well down there supporting all this life. That's a must."

"Yeah, you're right. Come on!" By this time I was waving him on, and I took off down into the valley. When I reached the trees, it was surprising how tall they were, and how they were so cleverly hidden from sight. There were several balled up masses of barbed wire fencing, evidently covering the wells and keeping them secured from wandering flocks and camels. In all, at a minimum seventy palms were visible, with multitudes of ancient trunks and pieces lying across the ground below the live ones where they'd fallen or been cut down years before. It was obvious that the sight had been there for a long, long time.

"Hey, look at this!" I yelled back at Jim. "The last place I saw something like this was Nuweiba Beach in Egypt."

"Oh, yeah." Jim answered. "Looks like all the different granite stones were mortared together by the water here, huh?"

"Yep!" It was certain that at one point in time, much water had coursed through this area, without question. There were granite stones from about hand-sized all the way up to about the size of a football that had been tumbled smooth by it, no doubt. We chatted as we continued to walk through the area, carrying on and spouting theories in a huge analysis of the place like we'd been doing this sort of thing all our lives. To us, at least, we felt like we'd finally found our course and we were loving every minute of it.

But Jim noticed away to the west, the sun had reached apex already some time ago, and was beginning its slow and steadfast arc toward the western horizon. "Well, enough leisure. We gotta find a closer place to that mountain wash I want to climb up, or we're gonna be hiking all afternoon just to get to where we can start."

"Oh, all right," I said, not all thrilled to be moving the truck again. I felt it was by an act of God we hadn't been caught thus far, so why push our luck by getting back out into the open?

But Jim was determined. There was no changing his mind. So out we went again, back past the quartz and the ancient holy site and due west, looking for any breaks at all we might find leading left toward the mountains. We poked up a few that looked favorable, just to find them ending in large boulders or the like.

The terrain was incredibly torturous to the poor little vehicle, and much more so to us humans inside it. Jim didn't help matters at all, with his "I only know two speeds" mentality, which meant wide open, slinging gravel, or dead stopped. We came to a particular place where there was almost nothing left of the track we'd been following, and only stone and rocks of a measurable size lay beneath us. The path dipped sharply down about four feet, and was at such an angle that when Jim tried to pass over it, the truck nosedived and lurched forward, causing me to crash my forehead suddenly and forcefully against the bar across the dash. I whipped my injured forehead around and let loose with an intense expression of indignation, concentrating it hard and sharp so that Jim would feel my eyes like an acetylene torch etching a hole in the side of his face.

"*Jiiiiiiiiiim!*" The tone of my voice was not far from the deep, low growl of a tiger. It would be wise of him not say another word for a while. People didn't call me "Tabasco" for nothing, and he knew it better than anybody! He grimaced and winced with sufficient sorrow and hurt for my hurt, however, thereby earning the ability to live and drive another day. So, with great effort to show me the true nature of his disgrace, he ever so slowly began moving forward again, this time with a great deal of cautious progress. God and God alone could help him if he slammed my head into that dash again! So he tried to put his mind back on what he was there for. Looking up ahead, he realized this path we were on was ending fast. It just looked like we weren't meant to get any closer to that range than we'd been when we saw the palms.

"Great. Now I've got to turn around again," he remarked with disgust.

"I have no comment." What else could I say? After all, I'd been convinced we shouldn't move the truck in the first place. I found myself in my own personal state of gloat that I'd been right, but I knew better than to say that much out loud to Jim. I could see the fringes of aggravation twitching in his facial expressions, and even I didn't have that much courage, even when I was mad. Besides that, my head still hurt.

Jim had a tough time turning the truck around, but he finally got it and began heading back the same way we'd come before all over again. It was the only way out because of the boulders literally everywhere.

We could both see the place where we had dropped off so suddenly and I'd cracked my head into the dash coming up, so he sped up a little to get the momentum he'd need to get back up that slope. He hit it all right, but halfway up, the little engine of the Toyota just didn't have the power to keep going. We slid right back down with a nasty thud, and sat there, completely stuck!

Now we were in a bit of a predicament. This was a rent truck, after all! Jim didn't have the usual series of implements he carried in our own truck for emergencies. At best, we had with us a small, folding campers' shovel. And in this situation, it was going to have to do. Out he went with it and started shoveling against the hard rocky basin, trying to level out enough of an area for the tires to get a grip. It took some time, but he finally got it, and the truck popped up and over the hill like there had never been a problem. We half-heartedly attempted to follow one more path to the left, which panned out just as miserably as all the others before it. The only thing that was memorable about this last track was the terrifyingly huge hornet that kept crashing into our windshield and trying to attack Jim. I laughed the whole way back to the same place I told him before we should have stayed in. My head was starting to feel better already!

Jim pulled back into the same tire tracks we had parked in earlier and turned the engine off. "Well, this is it then. We start from here. Let's get geared up. Go ahead and post the letters and I'll start securing the packs." He had written an explanation of sorts to put up in the truck window, along with a copy of our travel letter giving us permission to be in the area. He'd had a Saudi friend's wife translate his English into Arabic for the sake of those Bedouins who'd possibly see it, and it told of how we were just a family that loved the countryside there and would be in the mountains camping. We hoped it would keep our vehicle from being trashed. At present, I was already taping them to the inside of the windows, just like he'd asked me to do.

When I finished that, I started filling up the five-gallon collapsible jug we brought along with the water bottles purchased the night before at the Astra Supermarket. Each of our backpacks was equipped to hold two liter-sized water bottles, but we would need more than that for this journey. We would be saving the bottles for last, and drinking from this jug until it was gone first, thus lightening the load for Jim who would have to carry it alone. And water is heavy. Heavier than I ever dreamed!

When all was said and done, our backpacks looked like bloated ticks about to burst. Picking one of them up was almost impossible! I wondered how in the world I was going to survive just the weight of the pack, much less climbing with it on my back! But we could not cut down any further than we had already. We had to have our camping gear, the flashlights, the camera accessories, and the other things we'd packed. The only food we were carrying was the assortment of nasty looking energy bars from the health food store, and two packs of trail mix we'd found in a store in Al-Khobar near home. There just was no other option but to heave ho and go for it. So Jim hoisted up my backpack for me, and slung it on my back, while I struggled then to help him with his. We lay our hands upon the truck and asked God to protect it, gave each other an excitedly terrified and knowing look, and we were off.

The weight of the packs was absolutely disabling to me at first. I could go no further than a few hundred yards without having to adjust the straps, grab a sip of water, and rest. Jim had the added burden of the water jug, which sloshed and gurgled loudly as it swung from his hand. That and the sound of our labored breathing was really all we heard for a while, but for the continual and rhythmic crunch of the granite gravel under our feet. Conversation was completely out of the question, as it expended valuable energy and caused thirst at more regular intervals. All we could do was to keep plodding away at the series of ridges in front of us. Time was beginning to slow to a monotonous crawl.

This kind of hiking was the worst for wearing a body out quickly. We found ourselves climbing seventy-five to one hundred feet upward over the large boulders characteristic of the area, which made the progress slow and difficult anyway, and then having to crawl down the other side and face another just like the one we'd just gotten over. We had left the truck at about two o'clock. By four we had barely reached the last of the valleys before the ground level had risen to the upper plateau and we didn't have to lose altitude any more. Once we reached that point, it seemed like miles ahead of us to the base of the wadi-wash we intended to climb up the mountains themselves. It was very discouraging. The sun was already beginning to lose its brilliance, and we knew that dusk was going to stop our progress flat.

Up where we were now, though, at least the walking was on fairly flat ground. From time to time as I padded along behind Jim, I caught a whiff of the sweetest smelling fragrance I'd ever smelled, but I couldn't see any place from which it could be emanating. I was beginning to believe I was imagining it. I remembered Jim's mom telling me that a very sweet, heavenly smell accompanied angels' presence on the earth, and I decided to roll that thought around as I struggled against the straps of the pack, which were cutting deep grooves into my shoulders already.

Jim was on up about ten feet ahead of me, and keeping up a pretty good pace now that the climbing had a more even grade and we weren't going up and down and up again as we had been before. He noticed that the large shrubs we'd seen dotting the landscape over on the other side back in February were starting to appear here and there in the distance. The pack on his back and the dead weight of the water jug were burdening him, though, and I caught him looking back at me to see if it looked like I needed a rest yet.

He stopped for a moment and I felt my face go flush. I knew he was watching me; the short little woman plodding along behind him. And I must have looked ridiculous! My backpack was half as big as I was, and I knew I made a rather comical figure out here in this wilderness. I had my usually free-flying long curly hair pulled over to each side in braids like a twelve-year-old so that my back pack wouldn't rip it out of my head, and the way I was walking to compensate for the weight of the pack was hilarious, even to me. I would walk upright a few steps, then bend over and shift the weight forward so that the top of the pack hit me in the head. Then, I'd duck my head down, looking at the ground, and walk like a hunchback until that got uncomfortable. After that, I'd do it all over again. It kept either set of muscles from getting so fatigued that cramping would ensue. That was something I just couldn't have handled in addition to all this work!

"Penny!" He knew I needed to stop.

"Huh?" It was all I could get out of my mouth. Jim had caught me just as I leaned over and shifted the pack again, and I knew I must look really absurd with my head cocked to the side and my body all bent up. But I couldn't help it. I didn't want to tell him I was hurting all over already, and my heart was pounding so hard I thought I was going to pass out!

"Let's stop for a break up under that little acacia tree." He was smiling at me like I had multi-colored hair and a big round red nose. I would have probably looked better at that moment if I had!

"No arguments here," I replied, heaving a great sigh of relief. I truly did need to catch my breath, and get that hideous torture device off my back for a while. When I got to the tree, I slung the pack down and sat on it like a leather recliner, gazing up into the canopy above my head. I was all prepared to zone completely out for whatever break time Jim was going to allow us to take, when my eyes caught a slight movement in the thorny branches above me. There, not ten feet from my eyes, were two of the tiniest little black birds I'd ever seen, twittering and hopping about excitedly. Their song was so refreshing; warming my heart to the very core! With little legs not even as big as toothpicks, they were using them nonetheless to aid in the hurried preparedness of nesting. They were totally immersed in what they had been programmed by God to do on this earth and singing while they worked!

Jim came over to me with the jug, which was still impossibly heavy for me to both hold and drink out of at the same time. But between the sweet little birds and the water, I actually felt good enough to stand up and stretch and decided to wander about and have a look at the things near us. A very different looking small bush caught my attention, and I bent down to give it a closer look.

The bush was stripped of whatever leaves it should have had; I surmised that it possibly had not yet come forth with its new growth for the year. What lay beneath it is what I found so strange, and what caught my eye from all the way over by the acacia tree. Tiny little cream colored spheres were strewn all around it and piled beneath the bush, as if they'd all come off at one time. I reached down and picked up a handful, only to discover them to be as light as Styrofoam, and fuzzy to the touch. When I closed my hand tightly around them, they clung to one another and left a sort of an oily residue against my skin. I let that batch drop from my hand and picked up another group, held up my hand and slowly released them to see how they would react in the air. They delicately floated back to the ground again, most likely because of the extreme airiness and light weight they possessed. I was totally intrigued.

"Jim, get a load of this, will ya?" I couldn't wait to show him any longer.

"Whatcha got?" He was already on his way over to where I had been experimenting with this unusual substance.

"Well, I don't really know, but didn't one of those books we read say something about a plant they thought could have been manna? Wasn't it talking about a plant that had seeds that gathered in piles like this?"

"Yeah, I think so. I believe it said that it was supposed to look or taste somewhat like coriander seed."

I knew where he was going with this. But nothing he said was going to make me put any of this stuff in my mouth. I answered him back before he could tell me to try it. "Well, I'm not eating any of it. But get it on film, just in case it turns out to be important."

It was stupid of me to even ask him to get it on film. By the time I looked up, he had already gotten me both crushing the little round things in my hand, and letting them drop into the air. But that was it for the brief break. Jim reminded me that the sun was picking up speed the closer it got to the horizon, and we really needed to get moving again. I knew that. I knew all too well how late it was getting, and how far away we were, and how worn out I was already when we hadn't even started climbing. Heaving a huge sigh and a loud grunt, I swung the arduous pack onto my sore back and followed not so happily, but obediently.

He had to realize how tired I must be, I thought, because even his big frame was struggling to handle the load he was carrying. Before he got too far ahead of me, he yelled back and said, "Hey, nobody but you is crazy enough to be out here with me like this. You know that, don't you?"

A tremendous flock of butterflies suddenly leaped up into my heart. In an instant, the pack on my back was not the focus of my thinking any longer. The wilds all around me were. The crunching of granite under my feet, and the happy song of tiny birds. The endlessly blue sky and the extreme mountains we were about to ascend. The whispers running down the seam of the wind that presently moved the wisps of hair around my face, like dancing fairies full of unknown secrets! This had become paramount with Jim's comment to me, along with the knowing that there was no place on earth I would have rather been, aching body and all. "Yeah. I know!" I answered him beaming from the intensity of the rush I felt coursing through my veins. It was more than enough to keep my feet tracking steadily, one in front of the other.

It seemed like we hadn't gone on much further than few hundred yards before we came upon the first of the shrubs Jim had seen earlier. He didn't know what they were called, but their foliage resembled light green pine needles, except soft and profuse. They stood anywhere from two to six feet tall and waved pleasantly in the light breeze. That's when it hit us both square in the nose. The fragrance I thought I was imagining earlier blew into our faces so strongly that it almost knocked us over. Jim was overwhelmed with it, and exclaimed as though he'd run into a treasure.

"What's that fantastic smell?" He was wide eyed and incredulous.

I looked at the little white flowers covering the bushes and realized they had to be the source of the absolutely pungent, sweet aroma. These bushes, whatever they were, covered the east side of the mountain, whereas they were sparse on these hillsides. But on the other side where we had seen them before, they had never been in bloom. In fact, we had no idea until now that they even did bloom! We both hurried over and planted our faces in the luxury in front of us, to take in deep drafts of the exotic, celestial scent issuing forth from this humble, desert shrub.

I opened my eyes and felt an enormous smile spread over my face. "I've been getting little whiffs of this ever since we got up on this level, but I thought I was imagining things. This is a gorgeous smell! It's a good sign, mate!"

"I believe so, my dear." Jim responded. "But we gotta go. No time to stop now."

Onward toward the mountains we went, stopping only briefly here and there for a five-minute break. The sun was already behind the western peaks way off in the distance, and we were walking in shadows even though we had an hour or so left before sunset. We finally reached the edge of the wash Jim had targeted as our easiest access to the heights and began the painstakingly slow journey over the boulders that had collected over the centuries in this valley. On our left stood the majority of the highest peaks that Jim figured we had to

The peak named "The Cone"

cross before we'd be able to see the Lawz range. The sheer walls that made up their western slopes made climbing them directly impossible, so we would endeavor to get to the top of the long ridge and traverse it over to them via this way.

In the foreground between us and these jagged peaks to the left stood the most unique of the series of big mountains. We named it "The Cone" as soon as we came upon it, because that's just what it looked like—a polished, pointed cone. It was a high, pale gray, granite mountain that seemed to stand alone in the midst of all the others that were connected to one another, and it was the shape of a conical volcano, smooth as glass on top. It was almost as though the rough granite exterior the others exhibited had been carved away by a sculptor's knife on this one monolith on purpose. An easy reference point, I knew Jim was filing this thing away in his mind for later. I also knew that it seemed to be dreadfully and frighteningly high; and when I compared its height to the others on the range behind it, I was not at all amused. Their height surpassed this cone, and that already had me shaking in my sneakers just looking at it. How would I ever get up the others?

I looked over to the right, which was the side of the mountain we were headed toward and became aware of the fact that the slopes actually ran not only east to west, but from the westernmost point, turned abruptly and ran south to north. This section of the range was the one that had been blocking the light of the sun completely from us for a while now. We were basically hemmed in by the depth of the corridor we were climbing, and our tiny human forms were about to be hidden from view. It felt both safe and terrifying to me at the same time. Here we were, with darkness falling, all alone with only each other in the absolute middle of nowhere. But then again, the serenity and the strength of the massive mountain felt as though it was enfolding us and protecting us in a way. It was a strange paradox.

As I had been walking along behind him, I could see that with regularity, Jim had been keeping his eye on the sun, or the lack of its visibility thereof. He was watching the shadows completely enfold the eastern ridge to our left. I understood exactly why he was becoming nervous; we weren't nearly as far up this wash as we needed to be, and his legs were cramping up so badly now he almost couldn't go on. We had been carrying those dreaded backpacks for four-plus hours now, and it seemed like the top of this cut was just as far away as it had always been. Climbing in this crack was treacherous, too, and it was pushing our fatigued bodies to the very limit of what endurance we had remaining. So many times already, the boulders we had to traverse were much too high to climb, and we had to backtrack and clamber up onto the mountainside to go around each one of them before crawling back down into the v-shaped canal we were using as a road. Presently, however, a rest was demanded, and as we came over the top of a particularly large pink granite blob of rock, we found just the spot.

From some secretive corner to our left, I thought I could hear a trickle of water spilling onto the rocks. I had to stop walking to be certain, because it would be truly unusual to find any water source in this area that would last as far into the season as we were now, here in the beginning of April. Much to my surprise, my ears were not deceiving me. A small palm tree appeared, growing sideways right out of the side of the mountain, and I could now see that the water was seeping out of the cliff in a tiny stream below it. Everywhere the water cascaded, black-green ground moss was teeming. Several varieties of water plants were growing here and there, and a small pool had formed about five feet below the source. It was like we had stumbled into our own private Japanese garden, and we eagerly dumped the weighty packs to bask in the blissful peace and quiet here. In the little pool, several bright red flowers were blooming out of a plant of unknown origin, and I savored its beauty with admiration, determined never to forget the picture it now framed in my mind.

I wanted so much to be able to linger here! It took every ounce of strength and courage I could muster to pick up that pack again and leave this precious little oasis, but we had to get just a little bit further up this mountain. One look up that wadi and it began screaming out to me that we had at least another whole day to climb just to make the top, then another day to get over to the right area to hunt down Jebel Lawz. I knew we dare not even speak, for fear of what the other would say. I could feel the tentacles of discouragement beginning to sadistically stroke my temples.

Within fifteen or twenty minutes from the time we left the oasis, it was getting very difficult to see at all. The sun had not yet set, but had been hidden from our entire scope of vision for a long while now. I could see that directly in front of Jim was yet another huge boulder he was stopping to circumnavigate, and my heart sank when he dropped his pack and just stared back at me with a completely exhausted face. He'd already complained to me that his feet were killing him from his new hiking boots, and his legs were so cramped up now that he was actually slipping down from time to time just like I had been. Despair, the secret twin of discouragement, had just flown in to join us. The look on Jim's face was the final blow to my forward motion.

I had held my peace about this situation as long as I could. Fatigue was at an all time high, as I plodded miserably around the boulder with Jim. I wanted to just give this climb up. I started hearing my reasoning argue the salient points within my own soul. It was giving me a full blown power point presentation by this time as to why we should just turn around and leave. Now! There were plenty of other things we could go searching for in the truck on the ground; like the column we had heard was once posted at the Red Sea or the bitter springs of Marah. It was obvious in my rapidly collapsing mental state that we'd never make it to the top of this wadi. After all, we didn't have twenty days to spend here. And even if we did, there weren't enough provisions. Besides all that, my muscles were shot! I was losing my grip faster and faster, and the thought of a sprained ankle or worse all the way out here was too vicious to deal with.

"Jimmmmmeeeeeeeeeeee!" I was now officially in full blown whine mode, as I reached behind me and slung the object of my hatred to the ground with a thud. "I am worn completely out! It's going to take us fifty years at least to get way up there!" By this time I was waving my right arm wildly toward the towering peaks above us. "Can't we just spend the night and go back down in the morning and look for the other stuff? I can't climb any more!"

Jim heaved a weary sigh and stopped in his tracks right where he was. He had just gotten back down off the mountain edge and was heading back into the wadi when my loud complaining burst into the air. He turned slowly and wearily toward me.

"Babe, I don't know what to do yet," he all but whispered in the only voice he had left to answer me with. I could tell he was feeling every bit as worn down as I was. He looked up at me where I'd plopped myself down on the ledge where he'd just been, then over at my back pack where I'd thrown it up against the boulder.

"I'm not trying to complain! Honest I'm not, but you've got to look at the facts. We just don't have enough time to do this, and if we keep going as tired as we are, we're going to break a leg or something. That would be the worst. Then we couldn't even use the days we have to do anything else."

"Listen, I don't know what we're gonna do yet. Just stop it a minute and be quiet. I have to be able to think!" All Jim had on his mind was taking pictures of that holy sight at the foot of Jebel Lawz he had walked on in February. He had been so certain that we could just blaze up this wadi, hang over the edge, snap the pictures, and then zoom on out of here with the goods! Neither one of us had a clue as to how difficult this climb would be in reality, nor any concept of how to judge the distances in these big mountains. What seemed so close to us before was proving to be ever so far away.

To continue my argument against any further climbing, I reached out with my right hand, again trying to emphasize to him just how far away the top of this wadi was, when my eyes focused in on something so phenomenal that my words drizzled off to silence. A dazzling, white light had appeared almost all the way up the mountain near the top of the ridge. It shut me down immediately as I felt my skin flush with goose bumps, and all I could get out of my mouth was, *"What's that?"*

Jim was still looking at me and stumped about our situation, when I yelled out again.

"Look, up there by the top! What's that light?"

Jim whipped his head around and through tightly squinted eyes, glared up the wadi at the mysterious disc of brilliant light, which looked at a glance much like the appearance of gleaming metal, yet pure white. He scrambled for the binoculars that were hanging around his neck and jerked them up to his face. Just as soon as he got them in front of his eyes, he let out a loud cry.

"Arghhhhhh! I can't see out of these things!" The binoculars had been hanging around his neck the entire day, and as the sweat had broken out on his forehead, it had rolled down the side of his face and accumulated into each lens! The liquid had dried and left a salty residue in the eye-pieces, and he couldn't see out of them at all! Jim was fumbling trying his best to clean them off, and I was exclaiming at the top of my lungs about what it could be. Jim finally got one side cleaned out and lifted them again to his eyes. He still couldn't make out a particular shape, and the brightness was blinding. And before he could get a real good look, I couldn't stand it any longer and ripped the glasses out of his hands, and mashed my eyeballs up inside the lenses.

To me, whatever it was looked to be the shape of an arrow point, or a triangle of sorts with semi-curved sides. But the *brilliance* of this thing was the amazing part, especially knowing that the sun had been behind the mountains for a long time. We were not looking at a reflection caused by the sun here! This light was shining out from the shaded side of the mountain! Jim grabbed the binoculars back from me just in time to see the light growing smaller and smaller, until it finally disappeared.

We were both frozen in time against the ageless sky. Neither one of us dared speak just then, because it was perfectly clear in our spirits that we had just had a first hand encounter with something entirely supernatural. What on earth had we just witnessed? An angel of the Lord? A representation of the burning bush? Was it some sort of strange fire on the mountain? My mind raced through a million possibilities, all of which were re-igniting my spirit and recharging my heart and soul to keep on climbing!

After about a five-minute silence between us, Jim spoke out into the evening shadows. "I think maybe we ought to keep going tomorrow, babe."

"Yeah. I think we should. We've got to get up there and see what that was, or if it'll come back. I guess we have our sign to keep going, don't we?"

With that, I walked over to where I'd slung my pack in my earlier melt-down, and swung it back up onto my shoulders.

Somehow, it didn't feel nearly as heavy.

Within a hundred or so yards we reached an area where there was enough gravel surface to pitch the tent. We had to work quickly against the advancing night to set up for the evening. When all was ready, I went a little further up the path to take a break. I had spied the white bark of a tree there, and wondered what it was. It was very pretty to look at, and just beginning to blossom out into tiny green leaves everywhere. But with it as dark as it was, I couldn't tell what kind of leaves they were. I went on back to the little camp to find Jim perched up on a high boulder, chomping down some of the trail mix. When I joined him, a small owl came hooting and flapping out from another rock close to where we sat. It startled us enough to make us both duck and cover our heads, but then we had to laugh at ourselves, realizing it was only an owl! Soon we were settled into the quiet of the evening.

"You know, we've seen an awful lot today." Jim said softly, looking down into the camp fire.

"An unbelievable lot. That light! Wow! What in the world ...?" I was still befuddled and amazed all at the same time.

"Yep. Just when we almost gave up the climb, God Himself gives us a glimpse of things to come. That was the light of the Lord up there, Babe. Telling us to come on up."

I reached over to my pack and pulled out the little daily devotional that had spoken to us so plainly all throughout the trip to Egypt. I had brought it along again, and flipped through the pages here in the light of the campfire to read aloud the verse for April 2, 1992. And it couldn't have been any more timely: *"They looked ... and behold! The glory of the Lord appeared in the cloud"* (Exodus 16:10)!

Hearing that was about all the conversation we could muster. And the thought was so overwhelming there was nothing left to be said. Jim reached for my hand and led me and our bone-tired bodies down from the rock and into the tent where the goose-down sleeping bags neatly zipped together lay waiting for us. We were asleep almost before our heads hit the pillow.

CHAPTER THIRTY-TWO

The God of the Mountain

Jim opened his eyes. The first rays of dawn were filtering their soft glow into the earth, and in the wadi various sounds were beginning to become audible. The songs of the little birds that were hidden away came wafting into the tent like a morning hymn of the sweetest strain. And against that pure sweetness, now and again, what sounded like a miniature jet could be heard nearing the area where we were, growing louder and louder until it became a roar barely over our heads, and just as quickly began to diminish in the opposite direction. At present, one was coming that sounded particularly deep and rumbly, and it seemed to clip the top of the tent as it zoomed by. Jim couldn't help himself, and he laughed heartily out loud, just to find the sound of my giggles matching his from under our sleeping bag.

"Did you hear that?" Jim snorted.

"Did I hear it!" My voice came out all muffled and goofy from inside the puffs of goose down over my face. Slowly, ever so slowly, I began to try to move. "Ow! Ah! Ooooh! Youch! (Giggle.) Ahhhh! Oh, Jim, it hurts to laugh! It hurts to move! But those crazy sounding bees or flies or whatever are so hilarious! They sound like B-52 bombers!"

"I know it. They buzzed me all afternoon yesterday! Looks like they're getting an early start today!" he said as he reached over to unzip the tent flap and let in the crispy mountain air. His shoulder muscles screamed loudly at him in that instant, and he stopped halfway through his effort and let out a long moan. "Ahhhhhhhhhhhhhhhhhh!"

JIM AT THE TENT IN THE EARLY MORNING

"See—I'm not the only pile of pain this morning!" I grinned widely at him and finished the zipper off, which was a no-no. But he was too sore to argue with me for touching the zipper!

Outside, our whole view of things had changed considerably. Even as sore as we were, we had enjoyed a sound night's sleep, a night Jim would come to recall as one of the best ever in a tent. Coupled with the rest, and what we were sure was God's signal on the mountain last night, there was no place for discouragement within our hearts or minds this dawn. Looking about, all we could do was marvel at the beauty of creation around us.

The view now of where we had been climbing up the day before clearly showed that we had come up a lot farther than it had seemed. The hidden grove of palms that Jim had discovered yesterday was a minute green speck far down below. From up here, the major wadis with the tracks running through them looked like beige rivers criss-crossing the land, with the bumps of the boulder-pile jebels stacked up all along the sides. The most interesting thing, though, were the two landmarks that really stuck out, even from this altitude. We could see them easily still—the white quartz outcropping near the ancient circles in the valley directly below us, and the massive split rock just to the right and around the corner from the circles! Strange, how obvious they were from all the way up here! We lingered a while, trying our best to wake up without our usual three cups of coffee.

"Well, okay. So what do we have to eat around here?" He was afraid of the answer he was certain to get. He knew all we had left were those nasty energy bars, which were excellent nutrition but tasted like fossilized cardboard. Better still, the other option: the heartily dreaded trail mix. After a day's worth of the stuff yesterday, he didn't see how he could stomach saltless nuts mixed with shriveled up apricot halves even one more time.

"You really want me to answer that?" I asked him, with my lips curled up and a grossed out look on my face.

"Don't tell me. Just pass me one of the bars that has a high carb blend." Jim grimaced.

I went digging through my pack and surfaced with a couple of the kind he was looking for, along with the bag of trail mix. I pulled it out and set it aside on top of the rock next to me and threw one of the bars over to Jim. I opened one for myself, and we walked around chewing redundantly for the next few minutes, wishing the tasteless globs were coffee. We made a pact right then and there that never again would we put ourselves in this predicament; being on the mountain with no java! We had a long, hard climb ahead of us, and it surely would have been nice to start this day off with an added kick! In fact, it was going to be much more difficult in the actual climbing part than the day before because the terrain was soon to change. We would need the fuel in our bodies that the bland bars would provide to keep our muscles moving under the added strain, but they didn't have the ability to wake us up like the coffee did.

* * *

After a wide sweep of the camp site area, we finished the pitiful excuse for a breakfast and wound up right back at the rock I left the trail mix on. I was just about to grab it up and stuff it back in my back pack when out of the corner of my eye I detected some sort of movement inside the bag! I frowned at Jim and beckoned him over to investigate what I thought I'd just seen. Gingerly, I untwisted the tie holding the top of the clear plastic together, and opened up the bag and backed away. Much to our immediate shock and horror, four gray colored moths took to flight from inside the bag and disappeared into the fresh morning air!

"Gimme that water!" was all I could get out of my mouth! We gargled for several minutes before we could even muster the courage to start breaking camp.

It didn't take long for us to drop the tent, roll up our bags, and stuff the backpacks again. The Egyptian adventure had served to hone and refine our camping skills and ability so much so that we finished our set tasks within moments of each other. After looking around the site for anything we might be leaving behind, I strapped the cumbersome survival kit onto my back, and yelled out, "For-waaaaaard!" The command stuck, and followed us throughout the rest of the day each time we began again from a break.

Jim led the way as before and felt a new strength coursing through his body. The sight of the glowing light yesterday blazed brightly in his mind's eye, and it was calling him higher and higher. It must mean we were on the right track, he thought to himself—appearing there, just when we were about to give up like that. Visions of what it could have been were clicking through his conscious thoughts right and left. He had no permanent conclusions yet, but he was determined to get some.

I had been humming along behind him in my usual rhythm of walking upright for a time, then bending over and walking. The cramps from the sore muscles were causing me to see stars now and again, but I found that as I became more fully awake and I got warmed up, the strain seemed to ease a bit. I tried to memorize the scenery of where we were and what we were doing for future remembrance. As I looked all around, I could not believe I was really here, alone with Jim on an almost virgin mountain, backpacking my way up its side! What a blessing just to get this chance! The air was so clear and clean, the sky a deep azure, and a quiet so deep it roared in my ears. Except for the occasional bee and bird, Jim and I were making the only noise there was.

In front of me, I focused in on the wadi. From our vantage point in its center, I could see these now familiar pink and gray granite boulders as far up as the top. They were huge; bigger than any I had ever seen. For the most part, smaller ones had piled up against the big ones, so we were able to choose the steadiest and use them like steps to go over the top of each. Now and then though, a ten-feet-high or more boulder would stand all alone before us, and the only way up was going around it. It was just like we had to do the day before, only harder. These boulders were larger, and the mountain's angle was much more steep as we went higher. We had to scale one side of the boulders or the other, sometimes clinging precariously to the walls of rock in places, until we passed the boulder and could go back down into the bottom to continue the climb. It reminded me of a creek bed in places, the way the mountains were joined together at this wash.

As I surveyed the mass of the great chunks of mountain that had tumbled down into this valley of sorts, I wondered what had the power to do such a thing. These stones were so big it hardly seemed that even rains causing flash floods had the capability of doing it. Probably earthquakes, I figured. And in the very moment I thought it, I wished I'd never pondered the boulder situation. Now all of a sudden I couldn't shake off the earthquake idea. I was enveloped with visions of the ground shaking, and all these rocks dancing about like so many marbles thrown from a child's hand, then heading down the wash toward us in an avalanche of rock! If there was anyplace in the world I wouldn't want to be in an earthquake, this was it! I was now literally talking softly to myself out loud, but not so loud as to let Jim hear me. I knew he'd accuse me of being in "crisis mode" again. And that would just make us both mad.

So I stuffed the feeling the only way I knew how: I started singing hymns of praise and prayed prayers of protection!

It was nearly eleven when we reached the place that the wadi was becoming narrower and narrower in front of us. Before long we would run up against an almost solid rock wall, which seemed to be the end of our wash. The two mountains became one from there on out, and we were going to have to choose which of the two sides we'd have to try to climb up. This wasn't so easy, seeing as how we had no ropes nor climbing gear to use on difficult areas. And what we were looking at now was far more of a steep grade than we had counted on. But the way Jim figured, if we had made it up this far we could keep on somehow. He would chance it for sure, and he knew already that I'd be just nutty enough to follow him wherever he went, no matter what. So we stopped for a breather before deciding to take the ledge to the left.

Jim was also determined to search the area where we believed the source of the brilliant light we'd seen yesterday had come from. And we were just about to that place now. We dropped the packs and searched unencumbered for a few minutes but couldn't find a single thing that could have reflected such radiance as what we had both seen with our own eyes. This further evidenced a supernatural source, and I was greatly pleased to know it.

But once again time forced us onward. We noticed that within the wash, the color of the stones had been uniformly pink or grey, with small pieces of black and green from time to time. Now, crossing out of it and onto the mountain itself, the rock was just as uniformly brown. Scruffy, low lying bushes clung to the surface here and there; some with a pungent odor as thick as the spice markets in the old cities of Arabia. The angle of our climb was substantially more vertical now, and loose pebbles were starting to slow us down considerably. We had to be much more cautious in this sort of terrain, because one slip could cause an injury, and clinch the capabilities of moving onward. One spot not far from the top looked from a distance to be an easy walk, but we found out rather quickly that the rocky crags and jagged crevices were far easier to scramble up than the exposed spots where there were no side rocks to hold on to. Though our progress was agonizingly slow, at almost twelve noon I looked up to see Jim standing at the top of the ridge.

I was coming up behind him as fast as I could, but couldn't stand to wait any longer to see for myself what he must be seeing. But something was wrong. I fully expected a loud hoot and holler, a yippee, or at least a hurrah! But I heard no sound from my man on the top of that ridge. Presently, I saw him dump the backpack and the water jug, and his hands went to his hips. Still no exclamations of triumph. The air was perfectly quiet. "Well?" I ventured, cautiously; as I neared the place he stood.

Jim turned around and gave me a blank look, without saying anything, then looked back out over the top again. As I ascended the final few steps to the same spot he stood, I knew why he was speechless. We had fully expected to pop over this ridge and be glaring Jebel Lawz eye to eye. We had assumed we were on its western flank all along, and all we'd have to do would be to sneak over this edge to get all the pictures we needed of the ancient tabernacle sight. We expected to see the altar of the golden calf in the far off distance. What we saw in reality was nothing we recognized at all. The realization started an avalanche of discouragement and disappointment to come tumbling back down on us, as we sank to the ground and laid our heads on our packs. We were sitting at an altitude of around fifty-five hundred feet after a backbreaking effort to get up here, and we had no earthly idea where "here" was. Now everything was in jeopardy all over again!

About the only thing of interest in this spot was a pile of stones that were obviously man-made, which we were momentarily distracted by. Close to them on the ground to one side were two rams' horns, which was a bit out of the ordinary. But we were so puzzled by where we now found ourselves standing, we did not investigate the structure any more than on the surface. It could have been a grave, we surmised, but then again, it was a bit high placed for that. Maybe an altar of some sort? Disappointment had gripped us, and we just didn't have the energy to try and figure it out. We laid down on the rocks, worn out already.

Jim cringed as he leaned up from where we had laid down long enough to get his shoes untied and toss them aside. His socks were soaked with sweat, and the blisters on his feet were angry and red, causing him a considerable amount of agony. It had taken every mental faculty he had to overcome the pain that racked him everywhere, especially his feet, in order to keep going uphill. The notion that we were right on target where we'd climbed up, had been a constant that had been helping him move on. Now, he had not only lost the driving factor, he felt like the effort had been totally wasted. It was more than his tired body could handle just then. He slumped back down on the pack again, and closed his eyes.

I was horrified for him. I knew what this meant to him, and how sure he was that this was the right spot to climb. All the signs we had had along the way—the light calling us up—what was wrong? Had we misinterpreted all the signals? It was hard for me to be lighthearted all of a sudden, with my body aching acutely and my head hurting the way it did. I closed my eyes too, and we both napped quietly without discussing it for the space of about a half hour.

I opened my eyes to Jim shaking me and turned my head to see him point to the high ridge to our left. "Hey, babe, you see that peak up there?" he asked me in a weak and hoarse voice.

"Yes."

"That's where we're going now. Get geared up. I think Jebel Lawz is just hidden from our sight because of that peak up ahead there. Maybe we're not as far off as we think." Jim was fighting the overwhelming urge to give up. He remembered yesterday, how the light had appeared to keep us going. He wasn't going to try God's patience or mercy now. He'd keep on going. And I'd follow him wherever he went. Case closed.

So with our backpacks in place, we took our two weary souls and began another ascent. This time, the rocks underneath our feet gave way more quickly, as they were even smaller and looser than what we had yet experienced. There were no cracks, crevices, or bushes to hold onto; only what reminded me of a consistent plain full of stones, tilted at a steep angle lying in front of us. The resting breaks were by this time becoming quite frequent, as we became more and more exhausted from the altitude and the exertion of the climb itself.

I looked up in front of me and knew this was taking its toll on Jim. Where he'd thus far been ten to twenty paces ahead, I was now right on his heels, listening to his labored breathing. My own breath was searing my lungs I was sucking it in so fast and so deep. I wondered if we'd make this or not. Even our encouraging each other had come to an end, as talking was out of the question by this point. And even if we could have spoken, neither of us had any strength left inside with which to help the other. All I could do was follow.

As usual, in times of fatigue, the fear came again to plague me. The evil thoughts were beginning to come in, hauling their wicked loads to my brain. First I wondered what I could possibly do if Jim had keeled over with a heart attack or the like, from pushing himself too hard. Then I thought about myself, and remembered how I had only quit smoking some months ago. Now I was being tormented about having my own heart attack and dying young because of this strain. Then, those ideas fluttered away and a much more sinister one returned to torment me like it had earlier in the day. I began to look around me at how high up we were off the ground. The enemy reminded me of

PENNY AT A REST STOP HALFWAY UP THE MOUNTAIN

how heights were not at all where I enjoyed being. And then the zinger. "What if there's an earthquake way up where you are now?" the voice whispered. "You'd be crushed under the weight of all those boulders, as they bounce around, or better yet, you'll *fall!*"

I stood straight up and stopped for a minute. I shook my head violently and screamed at my mind to shut that mess down. I reminded myself of how big my God was, and how protected we were doing His work. In the middle of my silent conversation with myself, Jim turned around to me and said, "Penny, I just have to stop for a longer rest." He was pale and heaving his breath hard. "Let's get up there to that area of black looking rocks, and take a nap."

He got no argument from me. I was more than ready to lay my head down against the warm stones, which felt like heating pads to my aching muscles. I also needed to blank all those horrid thoughts out of my head.

Jim had already flung his backpack down, and was guzzling water when I pinched the buckles on the straps of mine and let it fall to the ground three feet away from him. I arranged the rocks for lying on and eye-balled where I'd land when I did. Jim lay down in almost the same breath. The heat against my back felt wonderful! I took a deep breath and was about to try to relax when I noticed my body was starting to vibrate all over. I thought for a minute, and then forced myself to believe it was only from the climbing, as after exercise. I might have convinced myself of that very fact had not Jim suddenly sprung up off of the ground in hopeless panic yelling, "Earthquake! Earthquake! Babe, it's an earthquake!"

I was immobilized in stark terror. What was actually the duration of only about five seconds seemed like a century to me before Jim yelled out wildly again, "Don't you feel the ground shaking? It's an earthquake!"

My conscious mind didn't know what to do. I felt like an actress watching myself on a movie screen! I felt that shaking, all right. I had felt it before he did! But I refused to admit that an earthquake was even a possibility! I just couldn't take it! I heard my own voice answering, "Jim! Shut up right now! It's no earthquake, that's your heart beating hard from the climb! There is no earthquake, you hear me? There is no earthquake!"

But Jim Caldwell was no idiot. He knew better than to think the heaving ground that swam before his very eyes was his own heart beating hard. He'd pushed himself physically for years in the health clubs, and he had never experienced anything like what he was feeling now. "Penny! There is no way possible that this is my heartbeat! You're shaking too!" And as soon as the words came out of his mouth, it stopped. No more waves along the ground. No more motion at all. Just the dead calm, quiet air, and his racing heart against mine!

I fell backwards and closed my eyes, just like I closed my thought processes down completely. It was too much. Too much that I had never told him the premonitions I'd had all morning about being in an earthquake! Too much that I'd felt my own body vibrating! Too much that I was nearing sixty-five hundred feet off the ground, and that I was nothing more than a speck of dust in this vast mountain range. I folded myself up and shut it all out, pretending I was safe at home in my warm bed, dreaming.

About an hour later, we awoke groggily having fallen dead asleep. Jim was trying to shake himself awake and it was no easy matter for him. He could have stayed here for another few hours sleeping easily, but he was only five hundred feet away from another summit, and he couldn't stand not making that last one after coming all this way. With the earth steady underneath us now, we geared back up and went for the distance.

Our bodies were not responding as quickly as we wanted them to anymore. My knees were literally buckling out from under me with only a few steps, and my ankles were turning under the weight of the back pack and the exhaustion. Jim's legs were cramping up and freezing: this was getting ugly. I knew, as the peak approached, that I just had to stop again. It was not my heart's choice, but my body's demand. It was giving out completely. I could only manage to struggle up to the top of the next ridge, just in time to see Jim look back at me and say, "Now I know where we are. Look over there."

I raised my eyes as I topped the ridge and my heart sank down into the bottom of my feet. I wanted to scream, but I had almost lost my voice by this time, and all I could get out was a breathless croak. "Oh, no, Jim, how could we have been this far off?"

It was impossible. Jim Caldwell may have been many things, but desert direction he never lost. His radar was as reliable as the sunrise. This was absurd. The pointy peak of the blackish-blue Jebel Lawz was another whole mountain climb away. It would take us another three days just to get there by foot: days we didn't have. Besides that, we didn't have enough water to last us that long without a supply reload. Little by little, the reality sank in.

It seemed we had made this agonizing climb for nothing. There would be no pictures to bring back home of the site we had felt to be so very, very holy on that first trip we had made after our return from Egypt. Everything we thought this trip's hardship was for had splintered into dust and had blown to the winds.

I fell sideways as I tried to sit down and dumped my backpack. There was no way to hide my feelings now. I wanted to cry and yell all at the same time. I had no control over the wet tears as they rolled down my cheeks and dripped in great drops onto my dusty jeans. As I sat there absorbed by misery, pondering this fate, I watched the slumped over figure of my worn-out husband slowly walking up the only remaining fifty feet or so to the highest rock formation on the plateau where we had just been. I was not only crying for our sakes; I was crying for him. I felt so badly for his mission's sake. I knew he was acting tough on the outside, but inside, that big heart of his was mashed. He had been so excited, so hopeful, so sure this would be the trip that he'd get back inside that fence that separated the holy from the profane. Now, here we were, dead-in-the-water. I kept watching him until his bent form disappeared over the edge of the rock formation in front of me.

My tears were ceasing all on their own, probably because of dehydration. It was certainly not because of a change of my mood. All I could do now was stare at the ground and listen to the roar of the quiet. Only the slightest breeze whispered among the scarce small bushes, and I just sat still on the rock, empty. Time was both standing still and passing by. It felt so unreal, all of it. Unreal.

And it had been a while now since I'd seen Jim, and I was beginning to get worried about him. The cliff he had painfully climbed up was fairly jagged and dropped off sharply on the side I could see, and I suddenly wondered if he'd slipped down on the other side and couldn't move, or something worse. About the time I was thinking of getting up and hunting him down, a low rumble drifted into my ears that made me forget Jim for the moment.

It was coming from the general direction of the cliff he should be on. A continuing rumble … and it grew, and grew, so intense, and so loud, it scared the daylights out of me! I could feel my heart pounding from what was a wild sensation of *vibration* within me, yet it was not the same as the ground-shaking experience. This didn't feel at all like the earthquake. It was different! Within the noise I could recognize a crisply distinct whirring, and a cyclical resonance that was almost unearthly. I had no idea what was causing it. The sound was now so loud that I felt completely enveloped in it; yet there was not a cloud in the sky, or a sign of anyone, or anything, on the mountain, or even in the tiny valley almost seven thousand feet below! I jumped up and ran over to the cliff ledge above me and screamed out, "Jim! Do you hear that? *What's that sound?*"

I got no response from him. In seconds I was scrambling up the same rocks he had, with a sheer adrenaline rush pushing me forward. Halfway up the formation I began to hear Jim's voice coming through the whirring: "Penny! Get up here now! "

Rocks and dust were flying out from under my feet as I scrambled up the rest of the ledge. I knew that I was going to find him hanging by his fingernails off the other side of the cliff, about to fall all the way down into the valley that was barely visible below. Just my head popped over the top and *I could see him*. Jim was standing, at the very edge of the precipice—his mouth was wide open, and there was a ghostly white pallor on his face.

And at that moment, abruptly, the whirring resonance ceased!

"Oh! Thank God you're all right!" I was coughing, and spitting, trying to get my voice to work against my heaving breath. "Why did you yell? You scared me out of my mind! I thought that you were hanging off the edge, about to fall off this mountain!

"What was that loud whirring noise I was hearing, Jim? Did you hear it? Why didn't you answer me ?" I was firing off at the mouth uncontrollably.

Between the bright light, the earthquake, and this mysterious sounding noise, my natural mind had blown a circuit.

As for Jim, he was in a state of pure awe. He simply stated: "You will never believe what just happened to me!"

He was wonderstruck! It was written all over his face. The despair was gone. The distress was gone. And strangely enough, I noticed that his hair was blown straight backwards!

He caught his breath and began in a hoarse whisper, "I was just standing right here, looking way off to the peak of Lawz, when over by this rock I started hearing this wild, loud noise! It sounded like the whirling blades of the big cooling tower fans we used to have out at Dow Chemical! So much so, in fact, that I walked over here, half expecting to look down into the huge exhaust vent of some hidden nuclear facility, or something like that." His voice was steadily rising now.

"When I got right here, the noise moved—directly in front of me—and it stood still…. So help me, Penny, *it just stood still in front of me!*"

I wasn't sure I understood what he meant, so I asked him, "What, you mean the noise stopped?" My eyes were glued on the lack of color in his face, and the obvious case of goose bumps on his arms, and still on that hair, blasted back from his eyes.

"No, no, no, I mean the noise wasn't *moving* anymore. It was still just as loud, but it was *hovering* right in front of my body! It was like a *presence* I can't really describe—like it had substance, but was invisible at the same time! It was sort of like the clear heat waves you can see out across the desert sometimes. I couldn't figure out what it was! But it was huge, I can tell you that! I felt like I could have been totally enveloped in it!"

He stopped for a moment to catch his breath again.

"I just stood there. Immobile. And I promise you, a thought overwhelmed me instantly. Penny, *if I had stretched out my right hand into this thing, it would have picked me up bodily and carried me over there to Jebel Lawz!*"

I swallowed hard, frowning all the more. It felt like my own eyes were bulging out of my head as Jim went on.

"As soon as I thought it, I looked at how far down the ground is down there, and fear hit me square in the heart! All I could see was you sitting on that rock down over there, then coming up here and not knowing what happened to me … and

JIM AT THE HIGH PLACE JUST BEFORE THE ENCOUNTER WITH THE WHIRLWIND

there I'd be, dead in the valley or on top of Jebel Lawz, carried away by this whirling presence!"

I could barely maintain myself by this time. I literally felt like I was about to faint in the light of this revelation. And still Jim was talking.

"It was too much! When I pictured your face, that's when I yelled for you to get up here. And get this! The very moment I yelled for you, the thing started moving again, and it moved over there, and it ripped those bushes all to pieces! All of a sudden I could see the whole thing, and Babe, it was a *tremendous whirlwind*! It filled up with dust and sticks and rocks and there it stood, *reaching as far up into the heavens as I could see*! Then it bounced a time or two, and, WHOOSH! Right off the mountainside! Can you believe it?"

I was transfixed hearing his story. But the scientific thinking popped out in my brain instantly when he said that his noise was being created by a whirlwind. That would explain the nature of the sound, all right, but there was a problem. We had seen hundreds of whirlwinds scouring their way through the desert before, and none of them were ever as loud as this was. But they also, by their very nature, must move along to retain their core of winds. Whirlwinds of the desert cease to be, no longer exist, when they stand still. I frowned at him even bigger, but continued to listen.

"I know what you're thinking. Whirlwinds don't just stand still; plus they kick up all kinds of dust and whatever else is on the ground below them, and you can see where they are because of the debris swirling around inside the funnel! Well, this one was invisible, Penny, and the most powerful one I've ever witnessed. And that's when I felt all my hair standing up.

"*It wasn't an earthly whirlwind, was it?*" I whispered the words, quietly, one at a time.

"No, Babe. *It wasn't!*" Jim's face was beginning to glow, radiant, and his smile was breaking out here and there between his words.

I was back to sitting down on the rocks by this time. Jim walked over to me and sat down alongside. For a long, long time, we just sat there in the stillness, staring southward in the direction the vortex had taken before it disappeared into thin air. We were two tiny breaths against this vast array of wilderness and mountains, perched high atop a ridge with an eagle's-eye view. From this height we could see clearly the lay of the land all the way to the Gulf of Aqaba. We could see the few cuts in the mountains down by the sea where the children of Israel could have come through to get to this place, which we now were convinced was the biblical Rephidim, where the rock Moses split was still in evidence down below us. And the significance of it all was dawning in our hearts and minds.

This trip had never been about taking photographs in the first place. *The plan from on High had always been a journey of revelation and destiny.* We had been called up here for a new perspective, a bigger one than we had had before. Called up higher to a new vantage point. From here we could see it all—and what we were seeing was profound. All at once we knew that this land had to be where the massive deliverance had been given by the hand of the Almighty to the children of Israel as He brought them out of Egypt. He was leading them to himself—to the mountain on which He had first appeared to Moses in the bush that burned with fire but was not consumed, the mountain in the land of Midian that we now knew was within our reach! *We were looking at the hidden things, now revealed!*

It would be up to us to make known the previously undiscovered item of great antiquity, the Split Rock at Horeb, and show that *it existed still,* in all its glory! The channels the water etched deeply into the rocks below it would someday get the attention of many, who would then come to believe that the biblical tales with which this had to do were not just mere allegory!

The circles of stone and the rock art we had discovered from the same area would prove to be exceedingly important in the years to come and would burst forth with their particular revelation at precise intervals, to be understood by many more than we could at present imagine!

But for now, we sat leaning on each other, just specks on a mountain top, filled with high joys and far views. Jim turned his gaze down to my face, and I looked up into his. The depth of what he had just experienced had engraved a permanent mark on his very soul and filled him anew with fresh visions and dreams. I could see it radiating out of his eyes as he looked at me. He had not imagined the events of this trip. I had been there with him as a witness. The fiery brilliance of the pure, white light up on the mountain; the ground-shaking, thunderous earthquake that rattled us both. And now this—the great and marvelous whirlwind that came and stood before him to crown his destiny with all things Sinai! Suddenly we understood the experience of Elijah as he stood before the Lord on Mt. Horeb, when a fire, an earthquake, and a great wind passed by—and then a still, small Voice spoke to him.

We sat motionless and listened intently as the Spirit of God—the Still, Small Voice—gave utterance in our hearts: *We felt the truth that God's Presence and purpose were still a part of this land.*

Jim had finally, after all these miles and months, heartaches and trials, despairs and defeats, looked upon the Guiding Hand that had been leading us all along, throughout Egypt and the desert and into this holy place. The pillar of cloud and smoke in the whirlwind had suddenly appeared before him on this day, April 3,1992, in a flash of intensity and power that would forever change the landscape of our destiny.

And we would never, ever be the same again. Though hidden within the whirlwind, the Presence had been made manifest. And Jim Caldwell had crested a rise and encountered the God of the Mountain!

THE END ... or is it?

No, it is really not the end. In fact, I believe that we are just at the beginning of understanding all that has been revealed to us by the Spirit of the living God. There are certain verses of Scripture that captivated our attention long before we ever set out on this incredible journey. Scriptures that we had no way of deciphering until now.

May you hear the Voice behind them: *And the Lord answered me and said,"Write the vision, and make it plain upon tables, that he may run that readeth it"* (Habakkuk 2:2).

I have tried my utmost to record the whole story of Jim's original vision as it unfolded in our lives. Did we actually find the Ark of the Covenant? No. Not yet. But we are more convinced than ever that we know *exactly* where it is waiting.

> *For the vision is yet for an appointed time, but at the end it shall speak, and not lie: though it tarry, wait for it; because it will surely come, it will not tarry.* (Habakkuk 2:3)

And so we wait for the appointed time.

We wait, gazing often upon the pictures we have of the mountain that calls us even now, sixteen years later. We ponder and study this enigmatic Jebel Lawz, whose very name means "Almond Mountain." Is it ironic, or is it divine intent, that between the two giant stone slabs at the top of the first ridge heading up the mountain, there sits that mysterious tree: the tree that still captivates us from the first time we saw it? The tree that we now firmly believe is an almond tree. The significance of this simple tree cannot be underestimated. The fact that it lives at all is a sign and a wonder in and of itself. But it's much, much more than that. Aaron's rod that budded was an almond rod, available here where he was. The menorah, the seven-tiered lampstand of Israel fashioned at Mount Sinai and placed in the tabernacle, was patterned after the almond branch and flower. And *this* mountain in northwest Saudi Arabia is called *Almond Mountain*! Take note of the Word of the Lord to Jeremiah the prophet: "Moreover the word of the Lord came unto me, saying, 'Jeremiah, what seest thou?' And I said, 'I see a rod of an almond tree.' Then said the Lord unto me, 'Thou hast well seen: *for I will hasten my word to perform it*'" (Jeremiah 1:11-12).

The Lord is there watching over His word, His plan, *even now*. The almond tree is alive, not dead. It is vital, full of life.

When the Lord spoke to Moses about leading the children of Israel into the promised land, He said that He would not be going. He said if He went, He'd end up destroying Israel along the way for their wicked ways. When Moses interceded on behalf of the sinful people, the Lord assured Moses His presence would go with them: He was going to send an Angel in whom He had placed His Name to go up with them. But He was not going to go.

> *Behold, I send an Angel before thee, to keep thee in the way, and to bring thee into the place which I have prepared. Beware of him, and obey his voice, provoke him not; for he will not pardon your transgressions: for My name is in him. But if thou shalt indeed obey his voice, and do all that I speak; then I will be an enemy unto thine enemies, and an adversary unto thine adversaries. For mine Angel shall go before thee, and bring thee in unto the Amorites, and the Hittites, and the Perizzites, and*

the Canaanites, and the Hivites, and the Jebusites: and I will cut them off. (Exodus 23:20-23)

And the faithful made it safely to the land promised to them.

Yes, the tree remains there. It lives on in spite of the harsh desert climate. It clings tenaciously to the surrounding rocky face of this mountain, set apart and defiant against the elements and the political gates of brass and bars of iron. It remains locked behind *for now*. A vibrant tree, pulsing with the residue of the glory of the Lord that once rested upon this place. A living sign that the Source of all life, and the sustaining thereof, is still there!

> *I will go and return to my place, till they acknowledge their offence, and seek my face: in their affliction they will seek me early.* (Hosea 5:15)

There is yet an appointed time of great significance for this Mount Sinai, the mountain we believe to be Jebel Lawz in northwest Saudi Arabia.

Its story is not over. It's all just about to begin!

JIM AND PENNY IN THE CLEFT OF THE SPLIT ROCK

A VIEW OF JEBEL MAQLA, BELIEVED TO BE MOUNT SINAI, FROM NORTH LOOKING SOUTH

LOOKING OUT OF WHAT COULD IN FACT BE ELIJAH'S CAVE, AT JEBEL LAWZ.

PETROGLYPH OF A BULL, POSSIBLY RELATED TO THE APIS BULL CULT OF EGYPTIAN WORSHIP ACROSS THE VALLEY FROM JEBEL LAWZ

WHITE MARBLE STONE PILLARS POSSIBLY REPRESENTING THE TRIBES OF ISRAEL AT JEBEL MAQLA

THE SPLIT ROCK IN THE FOREGROUND, AND THE APTLY NAMED
"CONE" MOUNTAIN IN THE BACKGROUND, ON THE WEST SIDE OF THE
JEBEL LAWZ RANGE

STONE STRUCTURES RELATING TO THE ALTAR OF MOSES NEAR THE FOOT OF JEBEL LAWZ.

A LARGE STONE WITH CRUMBLING STEPS SITUATED AT THE BASE OF THE SPLIT ROCK, A CANDIDATE FOR THE ALTAR JEHOVAH NISSI ON WHICH MOSES GAVE THANKS FOR VICTORY OVER THE AMALEKITES

Epilogue and Acknowledgements

I n the time since April 3, 1992, we have made another twelve trips out into northwestern Saudi Arabia, the region containing Mount Sinai, as well as many of the areas surrounding it. In fact, we have taken our journeys as far south as the border of Yemen and as far east as the Persian Gulf, sifting the sands and combing the mountains alike in search of the rich, magnificent history of Arabia that lay hidden there for centuries. The enormity of what we have discovered and documented was, by sheer volume, impossible to relate in this one book, which only deals with our first three ventures into the area.

The two mountains, Jebel Maqla, which we believe to be the biblical Mount Sinai, and Jebel Lawz, which we believe to be the biblical Mount Horeb, continued to call Jim and myself until we were finally able to decipher the pathways to their summits and stand high atop their magnificent pinnacles. In a completely unrehearsed and unplanned manner, we "just happened" to reach the summit of Mount Sinai on September 24, 1992, which also just happened to be Jim's thirty-eighth birthday, and likewise, the summit of Mt. Horeb on September 24, 1994, on Jim's fortieth birthday. The details of these two monumental journeys are best reserved for another book, which I am beginning to write even now.

Our quest for the truth has taken us from mountains and deserts to the vast, virtually unexplored regions under the seas that adjoin the Arabian Peninsula as well. We have hauled scuba equipment and air compressors literally the entire distance across Arabia to make numerous dives in the Gulf of Aqaba, as well as the main body of the Red Sea, on the hunt for relics of great antiquity that we know of a certainty, exist. And on almost all of these spine-tingling journeys, except the two climbs to the top of the high peaks, Lucas and Chelsea braved both the elements and the locals with us!

And these explorations were not easy ones to make, not only from a physical standpoint, but also from a mental one. Over the course of the fifteen mountain trips, as we refer to them, we have been harassed and assaulted personally, chased and accused, and yes, even captured and taken to jail on three separate occasions. We have had cameras and film confiscated, been run right off the highway twice, had an armed bandit hot on our tail for what ended up being a four-hour chase, and were even dragged before the Emir of a particular region of the country for pursuing these defining pieces of history connected to Mount Sinai! Even so, it was impossible for us to forsake the mission we know that we were sent to accomplish.

What we did not know in those early days was that the photographs and video evidence we were gathering would wind up encompassing the entire globe! We have, through these things, been so honored to meet and become acquainted with others who also share the knowledge of the profound matters with which we deal here. And every one of those meetings was absolutely divine in origin. I have learned only too well that coincidence is a word that does not have any place around these topics!

The first of those meetings would be with two gentlemen who lived in the 1800s. Of course I'm referring to Sir Richard Burton, whom we met by way of his book, *The Gold Mines of Midian,* and Dr. Charles Beke, from his book, *Discoveries of Sinai in Arabia and of Midian.* It was the opinion of Burton that Beke had indeed found reason to believe that Mount Sinai must of a biblical necessity be located inside northwestern Arabia, because the land of Midian where the mountain was located, has and always will remain inside the borders of what we now call Saudi Arabia. The ancient land of Midian has never been stretched across the Gulf of Aqaba and into Egypt properly, though some have tried to make the biblical story accurate by doing so. It is our absolute belief that Dr. Beke was the first one to name Arabia as the proper placement of Mount Sinai, and it is to him we will always refer as the originator of the theory.

Our next encounter would be with Ron Wyatt. We met Ron in February of 1992 in the country of Bahrain, where we began to show him the various things we had come across in Arabia. We also shared with Ron our own discoveries, which included potential sites for the biblical Marah, Elim, and the Split Rock, among others. Ron told us he had never been to the west side of the mountain range where all of these things are located, and therefore had never seen them until we shared our film with him for each discovery. He asked us for permission to use the images and video footage we had gathered in his private talks to various church groups. He promised he would not let the film or photos out to the public via any sort of media as we were still inside Arabia. Eventually, however, we began to find pictures of ours on the internet with us in the photos, and we became concerned that we could be discovered. At that point we stopped allowing any of our pictures or photographs to leave our own possession. We then began amassing a library of images and film that we simply kept with us in Arabia, until such time as we felt safe releasing them further.

And the first time we felt we could do just that was around the spring of 1995, when Jim and I had the privilege of sitting down with Dr. Chuck Missler of Koinonia House in Coeur d'Elene, Idaho. We had phoned his organization while we were stateside and explained a number of the things we were finding in Arabia to Mr. Bill Perkins, who, at our request, relayed the message to Chuck. Bill was particularly interested in the "identical snowflake" event, and as it turned out, so was Chuck! In spite of an extremely tight schedule, Chuck graciously arranged to spend several hours with us and patiently listened while we expounded of our experiences far out on the mountain. He made a suggestion to us that we should put together a short video to highlight the most important of our discoveries, and that advice was some of the best we have ever received! It was because of that little video that we would make a series of divine connections. Not only did Chuck figure prominently in that matter, he also very generously sent us out with numerous tape series and Bible study materials he had recorded, which we then took back to Arabia to share with the Christian community there. We would, in 1996, make a phenomenal trip to Israel with Chuck and his lovely wife Nan that will forever stand out as one of the highlights of our lives!

In March of 1998, as a direct result of the video Chuck inspired us to make, we met Bob Cornuke. Bob managed to get into Saudi Arabia with Larry Williams to investigate some of these things he'd heard about from Jim Irwin, the astronaut. Jim had been informed of the possibility that Mount Sinai was in Arabia from a man named David Fasold, who had been taken to Jebel Lawz by Ron Wyatt. Bob became convinced of the authenticity of the site, but only got out of Saudi Arabia with a few scant photos. When he was informed about us and our multiple hours of fresh video and photography, of not only the same site, but many others he and Larry had not seen, he contacted us immediately and we began sharing our findings and films with him. This culminated in the production of the documentary *The Mountain of Fire,* which highlights Jebel Lawz as a great candidate for the real Mount Sinai.

Through a crazy series of events which space will not allow me to go into here, we met a man by the name of Michael Rood at a seminar he was teaching in Gulfport, Mississippi, in the summer of 2002. Michael also staunchly believes that the real Mount Sinai is located in northwestern Arabia. As part of the seminar, he was using several of our photographs of the mountain and the Split Rock which he had obtained from Ron Wyatt in his power point presentation to illustrate the absolute accuracy and validity of the Scriptures. After the program was over, we introduced ourselves to him as the originators of those photographs, and the rest is history! Michael felt very strongly that we should meet up with one Tim Mahoney of Mahoney Media Group in Minneapolis, Minnesota, and he made the necessary phone calls to cause that to happen. And on a very fateful day in early September of 2002, we received a phone call from Tim that set us off on another adventure that continues to this very day.

Jim and I were sitting in our bedroom with the phone set to conference, and a number of voices came through from Minnesota on the other end. There was Tim Mahoney as well as another man by the name of Dr. Lennart Moller—and their families were in the background with them. Lennart, who is from Sweden, was in Minneapolis being filmed for Tim's upcoming film called *The Exodus Conspiracy.* Lennart is the author of *The Exodus Case,* in which he examines by scientific method the evidence from both the past and the present in relation to its biblical account. Having compiled probably the most comprehensive collection of data beginning from the time of Abraham and carrying through all the way to the time of Moses, Lennart is certainly one of the foremost scholars dealing with the topic today.

As we all introduced ourselves and became acquainted with one another, a great sense of connected destinies filled the room. One conversation led to another, and before we knew it, Jim was describing our wedding rings he had personally designed and had made for us in 1995. On either side of the rings are the dates we reached the summits of Mount Sinai and Mt. Horeb. Jim then related to our new friends the significance of those days, having been his thirty-eighth and his fortieth birthdays, respectively. The other end of the phone went completely silent for the space of about a full minute. In fact, we were just about to hang up and re-dial, certain of a lost connection, when Lennart spoke in a quiet voice, asking a question of Jim. "Jim, what year were you born?" I will never, ever forget what happened next. Jim replied, "Nineteen fifty-four. Why?" And again, the phone went silent. When Lennart spoke again, it was our turn to be at a loss for words. "Jim, my birthday is September 24, 1954!"

There we sat in Mississippi, on a phone call from Minneapolis, awestruck and stupefied to find out that a man who shares the same calling as Jim's was born on the opposite side of the world on the same day of the same year as Jim! What are the chances that a little baby boy born in Sweden and a little baby boy born in the United States on the exact same day would ever meet, much less share a destiny that would become joined over the sands of Saudi Arabia? Like I said before, coincidence has become an ignorant, meaningless word to all of us. Within a month of that call, Lennart was in our living room, and we spent a glorious week getting to know him and his work. We shared many thoughts and ideas that led us to create some mind-boggling projects, which we hope to be able to launch in the next two years. Lennart and his wife Marie have become the dearest of friends to us, and we are so very thankful for their presence in our lives!

Tim Mahoney is definitely another one of those miraculous connections we have been blessed with. After the initial contacts with Lennart, Tim flew down to meet us along with Dr. David Wessner, the executive producer. We gave them a tour of our information and particularly our photography and video work regarding the exodus and Mount Sinai, and they were convinced that the information we had gathered had a part in the new film. Over the time period from then until now, we have flown to Minneapolis numerous times to be filmed and share our information at Tim's beautiful studio.

During those visits we have spent many hours with Tim and his wife Jill and been brought into their family like long lost relatives. Aside from being perfectly yoked spiritually, Tim and Jim share a particularly great talent for being able to play just about any stringed instrument exceedingly well. Tim, who also writes his own lyrics, is proficient in the steel guitar, acoustic guitar, mandolin, fiddle, and lately, the banjo. Sharing a love for bluegrass music once landed us with Tim in a coffee house in Minneapolis on a Friday night, belting out Smoky Mountain music and singing harmony with the members of his regular friends in the band. If I am not mistaken I do also recall distinctly Swedish voices that joined us in that effort, after switching gears to Peter, Paul, and Mary's version of "Leaving On A Jet Plane." These are the moments between revelations that have so knitted our souls together with Tim and Jill, as well as Lennart and Marie. And we all know that there is so much more still to come.

There are, of course, other divine connections I would be remiss not to mention. During the same period as when we met Tim and Lennart, I received an email from a man who was most interested in the entire story and history of the exodus. He introduced himself and his interests in detail, and I was driven to phone Jim immediately to share with him what I was reading. This sounded like another with a calling to this quest! Jim also witnessed with his words, and I emailed our telephone contact information back to the man. And thus our great friendship with Dr. Glen Fritz was born! Glen was in the process of gathering a tremendous amount of information about Mount Sinai in Saudi Arabia, and at that time, was a Ph. D. student of Geography from San Antonio, Texas. He began to share numerous maps and fabulous satellite imagery with us, along with some specific research he was doing on the Gulf of

Aqaba. That research has led him to some exciting discoveries about the sea itself and its prominent place in defining the exodus routing that was previously unknown. Glen is the author of *The Lost Sea of the Exodus, A Modern Geographical Analysis*. He and his wife Carolyn have become dear friends of ours as well!

Once again, within the same few months of time as all these other connections were being made, we got a phone call from a man one afternoon that was in pursuit of Mount Sinai, but for quite a unique and different reason than all the others we had come in contact with. Enter Dr. Miles Jones into our lives! Miles was on a singular quest to find the real Mount Sinai, which he had already concluded was not the traditional mountain in the Sinai Peninsula of Egypt. Miles' research dealt with what he called "the writing of God," and he began to explain to us that he believed that the language and writing of God were given to mankind first at Mount Sinai—an alpha-numeric writing that was completely free of graven images. This work is astounding and on the cutting edge of his brand new revelation of historical facts, which will rewrite history concerning the origination of the alphabet. Miles' new book entitled *The Writing of God* should be ready for release soon.

One of the first amazing discoveries we made after we left Arabia was one that Miles not only confirmed, but enhanced with an added discovery of his own. Earlier in this book I mentioned an area near the Split Rock where we found numerous pairs of sandaled feet that had been etched directly into the rocks. These feet stayed in the back of my mind for years before I realized just what they signified. But in early 2002, I understood perfectly the broad scope of just why those feet had been placed upon those rocks!

Beginning with Abraham, a promise was given to him and his descendents in the Bible that a certain landmass would become their inheritance. This promise was to be defined by his leaving the country he had been born in and striking out toward a land he had never seen. He was told by God to walk the breadth and the length of the land involved and it would be given to him. The same promise was given to his son Isaac and to Isaac's son Jacob after him. Jacob fathered twelve sons, who inherited the original promise after their father's death. But their descendents would wind up in Egypt for hundreds of years and became a population of slaves in servitude to the Pharaoh. It would seem that the promise of a certain land belonging to them had been lost to history. But then Moses entered the scene. Moses wound up leading those descendents of Abraham out of Egypt in the Exodus to a new land wherein the mountain of God awaited them. That promise, so long before given to Abraham, was not only reiterated by God to Moses, it was also further defined. In Deuteronomy 11:23-24, Moses is advised that if he and the children of Israel will obey God, that He would cause them to possess nations greater and mightier than they were, and that the land they would inherit would be marked out by the soles of their feet! Oddly enough, it was November 24, 2002, when we put all these things together with Miles! All of a sudden finding multiple pairs of sandaled feet etched deeply into the rocks in Saudi Arabia took on a whole new meaning! It was quite plain to us from that point forward that these footprints, if you will, would some day in the future define a promise that had been given almost 4000 years ago!

We shared this theory with Miles Jones. As Jim shuffled through a number of slides we had taken of the footprints, Miles stopped Jim and asked him to return to one of the previous slides. It was a pair of the footprints all right, but Miles noticed something in the picture we had not. Three hash marks had been placed against the arch of the foot, and Miles immediately recognized this mark as an alphabetic character. As we began to go through all the rest of the pairs of feet we had captured, we noticed that every single one of them contained this triple hash mark in one form or another. Very excited about the possible meanings, we all scrambled up into my office upstairs where we had spread a huge amount of research material out onto the conference table already. Miles had brought numerous files with him which designated various experts and their theories on how this sort of ancient text, called Thamudic, was to be translated. But try as we may, we could not find a single chart of Thamudic text that contained this specific character we were finding on these footprints. In an act of desperation, I began a web search while Jim and Miles continued to pour over the charts, and much to my own surprise, I stumbled over a Thamudic chart that Miles had not previously seen. I printed this chart out immediately and was boggled by what my eyes saw! The triple hash mark on this particular chart was defined as being the proto Hebraic character *koph*, or *kaph*, which literally translated means "the cup of the palm of the hand" *and* the *"sole of the foot!"* Yes, that dictated a scream of excitement, and before the evening was over, Miles had detailed a chart showing the absolute progression of the Thamudic letter of the three hash marks from its origin to our current day letter *k*. But what was the most phenomenal to us was that a group had taken the time to etch these sandaled feet quite clearly upon these rocks thousands of years ago, and had also further defined their reason by placing the kaph on each one; thereby signaling to anyone of that day that the soles of their feet had tread there! And if you were promised a certain land by the mere act of defining where the soles of your feet had been, wouldn't you etch your feet upon the rocks as well? It will be very interesting to watch in the years to come, just what becomes of the sandaled footprints of northwest Saudi Arabia!

In another of these extraordinary path crossings, we were introduced to a couple by the name of Edgar and Yvonne Miles. These dear people came to see us at our home, and we shared our experiences with them over a wonderful day of visiting! Immediately they began to search for avenues by which they could bless our efforts to get the word out about all these magnificent discoveries in Arabia. They are solely responsible for the publication of *Jebel Maqla—Mount Sinai?* which was printed in 2003. Their constant encouragement and true understanding of the awesome significance of all these things has been an absolute treasure in our lives. We are so grateful to them for their deep and abiding friendship and all they have done for us!

In our most recent continuance of these incredible connections, December of 2006 found us on a plane to South Korea, and headed for the home of a man by the name of Dr. Sung Hak Kim. He and his wife Jenny, and their three children, had lived in Saudi Arabia for twenty years, and Dr. Kim was the personal physician to Prince Majed Bin Abdul Aziz! This Prince of Saudi Arabia was the chief of the Mecca region, an extremely high royal position inside the desert kingdom. And Dr. Kim was with him at all times, wherever he went. Dr. Kim explained to us that after he became aware of Jebel al Lawz in the northwest of the country, and the likelihood that it was indeed the biblical Mount Sinai, he began preparing his family to go and visit the place to see for themselves. He related to us his incredible journey from Jeddah to the mountain, and how he and his family had been treated in exactly the same manner as we were when we first attempted to visit the site; he had been chased off at gunpoint! Though he spoke fluent Arabic, and had high credentials as the physician to the Prince, this was a place that was off limits even to him!

But this did not deter Dr. Kim from continuing to plan further trips out to the mountain! He explained to us that it was as if the mountain itself was "calling to him," and he could not stop thinking about it at all times. And so, with great determination and courage, he gathered up his wife and children repeatedly to eventually make twelve trips out into the region! He has collected a tremendous amount of photos and video, as well as other pieces of evidence that he will soon be bringing to public light that will add an extremely significant amount of validation to the topic of Mount Sinai being in Saudi Arabia. His book, which details his riveting personal story about all these things, has just been published in Korea and is flying off the shelves as an immediate best seller! Best of all, Dr. Kim, Jenny, and their children have already become like members of our own family. The experiences we have shared are so incredibly similar in nature and calling that it defies logical explanation. We are greatly honored to know them and to have the privilege to call them our dear friends! They have been linked to us in such a way as only our Father could orchestrate.

In the midst of these incredible connections, a network of individuals has been brought together that we have been most fortunate to be associated with. We are certain that this body of information that has been accumulating through all of our various researches will some day make apparent the vast treasures that have, up to now, lain hidden beneath the shifting sands of ancient Arabia. It is our sincere desire that when this enormous volume of evidence has had a chance to be disseminated through the proper channels, it will be decided conclusively that Mount Sinai is indeed in Saudi Arabia, and the biblical record has been preserved true. And to have been allowed to be in the center of this whirlwind of controversy has been, and continues to be, the focal point and the greatest experience of our lives!

Dr. Charles Beke has a quotation in the beginning of his book *Discoveries of Sinai in Arabia and of Midian* that is appropriately revisited here, exactly as it was printed in 1878:

"The world may say I've fail'd; I have not fail'd
If I set truth 'fore men they will not see;
Tis they who fail, not I. My faith holds firm,
And time will prove me right."

May the body of research we have collected in Arabia be a part of the fulfillment of Dr. Beke's fondest prayer.

Penny Cox Caldwell
April, 2008

CONTACT INFORMATION

Split Rock Research Foundation
P. O. Box 6586
Diamondhead, MS 39525

Web: www.splitrockresearch.org

Email: office@splitrockresearch.org

To the God of the Mountain,
Who bore us up on eagle's wings
and carried us to Himself~

The One, True, Living God,

Who was,
and is,
and is to come . . . .

Two years ago, the word "adventure" began to surface with increasing intensity in my life. Little did I know that I was about to embark on an adventure so wild, and so holy that the first fifty years of my life would pale in comparison. Penny and Jim Caldwell have lived an extraordinary adventure for far longer than I. They have seen and done things that nobody on earth has experienced. Penny's new book, *The God of the Mountain*, gives the reader a rare glimpse into the lives of two people who have been led on a very special mission by God. To be sure, it isn't easy to follow the call to such an adventure. In fact it can be frightening, dangerous, physically and emotionally draining, and very confusing. But, they have persevered, prayed, and have listened carefully to God. In return for their obedience, they have been rewarded on a supernatural scale. They have walked in the ancient footsteps of God's chosen people and have been asked to bring this knowledge back to them—in Israel. Penny and Jim have been entrusted with much, and they were uniquely chosen for just such a time as this. You MUST read this book. It may change your life.

— **Pete Windahl**, Co-Producer *The Exodus Conspiracy*

If you combine Indiana Jones with the Swiss Family Robinson, and then turn those fictional Hollywood epics into fact, you will just begin to appreciate the husband and wife adventurers, Jim and Penny Caldwell, as they searched the ancient land of Midian for the true Mount Sinai. Faced with the constant threat of arrest, torture, and possible execution for their bravery, Jim, Penny, and their two children answered the call of the Lord and followed the ancient writings of Moses on the most amazing adventure of modern times— equal in every aspect to the search for Noah's Ark and the Ark of the Covenant. What Jim and Penny found is of supreme importance for both Christians and Jews. It is the very mountain where Moses received the Ten Commandments, where Aaron fashioned the golden calf, where Moses built the Exodus 24:4 altar and twelve pillars, and where God stood in the pillar of fire when Moses struck the rock that would supply the Hebrew slaves with life-giving water. Penny's moment-by-moment account of their adventure is a must read.

Congratulations, Penny, on a spectacular book!

— **Roger L. Johnson**, Commander, US Navy

There are books and there are *different* books. This is a different one. Penny Caldwell writes about her travels in Saudi Arabia, together with her husband and their children. Travels that few have experienced: strange events, remarkable discoveries, dangerous situations in the Land of Midian, in the territory of Moses. This is a personal travel log; it tells of travels that were personal to Moses and his people, and in the same way they are personal for Penny and her family. I know what she writes about because I have also been there—with Penny and her husband in the middle of nowhere—in the Land of Midian.

Penny describes her travels as "a journey of revelation and destiny." And I can tell you, this is not the end of a story—it is a beginning of the future.

— **Dr. Lennart Möller**, author of *The Exodus Case*

In my twenty years of life in Saudi Arabia, sixteen of which was spent as the private physician rendered to the former governor of Mecca, I traveled to the northern part of Saudi twelve times over a period of seven years. This is not a place for a Christian to share his or her faith. It is a country where one can get executed for believing in God. Ironically, this is where the Holy Mountain is located, protected with swords, guns, and modern weapons. From the world of religious repression inside Saudi Arabia, God chose two families, one from the East and one from the West to do His work. This book is the incredible story of the Caldwell family, and how they came to the Mountain. This is how it began in January of 1987 and 1988 when our two families moved there, and today it is God's grace that we returned to Korea and America safely.

That mountain called on us all the time. We both traveled there many times. We connected with Jim and Penny deep in our soul when we met. It was our experiences that brought us together and binds us to a common identity. Together we pray that all the nations in the world will come to know the hidden mountain, and the God of the mountain.

— **Dr. Sung Hak Kim**, South Korea

The God of the

of the
MOUNTAIN

THE TRUE STORY BEHIND
THE DISCOVERIES AT THE REAL MOUNT SINAI

PENNY COX CALDWELL

Bridge-Logos
Alachua, Florida 32615

Bridge-Logos
Alachua, FL 32615 USA

The God of the Mountain
by Penny Cox Caldwell

Edited by Ann Blanton

Printed in the Canada.

Library of Congress Catalog Card Number: 2008933165
International Standard Book Number 978-0-88270-605-4

Scripture quotations in this book are from the *King James Version* of the Bible.

The names of certain individuals mentioned in this book have been purposefully changed at the author's discretion.

BP 07-29-13

Who taught me the meaning of wonder
and how to dream among the stars.

CLAYTON CARLYSLE COX